THE SHERLOCK HOLMES BOOK

c. 2

THE SHERLOCK HOLMES BOOK

DK LONDON

SENIOR ART EDITOR
Helen Spencer

PROJECT EDITOR
Alexandra Beeden

DESIGNERS
Bobby Birchall, Vanessa Hamilton

EDITORS
Polly Boyd, Chauney Dunford,
Jemima Dunne, Joanna Edwards,
Sam Kennedy, Patrick Newman,
Carey Scott, Debra Wolter

US EDITORS
Christine Heilman, Margaret Parrish

DESIGN ASSISTANT
Renata Latipova

MANAGING ART EDITOR
Lee Griffiths

MANAGING EDITOR
Gareth Jones

ART DIRECTOR
Karen Self

**ASSOCIATE PUBLISHING
DIRECTOR**
Liz Wheeler

PUBLISHING DIRECTOR
Jonathan Metcalf

JACKET DESIGNER
Natalie Godwin

JACKET EDITOR
Claire Gell

**JACKET DESIGN
DEVELOPMENT MANAGER**
Sophia MTT

PRE-PRODUCTION PRODUCER
Gillian Reid

PRODUCER
Mandy Inness

PICTURE RESEARCH
Roland Smithies,
Sarah Smithies

ILLUSTRATIONS
James Graham,
Vanessa Hamilton

DK DELHI

JACKET DESIGNER
Dhirendra Singh

SENIOR DTP DESIGNER
Harish Aggarwal

MANAGING JACKETS EDITOR
Saloni Singh

PICTURE RESEARCH
Aditya Katyal

original styling by
STUDIO 8

First American Edition, 2015
Published in the United States by
DK Publishing, 345 Hudson Street
New York, New York 10014

Copyright © 2015
Dorling Kindersley Limited
A Penguin Random House Company
15 16 17 18 19   10 9 8 7 6 5 4 3 2 1
001—283947—Oct/2015

Published in Great Britain by
Dorling Kindersley Limited.

A catalog record for this book is available
from the Library of Congress.

ISBN: 978-1-4654-3849-2

DK books are available at special discounts
when purchased in bulk
for sales promotions, premiums,
fund-raising, or educational use.
For details, contact: DK Publishing Special
Markets, 345 Hudson Street, New York,
New York 10014
SpecialSales@dk.com

Printed and bound in China

A WORLD OF IDEAS:
SEE ALL THERE IS TO KNOW

www.dk.com

CONTRIBUTORS

DAVID STUART DAVIES, CONSULTANT EDITOR

David Stuart Davies is a crime writer, playwright, and editor. Regarded as an authority on Sherlock Holmes, he has written seven Holmes novels and several nonfiction works, including *Starring Sherlock Holmes* (Titan), and edited numerous collections dealing with the Baker Street sleuth. His latest Holmes title is *Sherlock Holmes & The Devil's Promise* (Titan). His own detectives are Johnny Hawke, a private detective operating in London during World War II; Luther Darke, a Victorian "puzzle solver"; and DI Paul Snow, a Yorkshire policeman in a series of novels set in the 1980s, the most recent being *Innocent Blood* (Mystery Press). His website is www.davidstuartdavies.com

BARRY FORSHAW, CONSULTANT EDITOR

Barry Forshaw is one of the UK's leading experts on crime fiction and film. His books include *Nordic Noir, Sex and Film*, and *The Rough Guide to Crime Fiction*. Other works include *Death in a Cold Climate*, *British Gothic Cinema*, *Euro Noir*, and the Keating Award-winning *British Crime Writing: An Encyclopedia*, along with books on Italian cinema and Stieg Larsson. He writes for various national newspapers and edits *Crime Time* (www.crimetime.co.uk).

DAVID ANDERSON

David Anderson is a researcher based in the Department of English at University College London, where he specializes in the literature and film of the city. He is a senior editor at *Review 31*, a staff writer at Connell Guides, and writer-in-residence at the Cob Gallery.

JOLY BRAIME

Joly Braime has been a magazine journalist, a guidebook and website editor, and a freelance writer who has worked on everything from financial books to articles about *Fifty Shades of Grey*. He has been a Holmes obsessive since acquiring *The Complete Sherlock Holmes* at the age of 11.

JOHN FARNDON

John Farndon is a Royal Literary Fellow at Anglia Ruskin University in Cambridge, UK, and an author, playwright, and composer. Among his many books are *Do You Think You're Clever?* and *Do Not Open*. He is the creator of *The Secret History of Objects* tales, which premiered at the Moscow Polytech Festival in 2015.

ANDREW HERITAGE

Andrew Heritage is a publishing consultant who specializes in cartography, current affairs, art, popular culture, and literary history. He has edited and contributed to over 100 titles including the *DK Atlas of World History*, *The Book of Codes*, *The Book of Saints*, *The Rough Guide to Crime Fiction*, and *Great Movies*.

ALEX WHITTLETON

Alex Whittleton is a freelance professional writer on a range of nonfiction subjects, including literature, lifestyle, media, and food. She has had academic work published in the *Thomas Hardy Yearbook* and has a particular interest in Victorian literature and culture.

LIZ WYSE

Liz Wyse is an author and editor who has written on a wide range of historical subjects, and recently created a range of books on etiquette and modern manners for Debrett's. She has edited a number of historical atlases, including *The Times Atlas of World Archaeology* and *The Historical Atlas of New York City*, and was Editor-in-Chief of *The Guinness Book of World Records*.

CONTENTS

INTRODUCTION

THE EARLY ADVENTURES

THE GREAT DETECTIVE

A LEGEND
RETURNS

HOLMES TAKES
A BOW

THE FINAL DEDUCTIONS

THE WORLD OF SHERLOCK HOLMES

FOREWORD

I n 1946, almost 70 years ago, Edgar W. Smith pondered in an editorial in the *Baker Street Journal*, "What is it that we love in Sherlock Holmes?" Nearly 130 years after Holmes first appeared, subsequently embedded in the hearts of millions, it is appropriate to reconsider this question.

First, Smith wrote, "we love the time in which he lived." When Smith wrote these words, that golden era, when it was "always 1895," was only a half-century earlier, and well within the living memory of Smith (who was born in 1894) and his contemporary readers. Now it is an alien country, as mythical and foreign as the era of the Roman empire, the battlefields of Napoleon, or the court of Elizabeth I. While it may be true that we do love the Victorian era, we love it as we love the Old West or the countryside of Arthur's Camelot, only as it exists in our imaginations, not in our memories. Even Smith knew that the late nineteenth century was no paradise but instead a time of great changes, for people of color, for women, and for the middle class. In the world of 1946, just righting itself from the cataclysms of war and the horrors of the Holocaust, how could Smith justify a love for a character as out-of-date as Sherlock Holmes?

Smith's answer was emblematic of 1946, when the world could still believe in heroes: "[Holmes] stands before us as a symbol," he wrote, "a symbol...of all that we are not but ever would be... We see him as the fine expression of our urge to trample evil and to set aright the wrongs with which the world is plagued.... [He] is the personification of something in us that we have lost or never had… And the time and place and all the great events are near and dear to us not because our memories call them forth in pure nostalgia, but because they are a part of us today. That is the Sherlock Holmes we love—the Holmes implicit and eternal in ourselves."

Those were stirring words for a world on the brink of peace and prosperity. The Allies had fought a terrible war, the last "good" war, and the madmen were defeated, by common men and women— heroes—from many lands. But if Holmes was only a hero, as Smith implied, he failed us, for he did not slay the dragon, at the Reichenbach Falls or later.

Seventy years later, we can see that the spirit of Moriarty did not die in a bunker in Berlin or in a palace in Tokyo. His hand is clear after 1946, in the wars in which so many died, in Korea, the Balkans, Afghanistan, and Iraq. Even today, his minions continue to foment crime, corruption, hunger, and poverty, in a world with factions no longer easily divided into good or evil.

And yet we return to Holmes. Smith was right in saying that Holmes appeals to us for "all that we are not but ever would be." But it is not Holmes's heroism that calls to us, for he was not a hero (or perhaps not just a hero). Rather, he was an individual, in an age when individuality seemed lost in the teeming masses of the Empire. Heroic or not, Holmes always did the right thing. Some have pointed out that he was arrogant, cold, high-handed, misogynistic, unfeeling, manipulative—and these are difficult charges to deny. Yet those are all merely facets of his single-minded character, unswerving in his pursuit of justice, without regard for the conventions of law or society. Holmes is what we dream of and yet hesitate to be: a man apart from the crowd. While he had only a single friend, Dr. John H. Watson, Holmes was very much a part of his world, as comfortable with the grooms and street urchins as with the bankers and nobility. In an age bound by rules and rituals for social circumstances of every sort, even death, Sherlock Holmes followed only his own rules.

The mystery writer Raymond Chandler, writing many years after the death of Conan Doyle, had little liking for the Holmes stories. His ideal detective, he said, lived up to a simple credo: "[D]own these mean streets a man must go who is not himself mean, who is neither tarnished nor afraid." Yet these words could not more accurately describe Holmes. Unafraid, untarnished, focused on his fixed goal, Holmes inspires all of us to believe that we need not be heroes; rather, we can make the world a better place by doing the right thing.

Leslie S. Klinger

INTRODU

CTION

Think of the silhouette: the deerstalker, the Roman nose, the pipe. Sir Arthur Conan Doyle's Sherlock Holmes is, quite simply, the most famous figure in all of crime fiction. What's more, he is one of the most recognizable fictional characters in the Western world—and beyond. And although he owes something to his literary predecessors in the detective fiction genre, Sherlock Holmes is the template for virtually every fictional detective that has followed him. Even those who did not emulate him were obliged to do something markedly different, so seismic was his impact.

The brilliant, impatient master of deductive reasoning who shared rooms at 221B Baker Street with his faithful chronicler, Dr. John H. Watson, is as popular today as when the young and ambitious author Conan Doyle created him. Without doubt, Sherlock Holmes is a figure for the ages, and this book is a celebration of the detective in all his myriad facets.

Early inspirations
When the American writer Edgar Allan Poe wrote about a proto-Holmes protagonist, C. Auguste Dupin, in a series of stories that virtually forged the detective fiction format, he had his rather remote sleuth utilizing observation, logic, and lateral thinking—all while demonstrating his skill to an awestruck unnamed narrator; the Holmes formula, in fact, in embryo.

Conan Doyle was a close reader of such Poe stories as "The Murders in the Rue Morgue" (1841), and he borrowed a variety of notions from Dupin and developed them far beyond anything Poe had ever dreamed of. Influenced also by his charismatic professor at Edinburgh University, Dr. Joseph Bell, Conan Doyle forged an imperishable canon of work over some 40 years with his stories and novels about the Great Detective, each brimming with atmosphere and invention.

No man... has brought the same amount of study and of natural talent to the detection of crime which I have done.
Sherlock Holmes
A Study in Scarlet (1887)

Conan Doyle inspired a reading public so obsessed with Holmes that the writer's attempt to kill off the character he had grown tired of (in the short story "The Final Problem," pp.142–47) was met with national outrage.

Writer at work
Conan Doyle's own life was often as remarkable as anything to be found in his more bizarre fiction, particularly in his later years, when his interest in spiritualism increasingly came to the fore. His feelings toward the character he had created in Sherlock Holmes were famously mixed. A well-known *Punch* cartoon of the day showed the author chained to the great detective, and Conan Doyle often expressed his frustrated wish to be remembered for something other than his famous protagonist. But it was Sherlock Holmes rather than the author's own preferred historical fiction that made Conan Doyle one of the most celebrated popular writers of his age.

The famous duo
Apart from the mesmerising genius of his detective, Conan Doyle's most durable achievement within the Sherlock Holmes stories and novels was the relationship he established

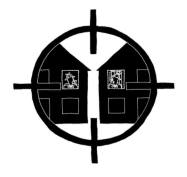

between the logical sleuth and his colleague Watson (the latter a surrogate for the reader), which the writer finessed into something immensely satisfying. Much of the pleasure of the stories and novels may be found in the interaction between Holmes and Watson as much as from the jaw-dropping revelations of the plots.

Holmes on the page

The Sherlock Holmes Book not only examines the complete canonical collection of 56 short stories and the four memorable novels (the most famous of which, of course, is *The Hound of the Baskervilles*, pp.152–61) but also applies the kind of forensic attention to all things Holmesian that the sleuth himself utilized in his cases— including the life and character of his creator, along with Conan Doyle's non-Holmes work.

Beyond the canon

While the original canon of Holmes stories and novels remains the key element in the detective's popularity, it is the infinite—and continuing—flexibility of Holmes and Watson as characters that has rendered them relevant and ripe for multiple reinterpretations even today, in a manner that

such Holmes imitators as Agatha Christie's Hercule Poirot could not begin to rival.

One reason for the longevity of the character is his immensely flexible appeal when adapted for drama—on stage, film, and television. Actors love to take up the magnifying glass, pipe, and violin, and surround themselves with the cozy clutter of 221B Baker Street. All the key actors who have taken on the mantle of Holmes are celebrated here, from the earliest portrayals to the most recent: Benedict Cumberbatch starring in a massively successful modern-day reimagining of Sherlock Holmes in the 21st century.

In these pages, you will also find the literary offshoots—the creation of adventures for the great detective by writers other than Conan Doyle, which began even when the author was still alive, and included such practitioners as his son, Adrian Conan Doyle. Over the years, there have been many Holmes pastiches, from retellings of canonical works to complete reinventions of the detective's cases.

Other areas for examination are the influence of Conan Doyle's writing on the crime fiction genre, along with the ways in which the Holmes stories provide insight into

historical and social aspects of Victorian England, 19th-century criminology and forensics, and the science and methods of logical thought and deduction.

The Great Detective

In short, *The Sherlock Holmes Book* provides a complete guide to all aspects of Holmesiana. It is a celebration of Conan Doyle's most fascinating creation, the Great Detective Sherlock Holmes. ∎

Barry Forshaw and David Stuart Davies
Consultant editors

When you have eliminated the impossible whatever remains, *however improbable*, must be the truth.
Sherlock Holmes
The Sign of Four (1890)

STEEL TRUE, BLADE STRAIGHT

SIR ARTHUR CONAN DOYLE

Arthur Ignatius Conan Doyle was born in Edinburgh on May 22, 1859. His mother, Mary Foley, was of Irish extraction; she could trace her ancestry back to the influential Percy family of Northumberland, and from there to the Plantagenet line. Mary recounted tales of history, high adventure, and heroic deeds to the young Arthur, which were to be the seeds of inspiration in his later writing career. The family was large—Arthur was the eldest of 10 children—and life was difficult for his mother, who struggled to bring up the family on the meager income provided by her unambitious husband Charles Altamont Doyle—a civil servant and occasional artist. Charles was prone to bouts of epilepsy as well as depression and alcoholism, which eventually led to his being institutionalized in 1893.

Education and influences

In order to help Arthur escape his depressing home background, Mrs. Doyle scraped enough money together to send him to Stonyhurst College, a strict Jesuit boarding school situated in an isolated part of Lancashire. It was at this

That love of books…
is among the
choicest gifts
of the gods.
Arthur Conan Doyle
Through the Magic Door (1907)

Conan Doyle is pictured here at work in the garden of Bignell Wood—the family's rural retreat in the New Forest, Hampshire—during the late 1920s.

establishment that he began to question his religious beliefs, and by the time he left the school in 1875 he had firmly rejected Christianity. Instead he began a lifelong search for some other belief to embrace—a search that eventually led him to spiritualism. It was also at Stonyhurst that he encountered a fellow pupil named Moriarty—a name that he would use to great effect later, in his writings. Conan Doyle was always picking up trifles and tidbits of information, ideas, and concepts that he encountered and stored away with the idea of possibly using them in the future.

After studying for a further year with the Jesuits in Feldkirch in Austria, Conan Doyle surprised his artistic family by choosing to study medicine at Edinburgh University. During his time at the university—1876 to 1881—he encountered two

professors who would later serve as models for his characters. In his autobiography, *Memories and Adventures* (1924), he describes Professor Rutherford with his "Assyrian beard, his prodigious voice, his enormous chest and his singular manner"—characteristics that Conan Doyle would later assign to the colorful Professor George Edward Challenger, the central character in his famous science-fiction novel *The Lost World* (1912). Even more significant was his association with Dr. Joseph Bell, whose method of deducing the history and circumstances of his patients appeared little short of magical. Here was the model and inspiration for Sherlock Holmes, and it is interesting to note that

Founded in 1891, *The Strand Magazine* was an illustrated monthly featuring short stories, including the highly popular Sherlock Holmes tales, which appeared in complete form.

the first collection of Holmes short stories, *The Adventures of Sherlock Holmes* (1892), is dedicated "To My Old Teacher Joseph Bell." It has been said that Conan Doyle looked upon Bell as a father figure because he lacked one at home.

To help to pay his university tuition and assist his mother with the upkeep of the family, Conan Doyle undertook many part-time jobs, including that of medical assistant in Birmingham, Sheffield, and Shropshire. He even served as a ship's doctor on an Arctic whaler, another experience that provided material for his writing—particularly the ghost story "The Captain of the Polestar" (1890), and "The Adventure of Black Peter" (pp.184–85).

From doctor to writer
After graduating in 1882, Conan Doyle became a partner in a medical practice in Plymouth, Devon, with Dr. George Turnaville Budd, who had been a fellow »

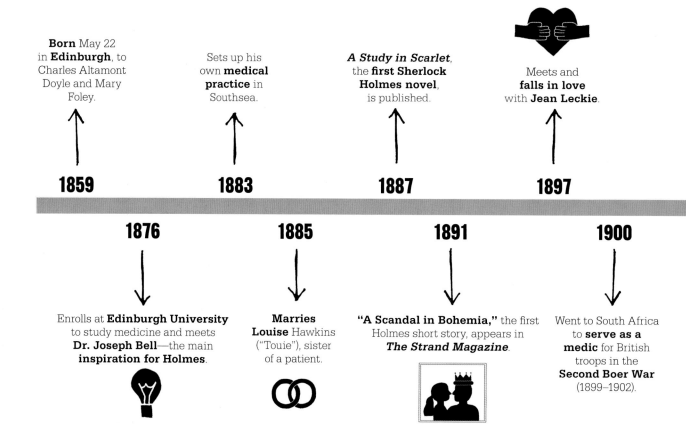

Born May 22 in **Edinburgh**, to Charles Altamont Doyle and Mary Foley.

Sets up his own **medical practice** in Southsea.

A Study in Scarlet, the **first Sherlock Holmes novel**, is published.

Meets and **falls in love** with **Jean Leckie**.

1859

1883

1887

1897

1876

1885

1891

1900

Enrolls at **Edinburgh University** to study medicine and meets **Dr. Joseph Bell**—the main **inspiration for Holmes**.

Marries Louise Hawkins ("Touie"), sister of a patient.

"A Scandal in Bohemia," the first Holmes short story, appears in *The Strand Magazine*.

Went to South Africa to **serve as a medic** for British troops in the **Second Boer War** (1899–1902).

student at Edinburgh University. Budd was an eccentric and volatile man and the partnership soon disintegrated, leaving Conan Doyle to pack his bags and set up a practice on his own in Southsea, Hampshire. By this time he had already tried his hand at writing fiction and had several short stories published, but it was while in Southsea that he made a more determined effort to achieve success as an author. As he slowly built up his medical practice, Conan Doyle toyed with the idea of creating a detective story in which the protagonist—a character called Sherrinford Holmes—solved a crime by deductive reasoning in the manner of Joseph Bell. In *Memories and Adventures* he observed: "Reading some detective stories, I was struck by the fact that their results were obtained in nearly every case by chance. I thought I would try my hand at writing a story in which the hero would treat crime as Dr. Bell treated disease and where science would take the place of romance." This idea materialized in the form of the novel *A Study in Scarlet* (pp.36–45), with Sherrinford becoming Sherlock—and a legend was born. It was published in *Beeton's Christmas Annual* in 1887; Conan Doyle accepted the meager fee of £25, and in so doing relinquished all claims to the copyright.

Following the publication of *A Study in Scarlet*, Conan Doyle turned his attention to historical fiction—his first love, inspired by his mother's stories and his admiration for the works of Sir Walter Scott. The result was *Micah Clarke* (1889), a tale based on the Monmouth Rebellion. It was a great critical and financial success, and it was this that convinced Conan Doyle that his future lay in writing.

The US-based *Lippincott's Magazine* commissioned a second Sherlock Holmes novel in 1890, and he produced *The Sign of Four* (pp.46–55) in less than a month. However, it wasn't until 1891, when *The Strand Magazine* began the series of 12 short stories (later known as *The Adventures of Sherlock Holmes*) that the character of Holmes really struck a chord with the public. It was Conan Doyle who had approached the *Strand* in the first instance: "It had struck me that a single character running through

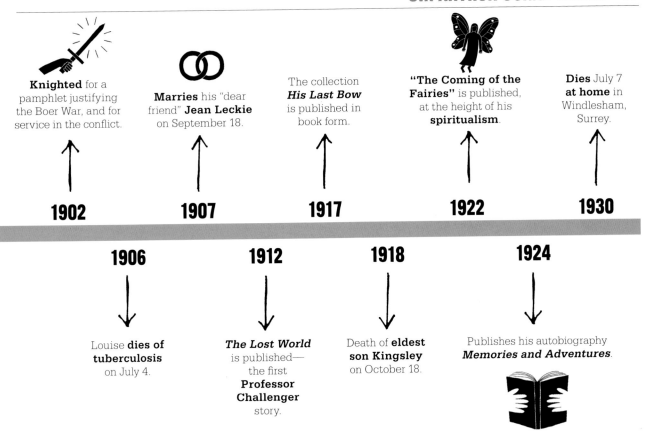

Knighted for a pamphlet justifying the Boer War, and for service in the conflict.

1902

Marries his "dear friend" **Jean Leckie** on September 18.

1907

The collection *His Last Bow* is published in book form.

1917

"The Coming of the Fairies" is published, at the height of his **spiritualism**.

1922

Dies July 7 **at home** in Windlesham, Surrey.

1930

1906

Louise **dies of tuberculosis** on July 4.

1912

The Lost World is published— the first **Professor Challenger** story.

1918

Death of **eldest son Kingsley** on October 18.

1924

Publishes his autobiography *Memories and Adventures*.

---

a series, if it only engaged the reader, would bind the reader to that magazine." And that is exactly what happened. Within six months of the Baker Street detective's first appearance in the *Strand*, in "A Scandal in Bohemia" (pp.56–61), the main selling point of the magazine was each new Holmes adventure.

Marriage and a break

Meanwhile, in 1885, Conan Doyle had married Louise ("Touie") Hawkins, the sister of one of his patients. It was a union that was dogged by Louise's constant ill health. In 1891, the couple moved from Southsea to Tennison Road in South Norwood, southeast London, so Conan Doyle could be closer to the literary world. However, after giving birth to two children, Mary

(1889) and Kingsley (1892), Louise was diagnosed with tuberculosis; her condition declined rapidly, and she remained an invalid for the rest of her life. In 1894, they left London and moved into a new house— Undershaw, in Hindhead, Surrey— since Conan Doyle believed the air would be better for Louise's health.

Despite the success of the first series of Holmes tales, Conan Doyle quickly became bored with his creation, and although he succumbed to the offer of an increased fee for a second series, he was determined that this should be the last. He wanted to spend more time writing historical fiction, which he saw as a more worthy pursuit, and one that would gain him greater recognition as a serious author.

In 1893, he visited Switzerland with Louise. It was while he was there that he visited the Reichenbach Falls and decided that this was a place that would "make a worthy tomb for poor Sherlock, even if I buried my banking account along with him." So in the last story of the second collection, *The Memoirs of Sherlock Holmes* (1893), he consigned his hero to the watery depths of the Reichenbach Falls, locked in the arms of the criminal mastermind Professor Moriarty.

Ignoring the public howls of complaint about his murder of Holmes, he concentrated on a wide range of other writing projects, including a tale of Regency life (*Rodney Stone*, 1896), a novel about the Napoleonic wars (*Uncle Bernac*, 1897), and many short stories. »

Conan Doyle's favorite stories

In 1927, *The Strand Magazine* ran a competition asking its readers to guess which of the Sherlock Holmes stories were Conan Doyle's favorites.

Conan Doyle announced his choices in a *Strand* article titled "How I Made My List." None of the stories from *The Case Book of Sherlock Holmes* were eligible, since it had not yet been published as a book. However, he began by listing "The Lion's Mane" and "The Illustrious Client" as his favorites from that collection.

The conclusive list of his favorites was as follows: first "The Speckled Band," "The Red-Headed League," and "The Dancing Men" for their original plots, followed by "The Final Problem," "A Scandal in Bohemia," and "The Empty House"—which respectively feature "the only foe who ever really extended Holmes," "more female interest than is usual," and "the difficult task of explaining away the alleged death of Holmes."

He then selected "The Five Orange Pips" and "The Priory School" for their dramatic moments, "The Second Stain" for its "high diplomacy and intrigue," and "The Devil's Foot," for being "grim and new." With its description of Holmes's early life, and "a historical touch which gives it a little added distinction," "The Musgrave Ritual" was also given a place on his favorites list. And finally, he added "The Reigate Squire," in which Holmes "shows perhaps the most ingenuity."

As Conan Doyle's stature as a writer and his wealth both grew, he became increasingly involved in public life and the literary scene. Among his distinguished friends and acquaintances was a set of authors who, like Conan Doyle, had created remarkable characters who would resonate with the public long after their deaths: Bram Stoker (Dracula); J. M. Barrie (Peter Pan); Robert Louis Stevenson (Dr. Jekyll and Mr. Hyde); and Oscar Wilde (Dorian Gray).

War and a resurrection

Conan Doyle was actively engaged in the Boer War (1899–1902), offering medical assistance at the Langman Field Hospital in Bloemfontein in South Africa

Conan Doyle on the way to the US in the 1920s with his second wife Jean and their children (from left): Lena Jean, Denis, and Adrian.

in appalling conditions and visiting the front; he later wrote up the history of the war and a pamphlet vindicating the actions of the British Army.

It was at the turn of the century that Conan Doyle hit upon a plot for a new mystery story—*The Hound of the Baskervilles* (pp.152–61). Constructing the framework of the story with the aid of his friend, journalist Fletcher Robinson, the author realized that he needed a central character to play detective, and so he resurrected Sherlock Holmes. The novel was set in 1889, two years before Holmes supposedly fell to his death at the Reichenbach Falls. It was first serialized in the *Strand* in 1901 and published in book form in 1902. In the same year, Conan Doyle was given a knighthood in recognition of his pamphlet on the Boer War and service at the front—although many felt that the honor was more

In the 1920s, magician and escape artist Houdini put on shows to expose false psychics and mediums. He had been friendly with Conan Doyle, but the two men fell out over a séance.

of a thank-you for bringing about the return of Sherlock Holmes. By 1904, the author succumbed to the offers of large fees and began writing more Holmes short stories.

A second marriage

Conan Doyle's relationship with his wife Louise was a strong friendship rather than a passionate romance, and it wasn't until he met Jean Leckie that he experienced the full emotional force of romantic love. He first encountered this attractive Scottish woman—14 years his junior—in 1897, and fell head over heels in love with her. He confessed to his mother how he felt about Jean and told close friends, too, who were divided on the subject; Conan Doyle's brother-in-law, E. W. Hornung (the writer of the Raffles detective stories), was furious at what he considered to be infidelity. However, Conan Doyle was not physically unfaithful to Louise. His strong personal code of chivalry forbade him to take his affair with Jean into the realms of sexual congress. Nevertheless, the strain must have placed Conan Doyle upon the psychological rack. His fondness and sense of duty to his invalid wife kept him by her side, while at the same time his passion for Jean tormented both his heart and mind.

Louise died in 1906, and Conan Doyle married Jean a year later. Shortly after the wedding, they moved to a new house—Little Windlesham, in Crowborough, Sussex. It was a happy marriage, and Jean bore Conan Doyle three more children: Denis (1909), Adrian (1910), and Lena Jean (1912).

On the side of justice

It was during this period that Conan Doyle became involved in a personal fight to establish the innocence of a Parsee, George Edalji, convicted of horse and cattle maiming in Warwickshire. Using the methods of his detective hero, Conan Doyle was able to establish that Edalji could not have performed the savage attacks on the animals because of his very poor eyesight. (The writer Julian Barnes, fascinated by the case, recounted the story in his 2005 historical novel *Arthur & George*, which was later dramatized and broadcast on television in 2015). »

In addition, there were other causes that Conan Doyle took up where he felt that injustice had been wrought. His moral standards prompted him to investigate matters where he believed that misjudgments had been made. Notably, he campaigned to have the death penalty lifted from Roger Casement, a traitor during World War I, but he was not successful. Similarly, he protested the innocence of Oscar Slater, a German Jew accused of murder: thanks to Conan Doyle's efforts, Slater was finally released in 1927 after serving 18 years of a life sentence.

Spiritualism

With the outbreak of World War I in 1914, Conan Doyle became instrumental in forming the local volunteer force—a forerunner of the Home Guard—and acted as a war correspondent, visiting the battlefronts. Perhaps it was the senseless slaughter of so many young lives that revitalized his

A man's soul and reason are his own and he must go whither they beckon.
Arthur Conan Doyle
Letter to *The Scotsman* (October 1900)

interest in spiritualism, for in 1916 he became convinced that he should devote his final years to the advancement of this belief. It was a decision that was further strengthened by the tragic death of his son, Kingsley, who passed away at the age of 26 after succumbing to pneumonia following his wounding on the Somme in 1918.

In the last decade of his life, Conan Doyle gave most of his time and energy to lecturing on

spiritualism in Australia, the US, Canada, and South Africa. He was careful and thorough in testing mediums, but there were occasions on which he was deceived, and his critics seized upon these to illustrate what they regarded as his credulity. Certainly, when two young girls claimed to have seen and photographed fairies in a watery dell near their home in Cottingley, Yorkshire, and Conan Doyle (together with Edward Gardner, a leading Theosophist) declared them to be genuine, he appeared very gullible.

It was Conan Doyle's obsession with spiritualism and his search for proof of a life beyond death that led him into a brief friendship with the magician Harry Houdini, who was also a spiritualist. The two men eventually fell out after a séance in which Lady Jean Conan Doyle (Arthur's wife), acting as a medium, apparently received a written message from Houdini's dead mother. As the magician's mother was a Hungarian Jew and couldn't speak or write a word of English, Houdini denounced the séance as being false. The magician also later wrote a mocking article about the incident, sealing the rift between the two men.

A fitting end

The spiritualist tours were arduous and physically draining, and Conan Doyle's health suffered as a result. He was now in his late sixties, but it appeared that he was making no allowances for his advancing age. In 1929, he suffered severe pains in

The "Cottingley Fairies" photos, faked by two young girls in 1917, fooled many people—including Conan Doyle—into believing fairies existed. The girls cut out illustrations from magazines, securing them in place with hat pins.

A new Holmes tale?

In 2015 a new Sherlock Holmes story was discovered in an attic in Selkirk, Scotland. "Sherlock Homes: Discovering the Border Burghs and, by deduction, the Brig Bazaar" may have been written by Conan Doyle in 1904 (though this has not yet been confirmed), as part of a booklet of short stories titled *Book o' the Brig*. The booklet was printed to raise money to replace a local bridge that had been destroyed by flooding in 1902. Conan Doyle regularly visited Selkirk, and may have contributed the story to assist locals in their fundraising efforts. He was involved in politics at this time, and seeking election as a Liberal Unionist.

In the story, Holmes uses his powers of observation and deduction to predict that Watson is about to travel to Selkirk to open a bazaar to raise money for a bridge. In typical Holmesian style, the detective announces that although Watson has not told him of his plans, his actions "have revealed the bent of your mind."

his chest and was diagnosed with angina. The doctors advised that he cancel all his spiritualist lectures, but the author was adamant that he would not let the public down by failing to honor his engagements. On his way to the Albert Hall, he suffered a violent attack, and from then on all physical exertion was forbidden. Some little time later he was discovered lying in the hallway of his home, clutching a single white snowdrop in his hand. He had seen the flowers through the window and had struggled from his sickbed to take one of the blooms.

My mother's and father's devotion to each other at all times was one of the most wonderful things I have ever known.
Adrian Conan Doyle
The New York Times (July 8, 1930)

By now, Conan Doyle knew he was dying. A few days before his death he wrote: "The reader will judge that I have had many adventures. The greatest and most glorious awaits me now." He informed his family that he did not wish to pass away in bed, so they helped him to a chair where he could look through the window at the Sussex countryside beyond, and he died there surrounded by his family on the morning of July 7, 1930. His last words were to his beloved Jean: "You are wonderful."

He was buried in the garden of his home at Windlesham, but his remains were later moved to the nearby churchyard at Minstead. The inscription on his gravestone is "Steel True, Blade Straight."

A man of many parts

Sir Arthur Conan Doyle was a remarkable man in all areas of his life. His literary output covers perhaps a wider range than any other writer of the 19th and early

Conan Doyle's final resting place is with his second wife Jean in the graveyard at the Church of All Saints in Minstead, Hampshire.

20th centuries: as well as detective stories, he wrote poetry, plays, domestic dramas, sea stories, historical romances, supernatural chillers, medical tales, and various spiritualist tracts.

However, as well as being a remarkable author, he was also a brilliant, energetic, innovative man with strong personal visions, attitudes, and ideas—a Victorian with a 20th-century outlook. His passion drove him to pursue a wide range of activities: he ran for parliament (unsuccessfully); he played cricket for the MCC, once capturing the wicket of the great W. G. Grace; he promoted cross-country skiing in Switzerland; he was one of the first car owners; he had a keen interest in photography and contributed articles on the subject to *The British Journal of Photography*; and, of course, he was also a doctor—a title that he prized above all others. With so many outstanding and fascinating qualities, it is not surprising that his most famous literary creation—Sherlock Holmes—was imbued with a similar kind of brilliance. ∎

MY NAME IS SHERLOCK HOLMES. IT IS MY BUSINESS TO KNOW WHAT OTHER PEOPLE DON'T KNOW

SHERLOCK HOLMES

Sherlock Holmes is the greatest fictional detective of all time; he is a man with exceptional powers of observation and reasoning, a master of disguise who is possessed of an uncanny ability to establish the truth. He is also an enigma.

The "emotional robot"

Initially, Holmes appears to be almost two-dimensional—a brilliant brain and human calculating machine with no personality or emotions. Even Conan Doyle said of him in an interview with *The Bookman* in 1892 that "Sherlock is utterly inhuman, no heart, but with a beautifully logical intellect." And in "The Adventure of the Mazarin Stone" (pp.252–53) Holmes himself declares, "I am brain, Watson. The rest of me is a mere appendix."

It may possibly have been Conan Doyle's intention to create a cold, robotic character with no human feelings and the mind of a computer. If so, he did not succeed—and thank goodness, since such a character would not have been very interesting, let alone inspire the affection, and often adoration, that Holmes does. This public fondness is, to some

Such is Holmes's popularity that a blue plaque has been erected at 221B Baker Street. In Conan Doyle's day, although Baker Street existed in real life, the house number 221 did not.

With his tall, gaunt frame, deep-set eyes, and aquiline nose, Sherlock Holmes is an instantly recognizable figure. Here, he features on a collectible cigarette card of the 1920s.

extent, due to a natural inclination to fill in the blanks about him in one's imagination—an innate tendency to believe that someone denying they have any feelings must be hiding a deep well of emotion. But it is also because of the undeniably deep affection Holmes inspires in others in the stories—Mrs. Hudson, Inspector Lestrade (eventually), and particularly Dr. John Watson. Watson may find Holmes's vanity occasionally irritating, but his unstinting loyalty and indisputable fondness—so unmistakable that some commentators have, with no real evidence, suggested that he and Holmes are even lovers—reinforce the sense that Holmes is so much more than a brilliant robot. And every now and then, Holmes gives fleeting hints that the loyalty and fondness are returned.

A complex interior

Conan Doyle also hints that there is a complex and deeply feeling character beneath the cool exterior. There is the drug use, which is an escape from boredom. There is the violin playing—so brilliant and yet so strange, which seems an outlet for emotions that cannot be expressed otherwise. And then there is the extraordinary river of compassion that runs through Holmes's dealings with the many people, including villains, in his cases. On several occasions, Holmes lets a culprit go free once he feels that natural justice has been served, rather than subjecting them to the full letter of the "official" law. The picture Conan Doyle creates, and

SHERLOCK HOLMES.
"THE ADVENTURES OF SHERLOCK HOLMES"

the one that makes Holmes so endlessly compelling, is the suggestion of hidden depths. He may be a person of extraordinary nobility who sacrifices his own feelings in order to serve the greater good by using his skills in detection. Or perhaps he is a man whose sense of inadequacy and interior pain lead him to bury his feelings and throw himself into his work. It is possible that both are true. In the BBC's recent television series *Sherlock*, the detective's difficulty with emotions is portrayed (by Benedict Cumberbatch) as a sign of mild autism.

Physical appearance

The one unambiguous thing about Holmes is his physical appearance, which was first brought to life by the Sidney Paget drawings in *The Strand Magazine*, which presumably Conan Doyle approved. In these, Holmes has sharp, angular features and is tall and thin, yet wiry and athletic, with reserves of strength »

The Solitary Cyclist

The Dancing Men

The Hound of the Baskervilles

The Second Stain

The Speckled Band

The Raigate Squire

The Boscombe Valley Mystery

The Red-Headed League

The Norwood Builder

The Abbey Grange

The Final Problem

The Bruce-Partington Plans

Sidney Paget, the first illustrator of the Holmes stories in *The Strand Magazine* (some of which are shown here), was largely responsible for creating the popular image of Holmes.

French artist Vernet—probably Charles Horace Vernet (1758–1836) as opposed to his father Claude Joseph (1714–1789). The only family member that the reader knows anything about is Holmes's elder brother Mycroft.

Holmes claims that he developed his skills in deduction as an undergraduate. Commentators have, therefore, speculated where he went to university, the writer Dorothy L. Sayers theorizing that it was Sidney Sussex College, Cambridge, while some scholars favour Oxford. There he had one true friend, Victor Trevor, who precipitated his involvement in "The *Gloria Scott*" case (pp.116–19). He does not seem to have made any other friends since, except Watson. In "The Five Orange Pips" (pp.74–9) Watson suggests, "Some friend of yours, perhaps?" and Holmes replies, "Except yourself I have none." His solitariness is lifelong.

In the 1870s, after university, Holmes moved to London and took up residence in Montague Street, near the British Museum. He had connections at St. Bartholomew's Hospital, which allowed him to conduct his experiments in the labs there, even though he was neither student nor staff. He was already developing his sideline as a consulting detective, but it was only after he met Watson in 1881 and moved into 221B with him as his co-lodger that the business became all-consuming.

Life with Watson
For eight years, Holmes and Watson were inseparable, and Watson was the witness and recorder of most of

that enable him to cope remarkably well in any physical tussle (aided by his knowledge of the martial art baritsu, p.165). Holmes's tweedy attire, cape, and his now famous deerstalker hat—created by Paget in the drawings rather than by Conan Doyle—are as iconic as his trademark cane and pipe.

Holmes's background
Conan Doyle gives away few details of Holmes's life, adding to the enigma. "His Last Bow" (pp.246–47), set in 1914, implies that Holmes is 60, meaning he was born in about 1854. His ancestors are "country squires", and his grandmother the sister of the

> I have chosen my own particular profession… I am the only one in the world.
> **Sherlock Holmes**

Holmes's brilliant exploits as a detective—although some were kept from Watson. Then, in about 1889, Watson fell in love with Mary Morstan and moved away from 221B Baker Street to set up his own medical practice in west London.

The relationship between Watson and Holmes became more distant after Watson's marriage, and we hear less of his cases—until the fateful one in "The Final Problem" (pp.142–47), in which Holmes appeared to meet his death at Reichenbach Falls on May 4, 1891 in a struggle with the archvillain Moriarty. Years later, to the total amazement of Watson (and the

reading public), he reappeared in London in "The Adventure of the Empty House" (pp.162–67). His account of his missing three years, called the "Great Hiatus" by Holmes enthusiasts, was scant and involved hints of gripping adventures in Tibet, Persia, and Khartoum before he settled in Montpellier in southern France, where he conducted scientific experiments. The lack of information has led Holmes enthusiasts to speculate that he spent at least some of that time doing undercover work for the British government, via Mycroft.

By the time Holmes returned, Watson had been widowed, and they resumed their relationship, until Watson again moved out of 221B and Holmes retired to a cottage on the south coast near Eastbourne to indulge in the joys of the quiet life and his passion for beekeeping. But he could not entirely resist the urge to do a little detective work on his new home territory, as depicted in "The Adventure of the Lion's Mane" (pp.278–83), set in 1907, and later carried out vital work for the Foreign Office in the build-up to World War I in "His Last Bow." After that, at age 60, Holmes finally vanished.

Inspiration for Holmes
Although Holmes's fame as a detective is unparalleled, he was by no means the first fictional sleuth. Edgar Allan Poe, Émile Gaboriau, and Wilkie Collins had all written about detectives, each of which can be seen, to some extent, in Holmes. From Poe, Conan Doyle drew upon the ideas of the "locked room mystery" and solving clues by clever deduction; from Gaboriau came forensic science and crime scene investigation; and from Collins something of Holmes's appearance.

But when Conan Doyle was asked about his inspiration for Holmes, he didn't mention any of these fictional figures. Instead, he referred to the real-life Dr. Joseph Bell (see p.43)—one of his former professors at Edinburgh University, who was renowned for his close observation and powers of deduction. Bell, too, had an interest in forensic science, and was often called as an expert for criminal trials. In 1892, Conan Doyle wrote to Bell, "It is most certainly to you that I owe Sherlock Holmes." But Bell wrote back, "…you are yourself Sherlock Holmes and well you know it". ∎

Mycroft Holmes

Holmes's elder brother Mycroft is a vibrant element in the Holmes canon—although, like Moriarty, he only appears directly in two stories. The reader is never told anything about his early life, except that he is seven years older than Sherlock Holmes, and, if anything, even cleverer. "He has the tidiest and most orderly brain," says Sherlock, "with the greatest capacity for storing facts, of any man living". His brilliance has given him a place at the heart of the secret government machinery in Whitehall, and he is a crucial source of intelligence. As Watson

remarks, Mycroft is "the most indispensable man in the country"—"Again and again, his word has decided national policy." Mycroft is considered by some critics to be the head of the secret service, although this is never specified.

The real-life inspiration for Mycroft Holmes may well have been Robert Anderson, whose role in government (as head of the secret service and the CID, and a key adviser on government policy in the 1890s) closely corresponds to that of Mycroft in the stories.

I WAS A WHETSTONE FOR HIS MIND. I STIMULATED HIM

DR. JOHN WATSON

Dr. John Watson is the narrator of all but four of the Sherlock Holmes tales. He is the essential witness to Holmes's brilliance, and the tireless biographer who records the detective's deeds and conveys them to the public in his memoirs. Holmes acknowledges Watson's considerable skills as a chronicler in the short story "A Scandal in Bohemia" (pp.56–61), when he urges Watson to stay and meet his new client, saying "I am lost without my Boswell." This likening of Watson to James Boswell (1740–1795), the

highly acclaimed biographer of Dr. Samuel Johnson, diarist, and lawyer, is an accolade indeed.

A key figure

Watson is a simple but ingenious literary device. With Watson addressing the reader directly, the narrative becomes immediate and engaging. He explains what is going on and the reader identifies with him, following his ups and downs as he witnesses Holmes in action, and experiences bafflement and wonder. And since Holmes's arrival at the truth generally takes

Watson by surprise, the reader also feels the thrill of discovery when the time comes for Holmes to reveal it.

But Watson is so much more than a mere observer. He is the warm-hearted and good-humored everyman to Holmes's cool and high-flown pragmatist. In an early version of *A Study in Scarlet* (pp.36–45), Conan Doyle gave Holmes a partner named Ormond Sacker before settling on the more down-to-earth name of John H Watson. Watson is loyal, steadfast, and utterly dependable. Holmes

The Baker Street household

Holmes and Watson rent their Baker Street rooms from the long-suffering landlady, Mrs. Hudson. Although she appears only briefly throughout the canon, her affection for the two men is unmistakable. Not only does she put up with Holmes conducting chemical experiments, firing a gun indoors, and taking drugs, she also answers the door at all hours to a string of miscellaneous visitors.

221B Baker Street is a suite of rooms on the second and third floors of the house, with the

sitting room on the second floor, overlooking the street, and Holmes's bedroom at the back; Watson's room is on the floor above, looking out over the rear yard. In fact, the address never actually existed; at the time, Baker Street ended at number 83. The house that is now home to the Sherlock Holmes Museum was then in Upper Baker Street, although it is very similar to the description in the stories. In 1990, it was officially given the number 221B.

Confidante and companion,
Watson (left) talks with Holmes in "The
Stockbroker's Clerk." The illustration is
by Sidney Paget from the March 1893
edition of *The Strand Magazine*.

" 'NOTHING COULD BE BETTER,' SAID HOLMES."

is sometimes rude to him, and
Watson, in turn, complains about
the detective's egotism, but, as
Holmes asserts in *The Hound of the
Baskervilles* (pp.152–61), "there is
no man better worth having at your
side when you are in a tight place."

In "The Adventure of Charles
Augustus Milverton" (pp.186–87),
Lestrade describes his suspect
as "a middle-sized, strongly built
man—square jaw, thick neck,
moustache," and Holmes replies
that this sounds like Watson, as
indeed it is. Watson is an army-
trained crack shot and was once
athletic, playing for the famous
Blackheath Rugby Club. But he
also has a war injury and a taste
for wine and tobacco.

Watson's past
In *A Study in Scarlet*, the reader
learns that Watson qualified as a
medical doctor at St. Bartholomew's
Hospital in London in 1878,
suggesting he was born around
1853. After qualifying, he signed up
as an army surgeon with the 5th

Good old Watson!
You are the one
fixed point in
a changing age.
Sherlock Holmes

Northumberland Fusiliers and was
posted to the Second Afghan War,
where he was shot at the Battle of
Maiwand in July 1880, in the arm or
the leg—the narratives are confusing
on this detail. While recovering in
the hospital, he became ill with
typhoid and was sent home with
his health "irretrievably ruined",
and was discharged from the army
with a meager pension.

With apparently no family to
turn to, Watson was left adrift in
London. It was at this low point that
Stamford, Watson's old friend from
medical school, introduced him to
Sherlock Holmes, who was looking
for someone to share his lodgings
at 221B Baker Street.

Thereafter, much of Watson's
life revolved around Holmes and
his escapades. At some point,
however, Watson moved out of
221B and became a successful
medical practitioner. Holmes has
such respect for Watson's
expertise that he keeps him at a
distance to stop him from seeing
through his feigned illness in
"The Adventure of the Dying
Detective" (pp.234–35).

Personal relationships
Watson's marital status is difficult to
establish. The reader learns that he
marries Mary Morstan, the young
woman who seeks Holmes's help
in *The Sign of Four* (pp.46–55), yet
in "The Adventure of the Empty
House" (pp.162–67) it seems she has
died. However, in some later tales,
Watson has a wife, and Holmesians
have often speculated on her
identity. Fans are also intrigued by
Watson's assertion that he has "an
experience of women which extends
over many nations and three separate
continents," though given that he is
comparing them to Mary when he
first meets her, this is probably just
the hyperbole of a man in love.

Watson is sometimes portrayed
as dull-witted. Even Conan Doyle
once called him Holmes's "rather
stupid friend." However, while he
may lag behind in brains, he more
than makes up for it in reliability
and integrity. Watson is Holmes's
rock and only friend, and Holmes
makes very clear in "The Dying
Detective" just how much Watson
means to him: "You won't fail me,"
he says, "You never did fail me." ∎

HE SITS MOTIONLESS, LIKE A SPIDER IN THE CENTRE OF ITS WEB

PROFESSOR JAMES MORIARTY

Conan Doyle created Professor James Moriarty simply to provide a fitting opponent with whom his hero could grapple during his goodbye to the world in "The Final Problem" (pp.142–47). Although Moriarty apparently died after his brief, dramatic encounter with Holmes at the Reichenbach Falls in Switzerland, and he only appears directly in one other story, *The*

Valley of Fear (pp.212–21)—set earlier in Holmes's career—his powerful specter seems to haunt the later tales. The character of Moriarty became established in readers' minds, and today we can hardly talk of Holmes without mentioning his nemesis—Moriarty is forever linked to the great detective's legacy.

Holmes's equal

The professor's power to terrify may stem from the fact that he is a mirror image of Holmes: the man the great detective might have become had he chosen to follow a sinister path. Moriarty is a spine-chilling version of Holmes: both men have high foreheads and sharp eyes, but in Moriarty's case everything is more drawn and exaggerated. Tall and thin, with sunken eyes and a protruding chin, his head moves from "side to side in curiously reptilian fashion." Moriarty came from a privileged background and received an excellent education that set him

Released in 1922, the movie *Moriarty* (originally titled *Sherlock Holmes* in the US) starred German actor Gustav von Seyffertitz as the brilliant criminal mastermind Professor Moriarty.

on a path toward respectability. Naturally brilliant at mathematics (a subject Conan Doyle hated), at the age of 21 he wrote a treatise on algebra that achieved recognition throughout Europe. He was also celebrated for his brilliant book on the dynamics of asteroids, which Holmes remarks is so advanced that "no man in the scientific press was capable of criticising it." On the back of this work, Moriarty became a professor of mathematics at an English university. But then unspecified "dark rumours" began

The greatest schemer of all time, the organiser of every devilry, the controlling brain of the underworld, a brain which might have made or marred the destiny of nations—that's the man!
Sherlock Holmes

to circulate about him, and he relocated to London to begin his criminal career. And what a career it was. Moriarty became the ultimate mastermind, drawing on his prodigious intellect to run a vast crime network, the largest ever seen, and yet remain invisible at its heart, entirely above suspicion, as the Professor Moriarty of mathematical celebrity. "Like a spider," he sat at the center, pulling the strings of this criminal web—"the organizer of half that is evil and of nearly all that is undetected in this great city." It took the equal genius of Holmes to finally trace the threads back to him.

Brain of the underworld

The brilliance of Moriarty's schemes means that no one can ever pin down the source of his criminal gains, whether it is burglary, extortion, or forgery. Holmes likens him to Jonathan Wild, who in the 18th century "was a master criminal… the hidden force of the London criminals, to whom he sold his brains and his organization on a fifteen per cent commission." Wild pretended to be a thief-taker, earning fame and money for the way his network caught criminals—but it

Sidney Paget's illustration of Moriarty first appeared in "The Final Problem," which was published in the December 1893 edition of *The Strand Magazine.*

was also he who was organizing the crime. Holmes scholars have identified various other candidates who may have provided Conan Doyle with the inspiration for Moriarty, but by far the strongest is the true-life criminal genius Adam Worth. Indeed, the similarity in their methods is so marked that the US detective William Pinkerton, head of the famous Pinkerton Detective Agency, believed that Conan Doyle should pay him royalties, as he had told the author all about Worth during a transatlantic voyage.

There are two major clues that lend weight to this theory. Firstly, in "The Final Problem" Moriarty is referred to as the "Napoleon of crime"—a moniker that was coined for Adam Worth. Secondly, in *The Valley of Fear*, Holmes reports that the professor has hanging in his study an incredibly valuable, and famous, painting of a coquettish young woman that he could only

have acquired through theft. It is easy to believe that this is Conan Doyle's reference to Worth's temporary "ownership" of Thomas Gainsborough's alluring portrait of Georgiana, Duchess of Devonshire, which he had personally cut from its frame in the gallery in which it was hanging, having reportedly become smitten with it. ∎

Adam Worth

German-born American super-criminal Adam Worth (1848–1902) was dubbed the "Napoleon of crime" by Scotland Yard's Robert Anderson for his skill in running a major crime network from his home in London. Like Moriarty, Worth was an expert operator, staying at arm's length from his crimes; unlike Moriarty, however, he was opposed to the use of violence, and treated the men who worked for him as family. Indeed, the only reason he finally served a prison term (for petty crime) was because he got caught while going to the aid of one of his gang.

Worth began his life of crime in the US, as a bank robber, before moving to London to set up as a respectable art collector and the head of a criminal syndicate involved in robbery and forgery.

For years, he outfoxed the world's police by conducting bloodless, well-executed crimes without leaving a shred of incriminating evidence. For example, there was nothing to link him to his theft of a Thomas Gainsborough artwork, which he carried with him for 25 years before shrewdly negotiating a $25,000 fee for its return.

I AM A PRACTICAL MAN, MR. HOLMES, AND WHEN I HAVE GOT MY EVIDENCE I COME TO MY CONCLUSIONS
INSPECTOR G. LESTRADE

Inspector G. Lestrade is the Scotland Yard detective who appears repeatedly throughout the Holmes canon. Many other police detectives make a fleeting appearance, from Inspector Stanley Hopkins in "The Adventure of Black Peter" (pp.184–85) to Inspector Bardle in "The Adventure of the Lion's Mane" (pp.278–83), but Lestrade is the only persistent presence. First appearing in *A Study in Scarlet* (pp.36–45) in 1887, Lestrade is still there in "The Adventure of the Three Garridebs" (pp.262–65), which Conan Doyle wrote 37 years later.

Conan Doyle seems to have gotten Lestrade's name from a fellow medical student at Edinburgh, Joseph Alexandre Lestrade, and the initial "G" may be an echo of the Prefect of Police known only as "G___" in Edgar Allan Poe's story *The Purloined Letter* (1845). Watson describes the inspector as "a little sallow rat-faced, dark-eyed fellow" and later as "a lean, ferret-like man, furtive and sly-looking." Very little

else is known about Lestrade, but he is probably part of the new breed of tenacious professional policemen who made their way up through the ranks from humble beginnings— the kind first depicted in fiction in the form of Inspector Bucket in Charles Dickens' *Bleak House* (1853) and Inspector Cuff in Wilkie Collins' *The Moonstone* (1868).

Fact or fiction?
Both Bucket and Cuff were based on the real-life Detective Inspector Jonathan "Jack" Whicher (1814– 1881), one of the eight original members of the Detective Branch set up at Scotland Yard in 1842. Whicher reached the pinnacle of his fame with the infamous Constance Kent murder mystery in 1860,

Inspector Lestrade arresting Jim Browner in "The Cardboard Box," first published in the UK in *The Strand Magazine* (1893).

> I really cannot undertake to go about the country looking for a left-handed gentleman with a game leg. I should become the laughing-stock of Scotland Yard.
> **Inspector Lestrade**

recalled in Kate Summerscale's 2009 book *The Suspicions of Mr. Whicher*. Readers both of the fictional stories and of the real-life crime reports at the time got a particular frisson from the way such lowly men probed behind the facade of well-to-do respectability to lay bare their corruption. Holmes, of course, has a more aristocratic brilliance, and when he first meets Lestrade, he can barely conceal his low opinion. "[Gregson and] Lestrade are the best of a bad lot. They are both quick and energetic, but conventional—shockingly so..." His ridicule soon becomes so marked it seems almost snobbery. But Conan Doyle may have been drawing inspiration from real life.

A tarnished reputation

By the 1880s, Scotland Yard's reputation, so bright in Whicher's day, had been tarnished by the way in which Inspector John Shore and his fellow detectives were given the runaround by Adam Worth, the real-life criminal mastermind who was one of the inspirations for Conan Doyle's Moriarty (p.29). Worth made Shore look flat-footed and incompetent, and Shore never caught his man despite years of dogged pursuit. Scotland Yard's reputation hit another low in 1888, when they failed to make any headway with the appalling Jack the Ripper murders (p.315).

Mutual respect

Over the years, however, Holmes's contemptuous attitude toward Lestrade seems to mellow. At first, Lestrade doesn't think much of Holmes either. So, perhaps sensing Holmes's ridicule, he declares himself to be a practical detective who deals in facts—in contrast to the abstract thinking of amateurs like Holmes. But as he sees Holmes solve case after case, he comes to admire the detective's methods. Holmes, in turn, begins to respect some of Lestrade's qualities, and allows the inspector to take the credit for his deductions.

In "The Cardboard Box" (pp.110–11), Holmes admits that Lestrade is "tenacious as a bulldog when he once understands what he has to do, and indeed, it is just this tenacity which has brought him to the top at Scotland Yard." And when Holmes comes back from the dead in "The Adventure of the Empty House" (pp.162–67), he trusts Lestrade enough to let him in on his secret. Lestrade returns the compliment, saying, "It's good to see you back in London, sir." By the time of "The Adventure of the Six Napoleons" (pp.188–89), it turns out that Lestrade regularly drops by at 221B Baker Street with updates and for advice. Lestrade even admits to a genuinely touched Holmes that "... we are very proud of you [down at Scotland Yard], and if you come down to-morrow there's not a man, from the oldest inspector to the youngest constable, who wouldn't be glad to shake you by the hand." ∎

The Baker Street Irregulars

Despite appearances, Holmes rarely works entirely alone. In a number of investigations the detective is aided by his invisible army of helpers— the motley crew of street urchins known as the Baker Street Irregulars. In *A Study in Scarlet*, Watson describes them as "half a dozen of the dirtiest and most ragged street Arabs that ever I clapped eyes on," but Holmes knows their value, calling them "the Baker Street division of the detective police force." Shabby they may be, but for the price of a shilling a day, they can "go everywhere and hear everything." No one but Holmes pays any attention to these dirty little children, led by a boy named Wiggins, but in many stories they provide crucial information. Besides the Irregulars, Holmes picks various other more humble members of society to help him—from the 14-year-old messenger Cartwright, who goes through hotel garbage cans in *The Hound of the Baskervilles*, to Billy the pageboy in *The Valley of Fear*.

THE EAR
ADVENT

LY
URES

Holmes solves his first case (see "The *Gloria Scott*," pp.116–19).

↑

1874

Holmes takes rooms by himself in London's **Montague Street** (see *A Study in Scarlet*, pp.36–45).

↑

1877

Holmes and Watson meet at **St. Bartholomew's Hospital**, London. They lodge together at **221B Baker Street** (see *A Study in Scarlet*, pp.36–45).

↑

JAN 1881

Queen Victoria celebrates her **Golden Jubilee**.

↑

JUN 1887

1876–1881

↓

Conan Doyle **studies medicine** at **Edinburgh University**.

JUL 1880

↓

Watson is shot and wounded at the Battle of Maiwand, **Afghanistan** (see *A Study in Scarlet*, pp.36–45).

JUN 1882

↓

Conan Doyle **moves to Southsea** to set up a medical practice. He also **renounces his Catholic faith**.

DEC 1887

↓

Conan Doyle publishes *A Study in Scarlet* (pp.36–45) in *Beeton's Christmas Annual*.

Event in the lives of Holmes and Watson

IN THIS CHAPTER

Sherlock Holmes and Dr. John Watson first entered into the public consciousness in 1887, when the novel *A Study in Scarlet* was published in England in *Beeton's Christmas Annual*. The story also featured two hapless inspectors, Gregson and Lestrade of Scotland Yard, along with Holmes's gang of informal assistants, the "Baker Street Irregulars." It was not a great success, but luckily found favor with the editor of *Lippincott's Magazine* in the US (who published *The Sign of Four* three years later).

A common device within the canon is established in *A Study in Scarlet* when American Jefferson Hope scrawls out the word "Rache" ("revenge") in his own blood, having come to England seeking vengeance: stories that begin in foreign lands must be unraveled and concluded by Holmes in London. Watson too sees himself washed up into the "great cesspool" of the British Empire, when he arrives in London after his wounding at the Battle of Maiwand in Afghanistan.

A quickening pace
Conan Doyle moved to London in March 1891; he had abandoned his struggling medical practice on England's south coast, and was planning to set up shop as an ophthalmic surgeon. The first four Holmes short stories were written during the following month, and began appearing in the newly founded *The Strand Magazine* soon afterward. This time, the sleuth was an instant success, and nothing could have prepared Conan Doyle for the readers' enthusiasm. Holmes's popularity also ensured the success

Watson marries Mary Morstan, and sets up a **new medical practice** (see "The Stockbroker's Clerk," pp.114–15).

JAN 1889

The Sign of Four appears in ***Lippincott's Magazine***. It is published as a novel in October.

FEB 1890

Holmes and Moriarty disappear into the Reichenbach Falls. The **"Great Hiatus" begins** (see "The Final Problem," pp.142–47).

APR–MAY 1891

The Strand Magazine begins publishing Holmes **short stories as serializations**.

JUL 1891

FEB 1889

Conan Doyle publishes *Micah Clarke* (p.344)—a **historical novel**.

MAR 1891

Conan Doyle **arrives in London**, by way of Venice, Milan, and Paris. He lodges at **23 Montague Place**.

MAY 1891

Conan Doyle **gives up his medical practice** and decides to make his living from **writing**.

OCT 1892

Conan Doyle publishes *The Adventures of Sherlock Holmes*.

of the *Strand* itself, since all of the detective's subsequent outings appeared there, before being published in book form. Conan Doyle was paid £300 for the last six stories in *The Adventures of Sherlock Holmes*—dwarfing the £25 for which he had sold *A Study in Scarlet*. And when the *Adventures* was published as a book in October 1892, the author dedicated it to Joseph Bell—the Edinburgh medical professor on whom Holmes had been partly based.

A complex character

Watson's famous list of Holmes's intellectual faculties is featured in *A Study in Scarlet*; indeed, at this point, it seems that the detective is a pure reasoning machine. However, in *The Sign of Four*, his cocaine use and violin-playing reveal other elements of his character, perhaps influenced by the cult of "aestheticism." Holmes displays a type of world-weariness so affected that it is known not as "boredom," but rather by the French term *ennui*. Yet, conversely, the second novel brims with the kind of physical action that is absent from the first. In fact, Holmes perpetually defies Watson's preconceptions: a result of Conan Doyle's occasional inconsistencies, perhaps, or even the detective's own evasiveness.

Yet for all the variations in his character traits, Holmes's physical appearance was set in these early years as Sidney Paget's drawings first appeared alongside the stories in the *Strand*. Holmes' image was based on the artist's brother Walter, and completed with the addition of the famous deerstalker hat.

Bringing it all back home

A thread of the exotic runs through the early stories, from the Indian backstory in *The Sign of Four* and Grimesby Roylott's Indian "Swamp Adder" in "The Speckled Band," to the penal transportation of British criminals to Australia in "The Boscombe Valley Mystery," and Elias Openshaw's exploits in the US Civil War in "The Five Orange Pips." There is also a marked sense of playfulness in these early stories. "The Red-Headed League," with its gullible pawnbroker Jabez Wilson, is a case in point, as is the duo's brush with European royalty in "A Scandal in Bohemia." In this story, Holmes's admiration for the "adventuress" Irene Adler also sets the tone for the frequent shift of sympathies between high-society clients and supposed criminals. ∎

THERE'S THE SCARLET THREAD OF MURDER RUNNING THROUGH THE COLOURLESS SKEIN OF LIFE

A STUDY IN SCARLET (1887)

IN CONTEXT

TYPE
Novel

FIRST PUBLICATION
UK: *Beeton's Christmas Annual*, December 1887

NOVEL PUBLICATION
Ward, Lock & Co. July 1888

CHARACTERS
Stamford Former medical colleague of Watson's.

Inspectors Lestrade and Tobias Gregson Scotland Yard policemen.

Enoch J. Drebber Elder of the Mormon church.

Joseph Stangerson Mormon elder, and Drebber's secretary.

Jefferson Hope Young American.

Constable John Rance Policeman.

Wiggins Leader of a gang of London street urchins.

Madame Charpentier Drebber's landlady.

Arthur Charpentier Naval officer, and son of Madame Charpentier.

Alice Charpentier Madame Charpentier's daughter.

John Ferrier Wanderer found by Mormons.

Lucy Ferrier John Ferrier's daughter.

Brigham Young Real-life leader of the Mormon church.

Chapter 1
Stamford introduces Watson to Holmes and **the two men agree to take rooms together**.

Chapter 3
Watson accompanies Holmes to a house in Brixton where an American named Drebber lies dead. **Holmes examines the scene** with a magnifying glass and tape measure.

Chapter 5
Holmes tries to **draw out the murderer** with a newspaper ad about a ring left at the scene, but is **outwitted by an accomplice** disguised as an old woman.

PART 1

Chapter 2
Watson studies Holmes, who **demonstrates his remarkable powers** of armchair observation and deduction.

Chapter 4
Holmes sends a telegram to the US police, then **interviews the constable** who discovered the body.

Chapter 6
Gregson arrests Drebber's landlady's son Arthur, but then Lestrade finds Stangerson **stabbed to death**, exonerating Arthur.

The year is 1880 and military surgeon Dr. John H. Watson has been discharged from the army after being wounded in Afghanistan. Back in London and living on a meager army pension, he is looking for someone to share lodgings with. An old colleague of Watson, Stamford, introduces him to Sherlock Holmes (who calls himself the world's only "consulting detective"), and the two men take up rooms at 221B Baker Street.

On receiving a request for help from the police, Holmes invites Watson to accompany him. The pair meet inspectors Gregson and Lestrade of Scotland Yard at a house in Brixton, where a body has been found. Holmes deduces from the sour smell on the man's lips that he has been poisoned. Documents identify him as Enoch Drebber, a US citizen, who is traveling with his secretary, Stangerson, and lodging with a Madame Charpentier.

A woman's wedding ring has been left at the scene, and after questioning Constable Rance, who found the body, Holmes suspects that a drunk seen hanging around the house was in fact the murderer

Chapter 7
Holmes **astounds Gregson and Lestrade** by luring the murderer, Jefferson Hope, to Baker Street and arresting him.

Chapter 2
A few years later, Ferrier is now a successful farmer in the Mormon stronghold of **Salt Lake City**, and Lucy falls in love with a non-Mormon, Jefferson Hope.

Chapter 4
Lucy, her father, and Hope leave under cover of darkness, heading for Carson City, **trying in vain to escape** the grip of the Mormons.

Chapter 6
Back at Baker Street, the arrested Hope **shows no remorse in avenging Lucy**, and recounts in brief his adventures in London tracking down his victims.

PART 2

Chapter 1
Many years earlier in the Utah desert, **Mormon pilgrims rescue** John Ferrier and his daughter Lucy, on condition they **convert to the Mormon faith**.

Chapter 3
When the Mormon leader, Brigham Young, says that **Lucy must marry either Drebber or Stangerson**, polygamist church elders, Ferrier and his daughter plan to flee.

Chapter 5
Stangerson kills Ferrier, and when Lucy is forced to marry Drebber **she dies broken-hearted**. Drebber and Stangerson are **exiled from the faith**, and Hope hunts them down in Europe.

Chapter 7
Hope dies before his trial, **Holmes tells Watson how he solved the murder**, and Watson vows to make the case public.

returning to claim the ring. Other evidence suggests to Holmes that the murderer is a cabbie, although he does not reveal this to Watson.

Gregson arrests the landlady's son, Arthur Charpentier, who had confronted Drebber over his coarse behavior toward his sister Alice. Lestrade suspects the secretary Stangerson, but finds him stabbed to death, killed while Arthur was in custody. A pillbox containing two pills is found with his body. Back at 221B, Holmes tests the pills on a sick terrier; the first is harmless, but the second kills the dog.

Learning from the police in the US that Drebber had sought protection from a man named Jefferson Hope, Holmes instructs a gang of street urchins, known as the "Baker Street Irregulars," to trace a cabbie by that name and lure him to Baker Street. When Hope arrives, Holmes arrests him before an astonished Gregson and Lestrade.

The second section of the novel begins in Salt Lake City, Utah, in 1847. Here, it is revealed that Hope had been in love with a young woman called Lucy, who had died of a broken heart after Stangerson

killed her father and she was forced to marry Drebber. The action then returns to Baker Street, where Hope reveals how he forced Drebber to make a choice between two pills; Drebber would take one while he would take the other. Drebber chose the poisoned pill and died. Hope accidentally left a keepsake, Lucy's wedding ring, at the scene.

Hope dies of a heart condition before he can be brought to trial. To Watson's indignation, a newspaper report gives all the credit for solving the case to Gregson and Lestrade, and barely mentions Holmes. ∎

T his is where the legend of Sherlock Holmes begins. Within the first few pages of his 1887 novel *A Study in Scarlet,* Conan Doyle establishes not only the eccentric and brilliant nature of his hero Holmes, but also the great detective's essential partnership with Watson and his atmospheric vision of Victorian London. The relationship between the two men and the setting of their adventures both played an essential role in the success of the many Holmes stories that would follow.

Before the two future partners meet, Watson's friend Stamford warns him that his potential fellow lodger "appears to have a passion for definite and exact knowledge," and may be a bit too scientific and cold-blooded for his tastes. He tells Watson that Holmes even beats corpses in the dissecting-rooms with a stick to see how a dead body bruises after death (in mentioning this, Conan Doyle is eager to show that his sleuth is at the forefront of current developments in criminal investigation). Holmes claims to have created a new and ground-breaking process for detecting

bloodstains—"the Sherlock Holmes's test". The fact that we never hear of this test again in any subsequent Holmes tale is not that important; Conan Doyle is simply trying to establish Holmes as the world's first forensic detective.

Holmes the magician
But Holmes's genius does not end with forensics. On first meeting Watson, he famously says, "You have been in Afghanistan, I perceive," revealing his remarkable powers of observation. Holmes is able to pick out minute details,

You have brought detection as near an exact science as it ever will be brought in this world.
Dr. Watson

Watson was injured at the Battle of Maiwand, July 1880, in the Second Anglo-Afghan war. This painting shows the British Royal Horse Artillery saving their guns from the Afghans.

assemble them in a rational and inspired fashion, and reach a conclusion that makes him seem like a magician performing an amazing trick.

Later, in 221B, Watson picks up a magazine and reads an article on "the Science of Deduction and Analysis" which says, "By a man's finger-nails, by his coat-sleeve, by his boot, by his trouser-knees, by the callosities of his forefinger and thumb, by his expression, by his shirt-cuffs... a man's calling is plainly revealed." When Watson dismisses this extract out loud as "ineffable twaddle" and "the theory of some armchair lounger," Holmes reveals that he was the author. He then explains how he knew Watson had recently been in Afghanistan.

Watson is a doctor, and this fact, combined with the details that Holmes observes about his person and clothing, enables Holmes to

A STUDY IN SCARLET

deduce that Watson has recently seen service in war-torn Afghanistan that ended in an injury (see below). "The whole train of thought did not occupy a second," says Holmes, with typical immodesty.

Creating a legend

Conan Doyle famously based Holmes's powers of observation on those of his mentor at Edinburgh University's medical school, Dr. Joseph Bell (see p.43). In the preface to *Sherlock Holmes—The Complete Long Stories* (1929), he later wrote: "Having endured a severe course of training in medical diagnosis, I felt that if the same austere methods of observation and reasoning were applied to the problems of crime some more scientific system could be constructed."

For Holmes to appeal to the reader, Conan Doyle knew that he had to be more than a scientific cypher: he had to be enthralling in his own right. To the hypocritical society of the time—which covered up the legs of a piano for the sake of decorum, yet allowed prostitution

> The most commonplace crime is often the most mysterious, because it presents no new or special features from which deductions may be drawn.
> **Sherlock Holmes**

to flourish in London's East End— there was nothing more fascinating than a flamboyant bohemian with a disregard for convention.

Conan Doyle imbued his sleuth with an array of idiosyncrasies. The reader learns quickly that Holmes plays the violin well, and is a boxer, a swordsman, and an expert in singlestick (a martial art that uses a wooden stick). He has written a monograph on cigarette ash, keeps

a tape measure and a magnifying glass in his pocket, and chatters to himself as he looks for clues.

Holmes is particularly proud of his "brain-attic," in which he stores only essential information. As he explains: "I consider that a man's brain originally is like a little empty attic, and you have to stock it with such furniture as you choose… It is a mistake to think that that little room has elastic walls and can distend to any extent." When Holmes declares, to Watson's amazement, that he did not know that the Earth orbits the sun, he tells Watson: "Now that I do know it I shall do my best to forget it."

The armchair detective

Holmes explains to Watson that when either the police or the many private detectives in London are stumped by a case, they come to him, and he puts them on the right track, without ever having to leave his armchair. In *A Study in Scarlet* more than in any of the subsequent Holmes stories, this is indeed his main role. Even before the start of »

Holmes observes Dr. Watson and forms a conclusion

Watson is a **medical type** with the air of a **military man**, so he must be an army doctor.

He has a **dark face, yet pale wrists**, showing that he is **deeply tanned**.

His **haggard face** clearly shows that he has undergone **hardship and sickness**.

He holds his **left arm** in a stiff and unnatural manner, showing that it has been **injured**.

Watson has been discharged from the army after military service abroad.

the central case, Watson notes how a stream of visitors of both sexes, and all ages and classes (police inspectors, "a young girl," "a Jew pedlar," "a railway porter," and an "old white-haired gentleman"), are redirected by private inquiry agencies to call upon Holmes at 221B for help.

When the main case in *A Study in Scarlet* does get underway, Holmes travels to the crime scene, where he investigates enthusiastically. "As I watched him," says Watson, "I was irresistibly reminded of a pure-blooded, well-trained foxhound as it dashes backwards and forwards through the covert, whining in its eagerness, until it comes across the lost scent." But for most of the story, the action occurs without direct involvement from Holmes, and the culprit is ultimately apprehended in his Baker Street sitting room.

Conan Doyle had to adjust this approach in later stories, allowing Holmes to go out and investigate crime, and be more of a man of action, or an "amateur bloodhound," as Watson calls him in *A Study in Scarlet*. However, he never fully loses his propensity for solving crimes from the comfort of his armchair.

> ...he was as sensitive to flattery on the score of his art as any girl could be of her beauty.
> **Dr. Watson**

Watson's notes on Holmes

1. Knowledge of Literature.—Nil.
2. Philosophy.—Nil.
3. Astronomy.—Nil.
4. Politics.—Feeble.
5. Botany.—Variable. Well up in belladonna, opium, and poisons generally. Knows nothing of practical gardening.
6. Geology.—Practical, but limited. Tells at a glance different soils from each other. After walks has shown me splashes upon his trousers, and told me by their colour and consistence in what part of London he had received them.
7. Chemistry.—Profound.
8. Anatomy.—Accurate, but unsystematic.
9. Sensational Literature.—Immense. He appears to know every detail of every horror perpetrated in the century.
10. Plays the violin well.
11. Is an expert singlestick player, boxer, and swordsman.
12. Has a good practical knowledge of British law.

Watson's vital role

Every genius needs someone more ordinary to illuminate their powers, and Conan Doyle uses Watson in this role, defining his character in the first few chapters. A man who is in the best of neither health nor spirits, Watson is friendless and has no real purpose in life at the beginning of the story. He says of himself "how objectless was my life, and how little there was to engage my attention." He fills his time closely observing his fellow lodger, even to the extent of making a list called "Sherlock Holmes—his limits." Many of its observations, such as that Holmes's knowledge of literature is "nil," prove in later stories to be inaccurate.

For a short while, Watson's study of Holmes becomes a kind of hobby—"this man stimulated my curiosity," he notes. But Watson very quickly assumes the role of Holmes's full-fledged assistant in investigating the Brixton murder. Presumably it is for his own interest that Watson makes detailed notes during the investigation. However, these jottings come in very handy when he decides to write up the notes to showcase the genius of Holmes in bringing the murderer to justice. It is also this act that seals the burgeoning relationship between Holmes and Watson: transforming himself from Holmes's companion to his biographer, Watson follows in the footsteps of the celebrated diarist James Boswell, who became the biographer of the famous writer Samuel Johnson a century earlier.

Holmes's London

While Conan Doyle recreates the streets and gardens of London in *A Study in Scarlet*, he had not lived in the city by that point; at the time he wrote the story he was residing in Southsea near Portsmouth, Hampshire. Instead, he must have acquired all his knowledge of the English capital from maps and gazetteers. The story takes us from Baker Street via hansom cabs to just a few well-known London areas, such as Brixton, Camberwell, Kennington Park, and Euston. Like Robert Louis Stevenson in *Strange Case of Dr. Jekyll and Mr. Hyde* (1886), Conan Doyle used his own home city, Edinburgh, as a model for London. The fictional Lauriston Gardens in Brixton, where the first corpse is discovered, was actually based on Lauriston Place in the

Scottish capital. But interspersed with these fictional locations are real-life London landmarks, some of which still survive. For example, in the first pages of the book, Watson waits for Stamford standing at the Criterion Bar in Piccadilly, which exists to this day.

Forgivable faults

It is easy to find fault with *A Study in Scarlet*. The structure is clumsy and the mystery itself somewhat contrived, and the central villain Jefferson Hope is a fairly featureless character too. Hope lacks any of the distinguishing qualities of the charismatic villains who were to cross Holmes's path in later stories; Conan Doyle merely uses him as a pawn to further his plot.

Another problem with *A Study in Scarlet* is that Holmes is such a brilliant detective that he very quickly sees to the heart of any case. Because he succeeds in solving the murder mystery and apprehending the culprit halfway through the narrative, there is little left for Holmes to do. Conan Doyle then takes the reader on a long flashback to the wilds of Utah, detailing the history of the links between Hope, Drebber, and Stangerson, and their connection to the Mormon church. As a result, Holmes necessarily disappears from the scene, and only returns in the last two short chapters.

The almost-too-quick genius of Holmes was a structural problem that Conan Doyle did not fully resolve in his later Sherlock Holmes novels either. He resorted to the flashback device once again in *The Sign of Four* (pp.46–55) and *The Valley of Fear* (pp.212–21). And Holmes is also absent for much of *The Hound of the Baskervilles* (pp.152–61), although Watson is on hand for the entire story. »

An inspirational teacher

In his 1924 autobiography, Conan Doyle explained the inspiration behind Holmes's amazing powers of deduction. "I thought of my old teacher Joe Bell…" At Edinburgh University's medical school, Dr. Joseph Bell (1837–1911) had made Conan Doyle his outpatient clerk, who recalled that Bell "…often learned more of the patient by a few quick glances than I had done by my questions."

On one occasion, Bell amazed the students gathered around him by pronouncing that the patient standing before them had served in the army, and had been recently discharged from serving as a noncommissioned officer in a Highland regiment on Barbados. Bell explained, "You see, gentlemen, the man was a respectful man but did not remove his hat. They do not in the army, but he would have learned civilian ways had he been long discharged. He has an air of authority and he is obviously Scottish. As to Barbados, his complaint is elephantiasis, which is West Indian and not British."

Victorian London was the backdrop for many of the Holmes tales, even before Conan Doyle moved to the city. The London settings included fictional places and real landmarks.

> There is a mystery about this which stimulates the imagination; where there is no imagination there is no horror.
> **Sherlock Holmes**

It may seem strange to the modern reader that Conan Doyle inserted such a long flashback into the middle of a detective story. At the time the author believed it would add an exotic appeal to the story, especially since the Mormons were very much in the news when Conan Doyle sat down to write this tale. The previous year he had attended a meeting of the Portsmouth Literary and Scientific Society, where the subject of Mormon polygamy had been addressed. By the time he was writing *A Study in Scarlet*, he had clearly carried out

some extensive reading on the church—so much so that he felt he could even include the real-life figure of Brigham Young in his cast of characters. Conan Doyle researched various volumes for his descriptions of Utah, as he did for London in the English section of the book. But he was not sufficiently careful in his placing of the Rio Grande, which appears to have wandered from its usual setting; "These little things happen," Conan Doyle is said to have admitted when this was pointed out to him.

Seldom bettered
While it is possible to pinpoint numerous holes in the plot of this tale if you look hard enough, in the end none of these faults are what really matters. What remains in the reader's mind is the well-defined central character of Holmes.

This brilliant characterization is most sharply demonstrated in the first part of *A Study in Scarlet*, in which the detective makes a succession of brilliant deductions about the corpse in the house in Brixton—a sequence that has rarely been bettered in crime fiction. On his arrival at the scene, Holmes

Holmes carefully examines the word "Rache" written in blood on a wall at the murder scene. The way the letters have been written gives him vital clues as to the identity of the killer.

immediately chastises Gregson for allowing everyone to trample over the pathway, destroying potentially vital footprint evidence. "If a herd of buffaloes had passed along there could not be a greater mess," he says. Inside the house, Holmes

Brigham Young

The only real-life historical figure Conan Doyle used as a character in a Holmes story was Brigham Young (1801–77). Born in Vermont, Young became a Methodist in 1823. He joined Joseph Smith's Church of Jesus Christ of Latter-day Saints after reading *The Book of Mormon*, and rose to become its leader. He was called the "American Moses" after leading his followers through the desert to the "promised land" of Utah, where the Mormons founded their headquarters in Salt Lake City.

Conan Doyle's depiction of both Young and Mormonism may be harsh, but he was never one to let facts get in the way of a good story, and at the time it was not regarded as particularly controversial. However, Conan Doyle was later criticized for defaming the faith, and years after his death, Brigham Young's descendant Levi Edgar Young claimed that Conan Doyle had privately apologized, saying that "he had been misled by writings of the time about the Church," and admitted that he had written "a scurrilous book."

flings himself to the ground with his magnifying glass before rattling off a list of facts to the dumbfounded Watson, Gregson, and Lestrade.

When Conan Doyle juxtaposes Holmes's powers with Watson's ordinariness, he makes those powers seem even more impressive; this effect is then amplified when Holmes is compared to the two bungling detectives. In their efforts to better one another, Lestrade and Gregson show just how far behind Holmes they are in terms of both acumen and perception. Neither of the two inspectors can explain the blood spattered around the murder scene, though Holmes privately surmises (correctly, it is later revealed) that the murderer must have had a nose bleed. Lestrade boasts to Gregson and Holmes that the murderer wrote "Rache" on the wall because he was disturbed before he could finish spelling the word "Rachel," but Holmes bursts his bubble by pointing out that *Rache* is German for "revenge."

Immortality beckons

In his 1947 essay "Lear, Tolstoy and the Fool," George Orwell wrote of Shakespeare that, like every other writer, sooner or later he will be forgotten. If the same applies to Conan Doyle, it is hard to envision his most famous creation suffering the same fate—Sherlock Holmes now has an identity beyond the pages of the novels and stories in which he first appeared.

Conan Doyle had great hopes for *A Study in Scarlet*, which it is believed took him only three weeks to write. But potential publishers

Beeton's Christmas Annual was a paperback magazine produced from 1860 to 1898. Only 10 copies of the magazine containing the first Holmes adventure are known to have survived.

were initially less enthusiastic: *The Cornhill Magazine* rejected it as reading like a cheap "shilling dreadful." In the end, Conan Doyle accepted the derisory one-time fee of £25 for it to appear in *Beeton's Christmas Annual* for 1887, which indeed cost just a shilling—five pence in modern money. To add insult to injury, its magazine debut

caused barely a ripple with the reading public. Having signed away the rights to it, Conan Doyle would never receive another penny for this, his first Holmes story, even when it was reprinted in book form just over a year later. However, *A Study in Scarlet* has remained in print ever since, just like every other Holmes story. ∎

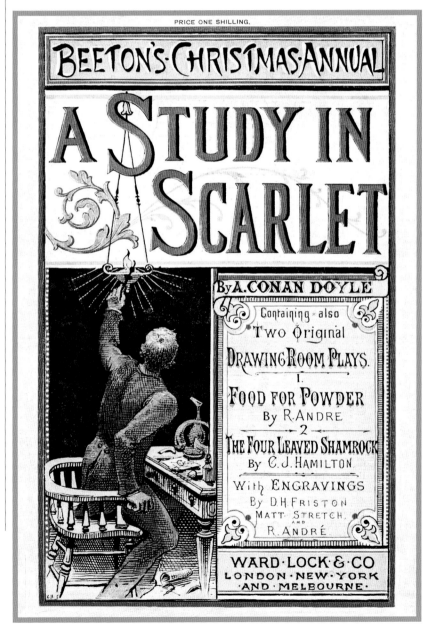

PRICE ONE SHILLING.

BEETON'S CHRISTMAS ANNUAL

A STUDY IN SCARLET

By A. CONAN DOYLE

Containing also
Two Original
DRAWING ROOM PLAYS.
I.
FOOD FOR POWDER
By R. ANDRE
2
THE FOUR LEAVED SHAMROCK
By C. J. HAMILTON.
With ENGRAVINGS
By D.H. FRISTON
MATT. STRETCH.
AND
R. ANDRÉ

WARD · LOCK · & CO
LONDON · NEW · YORK
· AND · MELBOURNE.

I NEVER MAKE EXCEPTIONS. AN EXCEPTION DISPROVES THE RULE

THE SIGN OF FOUR (1890)

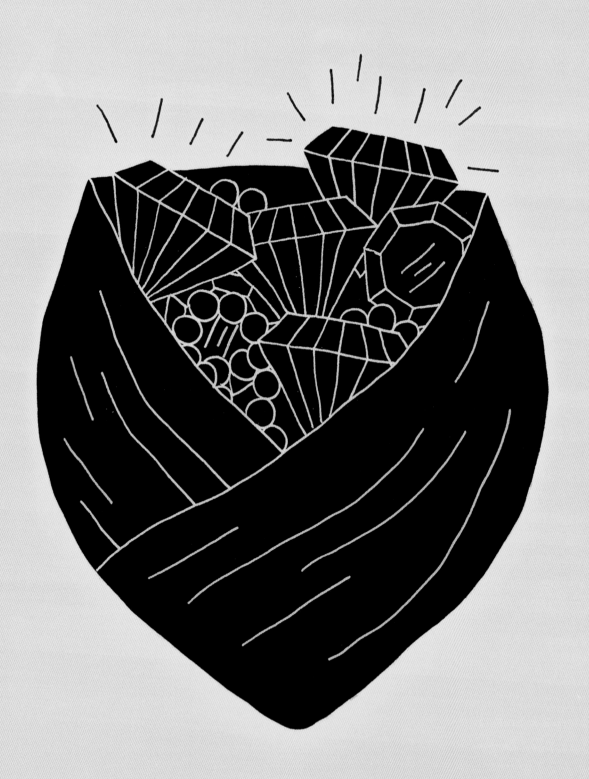

IN CONTEXT

TYPE
Novel

FIRST PUBLICATION
US: *Lippincott's Monthly Magazine*, **February 1890**

NOVEL PUBLICATION
Spencer Blackett publishers, October 1890

CHARACTERS
Mary Morstan
Young governess.

Captain Morstan
Mary's father.

Thaddeus Sholto
English gentleman.

Bartholomew Sholto
Thaddeus's brother.

McMurdo Pondicherry Lodge porter and gatekeeper.

Lal Rao Butler at Pondicherry Lodge.

Mrs. Bernstone Housekeeper at Pondicherry Lodge.

Major Sholto Thaddeus's and Bartholomew's father.

Jonathan Small Englishman.

Mahomet Singh, Abdullah Khan, Dost Akbar
Jonathan Small's associates.

Tonga
Native Andaman islander.

Athelney Jones
Scotland Yard detective.

Mordecai Smith Boat owner.

Mrs. Cecil Forrester
Mary Morstan's employer.

Chapter One
Watson rails against Holmes's drug use, The detective analyzes the story behind Watson's watch.

Chapter Three
Mary shows Holmes a plan of a building on which a note has been scribbled about the "sign of the four," found among her father's papers.

Chapter Five
Holmes, Watson, and Thaddeus find Bartholomew murdered by a poisoned dart and the treasure gone.

Chapter Two
Mary Morstan asks for Holmes's help in solving the twin mysteries of her missing father and an anonymous benefactor who now wants to meet her.

Chapter Four
Mary's benefactor, Thaddeus Sholto, reveals that her father is dead and that his own late father hid "the Agra treasure," which his brother Bartholomew has now found.

It is 1888 and Holmes, with no case to occupy him, resorts to cocaine, to Watson's dismay. But a puzzle for Holmes to solve appears with the arrival of Mary Morstan, the daughter of a former Indian Army officer who vanished in London 10 years earlier. At the time, his friend Major Sholto told Mary that he had no idea the captain was in the country. Four years after Captain Morstan's disappearance, Mary began to receive an annual, anonymous gift of a pearl, and now her mysterious benefactor wants to meet her.

Mary shows Holmes a paper that she found in her father's possessions, which is marked by four crosses and the words "The sign of the four—Jonathan Small, Mahomet Singh, Abdullah Khan, Dost Akbar."

That evening, Holmes, Watson, and Mary go to meet her benefactor, who turns out to be Thaddeus Sholto, the major's son. He explains that his father confessed on his deathbed that Captain Morstan had come to see him the night he disappeared, but died suddenly during an argument, and the major disposed of the body. The pair of

Chapter Seven
The murderer had stepped in creosote, so Holmes and Watson use Toby, a tracker dog, to follow the scent trail.

Chapter Nine
Disguised as a sailor, Holmes finds the boat and persuades Scotland Yard's Athelney Jones to provide a police boat.

Chapter Eleven
Watson takes the recovered chest to Mary, but it is empty; Small had thrown the treasure in the Thames. Mary and Watson declare their love for each other.

Chapter Six
Clues tell Holmes the murderer was tiny, and his accomplice a one-legged man who he surmises was Jonathan Small—one of "the four."

Chapter Eight
Toby leads Holmes and Watson to a boatyard, where Small has rented a launch called the *Aurora*, then hidden it. Holmes asks the Baker Street Irregulars gang to try to find it.

Chapter Ten
At nightfall the *Aurora* breaks cover, and Holmes, Watson, and Jones give chase in the police boat, eventually shooting dead Small's accomplice and arresting Small.

Chapter Twelve
Small tells the full story of the Agra treasure, and how Thaddeus's father stole it from "the four." Watson and Mary become engaged.

them possessed a chest full of the "Agra treasure"—but the major died before revealing to Thaddeus and Bartholomew, his brother, where it was. They had only the pearls, and argued over Mary's claim to them; this was when Thaddeus began to send the anonymous gifts.

Thaddeus tells the group that Bartholomew has found the chest at the family home. On arrival at the house, they find Bartholomew killed by a poisoned dart and the treasure gone. Holmes deduces that a wooden-legged man, who he surmises is Small, accompanied the murderer. Athelney Jones of Scotland Yard arrests Thaddeus. Holmes discovers that Small has rented a launch, the *Aurora*, but is lying low. When Thaddeus provides an alibi, a chastened Jones agrees to Holmes's request for a police boat.

That night, the *Aurora* roars off downriver, with Holmes, Watson, and Jones in pursuit. The "savage" fires at them with his blowpipe, but they shoot him dead and he is lost overboard. Finally, they catch up with Small, but he has thrown the treasure into the Thames. Small reveals that during the Indian Mutiny of 1857, he and Singh, Khan, and Akbar killed a man for the treasure, and hid it in Agra Fort, only to be arrested and sent to the Andaman Islands penal colony. Years later, they offered a share of the treasure to two guards, Major Sholto and Captain Morstan, in exchange for freedom. But Sholto took the treasure and betrayed them. Vowing vengeance, Small escaped with an islander (the "savage"), and tracked Sholto down.

The story ends on a happy note with Watson announcing his engagement to Mary to Holmes. ∎

Sherlock Holmes might have remained a one-book phenomenon had it not been for an invitation to dinner at the Langham Hotel in London's Regent Street that Conan Doyle received in August 1889. The invitation came from John Marshall Stoddart, the managing director of the successful American *Lippincott's Monthly Magazine*, who was in London to launch the UK edition. Stoddart had read *A Study in Scarlet* (pp.36–45) and enjoyed it. More importantly, he was canny enough to realize the detective story genre was about to bloom. This awareness was prompted, perhaps, by the high sales of Fergus Hume's 1886 *The Mystery of a Hansom Cab*, set in Melbourne, Australia.

What Conan Doyle did not know was that another writer would be at the dinner: Oscar Wilde. The pair would have made very contrasting dinner guests—the conventional and serious Scottish doctor set against the flamboyant aesthete. In his autobiography, Conan Doyle called it "a golden evening."

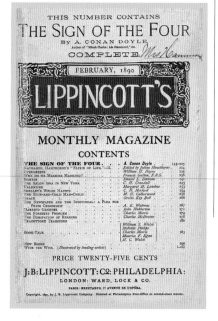

THIS NUMBER CONTAINS

THE SIGN OF THE FOUR
BY A. CONAN DOYLE
Author of "Micah Clarke; his Statement," &c.
COMPLETE.

FEBRUARY, 1890

LIPPINCOTT'S
MONTHLY MAGAZINE

CONTENTS

| THE SIGN OF THE FOUR | A. Conan Doyle | 145–223 |

During the course of the dinner, Wilde and Conan Doyle were each asked to produce a novella-length mystery for the magazine. Wilde came up with *The Picture of Dorian Gray*. Shortly after, Conan Doyle wrote to Stoddart: "As far as I can see my story will either be called *The Sign of the Six* or *The Problem of the Sholtos*. You said you wanted a spicy title. I shall give Sherlock Holmes of *A Study in Scarlet* something else to unravel."

Conan Doyle completed the book in less than a month. By then its title had become *The Sign of the Four* for the magazine, but when it was published later as a novel, the title became *The Sign of Four*.

A richly drawn Holmes

Conan Doyle was by now a more accomplished writer than when he wrote *A Study in Scarlet*, and

Lippincott's **magazine** gave *The Sign of the Four* top billing. It was renamed *The Sign of Four* when it was published in P. F. Collier's *Once a Week Library* in the US in March 1890.

Oscar Wilde had a sharp mind, outlandish dress and habits, and an apparent disdain for conventionalities, which left a lasting impression on the young Conan Doyle.

in *The Sign of Four*, he set about not only reestablishing Holmes in the consciousness of the reading public, but also adding more color, depth, and idiosyncrasies to the detective's character.

Conan Doyle's brush with Wilde prompted him to infuse Holmes with more bohemian extravagance than in the previous novel. In the opening paragraph of *The Sign of Four*, the reader discovers that the sleuth is a drug addict: "Holmes took his bottle from the corner of the mantelpiece, and his hypodermic syringe from its neat morocco case…" reports Watson. "Finally, he thrust the sharp point home, pressed down the tiny piston, and sank back into the velvet-lined armchair with a long sigh of satisfaction."

Holmes takes both morphine and cocaine, although he seems to favor the latter. He assures Watson that he indulges in this dangerous pursuit merely to offset boredom. Only when he has a problem to solve can he really come alive and dispense with artificial stimulants.

I abhor the dull routine of existence. I crave for mental exaltation.
Sherlock Holmes

Glass and silver syringes like this were used in the 19th century. Holmes kept his in a similar case, and preferred "a seven per cent" solution of cocaine.

Making Holmes a drug user was a clever way to embellish him as a character, making him immediately more edgy and interesting. For the first time, the reader also sees his theatrical side in his wonderfully convincing disguise as an old sea dog when trying to trace the *Aurora*, which leads Jones to observe, "You would have made an actor, and a rare one." In *A Study in Scarlet*, the villain's anonymous accomplice disguised himself as an old lady, but it is much more effective when the detective himself is in disguise. In his very next appearance, in "A Scandal in Bohemia" (pp.56–61), Holmes disguises himself as both a drunken horse-groom and a simple-minded clergyman.

A literary detective
In the early days of their friendship in *A Study in Scarlet*, Watson made a note that Holmes's knowledge of literature was "nil." In this tale, however, Conan Doyle has Holmes demonstrate a broad appreciation not only for British literature, but for foreign writers too. Holmes recommends that Watson read Winwood Reade's *The Martyrdom of Man* (1872)—an indictment of Christianity that was a favorite of Conan Doyle's. Holmes quotes the German writer Goethe (1749–1832) when he disparagingly says of Jones, "*Wir sind gewohnt dass die Menschen verhöhnen was sie nicht verstehen*" ("We are used to people making fun of things that they do not understand.")

This sophisticated literary knowledge, which may reflect Wilde's influence on Conan Doyle, serves no plot purpose. It is simply window-dressing intended to allow Holmes to impress the reader with his accomplishments. Another echo of that "golden evening" can be seen in Watson's portrait of Thaddeus Sholto, which is a veiled portrait of Wilde. "Nature had given him a pendulous lip," observes Watson, "and a too visible line of yellow and irregular teeth, which he strove feebly to conceal by constantly passing his hand over the lower part of his face." Wilde was well known for doing this.

Holmes is a genius
Conan Doyle's readers already knew that Holmes is clever, so it wasn't necessary to make him a master of so many academic disciplines. »

I cannot live without brain-work. What else is there to live for?
Sherlock Holmes

The Indian Mutiny

Conan Doyle would have learned about the Indian Mutiny at school in the 1860s and 1870s, when the affair was fresh in British minds. It began in 1857, when sepoys—Indian soldiers—in the Bengal army shot British officers, escalating into full-scale rebellions across northern and central India. For months, garrisons such as Agra were beleaguered, until British authority was restored in 1858. Conan Doyle may well have gleaned details about Agra from Major-General Alfred Wilks Drayson, his sponsor at the Portsmouth Literary and Scientific Society. Drayson commanded the 21st Brigade Artillery in India from 1876–78, and helped rearm several forts, including Agra. Conan Doyle's interpretation of the colonial mindset of the time, and how the rebellion revealed the true natures of those caught up in it, is fascinating. Small, Morstan, and Sholto alike are warped by their greed for the Agra treasure. Looting by British soldiers was common during the Mutiny, a subject Conan Doyle would revisit in "The Crooked Man" (pp.132–33).

"The SIGN of FOUR"

AN ADVENTURE OF SHERLOCK HOLMES

With an All Star Cast
including
ISOBEL ELSOM, ELLIE NORWOOD
and NORMAN PAGE
A Stoll Production

The Sign of Four was made into a silent film in 1923, starring British actor Eille Norwood (1861–1948) as Holmes and Arthur M. Cullin as Watson. Norwood played Holmes in 47 movies.

But the author was pleased with his embellished portrait of the detective. He wrote to Stoddart, "Holmes, I am glad to say, is in capital form all through. I think it is pretty fair, though I am not usually satisfied with my own things."

One aspect of Conan Doyle's characterization that remains unchanged from *A Study in Scarlet* is the opportunity that he gives Holmes to show off his skills of observation and deduction before the case even gets going. Conan Doyle would continue to use this technique in many subsequent Holmes stories. For example, Holmes would test Watson's own deductive skills using Dr. Mortimer's stick in *The Hound of the Baskervilles* (pp.152–61); Watson fails to make correct observations, but Holmes is able to determine that the doctor is young and owns a medium-sized dog. The repetition of the trick reminds readers already familiar with Holmes of his genius, while at the same time establishing it for new readers.

Here Holmes shows off his skills when he deduces from the color of the mud on Watson's shoes and the untouched stamps and postcards on his desk that the doctor has been to the Wigmore Street Post Office to send a telegram. He goes on to examine a watch Watson has recently acquired and declares, with typical insensitivity, that it had belonged to Watson's oldest brother, who, "taking to drink," must have recently died.

Rival relationships

Conan Doyle adds a new dimension to the dynamic between Holmes and Watson with the arrival of the female client Mary Morstan, with whom Watson promptly falls head over heels in love. Throughout the story, the doctor behaves like a lovesick teenager, giving the lie to his claim that he has "experience of women which extends over many nations and three separate continents." Any reader will wonder which nations and continents, and what kind of experiences. At one point he is so lovestruck that he babbles feebly to her about "how a musket looked into my tent at the dead of night, and how I fired a double-barreled tiger cub at it." When Thaddeus thoughtlessly tells Mary that her father is dead, Watson says that he "could have struck the man across his face." Yet when Thaddeus also reveals that Mary's share of the treasure will be worth a quarter of a million pounds, Watson is overcome by the thought that this will put her beyond his reach. So much so that, when the hypochondriac Thaddeus asks for his professional opinion on his health, "Holmes declares," says the doctor, "that he overheard me caution him [Thaddeus] against the great danger of taking more than two drops of castor-oil, while I recommended strychnine in large doses as a sedative."

Much more convincing is Conan Doyle's portrayal of the relationship between Watson and Holmes, a partnership that has moved on considerably since *A Study in Scarlet*. It is given real substance by the details of their domestic life together. The start of the story sees them bickering like old friends who are comfortable with each other and feel at ease in speaking their minds. Watson has no reservations at all about railing at Holmes's drug habit, because he cares about him.

A client to me is a mere unit, a factor in a problem. The emotional qualities are antagonistic to clear reasoning.
Sherlock Holmes

Mary Morstan

"What a very attractive woman!" Watson exclaims to Holmes after they first meet Mary. "Is she?" replies Holmes. "I did not observe." Watson extols Mary's radiant qualities, but to the reader she appears a rather unassuming figure. However, she shows strength of character when she learns that her father is dead, and has an instantly calming effect on Bartholomew Sholto's hysterical housekeeper. "God bless your sweet, calm face!" the old woman cries. "It does me good to see you." It is also obvious that her employer adores her. "She was clearly no mere paid dependent," observes Watson, "but an honored friend." The clincher is her relief on hearing that the treasure is lost.

When Watson tells Holmes of their engagement, he replies, "I really cannot congratulate you." But he concedes that Watson has chosen well, adding that she "might have been useful in such work as we have been doing." Clearly, her sole future role is to be a supportive wife.

In fine form

As in Conan Doyle's previous novel, *The Sign of Four* is dotted with inconsistencies and minor errors. Contributing factors to this were the haste with which Conan Doyle wrote it, and his loathing of looking back at previous writings to cross-check facts and details. For example, Watson's war wound migrates from his shoulder to his leg, and Watson now has an elder brother where before he had no living relatives. Of more concern is Conan Doyle's questionable depiction of the indigenous Andaman islander, Tonga, who he portrays as a bestial "savage." In an article in *The Quarterly Review*, 1904, Andrew Lang observed: "The [indigenous] Andamese are cruelly libelled [in *The Sign of Four*], and have neither malignant qualities, nor heads like mops, nor weapons." It may be that Conan Doyle deliberately ignored the facts and made Tonga repulsive so that the reader is not distressed when "the savage" meets his demise. Yet inaccurate portrayals of "savages" were commonplace in the Victorian era, so in his portrayal of Tonga, Conan Doyle was very much a man of his times.

Overall, however, both Conan Doyle and his finest creation are on sparkling form in *The Sign of Four*. Holmes rattles off the names of streets as the four-wheeler taking him, Watson, and Mary to meet Thaddeus itself rattles through the night, demonstrating his intimate knowledge of London: "Rochester »

The two men lounge in bachelor comfort, their rooms taking on the relaxed air of a gentlemen's club. The only female is Mrs. Hudson, their housekeeper (named for the first time)—a motherly figure who stays in the background. Their residence, 221B Baker Street, is a well-established haven amid the hurly-burly of the metropolis.

It is sad for the reader that this cozy state of affairs seems set to end when Watson announces his engagement. Watson is about to depart for domestic bliss, leaving a solitary Holmes with his hypodermic needle—or so the reader thinks. In later *Strand* adventures, however, Watson is either a frequent visitor to 221B, or the story is set back in the days of his bachelorhood. Eventually, in "The Adventure of the Empty House" (pp.162–67), we learn that Mary has died. And in "The Norwood Builder" (168–69), Watson has sold his medical practice and moved back in to 221B.

A penal colony was first established on Great Andaman Island in 1789. The British built a new prison after the Indian Mutiny to house their captives; here, prisoners take meals on the beach.

Row. Now Vincent Square. Now we come out on the Vauxhall Bridge Road. We are making for the Surrey side…" When they all arrive at Pondicherry Lodge, the ancestral family home of the Sholtos, Holmes once again behaves like a "trained bloodhound," launching himself into a frenzied forensic investigation of the murder scene with the same gusto that he showed in *A Study in Scarlet*. Watson notes: "He whipped out his lens and a tape measure, and hurried about the room on his knees, measuring, comparing, examining…" Through his deductive brilliance Holmes makes a complete fool of Scotland Yard's Athelney Jones, just as he did Gregson and Lestrade in the earlier tale, and manages to leave his partner Watson typically dumbfounded.

The villain's character

The Sign of Four also has a more memorable, complex villain than the bland, one-dimensional Hope of *A Study in Scarlet*. With his wild eyes and wooden leg—the result of a crocodile attack—Small was largely inspired by Long John Silver in Robert Louis Stevenson's

> I never guess. It is a shocking habit—destructive to the logical faculty.
> **Sherlock Holmes**

Treasure Island (1883). In Conan Doyle's essay "Through the Magic Door" (1907), he wrote of Stevenson: "…he is the inventor of what may be called the mutilated villain," and he "has used the effect so often, and with such telling results, that he may be said to have made it his own. To say nothing of Hyde… there is the horrid blind Pew, Black Dog with two fingers missing, Long John Silver with his one leg."

Small wrestles with his conscience throughout *The Sign of Four*, which makes him a sympathetic character. What happens to him in the end is not

clear. At worst he faces the gallows, the Victorians' preferred method of execution, and at best "digging drains at Dartmoor," as he puts it, presaging the looming presence of Princetown Prison in the later story *The Hound of the Baskervilles*.

A classic tale

Two images in particular remain long in memory after reading this tale. First, the description of the victim at the murder scene— Bartholomew's "ghastly, inscrutable smile," and the way that "not only his features, but all his limbs were twisted and turned in the most fantastic fashion." Second is Conan Doyle's extraordinarily atmospheric, almost Dickensian, evocation of Victorian London. "Down the Strand the lamps were but misty splotches of diffused light, which threw a feeble circular glimmer upon the slimy pavement," notes Watson in a particularly memorable passage. At the time, London was a thriving port, the hub of a great worldwide empire, and Conan Doyle's busy riverside scenes are full of atmosphere. "Somewhere in the dark ooze at the bottom

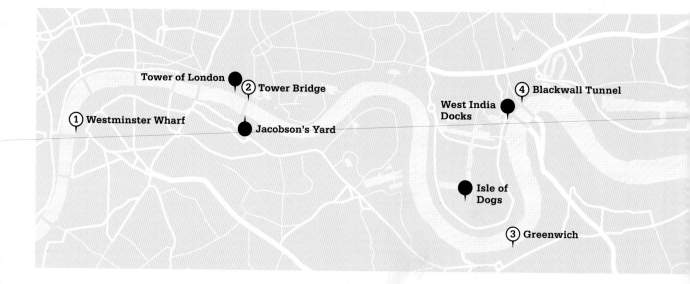

Tower of London ● ② Tower Bridge

① Westminster Wharf

● Jacobson's Yard

West India Docks ●

④ Blackwall Tunnel

● Isle of Dogs

③ Greenwich

of the Thames lie the bones of that strange visitor to our shores," says Watson, as he recalls Tonga's dramatic demise.

Unlike *A Study in Scarlet,* this tale was widely reviewed on both sides of the Atlantic. London's *Morning Post* commented rather pompously, "Mr. Conan Doyle has done better work… still, as a specimen of purely detective fiction, the tale has its merits." *The Daily Republican* in Pennsylvania expressed a more general view when it stated, "…[Holmes's] marvellous ingenuity in solving a

The Thames was a hive of activity in the 19th century, its banks lined with ships, as can be seen in this painting of Tower Bridge from Cherry Garden Pier by Charles Edward Dixon (1872–1934).

seemingly insoluble mystery is portrayed with so graphic a pen that Conan Doyle must take rank as a leader in the line of such writers as Poe and Gaboriau. *The Sign of Four* is bound to become a classic." However, by the time these reviews appeared, Conan Doyle had once again let Holmes slip from his mind, and was hard at work on one of his now long-forgotten historical romances.

Today *The Sign of Four* is indeed considered a classic. A 70-year-old Graham Greene wrote in the introduction to a 1974 edition of the book, "*The Sign of Four*… I read first at the age of ten and have never forgotten… the dark night in Pondicherry Lodge, Norwood, has never faded from my memory." ■

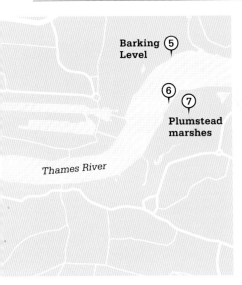

Barking Level 5

6 7

Plumstead marshes

Thames River

A police launch with "two burly police-inspectors" took Holmes, Watson, and Jones downriver in pursuit of the *Aurora.*

1 Westminster Wharf: Holmes and Watson pick up the police boat.

2 Tower Bridge: The police boat waits for *Aurora* to emerge from Jacobson's Yard.

3 Greenwich: Holmes is 300 paces behind the *Aurora* as they pass through here.

4 Blackwall Tunnel: Holmes is closing in; they are only 250 paces behind the *Aurora.*

5 Barking Level: The gap closes to a boat-length; Holmes sees Tonga on deck.

6 River bank: Chase ends; Tonga is shot.

7 Plumstead Marshes: Small is captured.

YOU SEE, BUT YOU DO NOT OBSERVE

A SCANDAL IN BOHEMIA (1891)

IN CONTEXT

TYPE
Short story

FIRST PUBLICATION
UK: July 1891
US: August 1891 (also as "Woman's Wit" and "The King's Sweetheart")

COLLECTION
The Adventures of Sherlock Holmes, 1892

CHARACTERS
Wilhelm Gottsreich Sigismond von Ormstein King of Bohemia.

Irene Adler American opera singer, and King Wilhelm's former mistress.

Godfrey Norton British lawyer who marries Irene.

The first of the 56 Sherlock Holmes short stories to be published in *The Strand Magazine*, "A Scandal in Bohemia" is the tale that introduces the beautiful Irene Adler—the most talked-about minor character in the Holmes canon after Moriarty.

Even in the story, Irene appears directly only briefly, yet a world of scholarship and speculation has built up around her. Many screen adaptations have developed her in their own ways: in the US series *Elementary* (p.339), Moriarty is Irene Adler in disguise, and in the BBC's series *Sherlock* (p.339), she is a high-class dominatrix who greets Holmes while naked.

Deep under cover in one of the convincing disguises he adopts when gathering evidence, Holmes (Jeremy Brett) finds himself accidentally caught up in Irene Adler's wedding ceremony.

Holmes and women

In the very first sentence of "A Scandal in Bohemia," Watson tells the reader that "to Sherlock Holmes she [Irene Adler] is always *the* woman," with "the" italicized to ensure the significance is clear. However, he then quickly stresses that "it was not that he [Holmes] felt any emotion akin to love for Irene Adler." In fact, the whole idea of love is "abhorrent to his cold, precise but admirably balanced mind."

And yet Conan Doyle has planted the irresistible hint that Holmes, emotionally cold and misogynistic, might have found his true love. It is a testament to Conan Doyle's brilliant realization of his creation that readers wish so much for the apparently emotionless detective to find his mate. Watson implies that Holmes has rejected the love of women in order to keep his mind focused on the rational work of detection, turning himself into a noble and almost tragic figure. It is no wonder that some literary commentators have likened the detective's behavior to that of the

In his eyes she eclipses and predominates the whole of her sex.
Dr. Watson

courtly knights of the Middle Ages, who desisted from sensuality in order to uphold their chivalric ideals. However, Holmes is a far more psychologically complex figure than any medieval hero.

Holmes the bohemian

Since his marriage and move away from 221B Baker Street, Watson has seen little of his former companion. However, he is aware that Holmes spends a lot of time in his lodgings, interspersing bouts of work with regular drug binges—alternating weekly "between cocaine and ambition, the drowsiness of the drug, and the fierce energy of his own keen nature." It seems that the detective needs a suitable outlet for his overactive brain when he is without a case to occupy his mind.

Although this story's title ostensibly refers to a potential scandal for the King of Bohemia, the first mention of Bohemia is in relation to Holmes, when Watson tells the reader that the detective "loathed every form of society with his whole Bohemian soul." The term

"bohemian" was in vogue at the time (see box, p.61), and referred to free-spirited individuals who led an unconventional lifestyle and rejected social norms. However, love and passion were also at the heart of the bohemian ideal— emotions that are anathema to Holmes. In calling this story "A Scandal in Bohemia," Watson is perhaps hinting that the real scandal may lie not within King Wilhelm's Bohemia but within Holmes, in a rare moment when a woman is able to capture both his respect and his admiration.

Holmes at work

After his lengthy, slightly wistful introduction, Watson sets the story in motion. He is standing in the street below the Baker Street rooms. He looks up to the window and spots Holmes: "his tall, spare figure pass[ing] twice in a dark silhouette against the blind." Holmes is remote and above the normal world, as he must inevitably be, but Watson can tell from his energetic pacing and alert posture » that he is at work again: "He had risen out of his drug-created dreams and was hot upon the scent of some new problem." Watson has already mentioned Holmes's indulgence in narcotics, and he stresses it a second time in order to portray the great detective as a dramatic, romantic figure who switches between light and dark—his career illuminated as if by flashes of lightning in the night.

Eager to reconnect with his friend, Watson makes his way up to the rooms. Holmes is as cool and incisive as ever, noting several things with unnerving accuracy: the amount of weight Watson has gained since they last met; that he has gone back into practice as a doctor; that he has been out in the rain a lot recently; and that he has an incompetent serving girl. When Watson, astonished, asks how he does it, the detective explains his method by demonstrating that it all depends on observation. Watson sees things, he says, but he does not observe. Ordinary people fail to notice life's minutiae, which is why Watson has no idea of the number of steps on the stairs up to 221B, but Holmes can tell him it is 17.

> A Frenchman or Russian could not have written that. It is the German who is so incourteous to his verbs.
> **Sherlock Holmes**

Such sharp observations are central to Holmes's method, and today this is still considered the principal skill of a detective. However, as Holmes points out, a detective also needs to understand exactly what he is seeing, as he demonstrates when he goes on to show the doctor an anonymous note that he has just received. Watson can deduce only that the writer is wealthy, whereas Holmes can also reveal that he is a native German speaker (as only the German language would construct sentences with the verb falling at the end) and that the notepaper comes from the German kingdom of Bohemia. Furthermore, when his client arrives a few moments later, giving a false name and with his face hidden behind a mask, Holmes realizes immediately that this large, flamboyantly dressed man is in fact Wilhelm Gottsreich Sigismond von Ormstein—the King of Bohemia.

The King and the diva

Holmes quickly makes his attitude toward royalty plain by adopting a curt, businesslike manner, aware that to anyone but the self-centered King, his disdain would be apparent. The King reveals that when he was Crown Prince he had a romantic liaison with a young American opera singer named Irene Adler, and was careless enough to have his photograph taken with her, thus leaving evidence of their affair. Recently, he has become engaged to a Scandinavian princess, and he is afraid that if her principled family were to be made aware of his past indiscretion, they will oppose the match. Irene has threatened to make the photograph public when the engagement is announced in a few days' time, presumably, the King says, because she does not want him to marry another woman,

Irene Adler

Critics are divided in their analysis of Irene Adler (portrayed here by Lara Pulver). Some say she reflects the emergence of a new kind of young woman in the late 1800s: smart, self-confident, and assertive, a phenomenon some scholars now call "first wave" feminism. Not all would join the suffragettes' campaign for votes for women, but these daughters of the middle class were beginning to believe in their right and ability to control their own lives. Increasingly, girls chose to go to the new women's universities—significantly, Irene comes from America, where women's education was further advanced than in Europe—and then to enter the workplace as teachers, doctors, and office clerks. However, others claim Irene represents a patriarchal Victorian view that only the most exceptional woman could match Holmes's intellect on his own ground. After her brief triumph, she must slip back into the shadows of marriage. Still others view her as a male fantasy figure, giving men the salacious illusion of submission.

Disguise is an ongoing theme in this story, and despite Holmes's usual mastery in the art of disguise, it is only Irene Adler who is completely successful in concealing her identity.

Failure: King Wilhelm tries to disguise his identity from Holmes, but fails immediately.

Failure: Holmes disguises himself as a clergyman, but Irene realizes who he is.

Success: Irene Adler disguises herself as a youth, and successfully fools Holmes.

and so he has been forced to seek Holmes's help in locating and recovering the incriminating photo.

The King refers to Irene as a "well-known adventuress," and many readers have taken his description of her at face value—the myth persists that she is a conniving blackmailer who uses her sexual wiles to make her way in the world. However, the King presents Irene in this way in order to justify his ill-treatment of her: he admits he has made several high-handed, even criminal, attempts to recover the photograph—including offering to pay for its return, hiring burglars to steal it, and even twice ransacking her home—all of which have failed.

When Holmes consults his biographical card index, it reveals Irene Adler to be a retired opera singer who has sung at La Scala in Milan and was prima donna at the Warsaw Opera. To have reached those heights, she must have been a serious artist, rather than an amoral gold-digger. When

the King admits Irene has not attempted to extort money from him, it is clear Holmes has already come to a different conclusion about Irene. Holmes yawns at the King's arrogance, and can barely wait for him to leave. Uncharacteristically, he also discusses his fee—making the point that his only interest in this case is financial.

Holmes's plan in action

The following afternoon, Holmes meets Watson after a morning's investigation. He is amused and excited about the success of his efforts, and by the astonishing turn that events have taken. Disguised as a groom, he has been chatting with the men caring for the horses in a mews behind Irene's house, and has learned a great deal about her.

The grooms, who would usually be first to spot anything salacious, described Irene respectfully as "the daintiest thing under a bonnet on this planet." Indeed, she seems to live a normal, ordered life, and their only noteworthy observation

is that she receives frequent visits from a handsome young lawyer named Godfrey Norton. Spotting Irene and Godfrey both leaving the house hurriedly in separate carriages, Holmes swiftly followed, only to find himself drafted in as witness to their legitimate and happy wedding in the Church of St. Monica in Edgware Road.

No wonder Holmes can barely contain his delight, especially as he has devised a "fool-proof plan" for recovering the photo, based on what he believes is his infallible knowledge of female psychology.

Later in the day, as per Holmes's scheme, Watson is standing outside Irene's house and watches the events that unfold: as Irene steps out of her carriage, a staged brawl between several men breaks out, and Holmes, this time disguised as a clergyman, comes to Irene's rescue. However, he soon collapses to the ground with blood dripping down his face. Concerned for his welfare, Irene has him carried inside the house, to recover »

Holmes's file on Irene Adler reveals that she was a talented contralto who once sang at the prestigious La Scala in Milan (pictured).

on the sitting room sofa. What Watson sees through the window is a lovely, kind young woman tenderly nursing the injured Holmes—not a femme fatale with a victim in her clutches. As he battles to decide what to do, Holmes gives him the pre-arranged signal to hurl a smoke bomb through the window and raise the alarm with a cry of "Fire!"

Just as Holmes has predicted, in the panic caused by the bomb Irene rushes to save the one thing that is most important to her—the photograph—and so reveals its hiding place in a recess behind a sliding panel. After confirming the fire was a false alarm, Holmes slips out of the house, intending to return the following day with the King to claim the picture. Holmes is so pleased with himself that he barely notices the young man who

greets him cheerily in a strangely familiar voice as he and Watson arrive at the front door of 221B.

A surprise for Holmes

The next morning, when Holmes and Watson arrive at Irene's home for their surprise visit, Holmes is amazed to find that the house-keeper has been expecting him—and to hear that Irene left for the Continent hours earlier, along with her new husband, taking

Male costume is nothing new to me. I often take advantage of the freedom which it gives.
Irene Adler

the photograph with her. In its hiding place, she has left a letter to Holmes, and a photograph of herself in evening dress for the King.

Irene's letter explains that she had realized the clergyman was Holmes in disguise the instant she betrayed the photograph's hiding place—although she congratulates him on his performance. But to be certain that he was indeed the famous detective, she had dressed up as a youth and followed him home, and it was she who had greeted him outside his door.

One of the fascinating things about this episode is the way that it focuses on Holmes's mastery of disguise—and yet Irene beats him at his own game. She tells Holmes that, as a trained actress, it is easy for her to wear "male costume," and that she has dressed up as a youth on many occasions, in order to enjoy the freedom of being incognito. In fact, it may not have been so unusual for a woman to disguise herself in male clothes to pass in a man's world. There is the renowned story of James Barry (born Margaret Ann Bulkley)—a woman who spent her entire life disguised as a man so she could pursue a career as a military doctor; likewise, there are many folk songs about women who joined the army in disguise.

The tradition of the undercover detective, though, goes back to the famous Eugène Vidocq (1775–1857), a French criminal-turned-detective in Napoleon's time (see box, p.317), whose amazing stories captivated 19th-century writers, such as Victor Hugo, Alexander Dumas, as well as Honoré de Balzac. They were surely an inspiration for Conan Doyle, too, together with the famous explorer Richard Burton (1821–1890), whose many exploits in disguise, such as sneaking into Mecca dressed as a Muslim, so intrigued Victorians.

A worthy adversary

In "A Scandal in Bohemia," Irene sees through Holmes's disguise, despite his brilliance, and it is she who pulls the wool over his eyes. She escapes with her picture, and it seems that for her—as so often with Holmes—winning the game is enough. Now happily married,

...the best laid plans of Mr. Sherlock Holmes were beaten by a woman's wit.
Dr. Watson

she declares in the letter that she has no interest in making the photo public, but will keep it as insurance should it ever be needed.

The King is certain that Irene will keep her word, and goes on to rue that she was not of his rank, as she would have made a great queen. "From what I have seen of the lady" Holmes responds coolly, "she seems indeed to be on a very different level to your Majesty." It is clear that in Holmes's opinion, she is far above him. The King offers Holmes an emerald ring as a reward for his work, but he asks instead to have Irene's photograph. Some readers insist that Holmes's choice

shows he is in love with Irene. But he never mentions her again in the stories, except to acknowledge, as in "The Five Orange Pips" (pp.74–9), that there was one woman who got the better of him. His regard for her is unmistakable, and the photograph is either simply for his files or a memento of a worthy adversary.

There is no doubt that Irene Adler is a fascinating character, and many feminist critics have commented on how she presents a challenge to the notion that reason, logic, and independent action are a male prerogative. American scholar Rosemary Jann believes that Irene "threatens male authority." Yet Holmes, although shaken, does not seem threatened. Instead, he demonstrates perfectly his dictum that one should not be blinded by preconceptions. Irene has opened his eyes wonderfully.

In realizing his error, and being aware that a woman can easily take control of a situation without resorting to sexual power games or emotionalism, Conan Doyle's Holmes seems far ahead of his time. More than a century on, it is a lesson that some adapters of this story have been slower to learn. ∎

The bohemians

Bohemia is a real place that was once a kingdom, but is now a region in the Czech Republic. However, "Bohemia" was also the imaginary spiritual home of the gypsy people, which is why, in the mid-19th century, the term "bohemian" came to refer to the unconventional, rootless lifestyle practiced by some artists, writers, and musicians. The bohemians were associated with romantic living—they were dedicated to artistic creation and free love— and some rejected material

wealth. With their soft, colorful clothes and unkempt hair, they were easy to recognize. Some bohemians were political rebels, but for many it was just a way of life. Most were poor and lived in run-down neighborhoods such as Montmartre in Paris, Soho in London, and Telegraph Hill in San Francisco, but there were rich bohemians, too—those who rejected society's values. Bohemianism appeared in cities in Europe and the US in the mid-1800s, and reached its peak in the 1890s, when Conan Doyle wrote "A Scandal in Bohemia."

I REALLY WOULDN'T MISS YOUR CASE FOR THE WORLD

THE RED-HEADED LEAGUE (1891)

IN CONTEXT

TYPE
Short story

FIRST PUBLICATION
UK: August 1891

COLLECTION
***The Adventures of Sherlock Holmes**, 1892*

CHARACTERS
Jabez Wilson Pawnbroker.

Vincent Spaulding
Assistant at Jabez Wilson's
pawnshop.

Duncan Ross
Man at the offices of the
Red-Headed League.

Peter Jones
Scotland Yard detective.

Mr. Merryweather
Chairman of the City
and Suburban Bank.

Although "The Red-Headed League" was written after "A Case of Identity" (pp.68–9), it was the first of the two to be published in *The Strand Magazine*. Some Holmesian scholars have surmised that the *Strand* considered "The Red-Headed League" to be the better story, and wanted to establish the detective's popularity as quickly as possible—it was certainly one of Conan Doyle's favorites. But there is another, perhaps more likely reason: "The Red-Headed League" took just seven days to write, and Conan Doyle finished the first three short stories during April 1891. There

Holmes's analysis of Jabez Wilson

Wilson's **right hand** is "quite a **size larger**" than his left, and his muscles are more **developed**.

He is wearing an **arc-and-compass** breastpin (an emblem of the **Freemasons**).

His **tattoo of a fish** is "quite peculiar to China," and he has a **Chinese coin** on his watch chain.

His **right cuff** is very **shiny**, and his **left cuff** has a **smooth patch** near the elbow where it **rests upon a desk**.

Jabez Wilson has worked in manual labor, is a Freemason, has been in China, and has done a considerable amount of writing lately.

is a good chance that "The Red-Headed League" and "A Case of Identity" were sent to the *Strand* together, resulting in a confusion about their intended order. Holmes's reference in this story to "the very simple problem presented by Miss Mary Sutherland" (who appears in "A Case of Identity") makes this mistake clear.

This is a story which focuses on gullibility and credulousness, and Conan Doyle brings attention to the bizarre, almost unbelievable nature of the case as a claim for its veracity. As Holmes remarks, "…for strange effects and extraordinary combinations we must go to life itself… always far more daring than any effort of the imagination."

Commonplace beginnings
Watson calls on Holmes one day to find him deep in conversation with Jabez Wilson, a pawnbroker, who

is a man florid of face, stout, and altogether an unremarkable example of "an average commonplace British tradesman"—that is, except for his mane of fiery red hair. Holmes swiftly realizes that Wilson is a Freemason. Conan Doyle was, at times, a member of this secret society, but here Holmes makes a pointed reference to "your order," showing the detective's aloofness

from it, contrary to speculation that Holmes himself was a mason. Holmes also observes that Wilson has been doing a great deal of writing; and this remarkable case revolves around this mundane task.

Little sympathy
It is unlikely that Wilson, as a pawnbroker, would have aroused much sympathy in contemporary »

Jabez Wilson (played by Roger Hammond in the 1984 Granada television production) is ushered through crowds of red-headed men.

readers, as his trade is the equivalent of today's thriving high-interest payday loan industry—a service to which poorer people were often obliged to turn, using jewelry and other valuables as security to borrow cash. Wilson himself remarks that his work is "mostly done of an evening, Mr. Holmes, especially Thursday and Friday evening, which is just before pay-day." Nevertheless, Wilson tends not to leave his premises very often.

Wilson's story

Wilson tells Holmes and Watson that two months previously, his new assistant, Vincent Spaulding, alerted him to an advertisement in the newspaper. It was placed by an organization called the Red-Headed League, based in the US in Lebanon, Pennsylvania, but with an office in (fictional) Pope's Court, off Fleet Street. The League sought "red-headed men... above the age of twenty-one years" to apply for a post involving "purely nominal services," at a weekly rate of £4. This amount was not to be sniffed at: Conan Doyle was only paid £25 for this

> Your case is an exceedingly remarkable one, and I shall be happy to look into it.
> **Sherlock Holmes**

story, even though he was soon able to command much higher fees. On the appointed day, says Wilson, Fleet Street was awash with men with red hair, and the thoroughfare looked like a "coster's orange barrow"—costermongers being a kind of greengrocer seen all over London (the name comes from a medieval word for apple). The image is both potent and bizarre. At the offices of this League, Duncan Ross (his name is taken from the Italian, *rosso*, meaning red) delightedly offers Wilson first refusal on the job. His "test" of the pawnbroker's hair is to tug on it

with all his might to make sure it is not a wig; this is a masterpiece of theater, as is his lament that "I could tell you tales of cobbler's wax [being used as a hair dye] which would disgust you with human nature." It transpires that the work requires copying out by hand the whole of the Encyclopaedia Britannica from 10 am until 2 pm every weekday. Fortunately, these hours do not interfere with Wilson's pawnbroking business. However, Wilson is told that if he leaves the office during the prescribed hours, he will instantly forfeit his new job.

Double deception

Wilson's assistant, Spaulding, began working for him a few months earlier. An eager employee, he was "willing to come for half wages, so as to learn the business." Holmes notes that Wilson is fortunate to have an employee who "comes under the full market price." But Spaulding disappears into the cellar of Wilson's shop for hours at a time, supposedly developing photographs. It becomes clear to Holmes that the real "league" is between Spaulding and Ross; the sole aim of their elaborate ruse

The Boylston Bank Robbery

Although Holmes declares "The Red-Headed League" to be a ruse without precedent, the heist itself was not so original. In November 1869, a remarkably similar bank robbery took place in Boston, Massachusetts. Charley Bullard and Adam Worth (who may have been the inspiration for Moriarty, pp.28–9) tunneled into the Boylston National Bank from a neighboring shop, then shipped their loot down the east coast to New York. The *Boston Tribune* called it "one of the most bold and successful robberies which has ever been perpetrated in this

city." For the six weeks prior to the theft, Bullard and Worth had operated the next-door premises as a hairdresser's, all the while secretly tunneling into the bank's vaults. Like the villains in this story, they had made the final moves over a weekend, so the losses were only discovered when the bank reopened the following Monday morning. The robbery's full details were later uncovered by Pinkerton's detectives, the same organization that would feature prominently in *The Valley of Fear* (pp.212–21) in 1914.

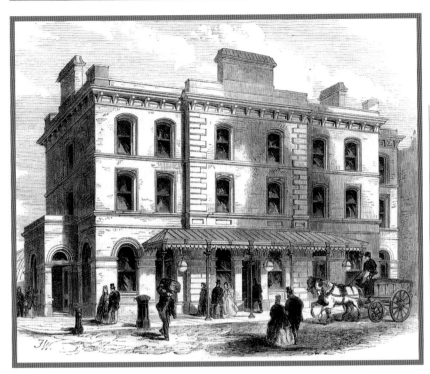

Aldersgate Street Station, one of the original Underground stations on London's Metropolitan Railway, opened in 1865. This engraving appeared in *The London Illustrated News* in 1866.

Holmes and Watson's journey to Aldersgate Street Station (now Barbican Station) on the oldest stretch of the London Underground network is the only recorded instance of them traveling by Tube: a remarkable fact, since there was (and still is) a Tube station at the end of Baker Street. "Saxe-Coburg Square," which Wilson gives as the location of his shop, does not actually exist. It has a royal name, and Conan Doyle might have been inspired by Bloomsbury's Mecklenburgh Square—named after the wife of George III—near Holmes's first London lodgings in Montague Street. However, while that square is fairly grand, the fictional Saxe-Coburg Square is "a poky, little, shabby-genteel place, where four lines of dingy two-storied brick houses looked out into a small railed-in enclosure."

On arrival at Wilson's shop, and certain that Clay will not recognize him, Holmes knocks at the door. Clay responds curtly to his request »

(which Conan Doyle returned to in "The Three Garridebs", pp.262–65) is to get Wilson out of his house, and keep him out, for some evidently nefarious purpose.

This unlikely tale sustains itself partly because it is so outlandish, and partly because it is hard to know what the two villains are cooking up. But Wilson's own recognition that it all sounds too good to be true also goes some way to relieving the reader's suspicions. In fact, to overcome his reservations, Wilson applies a reasoning rather like Holmes's: sometimes the truth is stranger than fiction.

For eight weeks, Wilson copied from the book and the money kept coming. Then, on the morning of his visit to 221B Baker Street, he had arrived at Pope's Court to find a sign pinned to the door, reading: "The Red Headed-League is dissolved, Oct 9, 1890." Wilson asked around, and discovered that Ross had also been going by the alias "William Morris." Wilson was given an address in King Edward Street, near St. Paul's: "I started off, Mr. Holmes, but when I got to that address it was a manufactory of artificial knee-caps, and no one in it had ever heard of either Mr. William Morris, or Mr. Duncan Ross."

The scene of the crime

Although Holmes declares the case to be "quite a three-pipe problem"—meaning that he would usually take the time to ponder and let his mind wander through all the elements of the mystery—he immediately recognizes Spaulding from Wilson's description, as the telltale white acid-splash scar on his forehead is so distinctive (the alert reader in 1891 would know that acid was used by coin counterfeiters). "Spaulding" is in fact John Clay, "one of the coolest and most daring criminals in London." It remains only for Holmes to visit Wilson's shop and find out what Clay is up to.

We are spies in an enemy's country. We know something of Saxe-Coburg Square. Let us now explore the parts which lie behind it.
Sherlock Holmes

The "real" John Clay is described by Scotland Yard's Peter Jones as a "murderer, thief, smasher, and forger." As his alias, Vincent Spaulding, he appears at first to be quite the opposite.

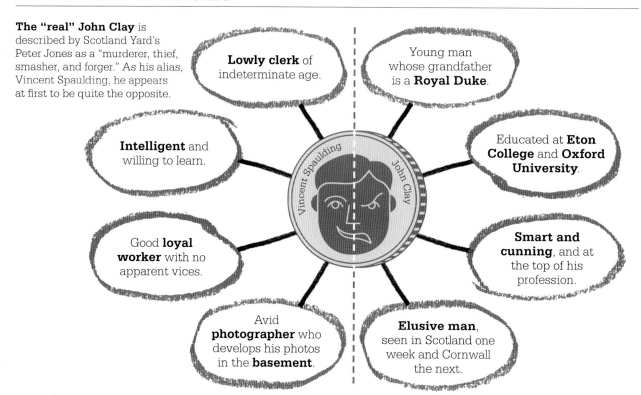

Lowly clerk of indeterminate age.

Young man whose grandfather is a **Royal Duke**.

Intelligent and willing to learn.

Educated at **Eton College** and **Oxford University**.

Good **loyal worker** with no apparent vices.

Smart and cunning, and at the top of his profession.

Avid **photographer** who develops his photos in the **basement**.

Elusive man, seen in Scotland one week and Cornwall the next.

for directions to the Strand. In truth, Holmes has only summoned him in order to get a look at his trouser-legs. Sure enough, the knees are dusty and worn—proof that something has been going on in the cellar. Holmes has already concluded that the only possible explanation is that Clay is digging a tunnel, so he raps his stick on the pavement outside to test for a hollow sound, but there is none. However, walking around the corner, Holmes realizes that the shop backs on to the Coburg branch of the City and Suburban Bank in the much finer grand parade of Farringdon Street.

Incidentally, as Holmes and Watson scout the scene, Holmes remarks, "It is a hobby of mine to have an exact knowledge of London." Conan Doyle would have done well to do the same, as his descriptions of London are often riddled with inconsistencies. For

instance, it does not make sense that Holmes and Watson go to Aldersgate Street Station to walk as far as Farringdon Street. It is also odd that St. Bartholomew's hospital, which is just around the corner, is not mentioned, since this is where Holmes and Watson first met in *A Study in Scarlet* (pp.36–45).

A considerable crime is in contemplation. I have every reason to believe that we shall be in time to stop it.
Sherlock Holmes

Time to "play"

Holmes now has all the pieces of the puzzle he needs, and he and Watson continue to St. James's Hall in the West End to hear the real-life Spanish violinist and composer Pablo Sarasate. Watson—still in the dark about the case—muses on the way Holmes's behavior fluctuates from "extreme languor to devouring energy." Building on the atmospherics in *The Sign of Four* (pp.46–55), this taps into 19th-century anxieties about the unconscious mind and can also be read as a reference to the idea of the "double life," a major literary trend of the time featuring in novels such as Oscar Wilde's *The Picture of Dorian Gray* (1890) and Robert Louis Stevenson's *Strange Case of Dr. Jekyll and Mr. Hyde* (1886). Holmes's "dual nature" also has roots in Detective C. Auguste Dupin's "bi-part soul" in Edgar

Allan Poe's "The Murders in the Rue Morgue" (1841). But perhaps Holmes is simply treating his brain as a machine, using a little music to stay relaxed—there is nothing to be done now until nightfall.

Caught in the act

Later that evening, Holmes and Watson meet at 221B, along with Peter Jones, "the official police agent," and Mr. Merryweather, head of the City and Suburban Bank. Jones reassures Merryweather by remarking on "that business of the Sholto murder and the Agra treasure" (events in *The Sign of Four*), showing that Holmes has become recognized at Scotland Yard.

The group heads to Farringdon Street and the vaults of the Coburg branch of the City and Suburban Bank, which is temporarily housing £30,000 worth of gold "napoleon" coins borrowed from the Bank of France. Merryweather strikes the flagstone floor with his stick and declares that "it sounds quite hollow." After a long wait, with Watson's army revolver cocked and the tension palpable, a "lurid spark" appears through a chink in the floor. When the two villains appear from their tunnel, Holmes collars Clay, while "Ross/Morris"—whose real name turns out to be Archie—tries to escape the way he came, but is arrested by the police officers waiting outside Wilson's shop.

Deep thinker

Back at 221B, Holmes remarks to Watson that the case has provided a welcome break from the tedium of everyday life: "It saved me from *ennui*. Alas! I already feel it closing in upon me." In the 1890s the word *ennui* (French for "boredom") carried connotations of decadent, *fin de siècle* world-weariness, recalling

This illustration, entitled "It's no use, John Clay... you have no chance at all," from *The Strand Magazine*, 1891, shows Holmes capturing Clay as he emerges from the tunnel.

the effete heroes of Oscar Wilde, J. K. Huysmans, and others. It is also reminiscent of the 19th-century French poet Charles Baudelaire, whose book *Le Spleen de Paris* (published posthumously in 1869) helped establish the appeal of affectedly melancholic boredom.

Holmes's final remark, a slightly misquoted aphorism from the French novelist Gustave Flaubert ("the man is nothing, the work everything"), suggests that the literary allusions might not have been accidental. It is clear that while the Holmes who appears in "The Red-Headed League" is relatively consistent with the Holmes of *The Sign of Four*, there has been a marked shift in his character since *A Study in Scarlet*. In that first story, Watson remarked of Holmes, "Of contemporary literature, philosophy and politics he appeared to know next to nothing." Yet earlier in "The Red-Headed League," when Holmes

explained how he had deduced that Wilson was a Freemason, the pawnbroker said bluntly, "I thought at first that you had done something clever, but I see that there is nothing in it after all." Holmes's erudite response to his client, a line from the Roman author Tacitus, not only displays his learning but would work equally well as a motto to this strange case: "*Omne ignotum pro magnifico*," which translates as "that which is most mysterious always seems most magnificent." ∎

John Clay

A young man "at the head of his profession," John Clay is a worthy adversary for Holmes, and the detective holds a certain admiration for Clay's cunning and the challenge he presents. Although Clay does not appear anywhere else in the canon, it seems that Holmes has met him before. After declining a reward at the end of this case, Holmes states that "I have had one or two little scores of my own to settle with Mr. John Clay... I am amply repaid by having had

an experience which is in many ways unique." In anticipation of the later villain Moriarty, the aristocrat of crime, Clay is the grandson of a royal duke. He was educated at Eton—one of Britain's most elite private schools—and Oxford University, where some Holmesian scholars believe the detective studied. Clay's snobbery is clear in his actions toward Jones, the Scotland Yard policeman—he insists that the officer call him "sir," and demands not to be touched by his "filthy hands" as he is handcuffed.

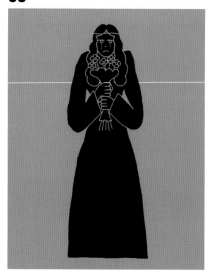

THE LITTLE THINGS ARE INFINITELY THE MOST IMPORTANT
A CASE OF IDENTITY (1891)

IN CONTEXT

TYPE
Short story

FIRST PUBLICATION
UK: September 1891
US: September/October 1891

COLLECTION
The Adventures of Sherlock Holmes, 1892

CHARACTERS
Mary Sutherland
Young woman seeking her missing fiancé.

James Windibank
Mary's young stepfather, a wine merchant.

Mrs. Windibank Mary's mother, who is 15 years older than her second husband.

Hosmer Angel
Mary's missing fiancé.

While Holmes and Watson sit by the fire in 221B Baker Street, Holmes remarks, "Life is infinitely stranger than anything which the mind of man could invent." The case that unfolds proves to bear this out. Rising to peer out of the window, Holmes observes a young woman with a "preposterous hat" and a "vacuous face" looking up nervously from the street below. She is soon being shown in by the bellboy, who announces her as Miss Mary Sutherland.

She is anxious to find her fiancé, Hosmer Angel, who disappeared on the morning

Holmes's observations of Miss Sutherland

Clearly defined **double line** above her wrist and the dents of a **pince-nez** on her nose.

Wearing **half-buttoned odd boots** but otherwise neatly dressed.

Both glove and finger clearly **stained with violet ink**.

Miss Sutherland is a short-sighted typist in a hurry, who had written a note just prior to leaving home.

Typewriters, which were common by 1891, offered standardized text. Yet the quirks specific to each machine enable Holmes to trace Windibank's letters.

of their wedding. Her story throws up a number of clues for the alert reader. Miss Sutherland lives with her mother and young stepfather, James Windibank. She has a small annuity of £100 left to her by an uncle, which she gives to her parents, and has her own income, since she works as a typist. Her meetings with Angel have occurred only when Windibank was away, during which Angel spoke in a whisper, wore tinted glasses, and had a bushy mustache and sideburns. He has sent her only typed letters (even typing his "signature"), and given only a post office address.

The investigation ensues
Holmes promises to investigate, but urges her to forget Angel. She claims this is impossible. He points out that Miss Sutherland is clearly short-sighted, but her real myopia signals a more profound blindness: her lack of suspicion has made her a victim of exploitation.

Angel's letters are a further opportunity for Holmes to show his acute powers of observation, as he identifies unique features in the way certain characters look,

which make them easily identifiable. He then invites Windibank to Baker Street and, as expected, sees from his acceptance letter that it was typed on the same machine.

Holmes corners his man
Windibank is confronted with the truth. He married Miss Sutherland's mother for her money, and has enjoyed Mary's annuity too. Fearing he would lose this annual income were Mary to marry, Windibank disguised himself as a suitor, then abandoned her in the hope that she would be paralyzed by loss and indecision for years to come, leaving him in control of her funds.

Unrepentant, Windibank sneers that the law cannot touch him. Holmes, raging that "there was never a man deserved punishment more," rushes at the "cold-blooded scoundrel" with a horsewhip, only for Windibank to flee. Laughing despite his anger, Holmes predicts that he will "rise from crime to crime" and end up on the gallows.

Undoubtedly, this tale is a clever demonstration of Holmes's opening assertion—closely observed truth is indeed stranger than highly wrought fiction. But Holmes's refusal to

The larger crimes are apt to be the simpler, for the bigger the crime, the more obvious, as a rule, is the motive.
Sherlock Holmes

reveal the truth to Mary, arguing that it would be dangerous to take away her delusions, is a troubling loose end. It effectively places her in the same position she was in at the outset—filled with longing for her so-called suitor—and she has gained nothing by seeking help. She is portrayed as a weak, comical figure, yet emerges from the story as a stoical and faithful victim whose innocence and naiveté are cruelly exploited by the people closest to her. Most disturbingly of all, her own mother has colluded in the deceit—a poignant betrayal. ∎

Women and property

For much of the 19th century, a woman who married ceased to be a legal entity in her own right, and as such was unable to formally own property—all her possessions would belong to her husband. All this changed with the three Married Women's Property Acts of 1870, 1882, and 1893, which gave married women rights to their own earnings and property, and to property, such as an inheritance, acquired during the marriage. These reforms made it harder

for greedy and unscrupulous husbands, like Windibank, to use marriage as a way of acquiring property. In "A Case of Identity," Windibank devised a convoluted and malicious plan to acquire the fortune of both his wife and stepdaughter. He first managed to convince his wife to sell her first husband's business, apparently at a loss. As a single woman, Mary had the right to bestow her income where she chose, but Windibank was able to prey on her innocence and generosity to appropriate it for himself.

THERE IS NOTHING MORE DECEPTIVE THAN AN OBVIOUS FACT
THE BOSCOMBE VALLEY MYSTERY (1891)

IN CONTEXT

TYPE
Short story

FIRST PUBLICATION
UK: October 1891

COLLECTION
***The Adventures of
Sherlock Holmes**, 1892*

CHARACTERS
Charles McCarthy Murder
victim, tenant farmer originally
from Australia.

James McCarthy Principal
suspect, and Charles
McCarthy's only son.

John Turner Wealthy,
widowed landowner, and
landlord of Charles McCarthy.

Alice Turner Daughter of
John Turner.

Inspector Lestrade Scotland
Yard detective.

**Holmes deduces the
position of a window**

Watson is known for
his characteristic
military neatness.

↓

He shaves every
morning by **sunlight**.

↓

His shaving is **less
complete on the left** of his
face, suggesting that the
right is better illuminated.

↓

**Watson's bedroom
window must be on
the right-hand side.**

As Watson is enjoying
a leisurely breakfast in
his matrimonial home,
a telegram from Holmes arrives,
summoning him to the 11:15am
train out of Paddington. Holmes
has not given him much notice,
and the doctor immediately panics,
despite living close to the train
station. Fortunately, as Watson's
wife points out, a neighboring
doctor, Anstruther, can cover
his comparatively busy medical
practice, freeing him to hightail
it for the train. There, Holmes is
waiting for him with the facts of
"one of those simple cases which
are extremely difficult."

A fatal quarrel
Charles McCarthy, a tenant farmer
from a rural country estate, has
been found murdered near a small
wooded lake called Boscombe Pool.
He has few friends in the area,
save for his landlord, John Turner,
who amassed a great fortune in
Australia many years earlier
and has been very generous to
McCarthy on account of their
acquaintance in those more
adventurous days. Suspicion has
fallen squarely upon the victim's
hot-blooded son, James, who was

seen having a heated argument with his father at the scene of the crime, before allegedly returning later to find the old man dying of his wounds, which were caused by a blow to the head.

James has refused to divulge the cause of their dispute, and when quizzed about old McCarthy's final mutterings, he recounts an unintelligible reference to "a rat." Furthermore, the young man appears wracked by guilt, and was seen carrying a gun, the stock of which could have been the heavy, blunt object used as the murder weapon. Holmes has been enlisted by Turner's daughter, Alice, who has known James since they were children, and who believes unquestioningly in his innocence.

A jaunt to the countryside

"The Boscombe Valley Mystery" is the first story in which Holmes and Watson head out into the English countryside, leaving the "great cesspool" of London behind them, and in his telegram, Holmes clearly tantalizes Watson with the promise of fresh air and perfect scenery. The trip also provides an opportunity for the characters to forgo their urban attire. Holmes cuts an "even gaunter and taller" figure than usual in his "long grey travelling-cloak," while there is a hint of comedy in the apparel of Inspector Lestrade of Scotland Yard, who meets them at the station—he is conspicuous as ever as a city detective "in spite of the light brown dustcoat and leather-leggins which he wore in deference to his rustic surroundings."

Another detective in town

Lestrade has already been on-site for some time when they arrive, and although it may appear that he is acting privately, he actually is still functioning at this time also as an official policeman. Like Holmes, he has ostensibly been hired to clear James of the crime. However, his priority is to persuade everyone around him of the young man's guilt. In his opinion, "McCarthy senior met his death from McCarthy junior and... all theories to the contrary are the merest moonshine."

Throughout the Holmes canon, Lestrade's relationship with Holmes is often a fractious one, and never

> What a tissue of mysteries and improbabilities the whole thing was!
> **Dr. Watson**

more so than during this particular case, where those occasional glimpses of mutual respect that appear in other stories are markedly absent. Lestrade is "indifferent and contemptuous" toward Holmes's methods, while Holmes berates the inspector most bitterly for trampling all over the crime scene. The two detectives snipe at each other incessantly (and enjoyably), and there is one moment, during a coach journey, where a string of jibes ends with Lestrade nearly losing his temper and snapping at Holmes ("with some warmth"). »

Sherlock Holmes's iconic deerstalker

The deerstalker—a soft cloth cap with peaks in front and behind, and ear flaps—has become an iconic accoutrement of Sherlock Holmes, although, surprisingly, this hat was never mentioned explicitly by name in any of the original stories. Here in "The Boscombe Valley Mystery," Conan Doyle refers to Holmes's headgear for his country trip as "a close-fitting cloth cap," while in the later story "Silver Blaze" (pp.106–09), he describes it as "his earflapped traveling cap." The full credit for Holmes's now-iconic image must in fact go to illustrator Sidney Paget, who first provided Holmes with his signature deerstalker in his illustrations of "The Boscombe Valley Mystery" for *The Strand Magazine*. It is odd that Paget should have picked such an incongruously rustic hat for a traveling city gentleman, but the deerstalker was Paget's favorite hat to wear in the country. As the reader later observes Holmes with his nose to the ground, tracking his prey through the muddy hollow of Boscombe Pool and completely absorbed by the chase, perhaps the deerstalker is not such an odd choice after all.

You know
my method. It is
founded upon the
observation of trifles.
Sherlock Holmes

Holmes's resolution of the case relies on a mixture of psychological insight and tenacious crime-scene analysis. Where others see guilt in James's remorse, reticence, and apparent invention, Holmes divines the predictable emotional turmoil of a grieving but innocent man. His interrogation of James is "off-camera" in the cells, but he returns with a full testimony. As is so often the case with earnest young men who refuse to give up information, James's silence had been because the honor of a lady is at stake.

Nevertheless, despite James's former reluctance to talk to the police, Holmes, the master manipulator, manages to wheedle some highly significant truths out of the young McCarthy.

More beast than man
The scene in which Holmes investigates the surroundings of Boscombe Pool is one of the most vivid portrayals of the great detective imitating a bloodhound. Picking his way along the trail, he undergoes a transformation, appearing more beast than man, as "his nostrils seemed to dilate with a purely animal lust for the chase." His body warps as he becomes tense and hunched, his steely eyes fixed on the ground, his veins standing out "like whipcord in his long sinewy neck." Indeed, his metamorphosis is so complete that, as Watson remarks, "men who had only known the quiet thinker and logician of Baker Street would have failed to recognize him."

Despite the obscured state of the crime scene, Holmes of course turns up a whole string of clues that

I find it hard enough
to tackle facts, Holmes,
without flying away after
theories and fancies.
Inspector Lestrade

everyone else has missed, eventually presenting Lestrade with the true murder weapon—a jagged stone—and announcing to the skeptical inspector that the criminal "is a tall man, left-handed, limps with the right leg, wears thick-soled shooting boots and a grey cloak, smokes Indian cigars, uses a cigar-holder, and carries a blunt pen-knife in his pocket." The solution is at hand, and Holmes has both murderer and motive.

Antipodean intrigue
Later, in a private meeting with Turner, Holmes reveals the truth. Turner's riches, it seems, had come not from enterprise, but from a lucrative spree as a highway robber in Australia, where he had been known as Black Jack of Ballarat—hence the dying man's garbled allusion to "a rat." McCarthy, a witness to one of Turner's violent crimes, had been blackmailing his landlord for years, but when he demanded that his son marry Turner's daughter Alice, it was too

Holmes's quest for clues can be so intense that he takes on the manner of a bloodhound, as captured in this *Strand* illustration during his exhaustive investigation of Boscombe Pool.

John Turner becomes a murderer when he cracks under the combined pressures of his past, present, and future. *Past:* as a former violent highwayman in Australia, one of his crimes was witnessed by Charles McCarthy and threatens to ruin Turner. *Present:* McCarthy then used his knowledge to blackmail Turner for money, land, and a home. *Future:* McCarthy finally is demanding the one thing Turner refuses to consent to—his daughter's hand in marriage.

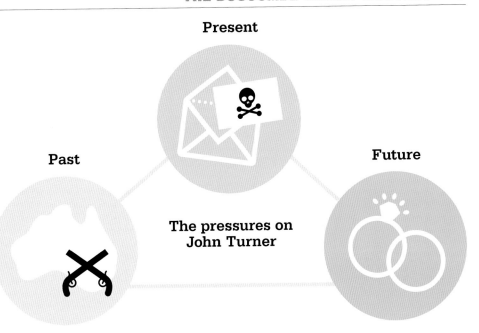

Present

Past

Future

The pressures on John Turner

much for the old man to bear. With his own health failing rapidly, and the very real prospect of his only child ending up at the mercy of his worst enemy, Turner was driven to silence McCarthy once and for all.

When anarchic and disreputable goings-on creep into Conan Doyle's ordered English society, they often appear to have originated from the younger nations. Primarily it is America that stands by with a ready supply of corrupt Mormons, Texan racists, and migrant Irish gangsters, but occasionally the trouble has its origins in Australia. At the time this story was written, the country had long since ceased to be a penal colony, with the last convict ship having disembarked on the coast of Western Australia some time before the young Conan Doyle's tenth birthday, but the notion of exile there, albeit voluntary, persisted.

Conan Doyle's Australia is a land of myriad opportunities and few questions, where new starts and fortunes can readily be made,

legally or otherwise. The return of a prodigal son from profitable yet dubious antipodean adventures, as with Turner in this case, was a theme to which Conan Doyle would return later in his career, and there are distinct echoes of "The Boscombe Valley Mystery" in "The *Gloria Scott*" (pp.116–19).

Getting away with it?
"The Boscombe Valley Mystery" is neither the first nor the last time that the trickiest aspect of the case, for Holmes at least, is the moral dilemma presented by its solution. In revealing the full details of what he has discovered, Holmes will clear James McCarthy, but as a consequence, both John Turner and his daughter will be ruined. Fortunately, there are some benefits to being a consulting detective rather than a police officer, and Holmes is able to use his discretion in this particular case.

Provided he fulfills his obligation to keep young McCarthy from the gallows, Holmes is free to stack

the odds in favor of a happy ending: having obtained, following their meeting, a signed confession from the ailing murderer, Turner, he promises not to use it unless absolutely necessary. In the end, Holmes manages to get the case thrown out on the strength of a number of objections, and young James and Alice are free to build a future together, happily ignorant of their turbulent family history. ∎

Your own deathbeds, when they come, will be the easier for the thought of the peace which you have given to mine.
John Turner

I AM THE LAST COURT OF APPEAL

THE FIVE ORANGE PIPS (1891)

IN CONTEXT

TYPE
Short story

FIRST PUBLICATION
UK: November 1891
US: December 1891

COLLECTION
***The Adventures of Sherlock Holmes*, 1892**

CHARACTERS
John Openshaw Young landowner from Horsham, West Sussex.

Joseph Openshaw John's late father and owner of a bicycle factory.

Elias Openshaw John's late uncle, who had emigrated to America before retiring back to Sussex.

Conan Doyle wrote "The Five Orange Pips" early in 1891, but was delayed in posting it to *The Strand Magazine* until May that year by an attack of influenza. It is one of the strangest and saddest of the Holmes tales—Holmes fails to prevent the murder of his young client or apprehend the murderers, and never quite gets to the bottom of the mystery. And yet Conan Doyle listed it as among his favorites.

Watson partially explains why when he introduces the story. He says that there have always been

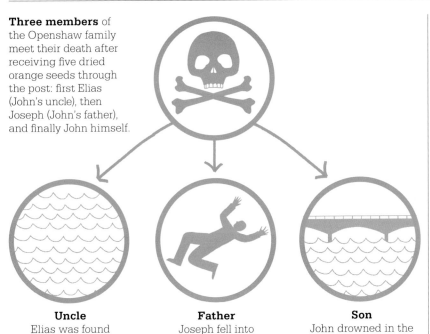

Three members of the Openshaw family meet their death after receiving five dried orange seeds through the post: first Elias (John's uncle), then Joseph (John's father), and finally John himself.

Uncle
Elias was found face-down in a shallow pool of water seven weeks after receiving the letter from India.

Father
Joseph fell into a chalk quarry three days after the letter from Dundee arrived.

Son
John drowned in the Thames River, near Waterloo Bridge, two days after receiving the letter from London.

cases that have been only partially solved, with "explanations founded upon conjecture and surmise." The strange case of "The Five Orange Pips," he says, is one of these, but its remarkable details convince him that it is a story worth telling. Indeed, it is the rich narrative that makes this story. Also, Conan Doyle most likely felt that including a failure helped to enhance the sense of realism in the stories as a whole and keep his readers engaged, since they could not always be sure that an adventure would end well.

A stormy case

The story is set in 1887 and begins in the middle of a violent September storm, which Watson describes in apocalyptic terms. It seems as if the whole world might easily be overwhelmed by chaos, and it needs the constant vigilance of

Holmes to keep its horrors at bay. As is so often the case in the Holmes tales, London is seen as a haven of rationality with danger lurking in the countryside beyond. But it is a fragile sanctuary that Holmes must be constantly on his guard to protect. No wonder he is in a dark mood.

As the storm reaches its height, there is a ring at the door. Such is the ferocity of the weather that it seems Holmes's usual prescience has deserted him. He considers it unlikely that the visitor is a client on such a night, and assumes it is a "crony" of his landlady. He is wrong.

The original illustration from the *Strand* depicts Joseph Openshaw—the second member of the family to fall victim to the Ku Klux Klan—receiving five dried orange seeds. Within three days, he was dead.

It *is* a client—a man in his early twenties, dripping wet from the storm and deeply worried.

Recovering his alertness, Holmes at once deduces that the man has come from somewhere southwest of London due to the mix of chalk and clay on his boots. As Watson later acknowledges, Holmes is thoroughly informed on virtually every branch of knowledge relevant to his detective work, and geology is one of them. It turns out that the young man is from near Horsham, in what is now West Sussex, where distinctive blue gault clay is found at the foot of the chalky South Downs.

A tale of three letters

His provenance established, the young man introduces himself as John Openshaw, and tells how his family has suffered a "mysterious and inexplicable chain of events." His father, Joseph, became rich making bicycles and inventing an "unbreakable tire"; John's uncle Elias, meanwhile, emigrated to America and made a fortune as a plantation owner in Florida, fought as a colonel in the American Civil »

'WHAT ON EARTH DOES THIS MEAN?'

The Ku Klux Klan

The Ku Klux Klan (or KKK) emerged in the southern United States during the late 1860s, in the aftermath of the Civil War, as resentment boiled over the freeing of slaves and their resultant inclusion in the political process. The KKK allegedly began when six former Confederate officers formed a social club in Tennessee in 1866. They named it the Ku Klux Klan in mockery of their Greek-named fraternities at college, and dressed up in white robes to frighten local black people. But what started as a joke soon escalated into violent terror, as white-sheeted vigilantes roamed across the South on horseback, killing black people and burning their houses.

Confederate general Nathan Forrest was the organization's first "grand wizard," but the mob attracted every white person with a grudge in the South. Tens of thousands of black people died as they were lynched, shot, or burned alive in their homes. It is unknown whether the encyclopedia article that Holmes cites is genuine, or whether the KKK really did use orange seeds as warnings. But the heart of the movement was certainly secretive and used every conceivable method, from intimidation to horrific violence, to instill terror and loyalty.

After a massive crackdown by the federal government of President Grant, clan activity did die down around 1870, just as Conan Doyle suggests in this story. But the KKK simply went underground, only to reemerge in the early 20th century, and then again more recently.

War on the Confederate side, and then, strangely, retired to a secluded Sussex estate around 1869. John says his reason for leaving America was a "dislike of the Republican policy in extending the franchise to negroes"; but, as we discover later, that is only part of the story.

The grumpy Elias was a recluse and seemed to care only for his adolescent nephew, John, to whom he gave complete control over his household—except for an attic that was always kept locked. Then, one morning in March 1883, Elias was struck by terror on receiving a letter from Pondicherry, India, which held just five orange seeds (pips), the mark "KKK" on the envelope, and a note that he refused to let John read. In a panic, Elias rushed to the attic and returned with a brass box with the same letters "KKK" on the lid. He burned all the papers inside, then made his will in favor of John's father, Joseph. Seven weeks later, Elias was found dead in a shallow pool. The verdict at the inquest was suicide, but John was unconvinced.

After Joseph took over the estate, nothing happened for more than a year, until in January 1885 he received a letter postmarked "Dundee" (Scotland), containing five orange seeds, with "KKK" and the words "Put the papers on the sundial" written on the envelope. Since Elias seemed to have burned the papers in question, Joseph did nothing. Three days later, he too was found dead, having apparently fallen into a chalk quarry.

John then inherited the estate, and for two years, all was quiet. But the day before coming to Holmes, he too had received an envelope with five orange seeds and the same message and "KKK" mark—this time with a London postmark.

The laugh was struck from my lips at the sight of his face. His lip had fallen, his eyes were protruding, his skin the colour of putty...
John Openshaw

The detective at work

Hearing John's story, Holmes is aghast, realizing at once the terrible danger his client faces. When told the police would not take the situation seriously, Holmes explodes: "Incredible imbecility!" John has a charred scrap of paper with some "enigmatic notices" written on it saved from the brass box, and Holmes advises him to go straight home at once and put it on the sundial, together with a note saying the rest of the papers have been burned and that this is the only one remaining.

As John sets off into the night, Holmes explains to Watson how he sees the case. He has, from just a few telling clues, worked out the nature of the threat. Holmes explains how just as the French naturalist Georges Cuvier (1769–1832) could describe a whole animal from looking at a single bone, "so the observer who has thoroughly understood one link in a series of incidents should be able to accurately state all the other ones, both before and after." Holmes was not the first fictional detective to be inspired by Cuvier in this way. Both C. Auguste Dupin, in Edgar Allan

> A man should keep his little brain-attic stocked with all the furniture that he is likely to use, and the rest he can put away in the lumber-room of his library, where he can get it if he wants it.
> **Sherlock Holmes**

Poe's "The Murders on the Rue Morgue," and Émile Gaboriau's character Monsieur Lecoq, invoke Cuvier as well.

This logic-based approach of a "new breed" of detective differed from that of the police, who would look at cases in isolation and work just with the facts before them, rather than drawing on information from other sources—including a broad knowledge base—and then making connections. This is one reason why, as here, the police often exasperate Holmes. Only in modern police investigations has a logical, scientific way of thinking become an official part of detective work.

The secret society

Holmes deduces that Elias must have had a strong reason for leaving America, and that his reclusiveness suggests he was in hiding. The efficiency of the murders suggests

an organization—rather than an individual—is behind them, and the letters "KKK" must be its initials. Holmes shows Watson an American encyclopedia that cites "KKK" as the initials for the Ku Klux Klan—a secret society that was formed by ex-Confederate soldiers after the Civil War (see box). In just a few years, they acquired a terrible reputation for their killings of their opponents and black people, often sending chilling warnings in the form of oak twigs, melon seeds, or—as in this case—orange seeds.

The seeds, Holmes believes, are a warning to do what the KKK demands or face the consequences. The surviving fragment of paper suggests to him that the burned papers were a list of those who had previously been sent seeds by the KKK and their resulting response. He guesses that Elias Openshaw's possession of this list must be a huge threat to the organization. Interestingly, his disappearance from the US in 1869 coincided with the sudden collapse of the real KKK.

Holmes has also worked out that the killer or killers take longer to reach the victim than the warning letter, because they are traveling by sailing ship, whereas the letter goes much faster by a mailboat steamer. The delay from Pondicherry would have been seven weeks, but it was just three days from Dundee. The London postmark on the most recent letter indicates the killers are now extremely close.

Disaster strikes

After his brilliant analysis, and feeling there is nothing more to be done that evening, Holmes picks up his violin and starts to play. However, unusually for Holmes, this time he has drawn the wrong conclusion. The following morning, he and Watson awake to a report in the newspaper of a tragic and fatal accident to young John Openshaw, who has been found drowned in the Thames River near Waterloo Bridge. "Holmes," writes Watson, "was more depressed and shaken than I had ever seen him." »

In 1945 the movie *The House of Fear* was released. Loosely based on "The Five Orange Pips," it features Holmes investigating a series of deaths at an old manor house, each death foretold by the delivery of orange seeds to the victim.

First, Holmes investigates every **shipping vessel** that docked in the **three ports** of Pondicherry, Dundee, and London.

Dates

He then deduces that **the dates** the ship was in port must **match the postmarks** on the letters: January 1883 (Pondicherry); January 1885 (Dundee); September 1887 (London).

Ports

Lone Star

American ships

Finally, the ship must be **American**—home of the KKK. Thus Holmes **finds the *Lone Star***—the Lone Star State being a nickname for Texas.

Holmes identifies the ship on which the murderers are traveling by a process of elimination. He begins with three facts about the ship: the ports in which it docked, the dates on which it docked, and the fact that it is American. A ship that matches all three criteria is the one he is looking for.

A poignant ending

Determined to avenge Openshaw, Holmes pledges to track down the killers himself. The police are not to be trusted. "I shall be my own police," he insists, "When I have spun the web they may take the flies, but not before."

Remarkably, he does just that, discovering from Lloyd's shipping registers that an American sailing ship named the *Lone Star* was in Pondicherry and Dundee on the corresponding dates—and has just left London bound for Savannah, Georgia. There are three Americans on board, including a Captain James Calhoun. Holmes sends a letter containing five orange seeds, with "SH for JO" written on the flap of the envelope, to "Captain James Calhoun, Bark Lone Star, Savannah, Georgia," knowing the mail steamer will arrive in Savannah ahead of the *Lone Star*. He then cables the police in Savannah to pick up the three wanted murderers as soon as they arrive.

It is one of the most brilliant pieces of detective work in the Holmes canon. Within 24 hours, from an envelope containing some orange seeds and some initials, he has identified and tracked down

It becomes a personal matter with me now, and, if God sends me health, I shall set my hand upon this gang.
Sherlock Holmes

the ringleaders of a frightening and murderous organization from across the Atlantic, and arranged for their arrest. However, for all of Holmes's successes here, the young man who came to him for help is dead, and, as it turns out, the *Lone Star* never reaches Savannah. The storms at sea were severe, and Holmes learns that "somewhere far out in the Atlantic a shattered stern-post of the boat was seen swinging in the trough of a wave, with the letters 'L.S.' carved upon it." The story has seen one of the greatest triumphs of Holmes's methods, and perhaps their most dismal resolution.

Reaction to the tale

Not long after the "The Five Orange Pips" was published, four brothers—Edmund, Dillwyn, Wilfred, and Ronald Knox—analyzed it in detail and found a string of inaccuracies and contradictions. They wrote to Conan Doyle to inform him of their findings, but the author did not reply for a long time. Twenty years later, in 1911, Ronald Knox wrote the first serious analysis of the Holmes stories entitled *Studies in the Literature of Sherlock Holmes*, and in the process launched a tide of studies known as the Grand Game (see p.326), which have grown ever since, and in which Holmes enthusiasts examine the tales and analyze any errors as if Holmes were a real person.

When Knox sent him the article, Conan Doyle finally broke his silence and replied: "I cannot help writing to tell you of the amusement—and also the amazement with which I read your article on Sherlock Holmes … That anyone should spend such pains on such material was what surprised me. Certainly you know a great deal more about it than I do, for the stories have been written in a disconnected (and careless) way, without referring back to what had gone before."

In their analysis of "The Five Orange Pips," the Grand Game enthusiasts have shown their disbelief that the infallible Holmes could let his client venture out into the night to his death. They have criticized the suicide verdict on Elias Openshaw as implausible, and found inconsistencies between the historical Ku Klux Klan and the KKK in Conan Doyle's story. They have also queried why the KKK didn't ever attempt to directly recover the incriminating papers.

Power and fallibility

Although those participants in the Grand Game were Holmesian in their thoroughness and research, their criticism and analysis of the

A view of Waterloo Bridge from Hungerford Bridge in 1888. It was from here that the final KKK victim, John Openshaw, fell to his death—yet it was officially recorded that he "had been the victim of an unfortunate accident."

story rather misses the point, as Conan Doyle would no doubt have agreed. "The Five Orange Pips" is deeply atmospheric. The five little seeds exert a terrifying symbolic power, as each appearance signals another death and the story gathers an unstoppable momentum, as dark events and secret conflicts across an ocean come home to roost in the quiet Sussex countryside.

In no other Holmes tale do we see the great detective so nakedly vulnerable and so keenly aware of the huge responsibility he has in his role as crime fighter. "I am the last court of appeal," he admits to his young client, and we see in this story that he knows the burden is a heavy one. His failure to prevent his client's death cuts him to the quick, and it is perhaps this fallibility and compassion that emerge briefly from time to time—in between his feats of brilliance—that has sealed Holmes in the hearts of readers all over the world for so long. ■

Elias Openshaw

In "The Five Orange Pips," Conan Doyle uses a device that is familiar in detective and horror stories of a ghost coming out of someone's past to haunt them or their offspring. In Elias Openshaw's case, the KKK are still coming to get him long after he believes he left them behind. His nephew recalls how he was a "fierce and quick-tempered, very foul-mouthed" man. Elias was a racist who made a fortune in Florida on a slave plantation and fought for the Confederates in the Civil War. Readers can only guess that he joined the KKK in 1866, that he was somehow involved in their violent campaigns, and that around 1869 he fled the US with papers that will incriminate many KKK members. Unusually for this kind of story, the reader never learns what Elias did, how the papers came into his hands, why he left America, or why the KKK is on his trail. By not providing the background story, Conan Doyle tantalizes the reader brilliantly with a past that remains an enigma.

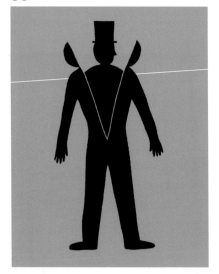

IT IS BETTER TO LEARN WISDOM LATE THAN NEVER TO LEARN IT AT ALL
THE MAN WITH THE TWISTED LIP (1891)

IN CONTEXT

TYPE
Short story

FIRST PUBLICATION
UK: December 1891
US: December 1891 (as "The Strange Tale of the Beggar")

COLLECTION
The Adventures of Sherlock Holmes, 1892

CHARACTERS
Neville St. Clair
Affluent businessman.

Hugh Boone
Disfigured beggar.

Mrs. St. Clair
Wife of Neville St. Clair.

Isa Whitney Patient of Watson's, addicted to opium.

Kate Whitney Wife of Isa and old friend of Mary Watson.

Mary Watson
Wife of Watson.

Holmes examines an envelope

The **name** is written in dark ink that dried naturally, indicating a **pause after writing**.

The **address** is grayish in color, showing that the ink here has been **blotted** immediately.

The writer knew the addressee's name but had to go and find out the address, which indicates that he was not familiar with it.

Unusually, this story begins in the home of Watson and his wife, Mary, when they are disturbed one evening by a distressed friend of Mary's, Kate Whitney. Her husband Isa is an opium addict and has been missing for two days; Kate suspects he is holed up in a opium den. As his doctor, Watson is dispatched to retrieve him. This scene provides a rare insight into Watson's domestic life; his tone seems to hold both affection and resignation when he remarks, "That was always the way. Folk who were in grief came to my wife like birds to a lighthouse."

Among the opium fumes
Watson arrives at the Bar of Gold, near London Bridge, and enters a "long, low room, thick and heavy with the brown opium smoke, and terraced with wooden berths, like the forecastle of an emigrant ship." He soon encounters Isa Whitney—in the sorry state his wife had predicted. To the doctor's sheer astonishment, he also sees Holmes among the mumbling addicts, disguised as a decrepit slave to the drug and clearly engaged in an investigation. Watson packs Whitney off in a cab home and joins his old friend on the hunt.

THE MAN WITH THE TWISTED LIP

Holmes reveals his mission to Watson: a respectable man of business, Neville St. Clair, has gone missing. He was last glimpsed in the upstairs window of this same opium den by his wife, who happened to be passing by sheer chance. Mrs. St. Clair gained access to the establishment, but found the upstairs room occupied only by a filthy, disfigured beggar named Hugh Boone. There was blood on the windowsill, and items of St. Clair's clothing and property were found concealed in the room and floating in the river outside. Boone was arrested, but in the absence of any further leads, Mrs. St. Clair has commissioned Holmes to get to the bottom of it. The detective is convinced that this will prove to be a straightforward murder case. He knows the opium den to be "the vilest murder-trap on the whole riverside" and its manager "a man of the vilest antecedents."

One and the same

Much to Holmes's surprise, however, his theory is proved incorrect when Mrs. St. Clair receives a note in her husband's handwriting assuring her that all is well. While Watson

sleeps, Holmes at last has the solution. Castigating himself for not seeing the truth sooner, he and Watson make their way to Bow Street police station, brandishing a bathroom sponge with which, quite literally, to clean up the matter.

As Holmes reveals by scrubbing the face of the imprisoned beggar, Hugh Boone and Neville St. Clair are in fact one and the same. A former actor turned journalist, St. Clair had discovered while researching an article just how much money a successful beggar might make, and for some years has been disguising himself grotesquely in the pursuit of easy cash. Unexpectedly sighted by his wife in his changing room above the opium den, he managed to preserve his secret, but at the cost of a murder charge. However, since no crime has actually been committed, St. Clair is released, promising an end to Hugh Boone.

"That rascally Lascar"

Charges of racism are occasionally leveled against Conan Doyle's portrayal of the lascar who runs the opium den. Lascars were Indian sailors working on British vessels, many of whom settled in London.

This engraving by Gustave Doré entitled *The Lascar's Room in Edwin Drood* conveys the seedy squalor of the Victorian opium den. It was made in 1872, two years after Dickens's death.

But Holmes's poor opinion of the lascar seems to stem more from his murderous criminality than his race, and the representation is far less uncomfortable to the modern reader than that of the crudely caricatured black boxer, Steve Dixie, in "The Adventure of the Three Gables" (see pp.272–73). ∎

Opium dens in Victorian London

Dr. Watson's evocation of the dreamy, seedy world inside the Victorian opium den is a captivating piece of writing, and the description may have been based on a real opium den at the time. London's best-known den in the 19th century was almost certainly known to Conan Doyle. It was run not by an Indian lascar but by a Chinese immigrant called Ah Sing. The clientele was mostly Chinese sailors, but curious gentlemen and members of the literary elite were also

visitors. Ah Sing's den was to be immortalized in Dickens's final work, *The Mystery of Edwin Drood* (1870), and Ah Sing liked to boast that the great novelist had visited his establishment.

However, there were far fewer opium dens in London than the literature and popular press of the day implied. The Pharmacy Act of 1868 restricted the sale of opium products to pharmacists, and many of London's addicts would not have been the stereotypical immigrant men smoking in a hazy

cellar, but could be anyone who was regularly prescribed laudanum (an opium tincture) for pain relief or other symptoms. Laudanum was so ubiquitous it is sometimes referred to as "the aspirin of the 19th century".

IN THE LARGER AND OLDER JEWELS EVERY FACET MAY STAND FOR A BLOODY DEED
THE ADVENTURE OF THE BLUE CARBUNCLE (1892)

IN CONTEXT

TYPE
Short story

FIRST PUBLICATION
US: January 1892 (as "The Christmas Goose that Swallowed a Diamond")
UK: January 1892

COLLECTION
***The Adventures of Sherlock Holmes*, 1892**

CHARACTERS
Henry Baker British Museum employee, and drinker.

Peterson Commissionaire.

Countess of Morcar Wealthy owner of the blue carbuncle.

Catherine Cusack Lady-in-waiting to Countess of Morcar.

Breckinridge Poultry seller at Covent Garden market.

John Horner Plumber accused of stealing the blue carbuncle.

James Ryder Attendant at the Hotel Cosmopolitan.

The story opens on a frosty morning two days after Christmas. Watson calls on Holmes one day to find his friend busy examining an old hat. This "battered billycock," has been found early on Christmas morning, along with a fine plucked goose for the pot, by a commissionaire named Peterson, who had witnessed their owner being attacked by a street gang. In the struggle that ensued, the victim had dropped the hat and goose before fleeing. Peterson picked them up and headed straight to Holmes to tell him of the events;

he left the hat with Holmes for examination and took the goose back to his wife to cook.

An extraordinary discovery
The reader soon learns the victim was a man named Henry Baker. On examining the hat, Holmes establishes that Baker is a middle-aged man with gray hair, which he anoints with lime cream and has recently had cut. More surprisingly, he deduces that Baker is intellectual, was once well off but has fallen on hard times (probably due to drinking), and is physically unfit, and that his

Jewel theft

Although jewel theft makes a compelling story, a glance through the Old Bailey's court records around the period when "The Adventure of the Blue Carbuncle" was written shows only a smattering of such cases. Most crimes were small-scale domestic burglaries, and there is certainly no prize approaching the value of the countess's famous carbuncle.

In the world of fiction, however, Conan Doyle's own brother-in-law was about to

create one of the greatest jewel thieves of all time. In 1898, E. W. Hornung, who was married to Conan Doyle's sister Connie, wrote the first of 27 stories dealing with the exploits of A. J. Raffles, the gentleman thief. Much as Holmes's work is chronicled by Watson, Raffles' adventures are recorded by his erstwhile companion Bunny Manders. The first volume of these tales, *The Amateur Cracksman*, was published in 1899 with a dedication to his brother-in-law that read "To A.C.D. This Form of Flattery."

home does not have gas lighting. Holmes's keen deductions are only slightly compromised in that he makes use of the now-debunked science of phrenology (see p.188), when he points out the size of the hat, saying "a man with so large a brain must have something in it."

Suddenly Peterson bursts into the room and announces excitedly that while preparing the goose for roasting, his wife found a large blue gem in its crop. Holmes at once recognizes the stone as the famous blue carbuncle, recently stolen from the Countess of Morcar at the Hotel Cosmopolitan. A suspect named John Horner, a plumber, is already in custody, but Holmes's interest is piqued, and when the hat's rather down-at-heel owner, Henry Baker, shows up, he unwittingly provides the detective with his first lead. Clearly ignorant of the goose's contents, Baker informs Holmes he bought the bird at a "goose club" set up by the landlord of the Alpha pub, near the British Museum.

Conan Doyle's footsteps

Holmes and Watson take a stroll through the "doctors' quarter" of Wimpole Street and Harley Street, bound for the Alpha pub, following a route that was once Conan Doyle's own daily commute. For a

> Chance has put in our way a most singular and whimsical problem.
> **Sherlock Holmes**

In the 19th century, Covent Garden market, where the goose in this story was sold, bustled with buyers and sellers hawking fresh food.

few months in 1891, shortly before writing this story, Conan Doyle lived just behind the British Museum and practiced medicine as an eye doctor in a clinic on Upper Wimpole Street. He rented a consulting room and a share of a waiting room, but patients were so scarce that, in his own words, "they were both waiting rooms." He soon abandoned medicine to focus on his burgeoning career as a writer.

Holmes the trickster

As well as good old-fashioned legwork, Holmes employs a fair bit of psychological manipulation in his pursuit of the jewel thief. On meeting the poultry butcher who first sold the goose to the pub, he capitalizes on the man's evident weakness for gambling to wheedle information out of him. Later, he utilizes carefully stage-managed shock tactics to prove one man's innocence and another's guilt.

At the story's denouement, the head attendant at the Hotel Cosmopolitan, James Ryder, is revealed to have himself stolen the gemstone with the help of Catherine Cusack, the Countess's lady-in-waiting. He then framed Horner, whom he knew to have a

criminal record. An inexperienced opportunist, Ryder took the gem to a criminal acquaintance who would sell it on his behalf. Fearful he would be stopped by the police, Ryder attempted to conceal the carbuncle by feeding it to a goose that his sister had promised him for Christmas, but somehow he ended up choosing the wrong bird from her flock. Meanwhile, the gem made its way via Covent Garden's poultry market, the Bloomsbury pub, and an unfortunate street altercation in Tottenham Court Road, safely into Holmes's hands.

The spirit of Christmas

"The Adventure of the Blue Carbuncle" is a sort of Sherlock Holmes Christmas special, with a heart-warming Dickensian dash of redemption. It is suffused with light, comedic moments, and Holmes gets so carried away with what he terms "the season of forgiveness" that he ends up letting the distraught and remorseful culprit go free. ∎

VIOLENCE DOES, IN TRUTH, RECOIL UPON THE VIOLENT

THE ADVENTURE OF THE SPECKLED BAND (1892)

IN CONTEXT

TYPE
Short story

FIRST PUBLICATION
UK: February 1892

COLLECTION
***The Adventures of Sherlock Holmes*, 1892**

CHARACTERS
Dr. Grimesby Roylott
Widowed former medical doctor, now living on his family estate in Surrey.

Helen Stoner Roylott's stepdaughter, who lives with him in Surrey.

Julia Stoner Helen's late twin sister, who died mysteriously two years before.

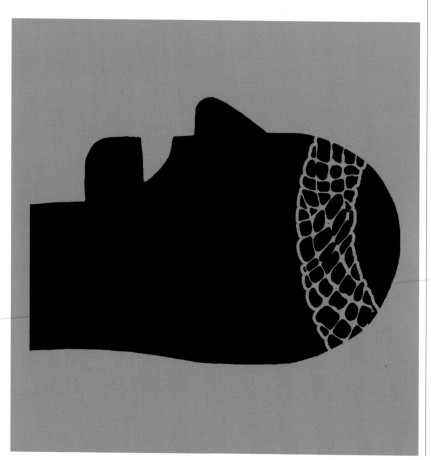

At the opening of this story, Watson clearly sets out to whet the reader's appetite for what is to follow: "I cannot recall any [case] which presented more singular features than that which was associated with the well-known Surrey family of the Roylotts of Stoke Moran." The time now has come, he says, to reveal a long-held secret, given that the embargo on revealing the truth has been lifted by the "untimely death of a lady." This is a classic literary device that draws in the reader and gives a sense of immediacy to a story set in the past. Although the lady he speaks of is not named in his introduction, it becomes apparent that she must

trouble one day when, in a fit of rage, he beat his butler to death. After serving a long prison sentence, he met and married a young widow, Mrs. Stoner—the mother of Helen and her twin sister Julia—and brought the family back to London, where he planned to set up a new medical practice. Soon after their return, Mrs. Stoner was killed in a railroad accident, leaving a considerable sum of money in her will. This was to remain in Roylott's hands until such time as Helen and Julia were married, after which each would be able to claim an annual income from their mother's estate.

Giving up the idea of living in London, Roylott used the money to relocate his family to his ancestral home in Surrey. At this time, Helen says, Roylott underwent a "terrible change." He became increasingly eccentric and reclusive, emerging only sporadically to wander off with the gypsies he allowed to camp on his land. He got into fights with several local men and became the »

be Helen Stoner, Holmes's client in the story, who has recently died from natural causes, some years after Holmes saved her life.

A cry for help
Early one morning in April 1883, a woman of about 30 years of age arrives at 221B Baker Street in a highly agitated state. It is so early, in fact, that Watson is still in bed. When Holmes quickly wakes him, he throws on his clothes and goes into the sitting room to see the lady, who is veiled and dressed in black.

Picking up on her anxiety, Holmes immediately helps her to relax, urging her to sit closer to the fire and ordering her a hot drink. Demonstrating his powers of deduction in order to reassure her, he says he knows that she got a dog-cart to the station and caught the early train to London simply from the pattern of mud spatters on the left arm of her jacket and the ticket in her hand. This is just what the frightened woman needs. "I have heard, Mr. Holmes, that you

can see deeply into the manifold wickedness of the human heart," she says. "You may advise me how to walk amid the dangers which encompass me." Confident that she has at last found someone who will take her fears seriously and be able to help her, she tells Holmes and Watson her chilling story.

Roylott of Stoke Moran
The woman's name is Helen Stoner, and she lives with her stepfather, Dr. Grimesby Roylott, who is the last living member of one of the oldest families in England. The Roylotts once enjoyed great wealth, but in recent centuries a succession of spendthrift heirs frittered this family fortune away, and by the time Grimesby came to inherit, all that remained was an old house with a big mortgage at Stoke Moran in Surrey. Roylott earned a degree in medicine and then emigrated to India, where he set up a successful practice. But while his finances improved, his "violence of temper approaching mania" got him into

He refused to associate himself with any investigation which did not tend towards the unusual, and even the fantastic.
Dr. Watson

LES ROMANS DE LA JEUNESSE
2.50 — 2.50

CONAN DOYLE
LA BANDE MOUCHETÉE
DESSINS DE MARTIN

BOIVIN & Cie, 5, RUE PALATINE, PARIS, 6e

Sherlock Holmes has long enjoyed international success, as this French book jacket (*c.* 1920) shows; today, the stories have been translated into more than 100 languages, including Braille.

"terror of the village," and also developed a passion for exotic animals. Helen explains that a baboon and a cheetah are still roaming loose in the grounds. She describes both pets as "Indian" (but as baboons live only in Africa and Arabia, this must surely be an error by Conan Doyle). Helen's dark description of Roylott clearly positions him as the story's villain.

Strange last words

Helen's story then shifts to focus on an intriguing puzzle, one which Holmes—and the reader—must unravel before Helen falls victim to Roylott. This puzzle element is crucial to the success of the Holmes stories, as it is in much of the best detective fiction. Here it centers on the sudden, unexplained death of Helen's sister, Julia, two years previously—just two weeks before her wedding. On a wild, windy night, Helen was awoken by her sister's scream: she rushed to Julia's bedroom, which was located between her room and that of her stepfather, where she found Julia convulsing in agony. She managed to shriek a few words—"Oh, my God! Helen! It was the band! The speckled band!"—before falling unconscious and dying.

The inquiry showed that Julia's door had been bolted shut from the inside (the girls always locked their doors before going to bed, as they were afraid of the cheetah and the baboon), the windows were barred, and there was no indication of how an intruder could have entered or left the room. Julia's body was left unmarked and there was no sign that she had been poisoned. She had been clutching a previously lit match and a box of matches when she died, so had clearly had some light and would therefore have been able to see something in the room. The only other clues were the odd sounds Helen had heard just before she found her sister: a low whistle and a metallic clanging. Apparently Julia too had been wakened by the same noises, always around 3am, during the nights leading up to her death, and she had also mentioned being troubled by the smell of cigar smoke coming from Roylott's room. These clues, though, made little sense. Helen believes her sister had died of fright, and wonders whether "the speckled band" she spoke of could be a reference to the "band" of gypsies camping outside, who wore spotted handkerchiefs on their heads. By now, the reader's mind is racing, trying to interpret all this carefully released data.

Helen says that two years have passed since her sister's death, and she herself is about to get married. But one night ago, she experienced a terrifying echo of the past. Roylott had asked her to sleep in Julia's old room while repairs were carried out on a wall in her quarters. Helen did as he asked, but in the early hours she had heard an eerily familiar sound: a low, clear whistle. She was so frightened, she stayed awake all night, and in the morning came straight to Holmes.

As Helen concludes her story, Holmes observes bruises on her wrist and realizes Roylott has been abusing her. He is now certain of

Dr. Grimesby Roylott

Dr. Roylott is one of the most colorful of all Holmes's villains, a huge and brutish man who keeps wild animals as pets and terrorizes all who cross his path. At the time, it was commonly believed that criminals were born, not made, and that they possessed certain physical characteristics that marked them apart—a theory called "anthropological criminology" (see pp.310–15), and Conan Doyle certainly gives Roylott a striking physiognomy: "A large face, seared with a thousand wrinkles, burned yellow with the sun, and marked with every evil passion" and "his deep-set, bile-shot eyes, and his high, thin, fleshless nose, gave him somewhat the resemblance to a fierce old bird of prey." He also has an explosive temper, which Helen believes has "been intensified by his long residence in the tropics," but when he unleashes this on Holmes, the detective uses humor to deflect it and refuses to be intimidated.

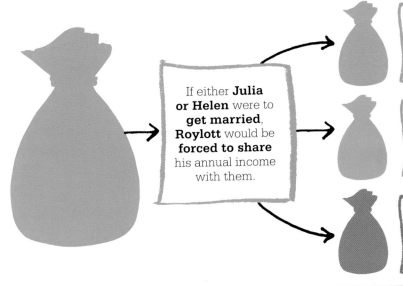

Roylott has total control of the family income from his wife's will, which enables him to give his stepdaughters enough money to live on, while retaining the vast majority for himself. He is desperate to prevent the girls from marrying, since they would gain the right to their own incomes.

If either **Julia or Helen** were to **get married**, **Roylott** would be **forced to share** his annual income with them.

Roylott's £750-a-year income splits by a third upon each marriage.

Julia's £250 claim reduces Roylott's share to £500.

Helen's claim of another £250 takes Roylott's share to £250.

the urgent need to protect Helen, and says he will visit Stoke Moran that afternoon, while Roylott is out. As Helen heads for home, Holmes is already forming various theories.

A logical process

At the time that Conan Doyle was writing "The Adventure of the Speckled Band," an American philosopher, Charles Sanders Peirce (1839–1914), was developing a new theory of logic that chimed perfectly with Holmes's way of working, although it was not widely known at that time. Previously, there had been just two recognized methods of reasoning: "deduction," in which the outcome is a logical, inevitable consequence, and "induction," in which there is good reason to expect a particular outcome but it is not certain. In his new theory, Peirce suggested there was a third type of reasoning, one which Holmes himself often uses: "abductive" reasoning. Abduction involves developing a theory based on all the available facts (see p.307). For example, if, following the sound of a gunshot, a body was found lying in a

pool of blood, it could be "abduced" that the dead person had been shot. Abduction provides an initial theory which must then be tested.

Holmes is convinced that Roylott is implicated in Julia's death, since the potential loss of income from his late wife's legacy, should his stepdaughters marry, gives him a strong motive. He speculates that Roylott may have asked a gypsy to get into Julia's room and kill her, and that the man must have made his escape through the window, making the metal bars on the shutters clang. However, Holmes knows he must also test this in situ.

At that very moment, Dr. Roylott, who has followed his stepdaughter, bursts ferociously into 221B. He warns Holmes not to interfere in his affairs and, to underline his point, grabs a poker and bends it into a curve as he leaves. Holmes laughs it off and calmly wrenches the poker straight again—an indication of his physical strength.

Holmes and Watson then ready themselves to investigate. As is so often the case, Holmes's use of understatement and wry humor

entertain the reader: "I should be very much obliged if you would slip a revolver into your pocket," he says to Watson. "Eley's No. 2 is an excellent argument with gentlemen who can twist steel pokers into knots. That and a tooth-brush are, I think, all that we need."

A locked-room mystery

At the house, Holmes inspects the room in which Julia died and Helen now sleeps. He immediately sees a flaw in his theory that the killer escaped through the window: »

Fancy his having the insolence to confound me with the official detective force!
Sherlock Holmes

there is simply no way that anyone could have entered or exited this room. The story now turns into a classic "locked-room" mystery—this is a major device in detective fiction in which a crime, usually murder, has been committed in a room from which there seems to be no possible way that the criminal could have gotten in or out. An early locked-room mystery appeared in Edgar Allan Poe's "The Murders

It is a wicked world, and when a clever man turns his brains to crime it is the worst of all.
Sherlock Holmes

in the Rue Morgue," in which a woman and her daughter are found murdered inside a room that is locked from the inside. In that case, the killer turns out to be an ape; Conan Doyle's inclusion of a pet baboon in "The Speckled Band" may be a tribute to Poe's story. Along with the cheetah and the gypsies, however, it is also a red herring.

A trail of clues

Conan Doyle now provides several key clues that will help the reader formulate theories about Julia's death. As he examines her room, Holmes spots two unusual items that Helen says were installed shortly before her sister's death: a small ventilator that opens into Roylott's room, rather than outside the house, and a fake bell-pull next to the bed that is attached to a hook above the ventilator. Later, Holmes tells Watson that he also saw that the bed was bolted into place, so it could not be moved from its position beneath the rope and

Sherlock Holmes, played here by Jeremy Brett in the 1984 television episode of "The Speckled Band," spots several clues inside Roylott's bedroom, including a saucer of milk, and then realizes his diabolical plan.

the ventilator; he also claims he knew there would be a ventilator between Roylott and Julia's rooms: how else would she have been able to smell his cigar smoke? When Holmes moves on to Roylott's room, he finds four further clues—an iron safe, a saucer of milk, a wooden chair, and a strangely looped "dog-whip." Holmes now has his theory, and perhaps the reader does too, but still, it must be tested.

Holmes decides that he and Watson must spend the night in the room in which Julia was killed. He explains his plan to Helen: when her stepfather gets home, she is to feign a headache and remain in her room. Once Roylott is in bed for the night, she is to send a signal via a lamp to Holmes and Watson—who will be watching from the window of a nearby hotel—and then sneak into her former bedroom.

As planned, just after 11pm, the duo enter Julia's old room. They extinguish the lamp, in case Roylott sees the light through the ventilator, and then wait in the dark. Watson's fears grow as the hours drag by, until at 3am they see a light glimmering through the ventilator, followed by a hissing sound, "like that of a small jet of steam escaping continually from a kettle." Holmes strikes a match and lashes furiously at the bell-pull with his cane as, ominously, Watson hears a low, clear whistle.

Killed by his own weapon

Moments later, a terrible cry of pain and fear comes from the next room. Warily, they enter and find Roylott sprawled dead in a chair with a "speckled band" wrapped around his head. The band begins to move: it is a snake, and from the pattern on its back Holmes can see it is a venomous "Indian swamp adder." He grabs the dog-whip and uses it to deftly capture the creature and return it to Roylott's safe. All that remains now is for Holmes to reveal how he solved the strange puzzle.

Homes explains how, when Julia became engaged, Roylott knew his income would diminish greatly, and so he hatched an ingenious plan to kill her, using one of his exotic pets as a weapon. For a succession of nights he stood on the chair in his room and carefully lifted a specially trained snake into the ventilator shaft, from where it would slither into the girl's room, and then climb down the dummy bell-pull and onto her bed. Before the light of dawn, he would whistle for the snake to return for its saucer of milk, and then the reptile would be stowed away once more in the safe— which closed with a metallic clang.

It took several attempts before the snake finally bit Julia, but when it did, the venom affected her so rapidly that she could identify it only as a "speckled band" before she died. Helen would have met the same dreadful fate if Holmes and Watson had not taken her place in the room. As the snake entered through the ventilator, Holmes drove it back with his cane, inciting it to attack the waiting Roylott. At the end of the story, Holmes admits that he is partly responsible for Roylott's death, but says he feels no guilt.

> I had never seen my friend's face so grim or his brow so dark as it was when we turned from the scene.
> **Dr. Watson**

Pick of the crop

During a visit to South Africa in 1900, Conan Doyle was asked by a journalist if he could name his favorite Holmes story. "Perhaps the one about the serpent", he replied. It is easy to see why he chose "The Adventure of the Speckled Band": it contains all the classic ingredients of a great detective story—a dastardly villain, a seemingly inexplicable death in a locked room, a young lady in great distress, moments of real danger, an injection of exotic and foreign "otherness," and some inspired and brilliant sleuthing. ∎

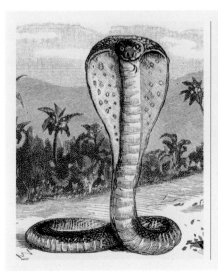

Roylott's snake

There has been much speculation about the species of the snake in this story. Holmes identifies it as a swamp adder—"the deadliest snake in India"—but this name is one of Conan Doyle's inventions. Some commentators have decided it must be an Indian cobra (*Naja naja*, pictured) since this matches the description of a reptile with a "diamond-shaped head and puffed neck." The Indian cobra's poison is suitably fast-acting, too: it blocks the transmission of nerve signals at the synapses (gaps between nerve endings) and can cause paralysis and heart failure, often within an hour but sometimes in just 15 minutes (although, inconsistently, Roylott himself dies within just a few seconds). It is the species most commonly used by India's snake charmers, too, and during the Hindu festival of Nag Panchami (in which devotees worship live cobras) snakes are fed milk, which may be where Roylott got the idea to reward his snake. However, since snakes are not mammals, they cannot digest milk and it is harmful to them.

EACH NEW DISCOVERY FURNISHES A STEP WHICH LEADS ON TO THE COMPLETE TRUTH

THE ADVENTURE OF THE ENGINEER'S THUMB (1892)

IN CONTEXT

TYPE
Short story

FIRST PUBLICATION
UK: March 1892

COLLECTION
***The Adventures of
Sherlock Holmes*, 1892**

CHARACTERS
Victor Hatherley
Young hydraulic engineer.

Colonel Lysander Stark
Middle-aged German man
who hires Victor Hatherley.

Elise Young German woman
who helps Hatherley to escape.

Mr. Ferguson
Stark's "manager."

As the reader is informed by Dr. Watson early on in "The Adventure of the Engineer's Thumb," this case is one of only two that he has brought to Sherlock Holmes's attention. Another unusual, although by no means unique, feature is the fact that the criminals manage to evade capture. In a few other cases, the perpetrators initially escape from Holmes, but then fate steps in to mete out justice. In this story, however, there appears to be no retribution for the crime.

An early-morning visitor

So many of Holmes's cases begin with a knock on the door of the detective's 221B Baker Street rooms, but here the victim arrives at Watson's home. As the doctor stresses, the events occur during a quiet, comfortable time in his life: following his recent marriage, he has established a medical practice close to Paddington Station and now only occasionally visits Holmes, for social reasons.

Watson has a useful ally at the nearby station—a train conductor, who directs a steady stream of patients toward his consulting rooms. Early one morning, the conductor arrives with a young man who has alighted from the morning train and asked to see a doctor.

The severed digit

Watson learns the patient is a hydraulic engineer by the name of Victor Hatherley. He is pale and agitated, and when the doctor suggests that his train journey might have been monotonous, Hatherley breaks into wild laughter that borders on mild hysteria. He soon reveals to Watson the reason for his distress: he has suffered a terrible injury—the loss of his thumb.

Holmes sat in his big armchair with the weary, heavy-lidded expression which veiled his keen and eager nature.
Dr. Watson

Some critics have suggested that this loss of a thumb could be seen as akin to a symbolic castration, and that Conan Doyle was using it to issue a warning. In the 1890s, many people worried that young British men were becoming rather decadent and effete. So here this "castration" may be a reminder of the need to maintain good moral fiber and resilience in a world that challenged Britain's dominance.

Many Holmes stories feature ruthless villains and gruesome crimes, some of which contain graphic descriptions of physical injury; yet, Watson's recollection of Hatherley's injury is shocking in its vividness: "There were four protruding fingers and a horrid red, spongy surface where the thumb should have been. It had been hacked or torn right out from the roots." Conan Doyle does not usually resort to such sensational detail to grab attention, but here it works. Like Watson, the reader is roused from the preceding, rather sleepy, narrative, and the tale suddenly gains momentum. In its way, this injury is as horrifying as a murder and, like the doctor, the reader is anxious for Holmes to step in as soon as possible.

An analytical mind
When Watson and Hatherley arrive at 221B, Holmes immediately instills calm. After producing some bacon and eggs, he listens with close attention to Hatherley's story. Holmes invites the young man to lie down on his couch while recalling the events: an approach that is strikingly reminiscent of a key technique that the esteemed psychoanalyst Sigmund Freud was using with his patients at the time Conan Doyle was writing this story. Of course, the author could not have known about Freud's

ideas, which were not revealed until 1895 with the publication of *Studies on Hysteria*, his groundbreaking book written with Joseph Breuer. Yet there is an uncanny similarity in the way that both Freud and Holmes listen to a narrative before working toward their conclusions through a steady process of logical deduction.

A tempting offer
Hatherley explains that he is alone in the world—both an orphan and a bachelor. He has been making little headway in his small business, so when a middle-aged German man, who introduced himself as Colonel

Victor Hatherley, illustrated here by Sidney Paget in *The Strand Magazine*, finds himself trapped inside the large hydraulic press that he was hired to repair.

Lysander Stark, visited him earlier that week and offered him a hefty fee—10 times his usual rate—to repair a hydraulic press, he was eager to agree. Hatherley admits to having had some misgivings about the new client's manner and his insistence that the work should be carried out in complete secrecy, saying he evoked "a feeling of repulsion" and "something akin to fear." However, he overlooked his »

When Hatherley is taken from the station to the house where the press is located, the journey takes an hour, so the police estimate it was a distance of about 12 miles. Holmes believes that because the horse was "fresh and glossy" the house is in fact located very close to the station— a belief that proves to be correct.

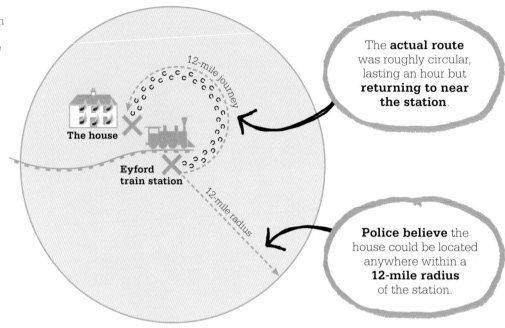

The **actual route** was roughly circular, lasting an hour but **returning to near the station**.

Police believe the house could be located anywhere within a **12-mile radius** of the station.

distrust and dislike because he so desperately wanted the work. Unsurprisingly, perhaps, given the warning signs, it is Stark who turns out to be the villain of the piece. Conan Doyle's choice of a German national for his evil-doer was probably no coincidence, since it may have been a reflection of the growing anti-German sentiment in Britain at the time. Germany was becoming increasingly militaristic under the ambitious and hostile rule of Kaiser Wilhelm, who was supporting the Boers in South Africa against the British during the Boer War (1899–1902).

A narrow escape
Hatherley explains to the group that Stark persuaded him to head out into the Berkshire countryside late that same evening, to examine and mend a hydraulic press being used to compact Fuller's earth— a clay used in the wool-making process. He was met by Stark at the isolated station and driven for

an hour through the darkness, in a horse-drawn carriage with frosted-glass windows, to the house where the press was located. At this point, Holmes interrupts to ask a seemingly trivial question about the carriage's horse—was it tired-looking or fresh? The response— "fresh and glossy"—gives the detective his first clue.

At the house, Stark briefly left Hatherley alone, at which point he was approached by a beautiful

In the silence I heard a sound which sent my heart into my mouth.
Victor Hatherley

young woman, later identified as Elise. In broken English, she repeatedly implored the young engineer to leave immediately. However, Hatherley was in desperate need of his fee, and determined to prove his toughness by seeing the job through, so he chose to ignore her warning.

Stark returned with his alleged manager, a Mr. Ferguson, and the pair took Hatherley to the press, located inside a small room. As they entered, the colonel explained that they were now standing inside the machine itself, and that it would be "a particularly unpleasant thing for us if anyone were to turn it on," since the ceiling would come down with crushing force to meet the floor. Hatherley examined the press, and after discovering a leak in the mechanism, he advised Stark on how to fix it. However, during his inspection it dawned on him that this device was not being used for crushing Fuller's earth; instead, it was being used to press metal. Upon hearing this, Holmes quickly realizes that it is a machine for making counterfeit coins.

Recognizing that Hatherley had seen through their ploy and afraid that he may have realized the true nature of their illegal work, Stark exited the room, locked the door, and turned on the press—intending to grind the engineer to a pulp. Hatherley screamed and begged to be let out, but his cries were ignored. The ceiling began its ominous descent and it was just a few feet away from Hatherley's body when the engineer suddenly spotted a concealed panel in the walls of the press. He threw himself through it, narrowly avoiding death.

Waiting on the other side was Elise, who led him to a second-story window and urged him to jump. As Hatherley clung to the windowsill by his hands, Stark arrived brandishing a cleaver and hacked off his thumb. The engineer fell into the garden below and then staggered into some rose bushes before passing out. He regained consciousness the next morning and, nursing his injury, made his way to the train station, which he was surprised to find close by.

> …every moment now is precious, so if you feel equal to it we shall go down to Scotland Yard.
> **Sherlock Holmes**

House on fire
After hearing the story, Holmes, Watson, and Hatherley set off by train for Eyford, with policemen in tow, to apprehend Stark. En route, they calculate the house's likely location, using Hatherley's estimate that it took an hour to get to the house, and therefore it was about 12 miles from the station. Yet Holmes insists the house is close to the station, surmising from Hatherley's assertion about the fresh state of the horse that the carriage had gone in a circle in order to confuse the engineer's sense of distance and direction.

Holmes's deduction is confirmed when, on arrival, they notice flames coming from a nearby house and, as they approach, Hatherley is sure it is the one he was taken to (the discovery by firemen of his severed thumb proves it). The oil lamp that Hatherley had used to inspect the press had started the blaze and it has destroyed all evidence of the counterfeiting gang's machine. The mysterious German, Elise, and Mr. Ferguson (who it turns out is really named Dr. Becher) have already fled, taking their hoard of counterfeit coins with them, and they are never apprehended.

A painful lesson
As they return to London, Holmes is remarkably sanguine about the case's outcome. When Hatherley complains that he has lost both his thumb and his fee, Holmes laughs and tells him to simply dine out on the experience. The story, it seems, is not meant to be one of the typical expositions of Holmes's brilliance, which is relatively modest here, but instead a salutary tale about how easy it is to get sucked into shady and dangerous dealings if one is tempted by easy cash. ∎

Coiners and smashers

Coins were counterfeited on a huge scale in Victorian London. It is thought that at the beginning of the 19th century there were nearly 50 mints churning out forged half-crowns and other coins, and that by 1850, more than one-fifth of all the trials held at London's Central Criminal Court (the Old Bailey) were for "coining" (counterfeiting coins). The guilty parties included both men and women.

The forgers who set up a press, like Colonel Lysander Stark and his accomplices, were known as "coiners" or "bit-fakers," while the low-life criminals who would subsequently pass the forgeries into circulation were called "smashers." The fake coins themselves were known as "snide," and the smasher's job was often referred to as "snide-pitching."

Counterfeiting was a labor-intensive and skillful business, since the forgers had to get hold of a press and all the metal they needed to make the coins, and then correctly set up the machine to churn them out. Yet it proved to be a profitable (if disreputable) business for many.

I HAD FORMED MY CONCLUSIONS AS TO THE CASE BEFORE OUR CLIENT CAME INTO THE ROOM
THE ADVENTURE OF THE NOBLE BACHELOR (1892)

IN CONTEXT

TYPE
Short story

FIRST PUBLICATION
UK: April 1892

COLLECTION
***The Adventures of Sherlock Holmes*, 1892**

CHARACTERS
Lord Robert St. Simon
Middle-aged second son of the Duke of Balmoral.

Hatty Doran Young American woman, recently married to St. Simon.

Flora Millar Former music-hall dancer and an intimate of St. Simon.

Francis ("Frank") Hay Moulton Wealthy American gentleman, formerly a mining prospector.

Inspector Lestrade Scotland Yard detective.

As the story opens, Watson is confined indoors by the seasonal ache of his war wound. His day is brightened by the arrival of an eminent new client: Lord Robert St. Simon, one of the highest aristocrats in the land.

The nobleman has recently married Hatty Doran, a free-spirited American heiress. However, during their wedding reception, the bride excused herself and fled, and has not been seen since. Flora Millar, a jealous chorus girl with whom St. Simon had once been intimate, tried to storm into the reception and was subsequently seen talking to Hatty in Hyde Park. Flora has been arrested but St. Simon does not believe she has done Hatty any harm, but he is anxious to find his wife, and so he engages the services of Holmes and Lestrade.

In the 1800s, high-society weddings, like St. Simon's, were lavish affairs, with brides wearing white—a new fashion made popular by Queen Victoria.

> My whole examination served to turn my conjecture into a certainty.
> **Sherlock Holmes**

An awkward situation

As usual, Lestrade is fixated on the first solution that presents itself: he thinks Flora lured Hatty away from her guests and then ambushed her. The discovery of a sodden wedding dress in Hyde Park's lake, with a note written by someone with the initials F. H. M. in its pocket, seems to prove his theory. Holmes is more interested in the fact that it was scribbled on an expensive hotel bill.

As Lestrade becomes ever more confused, Holmes announces that he has already solved the case. To him, two things are obvious: Hatty had been content to go through with the wedding but something had occurred immediately afterwards that made her regret it. She must have seen someone—given her origins, this was probably an American—and whoever it was must have been important to her, most likely a man. These clues enable Holmes to orchestrate a resolution to a story that began years earlier, in the gold fields of California.

Hatty Doran is, in fact, already married—to an American gold miner named Francis ("Frank") Hay Moulton. She thought he had been killed during an Apache Indian attack, but he escaped and has since made his fortune. Tracking her down on the morning of her second

wedding, Frank sneaked into the service and passed Hatty a note, signed with his initials. Shocked and confused to see her first husband alive, Hatty ran to him; Flora accosted her en route, but she ignored her. And, in an attempt to conceal Hatty's tracks, Frank tossed her wedding outfit in the lake.

Holmes locates the hotel that Frank had just left, and obtains his new address. There he finds the couple and, after hearing their story, encourages them to make peace with St. Simon. Faced with Hatty's request for forgiveness, the nobleman agrees to shake hands, albeit peevishly.

Holmes as mouthpiece

Among Holmes's socially diverse clientele, the upper classes do not always emerge particularly well. Lord St. Simon is fussy to the point of "foppishness" about his looks, and he is self-important and not very bright. Holmes takes evident enjoyment in gently mocking his intellect and exposing his various upper-class hypocrisies. However, the duke's son has escaped lightly compared to Flora. Holmes's worst characteristic in this story is arguably his careless snobbery in casting off the dancer so unfeelingly.

The story is also an opportunity for Conan Doyle to express his feelings about America. Although it is not always evident from his American villains, he was a great admirer of the US and toured there several times. In 1896, he penned a letter to *The Times* advocating closer ties with the country. In this story, Holmes gives a voice to his creator's vision of a future in which Britons and Americans are "citizens of the same world-wide country under a flag which shall be a quartering of the Union Jack with the Stars and Stripes." ∎

American heiresses

Britain's historic country estates were ruinously costly to run, and in the late 1800s the nobility were increasingly trading their titles for money from across the Atlantic. Just as television's fictional Earl of Grantham saved Downton Abbey through his wealthy American bride, so the real-life Duke of Marlborough secured Blenheim Palace's future by marrying Consuelo Vanderbilt (pictured) from New York. There was even a quarterly periodical called *Titled Americans*, listing all the ladies of America who had married old-world aristocrats, along with notable bachelors still on the market.

The American society ladies made their mark in political matters, too. Mary Leiter from Chicago became Vicereine of India and an early conservationist; Nancy Witcher Langhorne from Virginia (whose husband was US-born but ended up a hereditary peer) was later Viscountess Astor, the first woman to sit as an MP; and Jennie Jerome from Brooklyn became Lady Randolph Churchill and Winston Churchill's mother.

THERE ARE WOMEN IN WHOM THE LOVE OF A LOVER EXTINGUISHES ALL OTHER LOVES
THE ADVENTURE OF THE BERYL CORONET (1892)

IN CONTEXT

TYPE
Short story

FIRST PUBLICATION
UK: May 1892

COLLECTION
***The Adventures of Sherlock Holmes,* 1892**

CHARACTERS
Alexander Holder Prominent banker, who lives with his son and niece in Streatham.

Arthur Holder Son of Alexander, and a gambler in serious debt.

Mary Holder Niece and adopted daughter of Alexander.

Sir George Burnwell Disreputable friend of Arthur and lover of Mary.

This story is an excellent exemplar of Holmes and his methodology: logical but instinctive, methodical yet fearless. While those directly embroiled in the case find themselves blinded by suspicion and mistrust, Holmes is able to swiftly apply his ingenious logic and identify the true criminals in a masterful show of deductive superiority. And yet, while the crime is successfully solved, this is one of the few Holmes cases in which the perpetrators escape before they are brought to justice.

The client in question is an eminent banker, Alexander Holder, who has been entrusted with a precious beryl coronet to act as

It appeared to you to be a simple case; to me it seems exceedingly complex.
Sherlock Holmes

a guarantee against a substantial loan that is required by one of the "most exalted names in England"— Burdened by the responsibility, Holder takes the coronet back to his house in Streatham. That night, he is disturbed by a noise and wakes to see his son Arthur standing in his dressing room, holding the slightly mangled coronet. Crucially, three of its beryls are missing.

The Holder household
Holder is demented with anxiety and can only conclude that Arthur, an irresponsible gambler, is guilty. Holder is a widower who has overindulged his only child and now has little love for him. Holder reserves his affection for his adopted niece, Mary, an orphan with a loving, discreet, and loyal nature. Arthur is also devoted to Mary, and it is Holder's dearest wish that son and niece should marry, but Mary has twice refused Arthur's hand. It also transpires that a handsome and charismatic friend of Arthur's, Sir George Burnwell, is a frequent visitor to the Holder home.

Holmes is immediately skeptical about Arthur's guilt; why would he refuse to exonerate himself or give

The Beryl Coronet was one of the 47 silent films (45 shorts and two features) of the Holmes stories made by Stoll Pictures between 1921–23; all starred Eille Norwood as Holmes.

Adventures of
SHERLOCK HOLMES
"THE BERYL CORONET"

any explanation for the events of the night? How did he break the coronet without any audible noise? And where are the three beryls concealed?

A classic Holmes investigation ensues—various false clues are presented to him, but Holmes refuses to be thrown off the scent. He scrutinizes a windowsill with his magnifying glass, questions Mary, and observes a set of tracks in the snow that tell a complex tale.

Culprit revealed

Matters grow more complicated when Holder discovers a note from Mary telling him that she is leaving. Holmes soon reveals the truth behind her decision—and the crime. The true culprit is Sir George, "one of the most dangerous men in England—a ruined gambler, an absolutely desperate villain, a man without heart or conscience." The scoundrel has inveigled himself into the household and

become Mary's lover. He persuaded her to steal the coronet and pass it to him through a window. Arthur had witnessed the theft, pursued Sir George and grappled him for the coronet, leaving evidence of their struggle in the snow. The coronet had been damaged in the skirmish, and Arthur was trying to straighten it before returning it to his father's

bureau when he was caught. Out of love and loyalty for Mary, he refused to reveal the truth and her role in it.

During this fast-paced case, Holmes plays the part of a true action hero, disguising himself to glean information, accosting Sir George over the theft, threatening him with a gun, and buying the missing beryls back from a third party (to whom Sir George had already sold them) for £3,000.

Holder had let his love for Mary cloud his judgment, and decided wrongly that his son's lifestyle was a sign of his guilt. In fact, Arthur is unfailingly loyal to both his cousin, Mary, and his father. Mary, for her part, has foolishly abandoned the protection of her devoted stepfather and cousin for that of her dubious lover, and is likely to receive her retribution at Sir George's own cruel hand. "Whatever her sins are, they will soon receive a more than sufficient punishment," are Holmes's final, ominous words on the case. ■

The coronet

Coronets are simple crowns worn by the various ranks of the British peerage as well as minor royalty, each rank distinguished by a different configuration of strawberry leaves and silver balls. Beryl is a colorless gemstone that is often tinted by impurities to appear yellow (known as heliodor), green (emerald), red (scarlet emerald), or blue (aquamarine).

The gold coronet that features in this story, adorned with 39 "enormous" beryls, is

unusually elaborate. The man who entrusts Holder with the coronet estimates that it is worth around £100,000 ($12 million today), at least twice the value of the loan drawn on it. The reader does not learn the identity of the coronet's owner, only that "his name… is a household word all over the earth," which has led many to speculate that he is a member of the British royal family, probably the Prince of Wales (later Edward VII).

CRIME IS COMMON. LOGIC IS RARE

THE ADVENTURE OF THE COPPER BEECHES (1892)

IN CONTEXT

TYPE
Short story

FIRST PUBLICATION
UK: June 1892

COLLECTION
***The Adventures of Sherlock Holmes*, 1892**

CHARACTERS
Violet Hunter
Young governess.

Jephro Rucastle
Middle-aged landowner.

Mrs. Rucastle
Jephro's second wife.

Alice Rucastle
Jephro's daughter
by his first wife.

Toller and Mrs. Toller
The Rucastles' servants.

Mr. Fowler
Alice's fiancé.

A long and unusually revealing scene about Holmes's and Watson's relationship opens "The Adventure of the Copper Beeches." Holmes takes Watson to task about the way he writes about him in his memoirs, accusing the doctor of embellishing his reports with literary flourishes rather than simply detailing the detective's skill, and turning "a course of lectures into a series of tales." Indeed, it seems that the legendarily inscrutable Holmes is in a bad mood—and the famously placid Watson is quite offended and "repelled by the egotism" of his friend.

In a playful, self-referential manner, Conan Doyle has fun with the reader, and even has Holmes criticize the quality of the writing. It is so adroitly done that the reader almost forgets that Watson and Holmes are fictional characters, and Watson is not a real person writing about a real detective.

Holmes in a bad mood

Conan Doyle is clearly setting up the idea that something is preying on Holmes's mind. After the spat with Watson, Holmes rues the decline in the quality of the criminal mind, complaining sardonically, "As to my own little practice, it seems to be degenerating into an agency for recovering lead pencils and giving advice to young ladies from boarding-schools."

For the coolly logical Holmes, this seems strangely like an emotional outburst. It has all been triggered, it transpires, by a letter from a young woman named Violet Hunter, asking for advice on whether to take up a post as a governess, which he tosses to Watson to read. But is Holmes actually rather intrigued by this

The days of the great cases are past. Man, or at least criminal man, has lost all enterprise and originality.
Sherlock Holmes

THE ADVENTURE OF THE COPPER BEECHES

Violet Hunter, played by Natasha Richardson in the 1985 ITV adaptation, reads Holmes (Jeremy Brett) and Watson (David Burke) the letter from Mr. Rucastle imploring her to accept his job offer.

letter, instead of outraged? He has crumpled up the letter, but it is still in his hand to give to Watson. Does he suspect, as Watson reminds him of "The Adventure of the Blue Carbuncle" (pp.82–3), that what may appear at first to be "a mere whim" may turn out to be about something much more interesting?

A peculiar request

Just as Holmes has concluded his rant about the triviality of Miss Hunter's letter, Violet herself arrives at 221B Baker Street. Watson observes that his friend is immediately attentive and that he is "favourably impressed by the manner and speech of his new client." This observation may be intended to tantalize the reader into believing that Holmes might become romantically involved with the young woman. Violet confirms that she wants his advice on whether to take up a post as governess for a man named Jephro Rucastle at a house near Winchester called Copper Beeches. But, as Holmes sees at once, there is something more to this case than mere employment advice.

The pay is very good, but Mr. Rucastle has made some strange requests, including that she should cut off her long hair and wear any dress that he or his wife might ask her to put on. She initially rejects the offer, but needs the money and is curious about the situation, so she decides to accept it after all. Although Violet's mind is made up, she wants Holmes's opinion on the matter, and is checking whether she can contact him later should

anything untoward take place once she starts her new job. Fascinated by this enigmatic scenario, Holmes agrees to her request.

Two weeks after Violet has taken up the position, she telegraphs Holmes, imploring him to meet her in Winchester. The next morning, Holmes and Watson catch the train to see her, and she informs them of the strange progress of events.

Gothic setting

Copper Beeches, it seems, is a strange, rather eerie place. It is clearly Conan Doyle's intention to ramp up the atmosphere and sense of expectation by bringing all the familiar elements of the classic Gothic horror story into play—a remote location, a gloomy, decaying house, shadowy trees, a savage

dog, a morose housekeeper, and—most dramatic of all—a locked room containing a terrible secret.

The late Victorian era was a golden age for Gothic fiction and tales of the supernatural, with novels such as Bram Stoker's *Dracula* (1897) capturing the public imagination, and stories of encounters with ghosts and spirits receiving attention as never before. However, in stories such as "The Adventure of Wisteria Lodge" (pp.222–25) and "The Adventure of the Sussex Vampire" (pp.260–61), Conan Doyle takes the tropes of Gothic literature and allows Holmes to show that there is a perfectly rational explanation for each crime. That is why Holmes leads so neatly from the superstitions of the Victorian age to the rationality »

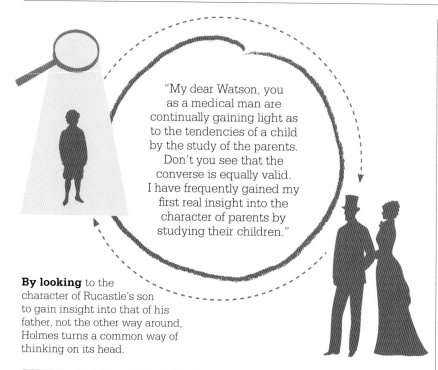

"My dear Watson, you as a medical man are continually gaining light as to the tendencies of a child by the study of the parents. Don't you see that the converse is equally valid. I have frequently gained my first real insight into the character of parents by studying their children."

By looking to the character of Rucastle's son to gain insight into that of his father, not the other way around, Holmes turns a common way of thinking on its head.

of the 20th century. Unlike many other fictional characters, he is not looking for evil spirits but for clues to real behavior.

The disturbed child

The emergence of psychology as a scientific discipline in the late Victorian era meant that many people were beginning to believe that to understand the present, you also had to understand the past. There was a shift toward a more scientific study of criminals, with new theories proposing that human behavior could be explained by inheritance and biology gaining wider currency.

So when Violet tells Holmes that the little boy in her charge is morose and cruel, and crushes cockroaches for fun, in a typical Gothic tale this might be a sign that the child is demonically possessed. But Holmes seeks a rational explanation. As he explains to Watson, in the bad behavior of the child he sees warning signs of the true nature of his father, Jephro Rucastle, and he is alerted to the peril Violet may be in.

The governess's story

Violet tells Holmes that she has learned that Rucastle also has a daughter, Alice, from his first marriage, who has gone away to Philadelphia. In her position as governess, Violet has been asked to wear a particularly striking electric-blue dress, and told to sit with her back to the window, either reading out loud or listening to Rucastle's stories while his wife sits in deadly silence. Sneaking a peek in a mirror one day, Violet glimpsed a mysterious young man watching her from the road.

She recounts other bizarre and unnerving matters—a huge mastiff, which is kept hungry, prowls the grounds at night; she finds a tress of hair very much like her own locked away in a drawer; and, strangest of all, there is a wing of the house kept locked and seemingly empty. Desperate to know what is going on, Violet sneaked into the locked wing and was terrified to see the shadow of someone moving in a barricaded room. Rucastle caught her and threatened to throw her to the dog if she did not curb her curiosity. Genuinely frightened by this, she had sent for Holmes.

The secret revealed

Holmes then surmises that Violet has been hired to impersonate Rucastle's daughter, Alice, who is not in Philadelphia at all but is instead imprisoned in the empty wing. He devises a plan to free Alice when the Rucastles are out that evening. Violet returns to the house, and, following the plan, lures the servant Mrs. Toller into the cellar and traps her there while Mr. Toller is drunk. Holmes and Watson arrive and break into the locked room, only to find it is empty.

Astonishingly, it seems that Alice has been taken out through the skylight. In one of his rare mistakes, Holmes believes that Rucastle has taken her away. At that moment, Rucastle surprises them in the locked wing and dashes

The lowest and vilest alleys in London do not present a more dreadful record of sin than does the smiling and beautiful countryside.
Sherlock Holmes

This illustration from *The Strand Magazine* depicts the moment Rucastle is savagely attacked by the huge mastiff.

out to set the mastiff on them, but the starving hound savages him instead. Watson manages to shoot the dog, but Rucastle is badly hurt.

As Watson tends to Rucastle's wounds, Mrs. Toller appears and reveals the truth. Alice was the sole beneficiary of her late mother's will, but she allowed her father to take care of the affairs. Upon meeting her fiancé Mr. Fowler, Rucastle tried to force Alice to sign the inheritance over to him before she married and he lost control of the finances. Distraught, she had an attack of "brain fever," suffering from the illness for six weeks. Alice recovered, but Rucastle locked her in the chamber. Violet was hired to act as Alice so that Fowler would believe she was well again, but no longer interested in him. Fowler was not put off, however, and it was he who rescued her.

Holmes the man

Although Holmes is attentive to Violet and seems to admire her, describing her as a "quite exceptional woman," to Watson's disappointment Holmes's brief interest in her is over as soon as the case is solved. Conan Doyle has teased the reader, momentarily hinting that emotion might lurk behind the detective's coolly mechanical facade.

The tale also reveals Holmes's somewhat bleak outlook on life. While traveling on the train to Winchester, Watson remarks on the beautiful countryside, dotted with charming farmhouses. Holmes admits that he can see only their desperate isolation in which unspeakable crimes may be concealed. Watson is appalled by his negativity, but the moment hints at the psychological complexity of Holmes that has enthralled readers for so long.

Interestingly, although Holmes says at the start of the story that Watson should tell tales that reveal his deductive powers, here they actually play very little part. Instead, the action is precipitated almost entirely by Violet, with Holmes taking a supporting role. ∎

Prisoners in the home

The immense control Victorian men had over their wives and daughters has been the stuff of Gothic horror stories ever since Charlotte Brontë wrote about mad Bertha Rochester being locked in the attic by her husband in *Jane Eyre* (1847). Legally, families were allowed to keep a family member confined if they were declared insane (to avoid a charge of false imprisonment)—but it was up to the family or a hired "doctor" to diagnose their insanity.

Brontë may have been inspired by a government report in 1844, which revealed shocking cases of the rural poor attempting to look after their unstable family members at home. The reason for the secrecy was partially the deep shame felt about mental illness; however, in some cases families were also trying to save their loved ones from the horrors of lunatic asylums. Nevertheless, many unfortunate people were locked away because of personal grievances or for financial gain. There were certainly many cases of unspeakable cruelty that never saw the light of day, and many others like Alice Rucastle whose terrible suffering remained hidden.

In 1879, the *British Medical Journal* observed that there was still "no law to prevent a Mr. Rochester from locking up his mad wife in the attic of a mansion, with a keeper." A rise in awareness followed, and 1890, the year in which "The Copper Beeches" is believed to be set, was the last year in which Rucastle could legally have gotten away with locking up his daughter.

THE GRE

DETECTI

AT
VE

The **"Great Hiatus"** continues; Holmes travels throughout **Asia and Europe** (see "The Empty House" pp.162–67).

The stories later collected in **The Memoirs of Sherlock Holmes** begin to appear in *The Strand Magazine*.

Conan Doyle publishes the **historical novel The Refugees** (p.344).

"The Final Problem" (pp.142–47) appears in *The Strand Magazine*. **Holmes's death** is met with a **stunned response**.

1892   **DEC 1892**   **MAY 1893**   **DEC 1893**

OCT 1892   **1893**   **OCT 1893**

Event in the lives of Holmes and Watson

Conan Doyle publishes **The Great Shadow**, a novel about the Napoleonic wars.

Conan Doyle's **first wife**, Louise, is diagnosed with **tuberculosis**.

Conan Doyle's **father**, Charles Altamont Doyle, **dies at age 61**.

IN THIS CHAPTER

COLLECTION
***The Memoirs of Sherlock Holmes**, 1894*
Silver Blaze
The Cardboard Box
The Yellow Face
The Stock-broker's Clerk
The *Gloria Scott*
The Musgrave Ritual
The Reigate Squire
The Crooked Man
The Resident Patient
The Greek Interpreter
The Naval Treaty
The Final Problem

Less than two months after *The Adventures of Sherlock Holmes* was published, *The Strand Magazine* began serializing the short stories of what would be that book's successor, *The Memoirs of Sherlock Holmes*. This collection would culminate in an event that horrified readers— Holmes's untimely death, in the thrilling "The Final Problem."

Faithfulness and fallibility
In both "The Yellow Face" and "The Cardboard Box," Holmes displays a new awareness to criminals' own sense of victimization. In fact, in this collection of stories, the detective seems more in tune with human psychology in general. One sequence in "The Naval Treaty," in which Holmes hints at his thoughts on religious faith, illuminates a

new, more wistful side to his personality. And in "The Reigate Squire," he seems more human, too, as he succumbs to burnout due to overwork. Meanwhile, Holmes's wide misreading of the facts in "The Yellow Face" reveals for the first time his fallibility as a detective, and elicits an unusually contrite reaction.

A strong theme of betrayal runs through the *Memoirs*. "The *Gloria Scott*," "The Crooked Man," and "The Resident Patient" all attest to this. Suggestions of adultery fuel "The Cardboard Box," and in "The Yellow Face" Grant Munro's behavior is driven by the fear that his beloved wife is being unfaithful. Continuing this theme in "The Musgrave Ritual," the butler's jilting of one woman for another is key to his mysterious disappearance.

Following the **death of his wife**, Watson sells his practice and **moves back into 221B Baker Street** (see "The Norwood Builder," pp.168–69)

Conan Doyle publishes **Round the Red Lamp**—a collection of **short stories** on medical themes.

Conan Doyle publishes **The Medal of Brigadier Gerard** in *The Strand Magazine*— the first of a series.

↑ ↑ ↑

1894   **OCT 1894**   **DEC 1894**

DEC 1893   **FEB 1894**   **1894**

↓ ↓ ↓

Conan Doyle publishes **The Memoirs of Sherlock Holmes**.

Holmes returns to London, marking the end of the **"Great Hiatus"** (see "The Empty House," pp.162–67).

Conan Doyle embarks on a successful **lecture tour of the US** with his brother Innes.

The first ending

Two key characters are introduced in the *Memoirs*: Holmes's brother Mycroft—unmentioned before "The Greek Interpreter"—and the detective's nemesis, Moriarty, who unexpectedly materializes for the first time in "The Final Problem," which narrates the destruction of Holmes and Moriarty at the Reichenbach Falls in Switzerland. Sidney Paget's full-page rendition of the horrifying scene prefaced the story in the *Strand*.

The public response was instant and powerful: "I heard of many who wept," said Conan Doyle. In the story, the author describes Moriarty as "the Napoleon of Crime"—and it is interesting to note that the "better things" to which Conan Doyle wished to dedicate his time also centered on the Napoleonic

era. His historical novel *The Great Shadow* had been published just 13 months before "The Final Problem," and in 1894 he began his stories set during the Napoleonic wars: the "Brigadier Gerard" series.

Gone for good?

Conan Doyle is known to have grown tired of Holmes, but aside from the fulfillment of his higher literary ambitions, there may have been other reasons for killing off his most famous creation at this difficult time in his personal life— his wife had been diagnosed with tuberculosis, and in October 1893, his alcoholic father died in an asylum. However, did Conan Doyle really plan to permanently shelve Holmes? The mystery surrounding the Reichenbach Falls incident left open the possibility of a plausible

resurrection. And 10 years later, that is exactly what happened. Holmes's fictional interlude—between his "death" in April 1891 and his return in February 1894—became known as the "Great Hiatus."

The deeper question of whether Conan Doyle created this mystery deliberately for economic reasons, or whether he had greater affection for Holmes than he let on and could not bring himself to narrate a clear-cut death, will probably never be answered. What is certain is that Conan Doyle was paid £1,000 for the stories in *The Memoirs of Sherlock Holmes*—earnings a world away from the early days of his writing career, when he got by on a shilling a day and, as he recalled, subsisted on "bread, bacon and tea, with an occasional saveloy—what could man ask for more?" ■

THE REAL MURDERER IS STANDING IMMEDIATELY BEHIND YOU

SILVER BLAZE (1892)

IN CONTEXT

TYPE
Short story

FIRST PUBLICATION
UK: December 1892
US: January/February 1893

COLLECTION
***The Memoirs of Sherlock Holmes*, 1894**

CHARACTERS
John Straker Racehorse trainer and retired jockey.

Fitzroy Simpson Wealthy London bookmaker and profligate gambler.

Colonel Ross Owner of the racehorse Silver Blaze.

Inspector Gregory Official investigating officer.

Silas Brown Trainer at Mapleton stables.

Ned Hunter Stable lad at King's Pyland stables.

One of the most commonly reproduced images of Sherlock Holmes is a Sidney Paget illustration from "Silver Blaze," showing a deerstalker-clad Holmes sitting in a train car. He is gesticulating with his long fingers as he expounds the mystery of a missing racehorse and its apparently murdered trainer to a cigar-toting Watson. Prior to this explanation, he (rather improbably) declares the train's speed to be exactly 53½ miles an hour, based on the telegraph posts alongside the track being 60 yards apart. "Silver Blaze" is bookended by train journeys, during which both the exposition and the final explanation of the case take place.

A vanished favorite

The racehorse Silver Blaze, so named for his distinctive white forehead, has gone missing from his stable at King's Pyland on Dartmoor, a week before he is due to run as odds-on favorite in the Wessex Cup. His trainer, John Straker, has been found dead out on the moor, his skull staved in and his hand gripped around a peculiar knife. Fitzroy Simpson, a bookmaker, is already in custody

as prime suspect, having attempted to bribe his way into the stable on the evening in question. Furthermore, that same night he had dined at Straker's house, where a portion of their curried mutton had been laced with opium and used to drug the stable boy who should have been guarding Silver Blaze. Simpson's presence at dinner could have given him the opportunity to drug the food in order to later steal the horse. Simpson claims that in attempting to enter the stables he had merely been looking for some inside tips on the race, but his heavy palm-wood walking stick, a "Penang lawyer,"

…nothing clears up a case so much as stating it to another person.
Sherlock Holmes

Holmes is depicted here in his iconic deerstalker, in *The Strand Magazine*'s illustration from "Silver Blaze." The watercolor version of this scene sold at Christie's for $90,000 in 2014.

is a good fit for the murder weapon, and he seems entirely guilty of both the abduction and the killing—to everyone except Holmes, that is.

Dartmoor location

This case sees Holmes and Watson's first encounter with Dartmoor, an evocative location to which they would return nine years later in *The Hound of the Baskervilles* (pp.152–61). But whereas the Dartmoor of the later story is described as "forbidding," "desolate," and "melancholy"—a fitting setting for the chilling menace of the hound— here it is an invigorating place of unkempt beauty. As the two friends stroll across to the neighboring stables at Mapleton, Watson briefly describes how "the long sloping plain in front of us was tinged with gold, deepening into rich, ruddy brown where the fading ferns and brambles caught the evening light." He bemoans only the fact that "the glories of the landscape were all wasted upon my companion," although in fact even Holmes is not immune to its appeal, later thanking his hosts for "a charming little breath of your beautiful Dartmoor air." In spite of this, the locals do seem to have an alarming propensity to set their dogs on strangers, and perhaps this is a subliminal hint of things to come.

An uncommon policeman

The investigating detective is Inspector Gregory, a policeman to whom Holmes is uncharacteristically complimentary, describing him as "an extremely competent officer."

Holmes is very impressed at the way Gregory has preserved the clues at the site of Straker's apparent murder by instructing his men to stand on a piece of matting at the edge. This admiration for Gregory's methods is in striking contrast to the ire Holmes expresses toward Lestrade when inspecting a crime scene in "The Boscombe Valley Mystery" (pp.70–3): "Oh, how simple it would all have been had I been here before they came like a herd of buffalo and wallowed all over it."

Gregory is consistently able to aid Holmes's investigations— whether through appropriate snippets of information, a handy bag of boots, or a photograph produced from his pocket in timely fashion—which prompts the delighted detective to observe, "My dear Gregory, you anticipate all my wants." Like another

promising young inspector, Stanley Hopkins, who would not turn up at 221B Baker Street until more than a decade later, in "The Adventure of Black Peter" (pp.184–85), Gregory makes great efforts to adopt Holmes's own methods. And yet despite being a man who "was rapidly making his name in the English detective service," the tall, leonine Gregory never appears again after "Silver Blaze."

Facts that suit theories

Holmes's one criticism of Gregory is his lack of imagination, and the value of this particular asset to an investigator is a point he returns to later on in the story. Yet this is a curious criticism for Holmes to make given that in "A Scandal in Bohemia" (pp.60–1), he remarks that "It is a capital mistake to theorise before one has data." In "Silver Blaze," »

The Epsom Derby was one of many popular races in Victorian England. The Wessex Cup in this story is fictional, yet the story has inspired several Silver Blaze Wessex Cup races globally.

Holmes in fact advocates the exact opposite: he contrives a theory as to the missing horse's whereabouts, then goes in search of proof. When he finally finds it, he crows, "See the value of imagination… We imagined what might have happened, acted upon the supposition, and find ourselves justified."

Holmesian methods

Holmes employs a number of his stock deductive methods as he proceeds to unravel the crime at King's Pyland. First, there is the sifting of information: he plows through all the accounts in the popular press in an effort "to detach the framework of fact—of absolute, undeniable fact—from the embellishments of theorists and reporters." In doing this, he trims off the suppositions of others, leaving the reader with the impression that perhaps imagination is a grand thing—so long as it is Holmes's own.

Once Holmes has arrived at the scene, there is the inevitable observation of small clues, in everything from the dead man's effects to the environs of the stables and the murder scene. Various odds and ends of Holmes's vast residual knowledge are here brought into play too, notably the fact of his being, as alleged in *A Study in Scarlet* (pp.36–45), "well up in belladonna, opium, and poisons generally." Most famously,

there is Holmes's last, tantalizing exchange with Inspector Gregory concerning the stable dog (see right), before he leaves Dartmoor.

A flair for the dramatic

The matter of the stable dog's silence as Silver Blaze was led out of his stall is one of several clues upon which the solution hangs, and soon Holmes has a firm handle on them all. The silent dog indicates its familiarity with the intruder; the curry used to mask the taste of opium and drug the stable boy in fact exonerates Simpson, as (being a guest) he could have had no hand in its preparation nor in its devising as a meal; and the "singular knife"—suited to surgical procedures—that was found on the dead man hints at a dark and specific purpose. It is well within Holmes's power to resolve the matter before he leaves Dartmoor, but he chooses not to. Instead he assures Colonel Ross, the horse's owner, that Silver Blaze will run in the Wessex Cup, and arranges to meet him at the Winchester Racecourse in four days.

Victorian horse racing

Horse racing was a hugely popular pastime in the Victorian era, one of the few events at which aristocrats and ordinary people met and mingled. Holmes has a shrewd understanding of the psychology of the betting man. In "The Adventure of the Blue Carbuncle" (pp.82–83), he tricks a wary poultry merchant into giving up information for a wager, observing that "when you see a man with …the 'Pink 'un' protruding out of his pocket, you can always draw

him by a bet." The "Pink 'un" was another name for *The Sporting Times*, one of several racing papers of the era. By the 20th century, however, the sport's popularity had declined, and many of the smaller racecourses had disappeared, among them Winchester Racecourse at Worthy Down. In use since the 1600s, and patronized at one time by Charles II, its last race was run on July 13, 1887. By the end of World War I, it had been turned into an airfield.

> I was marvelling in my own mind how I could possibly have overlooked so obvious a clue.
> **Sherlock Holmes**

Holmes justifies this delay as a playful form of retribution toward Ross, who has been dismissive of his abilities and somewhat prickly toward him: "The colonel's manner has been just a trifle cavalier to me. I am inclined now to have a little amusement at his expense." Whether we believe him entirely, of course, is a rather different matter, but Holmes is fond of a dramatic denouement and, as he remarks to a fellow detective in *The Valley of Fear* (pp.212–20), "surely our profession… would be a drab and sordid one if we did not sometimes set the scene so as to glorify our results."

Whatever Holmes's motivation, the reappearance of the racehorse and the unmasking of the villain are beautifully staged. Silver Blaze turns out to have been both victim and killer, having fatally kicked his trainer in the head while the debt-ridden Straker attempted to rig the race by laming him with a "slight nick upon the tendons." Since then, Silver Blaze has been hidden away at Mapleton, after being found wandering the moor by Silas Brown, Straker's rival trainer, and subsequently disguised with dye to conceal his true coloring. Holmes neglects to reveal this fact to Ross, but as a bay-colored Silver Blaze dashes to victory at Winchester, the colonel is happy enough.

A vice revealed

At the races, Holmes cannot help indulging yet another vice: "But there goes the bell, and as I stand to win a little on this next race, I shall defer a lengthy explanation until a more fitting time." His enthusiasm for the races is evidently shared by Watson who, in "The Adventure of Shoscombe Old Place'"(pp.288–91), confesses that he spends half his pension on betting. It is, however, unlikely that Conan Doyle was an enthusiast himself. In his biography, *Memories and Adventures*, he acknowledges how his ignorance of horse racing "cries aloud to heaven" in "Silver Blaze," which was at the time criticized by experts because had his characters really acted as he described, they would have either ended up in prison or been banned from the sport. "However," Conan Doyle retorted, "I have never been nervous about details, and one must be masterful sometimes." ∎

A key clue for Holmes was the lack of noise made by the stable dog, which allowed the thief to lead Silver Blaze from the stable unheard. His deductions in this case gave rise to the phrase "the curious incident of the dog in the night-time," later immortalized by Mark Haddon in his novel of the same name.

Inspector Gregory:
"Is there any point to which you would wish to draw my attention?"

Holmes:
"To the curious incident of the dog in the night-time."

Inspector Gregory:
"The dog did nothing in the night-time."

Holmes:
"That was the curious incident."

THERE IS NO PART OF THE BODY WHICH VARIES SO MUCH AS THE HUMAN EAR
THE CARDBOARD BOX (1893)

IN CONTEXT

TYPE
Short story

FIRST PUBLICATION
US: January 1893
UK: January 1893

COLLECTION
***The Memoirs of Sherlock Holmes*, 1894**

CHARACTERS
Susan Cushing Quiet and respectable retired spinster.

Sarah Cushing Sister of Susan; a proud, fierce woman.

Mary Browner Third Cushing sister; married to James Browner.

James Browner Tempestuous, heavy-drinking ship's steward.

Alec Fairbairn Dashing, swaggering competitor for Mary's affections.

Inspector Lestrade Scotland Yard detective.

The story opens on a "blazing hot day in August" and Watson is dying to get out of the sweltering city. Restless and bored, his gaze wanders to two portraits on the wall. Moments later, Holmes makes a comment that is so in tune with his thoughts, it is as if he has read the doctor's mind. The detective explains the trick: he had followed his friend's facial expressions and, from a mere quiver on his lips, had deduced that Watson had been musing on "the preposterous way" of settling arguments through violence. This observation neatly foreshadows the action to follow. Holmes announces

The 1994 television adaptation of "The Cardboard Box" was set during a snowy Christmas. It starred Jeremy Brett at the end of his Holmes career, due to his declining health.

Conan Doyle's self-censorship

When the stories published in *The Strand Magazine* between December 1892 and November 1893 were compiled as *The Memoirs of Sherlock Holmes*, "The Cardboard Box" was left out at Conan Doyle's insistence. The story was included in the first American edition of the *Memoirs*, but removed in a revised second printing, and the original edition destroyed. Debate about Conan Doyle's reasons has raged among Holmesians ever since. As Christopher Roden points out, the author offered various excuses: "that it was out of place in a collection intended for boys; that it was more sensational than he cared for; and that it was a weak story." However, salacious content appears elsewhere in the canon, and the tale is a compelling one. Whatever the reason, there was one part of the story that Conan Doyle thought too good to lose. For the *Memoirs* publication, the opening mind-reading passage of this story was moved to the start of "The Adventure of the Resident Patient" (pp.134–35). While "The Cardboard Box" was eventually included in 1917's *His Last Bow*, most modern editors return it to the *Memoirs* and, to avoid duplicating the opening passage, restore both stories to their original versions.

his involvement in a sensational new case, which "may prove to be more difficult of solution than my small essay in thought reading." An innocuous spinster, Susan Cushing, has received a very grisly package of two severed human ears. Lestrade suspects it is no more than a prank by her former lodgers (three medical students) but, as usual, he turns out to be wide of the mark.

Unpacking the box

At Susan's home, Holmes's major deductions revolve around the package, the cardboard box of the title. To the sharp-eyed detective, this box yields a host of clues— including tarred twine and an especially well-executed knot— to the sender's identity. The ears themselves are preserved in rough salt, which is not a substance that a medical practitioner would use, and they are not a matching pair: one is a woman's, the other a man's. Holmes deduces that this is no student joke—it is a double murder.

Susan then unwittingly provides almost all the extra information Holmes needs to solve the case, telling him that she has two sisters, Mary and Sarah. Mary lives in Liverpool with her sailor husband James Browner; her other sister Sarah had once lived with the couple, but after a "quarrel" she returned to London to lodge with Susan (although she has recently moved out). As they talk, Holmes notes a strong resemblance between Susan's ear and one in the box.

En route to sister Sarah's house, Holmes wires a police contact in Liverpool. Sarah is ill and cannot meet them, but Holmes says that he had only wanted to "look at her," and that he already has the information he needs. Back at Scotland Yard, he receives a response to his telegram, and tells Lestrade that Browner sent the parcel, and can be apprehended when his ship next docks in London. By now, Holmes is convinced that one of the ears belongs to Mary Browner, and the other to her lover.

A husband's betrayal

Once under arrest, Browner readily admits to his crime in a confession that portrays him more as the victim of the case, rather than the villain, confusing the story's morals. Sarah was in love with him, but when he gently spurned her advances, she became vengeful, poisoning his marriage and encouraging Mary to have an affair with a dashing seaman, Alec Fairbairn.

One day, Browner saw the lovers, and, in a jealous rage, he armed himself with a heavy stick and followed. When they rented a boat and rowed out to sea, he did the same and, after a confrontation, he killed them both. He hacked off their ears, later sending one of each to Sarah, in a crazed bid to show her where her "meddling" had led. All of this precipitates a melancholic closing remark from Holmes, echoing Watson's thoughts on "the sadness and horror and useless waste of life" involved in violence. ∎

> What object is served by this circle of misery and violence and fear?
> **Sherlock Holmes**

ANY TRUTH IS BETTER THAN INDEFINITE DOUBT
THE YELLOW FACE (1893)

IN CONTEXT

TYPE
Short story

FIRST PUBLICATION
UK: February 1893
US: February 1893

COLLECTION
***The Memoirs of Sherlock Holmes*, 1894**

CHARACTERS
Grant Munro ("Jack") Hop merchant living in Norbury.

Effie Munro Grant Munro's wife, who previously lived and was married in Atlanta, Georgia.

John Hebron Effie's late husband, an American lawyer.

Lucy Hebron Effie's daughter.

This tale opens with a lull in business for Sherlock Holmes, and a remark from Dr Watson on the detective's habit of turning to cocaine during slow periods. He refers to Holmes's casual drug use as "a protest against the monotony of existence when cases were scanty." Yet it has now become more of an affectation than a true habit, and Conan Doyle's previous depictions of Holmes as a misanthropic decadent, influenced by Oscar Wilde's novel *The Picture of Dorian Gray* (1891), are giving way to a more well-adjusted persona.

Evasion and lies

Holmes and Watson return from a stroll to find they have just missed a caller—Grant Munro. When he returns, Munro explains his situation: his wife, Effie, has been deceiving him, causing a rift in their otherwise perfect marriage, and he wants Holmes's advice.

Six weeks earlier, Effie had asked Munro to give her £100, insisting he not ask about its purpose. Then, last week, he was returning to their home in Norbury when he saw that a nearby cottage had new occupants; he caught a

Interracial marriage

In the United States in the 19th century, interracial marriage and miscegenation (breeding between races) were highly taboo. The Hebron family would certainly have had to leave their home in Atlanta, Georgia, where laws against miscegenation still applied until 1967.

Munro's acceptance of his mixed-race stepdaughter reflects the softer attitudes in Britain at the time: interracial marriage might have been frowned upon by society, but

it was not illegal. Interestingly, in the British edition of the story there are two minutes of silence before Munro's heart-warming declaration of acceptance; in the American version it was adjusted to 10 minutes.

In 1882, Conan Doyle met the American minister and black anti-slavery leader Henry Highland Garnet. Conan Doyle's sympathies as set out in "The Yellow Face" may have resulted from what he came to learn as a result of their friendship.

Many serious outbreaks of yellow fever occurred in southern states of the US in the 19th century. In severe cases, patients developed jaundice, which turned their skin yellow, and often died.

until her mother arranged their passage to England, using the money Munro had given her. Fearing Munro would no longer love her, Effie tried to keep her daughter's existence a secret from him and made Lucy stay inside the cottage, wearing a mask to disguise the color of her face.

After hearing this pitiable tale, Munro declares, "I am not a very good man... but I think that I am a better one than you have given me credit for being." He lifts up little Lucy and kisses her, a noble gesture given social conventions of the time, then goes to his wife.

This case is unusual both in that no crime has been committed, and also in that it is one of only a handful where Holmes's deductions are proved wrong. But most striking is Conan Doyle's progressive anti-racism message, which would have been at odds with attitudes of many 19th-century readers. ∎

glimpse of an eerily inhuman "yellow livid face" peering out of an upstairs window. That night, he awoke to discover his wife slipping out of the house at 3 am, and when she returned, she was vague about where she had been.

The following day, Munro saw Effie coming out of the cottage and asked her what business she had with its occupants. Again she would not tell him, but implored him never to enter the house, saying that their marriage would be over were he to do so. She swore she would not go there again, but three days later she did, so Munro rushed over there. The cottage was empty, but in the upstairs room he found a photograph of his wife.

For Holmes, the case hinges on Effie's past. Munro reveals she had emigrated to the United States, but returned after the death of both

her first husband and her child from yellow fever. When she married Munro, she signed her ex-husband's income over to him. Munro says he has seen the first husband's death certificate, but Holmes suspects foul play. He is sure this is a case of blackmail, and that Effie's first husband must be alive and has tracked her down to extort money: the face at the window is his. Then Munro summons Holmes and Watson to Norbury because the cottage's residents have returned.

Love conquers prejudice
Holmes and Watson help Munro enter the cottage, where they discover that the "yellow face" is a mask being worn by a young black girl named Lucy—Effie's daughter. The first husband, an African American lawyer, did die, but the child survived and lived with a nurse

Watson... if it should ever strike you that I am getting a little over-confident in my powers... kindly whisper 'Norbury' in my ear, and I shall be infinitely obliged to you.
Sherlock Holmes

HUMAN NATURE IS A STRANGE MIXTURE, WATSON
THE STOCKBROKER'S CLERK (1893)

IN CONTEXT

TYPE
Short story

FIRST PUBLICATION
UK: March 1893
US: March 1893

COLLECTION
***The Memoirs of Sherlock Holmes*, 1894**

CHARACTERS
Hall Pycroft Young stockbroker's clerk.

Arthur Pinner Financial agent based in London.

Harry Pinner Owner of a newly established hardware distribution company, based in Birmingham.

Beddington Criminal who has just been released from a five-year prison sentence.

When Conan Doyle wrote "The Stockbroker's Clerk," his earnings from the Sherlock Holmes stories were reaching a level at which he had money of his own to invest. He began to deal with the brokerage of Pim, Vaughan and bought shares in ventures such as the Portsmouth Tram Company and Australian mines. Doubtless, therefore, he was well aware that fraud was rife in the financial world at the time. In this story, he displays a knowledge of how businesses worked, using a plot that turns, plausibly, on the pitfalls inherent in the way London firms like the fictional Mawson & Williams hired their staff.

A dream job turns sour
The stockbroker's clerk in the title is young Hall Pycroft, and he is traveling to Birmingham by train with Holmes, whose services he has engaged, and Watson. During the journey, he tells them about the case. He was let go from his clerk's job a while ago, and after a long and desperate search for a new job he finally landed a post at major London stockbrokers Mawson &

Financial felons
The financial world of the late 19th century was highly corrupt. At least one in six company launches on the stock market was fraudulent, with swindlers taking investors' money and then vanishing. Banking was just as corrupt as the stock market, with 242 out of the 291 private banks formed between 1844 and 1868 failing, often because of fraud. When the giant City of Glasgow Bank failed in 1878, it transpired that the directors had lent millions to friends and family with no collateral, and cooked the books to cover it up. However, the police almost never investigated what is known today as white-collar crime, concentrating instead on the working-class felon. Such was the level of theft and corruption in the business world that Beddington, posing as a clerk, would hardly have needed to murder the security guard and carry the bonds off in a bag. Huge sums of money were hemorrhaging each day through the slippery hands of "legitimate" employees.

In a dramatic scene, illustrated here in *The Strand Magazine*, Holmes, Watson, and Pycroft force their way into Pinner's office and find him attempting to commit suicide.

Williams. However, shortly before Pycroft was due to take up the position, he was offered a better-paying job by a man named Arthur Pinner, who instructed him to travel to Birmingham to meet his brother Harry, the "promoter" of the Franco-Midland Hardware Company, at their offices. Flattered by the offer, Pycroft accepted the job, signing a declaration stating his willingness to join the company, and agreeing to not officially resign his post at Mawson & Williams.

In Birmingham, Harry took Pycroft to the company's office, which turned out to be a couple of small, dusty, and sparsely furnished rooms. Pycroft began to work, but soon felt a vague sense of unease. He then observed that Harry had a gold filling on the same tooth as his brother, and suspected that they must be the same man. His suspicions aroused, Pycroft consulted Holmes, who agreed to probe his mysterious new employer.

When the trio arrive at Pycroft's Birmingham office, with Holmes and Watson posing as job-seekers, they find Pinner reading a newspaper and looking highly distraught; he asks them to leave him alone for a moment. Hearing strange sounds,

they burst back into the room and find him hanging from a hook on the door. After cutting him down and reviving him, Holmes deduces that Pinner has devised a fictitious post for Pycroft in Birmingham, to get him out of the way so a crime could be committed at Mawson & Williams in London.

A murderous thief

The newspaper Pinner was reading reveals both the details of the crime and the reason for Pinner's despair. His real brother, a notorious forger and safe-breaker called Beddington, had taken up Pycroft's position at Mawson & Williams; it was easy to impersonate the young clerk, since no one in the company had actually met him. Then, the previous Saturday, Beddington had dallied in the office, murdered the guard, and tried to make off with a bag stuffed with almost £100,000 in bonds. But an astute policeman, surprised to see a man leaving the office so late with a bag, arrested him, and the crime was discovered. All that remains, the paper reports, is to catch Beddington's brother, who usually works with him. "We may save the police some little trouble in that direction," remarks Holmes.

Holmes seems surprisingly sympathetic toward Pinner, who, having been driven to suicide on hearing of his brother's arrest, is now facing prison for his role in the crime. In fact, Holmes often stands outside the law, and is happy to see natural justice done instead. It is, of course, what puts him in Scotland Yard's bad books, but it also saves him the trouble of having to build

a legal case—once he has explained it, the reader is satisfied that justice has run its course. However, Holmes knows that in this case they must hand Pinner over to the police. The tale is also unusual in that, when he arrives at the solution, Holmes is far from the crime scene, and is only able to apprehend the accomplice. The felony itself took place within London, and it was only the sharp eyes of a policeman that led to the arrest of the perpetrator. ∎

Holmes's deduction of Watson's health

Watson has **new slippers** with slightly **scorched soles**.

↓

The slippers haven't been **wet**—the shop's **paper label** is still attached.

↓

They weren't scorched **while drying**, so he has been sitting **by the fire** with his feet outstretched.

↓

He would not do this in **summer** if he was in **good health**.

↓

"I perceive you have been unwell lately. Summer colds are always a little trying."

AND THEN IN AN INSTANT THE KEY OF THE RIDDLE WAS IN MY HANDS
THE *GLORIA SCOTT* (1893)

IN CONTEXT

TYPE
Short story

FIRST PUBLICATION
UK: February 1893
US: April 1893

COLLECTION
***The Memoirs of Sherlock Holmes*, 1894**

CHARACTERS
Victor Trevor senior
Justice of the Peace in
the Norfolk Broads.

Victor Trevor junior Son
of Trevor senior, and an old
college friend of Holmes.

Beddoes Fellow prisoner,
mutineer, and friend of
Victor Trevor senior.

Hudson Sailor on the
Gloria Scott.

Jack Prendergast Leader
of the mutiny on board the
Gloria Scott.

nlike most Holmes stories, "The *Gloria Scott*" is told by Holmes himself, not Watson, as the two friends sit by the fire one winter's night in 221B Baker Street. Holmes had many cases before he met Watson in 1881, but of those investigations this was one of only two that Watson recorded in his annals – the other being "The Adventure of the Musgrave Ritual" (pp.120–25). Indeed, Holmes declares it to be the very first case he was ever engaged in. It features two of Conan Doyle's favorite themes:

He was the
only friend I made
during the two
years I was at
college. I was never
a very sociable
fellow, Watson.
Sherlock Holmes

seafaring, and the haunting of a good, respectable citizen by a disreputable past in distant climes.

A hidden past
Holmes recalls how in his student days, during the long summer vacation, he went to stay on the Norfolk Broads at the grand house of Victor Trevor, his only friend at university (probably Oxford or Cambridge, but this is a point of debate). Over a glass of port one evening, young Victor's father, Victor Trevor senior, asked Holmes to demonstrate his deductive powers, which his son had been extolling. "Come, now, Mr. Holmes," he said, "I'm an excellent subject, if you can deduce anything from me."

Trevor senior, a justice of the peace with a reputation for leniency, was taken aback by Holmes's perception that in recent months he had been going about in fear of attack. Holmes's remarkable insight was based on a shrewd observation of Trevor's walking stick: he could tell from the inscription that the stick was less than a year old, and further noted that it had been hollowed out at the top and filled with lead—presumably in order to be used as a weapon.

Holmes also observed from his host's flattened and thickened ears that he was once a boxer (a shared enthusiasm), while his callused hands suggested digging. Trevor senior explained that he had made his fortune prospecting for gold.

Holmes, who had earlier observed a semi-erased tattoo on the man's arm, then added, "And you have been most intimately associated with someone whose initials were J.A., and whom you afterwards were eager to entirely forget." At this, to both Holmes's and Trevor junior's astonishment, Trevor senior slowly stood, stared wildly at Holmes, then fainted. When he came to, Trevor senior declared in admiration of Holmes's

Tea clippers like the *Gloria Scott* were built for speed, and designed to carry light loads. The only surviving intact example is the *Cutty Sark* (below), now moored in Greenwich, London.

> It seems to me that all the detectives of fact and of fancy would be children in your hands.
> **Victor Trevor senior**

astute, albeit unofficial, detective work, "That's your line of life, sir, and you may take the word of a man who has seen something of the world." And that, describes Holmes to the listening Watson, was the moment he realized that he might make a profession out of detective work.

Once recovered, Trevor senior claimed, rather unconvincingly, that "J.A." was an old flame. Yet afterward he was so uneasy that Holmes resolved to leave. However, the day before his departure, an uninvited guest arrived—an "acid-faced" old sailor named Hudson. Trevor senior clearly knew the sinister-looking man, and poured himself a large brandy. "Why, it's thirty year and more since I saw you last," said Hudson. "Here you are in your house, and me still picking my salt meat out of the harness cask." When he mentioned a mutual acquaintance called Beddoes, Trevor senior, clearly in shock, drank himself into a stupor.

A fatal message

Seven weeks later, back in London, Holmes received a telegram from Trevor junior imploring him to return to Norfolk, where his father had suffered a massive stroke. »

Beddoes warns Trevor senior

by way of a cryptic code. The full coded message is shown here, but Holmes deduces that taking every third word (in bold) reveals its true meaning. The use of coded messages for secret communications was common in Victorian Britain.

> *The supply of game for London is going steadily up. Head-keeper Hudson, we believe, has been now told to receive all orders for fly-paper and for preservation of your hen pheasant's life.*

But by the time Holmes reached Trevor's hamlet, the old man was dead. It transpired that, since Holmes's last visit, Hudson had exerted a strange hold over Trevor senior and for weeks had terrorized the household. Things came to a head when an argument broke out between Hudson and Trevor junior. Young Victor had then refused to apologize, at which Hudson left for Beddoes' Hampshire estate. And it was a brief, cryptic message (see above) from there, received the day before Holmes's return to the house, that had brought on the stroke.

The budding detective took some time to decipher the strange message. He read it backward, then tried alternate words, before realizing the key lay in every third word, starting with the first: "The game is up. Hudson has told all. Fly for your life." No wonder Trevor senior was so affected. But why the bizarre "Head-keeper" and "hen pheasants," and what secret was Hudson harboring? The odd choice of filler words seemed to

The murder of the ship's captain, illustrated here by Paget in *The Strand Magazine,* is part of the violent and bloodthirsty mutiny that led Armitage and Evans to flee the ship.

validate the message's authenticity, confirming that Beddoes, an avid hunter, wrote it. But Hudson's role remained unexplained.

A deathbed confession

As Trevor senior gasped his last breath, he told his doctor where to find a letter he had written for his son in the event of his death. The

letter revealed that his real name was James Armitage—"J.A."—and explained how, as a young man working in a London bank, he had stolen money in order to pay a debt, intending to return it before anyone noticed. However, he had been caught, tried, and sentenced to transportation aboard the *Gloria Scott*, bound for Australia.

Here the plot thickened. It was October 1855, and transportation ships had been enlisted for military uses because of the Crimean War (1853–1856). The ship carrying Armitage was, in fact, a repurposed tea clipper, a lightweight vessel overloaded with almost a hundred crew, prisoners, and soldiers.

At sea, an inmate named Jack Prendergast let Armitage in on an elaborate escape plot. It was already well prepared and financed, and Prendergast's partner was busy masquerading as the ship's own chaplain, and secretly bribing the

> Those are the facts
> of the case, Doctor,
> and if they are of any
> use to your collection,
> I am sure that they
> are very heartily
> at your service.
> **Sherlock Holmes**

crew and bringing weaponry into the 38 inmates' cells. They seemed so certain to overwhelm the 18 soldiers and a mere few others that Armitage decided to join in.

A violent mutiny

The violence of the mutiny that took place is described in full, gory detail. Conan Doyle, who twice served as a ship's surgeon—in the Arctic on the whaler *Hope* in 1880, and off the West African coast on the steamer *Mayumba* in 1881—has Prendergast ruthlessly cut the throat of the bound and gagged convict ship's surgeon. Interestingly, however, there is a curious difference between the original British and American descriptions of the murdered ship's captain. In the British edition, he "lay with his head on the chart of the Atlantic," whereas the American edition described "his brains smeared over the chart of the Atlantic." The jury is still out as to which of these was Conan Doyle's original.

Uneasy with all the wanton bloodletting, several men, including Armitage and another friend named Evans, wanted no more part in it.

They escaped in a lifeboat, but as they rowed away the *Gloria Scott* exploded and they turned back to search for survivors. There was only one amid the wreckage: Hudson. It transpired that a bullet had ignited the ship's gunpowder.

The men were picked up off Cape Verde by a brig heading for Australia, and managed to convince their rescuers they were from a foundered passenger ship. Once in Australia, Armitage and Evans created new identities, renaming themselves Trevor and Beddoes, respectively, and both made their fortunes. Returning later to England, with their pasts safely buried, it was clear why the return of Hudson, with his knowledge of their part in the mutiny, was so disconcerting.

In concluding his reminiscence, Holmes tells how Victor junior—heartbroken about his father's disreputable past—became a tea planter in India. And it turned out that Beddoes' warning that Hudson had "told all" had been wrong. Both Beddoes and Hudson vanished, but although the police thought Hudson had killed Beddoes, Holmes himself suspected the opposite, and that Beddoes had fled the country.

A likely inspiration

Apart from this surmise, Holmes does little more in this case than decode the cryptic message and read a confessional letter: indeed, the whole case is largely a frame for a pirate story (Conan Doyle was enthusiastic about the genre, and in 1922 wrote a collection called *Tales of Pirates and Blue Water*).

"The *Gloria Scott*" may have been inspired by a real-life case of mutiny, aboard the convict ship *Cyprus* in 1829, in which some convicts refused to take part. Two rowed away—and the captain who picked them up was named Hudson. ∎

Transportation

The transportation of British criminals to the far reaches of the Empire was a staple of 19th-century justice, and had been since Elizabethan times. Convicts were usually forced to do hard labor—a practice that was seen to kill two birds with one stone, since it not only removed the convict from British society but also provided the colonies with a supply of workers. In the early days, felons were sent to work for the Virginia Company in America, but after American independence, Australia became the focus, the first 700 convicts landing in Botany Bay, near Sydney, in 1788. Although the practice ended in New South Wales by 1851 and in Tasmania by 1853, it continued in Western Australia until 1868, by which time over 160,000 convicts had been delivered to the country. Had Trevor senior's crime been committed 33 years earlier, his story would have been very different. As his confessional letter from the 1880s states, "The case might have been dealt with leniently, but the laws were more harshly administered thirty years ago."

IN MY INMOST HEART I BELIEVED THAT I COULD SUCCEED WHERE OTHERS FAILED

THE MUSGRAVE RITUAL (1893)

IN CONTEXT

TYPE
Short story

FIRST PUBLICATION
UK: May 1893
US: May 1893

COLLECTION
*The Memoirs of
Sherlock Holmes*, 1894

CHARACTERS
Reginald Musgrave Old
acquaintance of Holmes and
owner of Hurlstone estate.

Richard Brunton Former
butler at Hurlstone; a widower
and womanizer.

Rachel Howells Second
maid at Hurlstone and
Brunton's former fiancée.

I t is no surprise that "The Musgrave Ritual" was one of Conan Doyle's favorite stories. Brimming with intrigue, it features buried treasure, a baffling coded message, and even a link to the English Civil War that adds a piquant element of historical drama.

Although the story begins with Watson addressing the reader in the usual way, it is actually Holmes who narrates most of the action, since it occurred long before the doctor moved into 221B Baker Street. In fact, it is the second-earliest case in the Holmes canon, following on from "The *Gloria Scott*" (pp.116–19).

An untidy flatmate

On a winter's evening in 1888, at 221B, soon after the publication of *A Study in Scarlet* (pp.36–45)

The 1943 movie *Sherlock Holmes Faces Death* takes the name and ritual from "The Musgrave Ritual," but bears little resemblance to the original story.

and around the time of the events in *The Valley of Fear* (pp.212–21), Watson is berating Holmes for his untidiness and famous domestic peccadilloes: his habit of keeping cigars in the coal scuttle, stashing tobacco in a Persian slipper, and pinning letters to the mantelpiece with a jackknife. It is hard to disagree with Watson's complaint that pistol practice is best saved for outdoors. Yet Holmes's decoration of the wall with bullet holes that spell out "VR" (Victoria Regina) is not only evidence of his patriotism, it is also a deft piece of contextual data from Conan Doyle, as June 1887 had marked Queen Victoria's Golden Jubilee.

It is Holmes's lackadaisical housekeeping that prompts him to tell Watson about the "Musgrave Ritual." Ruefully accepting Watson's suggestion to tidy up, Holmes starts with a box containing a record of his earlier cases and chances on one that "really is something a little recherché," withdrawing a set of perplexing items: an old, crumpled piece of paper, a weathered key, a wooden peg attached to some string, and some rusty metal discs—the residual traces of the case.

A familiar new client

After his success as a student in the case of "The *Gloria Scott*," Holmes earned a reputation as an investigator at university, spurring several fellow students to offer him investigative work. Reginald Musgrave—a shy and aristocratic man—was one of them. Having been out of touch for four years, Musgrave visits Holmes at his Montague Street lodgings, near the

British Museum (and close to where Conan Doyle once lived). Musgrave tells Holmes that his father died two years ago, and that he is now in possession of Hurlstone, the family home. In response to an enquiry about his career, Holmes remarks, "I have taken to living by my wits," making him a paradigm of the self-made man. Musgrave is pleased to hear it, since there is a mystery to be solved and the police are unable to shed any light on the matter.

A butler and a battle-ax

Musgrave explains that the mystery concerns the disappearance of his butler, Richard Brunton, an educated man who has served the family for over 20 years. He is a notorious womanizer and recently broke off his engagement to a maid, Rachel Howells, in favor of another servant, causing great uproar.

In the small hours of the previous Thursday night, Musgrave had been unable to sleep, and had gone to » retrieve a book from the billiards room. He was alarmed to see a light coming from under the door of the library and, suspecting burglars, he picked up an old battle-ax from a wall display and peeped in through a crack in the door. He was amazed to see his butler examining "a slip of paper which looked like a map." Musgrave then watched as Brunton headed to the bureau, removed a second document, and began to study it carefully and meticulously. Furious, Musgrave confronted Brunton, who turned "livid with fear" and thrust the maplike paper into his pocket. Musgrave fired him on the spot, but Brunton managed to barter for a week's notice.

Musgrave explains to Holmes that the document taken from the bureau was a strange old family "observance" called the Musgrave Ritual. This document is no secret, and consists of a series of arcane-sounding questions and answers that, for generations, each Musgrave has read out upon reaching maturity. Musgrave is certain the Ritual is of no relevance to the case, saying it is of "no practical use whatever." Holmes clearly has other ideas, but allows his client to continue.

> If we could find that spot we should be in a fair way towards finding what the secret was...
> **Sherlock Holmes**

The disappearances

It was three days later that Brunton mysteriously vanished. His bed had not been slept in, and no one knows how he could have left the house—the doors and windows were locked. Also, his effects (except for a black suit and slippers) were all left behind. A thorough search of labyrinthine Hurlstone, parts of which date back to 1607, proved fruitless—no trace of the butler could be found.

In the meantime, another curious incident had occurred. When Rachel Howells, the second maid and Brunton's snubbed fiancée, told Musgrave that the butler was missing, she suffered a hysterical attack and had to be confined to bed. Three days later, she too disappeared. Footprints ran from her window, across the lawn, and stopped at the edge of a lake. Musgrave and the staff suspected the worst of the "poor demented girl," but dredging the lake had revealed only an old linen bag filled with "a mass of old rusted and discoloured metal and several dull-coloured pieces of pebble or glass."

Holmes's curiosity is aroused, and he says he must see the Ritual. Although Musgrave cannot see its relevance, he duly brings the document with him to Montague Street to show Holmes, pointing out that there is no date inscribed on it, but that the spelling is of the mid-17th century—almost the same age as the house itself. Holmes instantly grasps the document as being "immensely practical," declaring the butler an extremely clever man with "a clearer insight than ten generations of his masters."

Over the oak, under the elm

That afternoon, Holmes travels down to Hurlstone with Musgrave. As he describes his journey, he intones to Watson that it had already

Richard Brunton

Originally a schoolmaster, Richard Brunton was first employed by Musgrave's father. The description we are given is initially rather humorous—one can picture this flamboyant intellectual in "a quiet country district," dazzling the local ladies with his "splendid forehead" and flair for music and languages. Musgrave compares him to Don Juan, the mythic European libertine. This legendary lothario was a stock figure in celebrated works by Byron, Mozart, Pushkin, and others. It is interesting that Brunton, with his "insatiable curiosity," recalls Holmes himself. However, unlike the detective, he is scuppered by his inability to control himself: a fatal flaw reminiscent of pride or hubris in classical drama.

Although Conan Doyle has been criticized for thin characterization, Brunton comes across vividly, even if Holmes encounters him only as a barely recognizable corpse. So vividly, in fact, that the reader might forget he is described in three layers of narration: Musgrave's, Holmes's, and Watson's.

After examining the Musgrave Ritual, Holmes deduces what Brunton had already discovered, that the Ritual contained directions to a hidden treasure, entrusted to the Musgraves centuries ago. At a certain time of year, the directions can be followed using the shadows cast by the trees in the grounds of Hurlstone, Musgrave's estate.

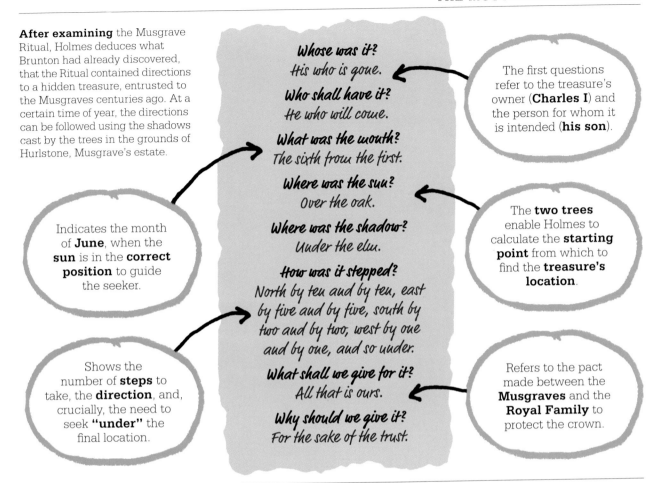

> Whose was it?
> His who is gone.
>
> Who shall have it?
> He who will come.
>
> What was the month?
> The sixth from the first.
>
> Where was the sun?
> Over the oak.
>
> Where was the shadow?
> Under the elm.
>
> How was it stepped?
> North by ten and by ten, east by five and by five, south by two and by two, west by one and by one, and so under.
>
> What shall we give for it?
> All that is ours.
>
> Why should we give it?
> For the sake of the trust.

The first questions refer to the treasure's owner (**Charles I**) and the person for whom it is intended (**his son**).

Indicates the month of **June**, when the **sun** is in the **correct position** to guide the seeker.

The **two trees** enable Holmes to calculate the **starting point** from which to find the **treasure's location**.

Shows the number of **steps** to take, the **direction**, and, crucially, the need to seek **"under"** the final location.

Refers to the pact made between the **Musgraves** and the **Royal Family** to protect the crown.

---

become clear to him "that there were not three separate mysteries here, but one only": the Ritual, as well as the disappearance of Brunton and Howells, all share a common denominator. To Holmes, it is clear that the Ritual (see above) is in fact a cipher, giving measurements that plot a course to a particular spot. If Holmes can find that, then he will almost certainly discover the secret that will enable him to solve the entire mystery.

The detective works through the document, applying his usual logic. The oak tree is easy to identify—it is situated directly in front of the house and extremely ancient, so it would have certainly been there when the Ritual was drawn up. He

asks Musgrave if there is an elm, and learns that one was cut down after being struck by lightning 10 years before, but a mark on the lawn shows where the tree once stood (midway between the oak and the house). When questioned on the height of the tree, Musgrave conveniently recalls from his trigonometry lessons that it was exactly 64 feet tall. Holmes enquires if the butler ever asked him the same question and Musgrave, astonished, recalls that he had indeed, only a few months ago.

Stepping it out
Holmes intuits from the wording of the Ritual that the starting spot must be the point that the elm's

shadow would have reached at the exact moment when the sun is just higher than the oak. He puts a rod into the ground where the elm had been, and follows its shadow to a point calculated on the basis of the elm's 64-foot height. This takes him to a spot by the house that is marked by a "conical depression"— more evidence of Brunton having also followed the same path. From this starting point, Holmes begins to step north, east, south, and west, following the words of the Ritual. They lead him through a heavy old door in the house's oldest part and into a stone passageway behind it where the "sun shone full upon the passage floor." Holmes is convinced he has found the correct location. »

This illustration by Sidney Paget first appeared in *The Strand Magazine*. It shows Holmes, right, examining the ancient oak tree that was the first step mentioned in the Musgrave Ritual.

story since its publication. For instance, in the original version of the story, the reference to the time of year (June) was absent from the Ritual; Conan Doyle added it later, presumably after realizing that it would have a vital effect on the shadows' trajectories. Yet even with this addition, the Ritual still doesn't specify the time of day, which would put the elm's shadow in an opposite direction depending on whether it was morning or evening. The story also does not account for new trees growing during the three centuries since the Ritual was penned; and the final two steps that lead into the corridor are made moving west, even though "the setting sun shone full upon the passage floor." However, such discrepancies play no part in the thrilling climax of this story.

Beneath the flagstones
However, when he looks down, hoping to see evidence of a hiding place beneath the paving—as the Ritual implies—to his dismay he sees that the paving stones were cemented together many years ago and Brunton cannot possibly have moved them. But Musgrave tells him that there is a cellar hidden beneath, and leads him down. Now it is clear they have found the correct spot—and they are not the only ones to have visited recently.

Here, in the dark cellar, they find Brunton's "shepherd's-check muffler" tied around an iron ring that is attached to a large, heavy flagstone in the floor. Although it might strike the reader as odd that this room was never investigated in the supposedly "cellar to garret" search, the intensifying excitement

leaves no time to wonder about such intricacies. Anticipating what they might find, Holmes asks Musgrave to summon the county police. Then, with a police constable, Holmes lifts up the flagstone and peers into the hole beneath. There he sees a square chamber, a little deeper than the height of a man: on one side is a "brass-bound wooden box," with an old key in its lock. On the other, a gruesome, black-clad corpse: the over-inquisitive butler.

The reality of the Ritual
Although the Ritual wording is beguiling, Holmesian experts agree that, in reality, there is no way the L-shaped house, the oak tree, and the elm could have been arranged in such a way that the Ritual makes sense; in addition, there are various other issues that have plagued the

The mystery accomplice
The discovery of Brunton's body is tantalizingly inconclusive: Holmes has only solved part of the mystery. He reaches the full solution by using his trademark technique of putting

No man could have recognized that distorted liver-coloured countenance.
Sherlock Holmes

Here was the secret of her blanched face, her shaken nerves, her peals of hysterical laughter on the next morning.
Sherlock Holmes

"myself in the man's place." It is an apposite remark, since he has literally been tracing Brunton's steps to the letter, following the felon's every move in a manner more pronounced than anywhere else in the canon.

There is a moment of cheeky braggadocio from Holmes when he tells Watson that "the matter was simplified by Brunton's intelligence being quite first-rate," meaning (given Holmes's own intellect) he didn't need to take "the personal equation" into account. This was originally an astronomers' term, coined when they realized that scientific measurements could be affected by subtle personal bias. Holmes's use of the word preempts its employment in the 20th century by psychologists like Wilhelm Wundt and Carl Jung, who highlighted the effect of individual subjectivity in psychological judgments.

Holmes establishes that Brunton would have needed an accomplice to lift the flagstone, and correctly surmises that he had sought the help of his old flame, Rachel Howells. But Brunton had not counted on his former lover vindictively kicking away the wooden wedge keeping the stone raised, leaving him to suffocate in the airless chamber.

A regal discovery

It is clear that the "treasure" Brunton was after was the bag of objects found in the lake, where Rachel must have thrown them before she fled. Having earlier painted her as hysterical, Conan Doyle now relies on another stereotype: her impulsive vengeance is written off as a sign of her "excitable Welsh temperament."

The dirty coins beside Brunton's corpse are from the time of Charles I, so Musgrave's general dating of the Ritual was correct. He then says that his ancestor Ralph Musgrave had been a prominent Cavalier and "right-hand man to Charles II in his wanderings." With a quick polish, Holmes achieves a dazzling shine on one of the old gems, and realizes the "double ring" of rusted metal is in fact the lost crown of the Stuarts, and the dull stones are its gems. All had been safely stored at Hurlstone in anticipation of the restoration of the monarchy after the Civil War.

In reality, the Stuart crown was melted down, but Conan Doyle exploits an alluring—and even historically plausible—possibility. Nevertheless, the "unfortunate oversight" of whichever Musgrave descendant failed to communicate the significance of the Ritual as successfully as the Ritual itself, meaning Charles II never reclaimed his crown, is a little perfunctory.

Holmes's comment that "nothing was ever heard" of Rachel is a loose end as uncharacteristic of the detective as of Conan Doyle—chiefly given that she is surely guilty of the worst transgression. However, it is also worth noting there is one more crime that goes unpunished: Holmes never did get around to tidying up his room. ∎

A nation in conflict

The English Civil War (1642–1651) began as a result of irreconcilable differences between King Charles I and his parliament. In one of the most dramatic episodes in English history, the Civil War divided the country between those supporting the King (the Cavaliers) and those supporting the Parliamentarians (the Roundheads) under Oliver Cromwell. It culminated in the execution of King Charles I in 1649, the exile of his son (later Charles II), and the monarchy's replacement with a republic. The "wanderings" of Charles II that Musgrave refers to is the period when he had fled from England.

Within a decade, Cromwell's government was falling apart, and his death in 1658 threw the country into disarray. The Royalist general George Monck, who had in fact been a good friend of Cromwell, arranged for Charles II's return from exile. On May 1, 1660, Charles II was restored to the throne and England's brief years as a republic came to an end.

THE RESULTS SHOW THAT THE TRAP WAS SKILLFULLY BAITED

THE REIGATE SQUIRE (1893)

IN CONTEXT

TYPE
Short story

FIRST PUBLICATION
UK: June 1893
US: June 1893 (as "The Reigate Puzzle")

COLLECTION
The Memoirs of Sherlock Holmes, 1894

CHARACTERS
Colonel Hayter Old Military friend of Watson's.

Inspector Forrester Local police detective.

Old Mr. Cunningham Elderly local squire and justice of the peace.

Alec Cunningham Mr. Cunningham's son.

Mr. Acton Neighbor in a land dispute with the Cunninghams.

William Kirwan Victim.

W hen it was originally published in *The Strand Magazine* in June 1893, Conan Doyle's story about a landowning father and son was called "The Reigate Squire," referring to the father, Old Mr. Cunningham, only. When it was included in *The Memoirs of Sherlock Holmes*, however, it was retitled "The Reigate Squires," to include the son as well. To complicate matters further, when published in the US in *Harper's Weekly* (at the same time as the UK *Strand* publication) it was called simply "The Reigate Puzzle." Interestingly, this was also the title used by *Strand* illustrator Sidney Paget in his account book in March

To prove that the earth is spheroid, Pierre-Louis Moreau de Maupertuis, the model for Conan Doyle's villain, did experiments in Lapland in 1736.

1893, so it may be that "The Reigate Puzzle" was in fact Conan Doyle's original, working title.

Whatever title Conan Doyle preferred, the idea for the story came from "Health and Handwriting," an article published in the *Edinburgh Medical Journal* in January 1890 and sent to him by its author, Alexander Cargill. He wrote to Cargill in 1893, saying, "I would like now to give Holmes a torn slip of a document, and see how far he could reconstruct both it and the writers of it. I think, thanks to you, I could make it effective."

In 1927, Conan Doyle had to choose between this story, "The Adventure of the Bruce-Partington Plans," "The Crooked Man," "The Man with the Twisted Lip," "The *Gloria Scott*," "The Greek Interpreter," and "The Resident Patient" for the final spot in his list of his 12 favorite Holmes stories (see box, p.18). "I might as well draw the name out of a bag…" he wrote, "…they are all as good as I could make them." But in the end he chose "The Reigate Squire," on the basis that it was the story in which Holmes had shown the most ingenuity.

The exhausted hero

The setup for the story is unusually dramatic, and lays the ground for the parochial crime that follows. Holmes has just broken a major international conspiracy. The villain of the piece was "the most accomplished swindler in Europe," one Baron Maupertuis— named, with delicious irony on Conan Doyle's part, after one of the greatest French scientists and adventurers. Pierre-Louis Moreau de Maupertuis (1698–1759) was the leading champion of Newtonian science in 18th-century France, and led an extraordinary expedition to the Arctic to prove Newton's ideas »

Graphology

There was huge interest in the "scientific" study of personality in late Victorian times. Many people believed personality was revealed by physical traits, such as the pattern of bumps on the head— a now discredited idea called phrenology (see p.188). Others believed in handwriting analysis, with some experts claiming that subtle differences in handwriting could reveal life stories. The theory originated with French priest Jean-Hippolyte Michon (1806–1881) and his followers, who, from 1830, established the "science" that came to be called graphology.

In the same year that Conan Doyle wrote "The Reigate Squire," French psychologist Alfred Binet (1857–1911, pictured) published a key text on the subject, which he considered to be "the science of the future." Just a year later, graphology received a major blow when handwriting "experts" in France were exposed for their role in the conviction of Jewish artillery officer Alfred Dreyfus, wrongly accused of treason. Graphology never proved itself, and today it is considered a pseudoscience, like phrenology.

The deceptive letter that lured Kirwan to his death offers many clues to Holmes. Whoever wrote it was involved in the crime, and the time it occurred is clear. As Holmes observes, "Why was someone so anxious to get possession of it? Because it incriminated him."

The **corner** of the letter was "found between the **finger and thumb** of the dead man."

If you will only come round to the east gate you will will very much surprise you and be of the greatest service to you and also to Annie Morrison. But say nothing to anyone upon the matter.

at quarter to twelve learn what maybe

The varied **handwriting** shows that it was written by "**two persons** doing **alternative words**."

Holmes finds the **other part** of the letter in the **Cunninghams'** house.

about the shape of the world, during which he survived the winter conditions by sheltering in a tent.

Watson does not explain what Maupertuis's evil namesake, the baron, has actually done, stating that his schemes are not "fitting subjects for this series of sketches." However, it seems Holmes's success in bringing him down was such a feat that all of Europe is "ringing" with the detective's name, and his hotel room in Lyons is "ankle-deep with congratulatory telegrams."

Holmes, though, was so utterly worn out by the struggle that Watson had to rush to his side and escort him back to 221B baher Street. Caring as ever, Watson has decided that they should take up the offer of a quiet stay in the Surrey countryside around Reigate, at the home of Colonel Hayter, "a fine old soldier" and Watson's friend from his army days in Afghanistan.

And so, by the time they arrive at Colonel Hayter's house, we have a complete picture of Holmes, the exhausted hero of international crime fighting, and of the dependable Watson. The shift from Lyons to Reigate also allows Holmes to solve a local murder rather than a grand crime, without being any less the great detective.

I have usually found that there was method in his madness.
Dr. Watson

And so it begins

Their sojourn in Reigate has barely begun before news of a crime reaches Holmes's ears. There has been a break-in at the nearby home of old Mr. Acton, during which some very odd things were stolen, including a ball of string. The very next morning they hear news of a murder at the "fine old Queen Anne house" of some other neighbors, old Mr. Cunningham and his son Alec: the Reigate squires. Moments later, Inspector Forrester—"a smart, keen-faced young fellow"—arrives. He has heard that Holmes is staying locally and is eager for him to help with the investigation. Watson tries in vain to persuade Holmes to stay out of it for the sake of his health. But, as Holmes teases him, "The Fates are against you, Watson."

It is an intriguing case. The Cunninghams have both apparently witnessed a man wrestle with their coachman, William Kirwan, outside their house, shoot him dead in the struggle, then leap over the hedge and run away. The only clue is a scrap of paper found gripped in the dead coachman's fingers, on which is written "at quarter to twelve learn what maybe." This immediately sets Holmes's mind racing, but he keeps his ideas to himself for now.

Meeting the squires

Holmes and the inspector head off to investigate the murder scene, where Holmes observes another clue that he keeps to himself. Holmes, Watson, the inspector, and Colonel Hayter then return to the Cunninghams' house, where they are received by the father and son, the former elderly and with a "heavy-eyed face," the latter a cheery, flashily dressed young man.

The two men inquire about the investigation, and Inspector Forrester is about to tell them about the scrap of paper when Holmes falls to the ground as if in a fit. Inside the house, however, he quickly recovers, and explains that he has recently been under a great deal of stress. He then composes an offer of a reward for information, but makes an uncharacteristic error when writing "at a quarter to one" instead of "at a quarter to twelve." Old Mr. Cunningham happily corrects the text for him. Watson puts the apparent mistake down to Holmes's illness, but Holmes has in fact, with his customary ingenuity, erred deliberately in order to get the old man to write down the very same phrase,

"quarter to twelve," so that he can compare his handwriting with that on the piece of evidence.

Holmes then asks if he might be shown around the Cunninghams' home. When they are in old Mr. Cunningham's bedroom, he hangs back with Watson, and, when no one else is looking, he deliberately knocks over a small table with a carafe of water and a dish of oranges on it, before loudly blaming Watson. As a confused Watson and the inspector stoop to clear up the mess, they hear a sudden cry of "Help! Help! Murder!" coming from Alec's dressing room. Rushing in, they find Alec strangling Holmes,

with his father trying to wrestle a piece of paper from Holmes's grasp. Alec then tries to pull out a revolver, but within seconds both he and his father are under arrest. All that remains is for Holmes to explain how he solved the case.

Holmes tells all

Back at Colonel Hayter's house, Holmes explains his methods. The key to solving the case was to concentrate on the scrap of paper, rather than allowing himself to be distracted by the Cunninghams' witness statements. "It is of the highest importance in the art of detection," he insists, "to be »

In a rare physical attack, as drawn by Sidney Paget for *The Strand Magazine*, Holmes is overpowered and throttled by Alec Cunningham until Watson and Forrester rush to his aid.

Alec Cunningham

Young, energetic, and full of life and cheeriness—Alec Cunningham seems to be the very opposite of how a murderer would be expected to look and behave. When Watson first encounters him, he describes Alec as "a dashing young fellow"; there seems nothing furtive or dangerous in him. But, as Holmes is quick to realize, looks can be deceptive; indeed, Alec is a perfect illustration of Holmes's policy of the need to be wary of any kind of prejudice.

Alec is not only involved in the murder but is also the leader who bullies his elderly father into going along with him. Alec's *bonhomie* and fashionable clothes are a perfect mask for his brutal personality. He is perhaps the epitome of the rapacious English landowner with a sense of entitlement. His performance is so convincing that Inspector Forrester still thinks he is innocent even after seeing him try to strangle Holmes. Only when Alec pulls out his revolver does Forrester finally see the truth.

writers are related. It must have been that Alec coerced his father into writing the note with him, so that they were equally responsible.

Holmes's inferences are entirely plausible, but this is one instance in which Conan Doyle was wrong. Graphology has not turned out to be the exact forensic science that Holmes claims it to be, and it very rarely proves much help in criminal investigations. Experts can identify someone from their handwriting, even when that person tries to disguise it, but it is not possible to tell a person's age, character, or gender from their handwriting.

able to recognize, out of a number of facts, which are incidental and which vital."

Someone, Holmes says, must have torn a piece of paper from the murdered coachman's grip, leaving just the fragment found in his hand. If the murderer fled instantly, as the Cunninghams had said, it could not have been him. Could it therefore have been Alec, who was first on the scene?

Holmes explains how Forrester ignored this possibility because he assumed such respectable landowners could not be involved. "I make a point," Holmes says, "of never having any prejudices, and of following docilely wherever fact may lead me." This is a central plank in Holmes's methods. He knows how easy it is to be blinded by preconceptions and so miss vital clues, which is why the police so often get it wrong. Even he must be vigilant to ensure he does not fall into the same trap.

The handwriting on the scrap of paper yielded key clues to Holmes's sharp eyes. Holmes, it seems, is an expert in graphology: determining someone's character from their handwriting (see box, p.127). He

explains how differences in the shape of the letters reveal that the writing was the work of two people. One has a stronger hand, and wrote parts of the message first, leaving the weaker hand to fill in the gaps. Holmes asserts that the stronger hand is that of the ringleader; that it is firmer and steadier also suggests that it was written by the younger of the pair. Similarities in the shaping of the letters also indicates that the

Henry George (1839–1897) was an influential writer and politician who argued that the benefits derived from resources and opportunities belonged to all—not just wealthy landowners.

On closer inspection

An examination of the crime scene confirmed to Holmes that Alec's witness statement was false on at least two counts. Firstly, the nature of the murdered man's wound and the lack of powder-blackening around it showed Holmes, a pioneer in the science of ballistics, that the gun must have been fired from at least four yards away, and not at point-blank range. Secondly, there was no trace of any boot marks beyond the hedge that Alec claimed the murderer had leapt over. Alec, therefore, was lying, and must himself have been the murderer—in which case, he must also have torn the piece of paper from the dead man's hand, and most likely thrust it into his dressing-gown pocket.

With the Cunninghams firmly in his sight, Holmes then sought a motive—and in the initial burglary he found one: the men were looking to destroy a document that proved Mr. Acton's claim on half their land. When they could not find it, they took the strange items to make it seem like a burglary.

Land ownership was a hot issue at the time Conan Doyle was writing. In 1873, the UK government had commissioned "a second Domesday book" to record who owned each piece of land in the country. It was not only a huge work, but also political dynamite, since it revealed that just 4.5 percent of people owned all of the land in the UK, while 95.5 percent owned nothing. At the same time, 100,000 copies of American land reformer Henry George's radical book *Progress and Poverty* were sold in the 1880s. In 1889, the Land Nationalization Society was formed to campaign for land to become the common property of all, and then in 1892 Alfred R Wallace wrote the best-selling *Land Nationalization*. Thus greedy, conniving landowners were very much in the spotlight.

Diversionary tactics

With a motive established and strong evidence pointing to the two men, Holmes needed the piece of paper that had been torn from

I tumbled down in a sort of fit and so changed the conversation.
Sherlock Holmes

Kirwan's hand. Once inside the Cunninghams' house, Holmes had to create a diversion that would enable him to slip into Alec's room and find the piece of paper—hence he knocked over the table and pinned the blame on Watson. However, the Cunninghams followed him, and, seeing that he had found the note, they had become desperate.

Evidently, Kirwan had seen the Cunninghams in Mr. Acton's house as they searched for the document, and had attempted to blackmail them as a result. The torn paper was a letter primarily designed to lure Kirwan to his death, but also cleverly worded in order to imply that he was guilty of the theft, thus staining his character too. The idea had been Alec's—"a stroke of positive genius on his part," says Holmes admiringly.

Having solved the crime, Holmes feels entirely rejuvenated. "Watson," he says cheerfully, "I think our quiet rest in the country has been a distinct success, and I shall certainly return much invigorated to Baker Street tomorrow." ∎

Disputes of land ownership, such as that between the Cunninghams and Acton, were common in the 19th century, as ownership of land was based on voluntary registration.

ONE OF THE STRANGEST CASES WHICH EVER PERPLEXED A MAN'S BRAIN
THE CROOKED MAN (1893)

IN CONTEXT

TYPE
Short story

FIRST PUBLICATION
UK: July 1893
US: July 1893

COLLECTION
The Memoirs of Sherlock Holmes, 1894

CHARACTERS
Colonel James Barclay Commander of the Royal Mallows.

Nancy Barclay (neé Nancy Devoy) Colonel Barclay's beautiful wife.

Miss Morrison Young friend of Nancy Barclay.

Corporal Henry "Harry" Wood Formerly of the Mallows, and an old comrade of Colonel Barclay.

While it did not feature on the official list of Conan Doyle's favorite Holmes stories (see p.18), "The Crooked Man" is one he held in particularly high regard. Although narrated by Watson, much of the story is in fact recounted by Holmes himself, when he calls on his friend one evening. In a clever move by Conan Doyle, strategic gaps in Holmes's story allow Watson to save key details and keep the reader guessing.

Yet, before embarking on his tale, Holmes remarks that Watson must have had a busy day. When

The Indian Rebellion of 1857 saw several states rise up against the ruling East India Company. It lasted a year, and once it was quashed, Britain imposed direct rule as the new British Raj.

the astonished Watson asks how he knew, Holmes replies, "Elementary," before citing a few simple clues he has observed. It is the closest he ever comes to uttering the immortal catchphrase, "Elementary, my dear Watson." Although Holmes often refers to the doctor as "my dear Watson," never in any story does he use the full, now iconic, phrase.

Holmes's story

The story Holmes has to tell Watson concerns his investigation of the mysterious death of Colonel Barclay in Aldershot. After the colonel's wife, Nancy, returned home, much distressed, from a church errand with her friend Miss Morrison, the couple had been heard arguing in the morning room. Nancy was heard to shout "David!" twice—odd since the colonel's name is James. A crash and a piercing scream led her servants to try to break down the door, but it appeared to have been locked from the inside, so the coachman entered through the open French windows. Mrs. Barclay lay insensible on the couch and Colonel Barclay was dead, with blood streaming from his head and a ghastly expression on his face.

It seems like murder, and Mrs. Barclay is the prime suspect, but the facts don't add up. Holmes persuades Miss Morrison to reveal what upset Nancy. She tells of an earlier encounter with a deformed man ("a dreadful-looking creature") who was known to Nancy. Holmes tracks down the man's lodgings, finds that his name is Henry Wood, and deduces from an Indian rupee given to his landlady that Wood is connected to the Barclays' past in India, where they met and married.

Betrayal in Bhurtee

The following morning, Holmes and Watson set off to Aldershot to call on Wood. Hearing that Nancy Barclay could be tried for murder, Wood tells his story. Thirty years ago, he and the colonel were young officers in the same corps in the British Army in India, and both fell in love with Nancy. It was Henry that Nancy loved, but her father was set on her marrying Barclay, who was destined to be an officer. During the Indian Mutiny of 1857, Barclay saw a chance to dipose of his rival, and betrayed Wood to the rebels. Wood escaped, but was disfigured as a result of being tortured. He roamed India as a street entertainer before returning to England. Then, by chance, he had seen Mrs. Barclay and followed her home. When Wood burst in through the French window, Barclay had dropped down dead, hitting his head as he fell. The "bare sight of me was like a bullet through his guilty heart," claims Wood. Mrs. Barclay had fainted, so Wood hurried to unlock the door and call for help, then realized how things looked, and fled, taking the key.

An autopsy exonerates Mrs. Barclay, and Holmes allows the matter rest—natural justice has been done, so why involve the police? When Watson asks why Mrs. Barclay called her husband David, Holmes refers him to "the small affair" of David and Bathsheba in the Old Testament. So "the crooked man" in the story's title may not be the deformed Wood after all, but in fact the morally corrupted Barclay. ∎

> …the problem was already one of interest, but my observations soon made me realise that it was in truth much more extraordinary than would at first sight appear.
> **Sherlock Holmes**

David and Bathsheba

Holmes believes that when the churchgoing Mrs. Barclay calls her husband "David," she is invoking the Old Testament story of King David (Samuel 2, Chapter 11). The king spied Bathsheba, wife of Uriah, who was one of the king's soldiers, bathing one day, and he made love to her. When Bathsheba became pregnant, David tried to persuade Uriah to sleep with her so he might think the baby was his. But Uriah, as a soldier on duty, refused. In desperation, David had Uriah sent to the front line in battle, where he was certain to be killed. With Uriah dead, David married Bathsheba. But he was racked with guilt, inspiring Psalm 51, (*Miserere Mei, Deus*: "Have Mercy on Me, Oh God"). Apparently Barclay had suffered the same guilt, for Holmes learns that he was often "sunk in the deepest gloom" for days at a time. The parallels with the situation between Barclay, Wood, and Nancy in India are striking, and suggest Conan Doyle may have used the Old Testament story as a basis for the plot of "The Crooked Man."

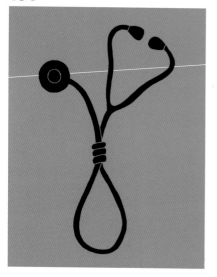

I CAN READ IN A MAN'S EYE WHEN IT IS HIS OWN SKIN THAT HE IS FRIGHTENED FOR
THE RESIDENT PATIENT (1893)

IN CONTEXT

TYPE
Short story

FIRST PUBLICATION
UK: August 1893
US: August 1893

COLLECTION
***The Memoirs of Sherlock Holmes*, 1894**

CHARACTERS
Dr. Percy Trevelyan
Recently qualified doctor.

Mr. Blessington Percy's "resident patient" who sets him up in a medical practice.

Russian count and his son Percy's new, cataleptic patient, whose son accompanies him to the practice.

With its violent backstory, this murky case is one of several in *The Memoirs of Sherlock Holmes*—including "The Gloria Scott" (pp.116–19) and "The Crooked Man" (pp.132–33)—that turns on revelations of a character's criminal past. It is also notable for its inclusion (in certain editions) of a passage on mind-reading, which first appeared in "The Cardboard Box" (pp.110–11). When Conan Doyle excluded "The Cardboard Box" from the first published collection (see box, p.111) he was loath to lose this passage and included it here.

A case of the jitters
Holmes has been approached by a doctor, Percy Trevelyan. Only recently licensed and low on funds, he had accepted a business offer from a Mr. Blessington, a man with "thousands" to invest, who set Trevelyan up in a practice, in return for lodgings, a profit share, and the supervision of his heart condition.

Trevelyan consults Holmes because his "resident patient" has recently become inexplicably jittery. After a burglary nearby, Blessington insisted they increase the house's security, and then, a few days ago,

Catalepsy

Holmes remarks to Watson that catalepsy—the Russian count's fraudulent ailment—is "a very easy complaint to imitate." Catalepsy causes debilitating muscle spasms that turn the body stiff and unresponsive to stimuli. It is often associated with psychological conditions, such as schizophrenia. Although medical knowledge of nervous complaints was growing in the 19th century, catalepsy was often employed by writers to help suggest an atmosphere

of intense anxiety, even insanity. Its morbidly compelling effects are employed in Edgar Allan Poe's "The Fall of the House of Usher" (1839) and in Dickens's 1853 novel *Bleak House*.

Trevelyan himself takes notes when his patient appears to fall into catalepsy's grip, but his treatment—the inhalation of amyl nitrite—was not a common one. This substance was in fact normally used as a remedy for heart complaints, as it increases the heart rate. Today, amyl nitrite is more often used as a recreational drug ("poppers").

an odd incident had left him in tears. Trevelyan had received a new patient—an elderly Russian count with catalepsy. His son had brought him, and remained in the waiting room. During the examination, the patient had a fit, so Trevelyan left to get medicine—only to discover both men had vanished when he returned.

The next day the men came back to resume the consultation, apologizing for their abrupt exit. Later, when Blessington returned from a walk, he claimed an intruder had been in his room. A footprint on the carpet confirmed this, and Trevelyan realized that the count's son must have slipped upstairs from the waiting room. The incident had left Blessington crying and almost incoherent with fear.

Holmes accompanies Trevelyan to the practice. He is sure that the men were after Blessington himself, rather than anything in the room, but Blessington insists he has no idea who the intruders are. Holmes leaves, disgusted, saying that he cannot help if he refuses to tell the truth.

Criminal justice
The next day, Blessington's corpse is found hanging from a noose hitched up in his room. In spite of the police's initial verdict of suicide, Holmes's

> It was a dreadful sight which met us as we entered the bedroom door… he was scarce human in his appearance.
> **Dr. Watson**

deductions show that this is murder. Four cigar ends in the fireplace, as well as footmarks on the stairs, show that three people had surreptitiously made their way upstairs during the night. A screwdriver and screws left in the room suggest that the three felons had planned to build a set of gallows, before deciding to make use of a light fixture to "execute" Blessington.

Investigations reveal that the trio were in the notorious "Worthingdon bank gang"—a group of murderous robbers. Blessington (whose real name is Sutton) was a key member, but when the gang was caught, he had turned informer and escaped prison. His sordid death was a vengeance 15 years in the making: on their release, the men had hunted him down, two of them posing as the Russian count and his son. The three assailants are not caught at the time, but Watson

Cavendish Square, close to Harley Street, was—and still is—a well-known site for medical practices. Blessington's patronage enables Percy Trevelyan to practice in the vicinity.

reports at the end of the tale that they were later aboard an "ill-fated steamer" that vanished at sea.

The proceeds of crime
Trevelyan shares some similarities with his creator. Conan Doyle had also struggled with a "want of capital" when trying to establish a medical practice. Trevelyan has the look of "an artist rather than of a surgeon," and has written a monograph on obscure nervous lesions—the subject of Conan Doyle's own university thesis. And both the author and his character are supported by the proceeds of crime, whether Blessington's stolen loot or Holmes's commercial success. ∎

TO THE LOGICIAN ALL THINGS SHOULD BE SEEN EXACTLY AS THEY ARE
THE GREEK INTERPRETER (1893)

IN CONTEXT

TYPE
Short story

FIRST PUBLICATION
UK: September 1893
US: September 1893

COLLECTION
***The Memoirs of Sherlock Holmes*, 1894**

CHARACTERS
Mycroft Holmes Sherlock Holmes's older brother and influential government official.

Mr. Melas Mycroft's neighbor, a linguist and interpreter.

Harold Latimer Young Englishman.

Sophy Kratides Harold's Greek girlfriend.

Paul Kratides A Greek national and brother of Sophy.

Wilson Kemp Latimer's associate.

At the outset of this story, Watson says he has long suspected that Holmes might be an orphan, given his great reluctance to talk about his past. However, as the duo are discussing the recurrence of traits within a family line, Holmes suddenly reveals that he is descended from "country squires," and that his grandmother's sister was a French artist (the "Vernet" he cites was a real person, with a special talent for making precise drawings from memory). And, while musing that his deductive skills may have been hereditary, he casually mentions that his brother possesses the same gift. It is a wonderfully understated

Some of my most interesting cases have come to me in this way through Mycroft.
Sherlock Holmes

dramatic turn—up until this point, Watson has never heard of Mycroft Holmes. The detective goes on to describe his older brother as by far the superior thinker, but with a lethargic personality that makes him unsuited to detective work. Mycroft rarely ventures beyond his club, or Whitehall, where he puts his "extraordinary faculty for figures" to use in the civil service.

A forced interrogation
Mycroft Holmes comes up in the conversation because he has just summoned his brother to his club, in order to pass on a case brought to him by his Greek neighbor, Mr. Melas, who works as an interpreter. Two days earlier, Melas was hired by a menacing young man called Harold Latimer. He was whisked off in a blacked-out cab to a grand house outside of London, where Latimer and his associate, Wilson Kemp, forced him to relate a set of demands to their "visitor," a gagged and emaciated Greek man, and get him to sign a legal document.

The man was stubbornly uncooperative, but Melas managed to extract information from him surreptitiously in Greek, without revealing it to the men: his name

Holmes (Jeremy Brett) worked with his larger-than-life yet shadowy sibling Mycroft (Charles Gray) to uncover the motives of a brutal duo, in an episode from the 1985 British television series.

was Paul Kratides and he was being held captive and starved. The interview broke off when a young Greek woman entered the room unexpectedly; it was apparent that she knew Paul, although she seemed astonished to see him.

Melas was then deposited back in London, with a strongly worded warning that he should tell no one of his visit. However, despite his timidity, he was anxious to help his countryman, so he went to the police, and also to Mycroft, who placed a newspaper advertisement offering a reward for information about the whereabouts of two Greek nationals: Paul Kratides and a woman called Sophy.

Murder and vengeance

Later that day, a man responds to the advertisement. He provides the address of a house in Kent where Sophy (and Paul) are located, and the brothers and Watson set off to investigate. En route, they go to pick up Melas, but he has been abducted by Kemp. When they arrive in Kent, the house is dark and apparently deserted. Holmes observes two sets of wheel tracks in its driveway—the outbound ones are much deeper, which confirms the villains' recent departure, along with Sophy, in a luggage-laden carriage.

They find Melas and Kratides tied up in an upstairs room, where they are slowly being poisoned by carbon monoxide fumes from a charcoal brazier. It is too late to save Kratides, but Melas recovers. Mycroft's correspondent then fills in the gaps: during a visit to England, wealthy Sophy Kratides had been seduced by Latimer. When Paul, her brother, arrived to halt their affair, Latimer and Kemp held him prisoner, but the language barrier thwarted their plans for him to sign over the family's money.

The story ends ambiguously: months later, Holmes learns that two Englishmen have been found dead in Budapest; the police think the pair stabbed one another, but Holmes hopes Sophy has somehow managed to avenge Paul's death. ∎

Victorian gentlemen's clubs

Mycroft's members-only club, the Diogenes, is fictitious, but its location in the aristocratic St. James's area of the West End, and its strict rules and emphasis on privacy and exclusivity, are an accurate representation of the gentlemen's clubs that flourished during the Victorian era, some of which are still going strong today. Watson says that the Diogenes is a few doors down from the Carlton Club, a genuine institution that had been a meeting place for Conservative politicians since its 1834 founding. Mycroft's club was possibly based on the real-life Athenaeum, founded in 1824 for those who enjoyed "the life of the mind," since it too had a "Strangers' Room," the only place where conversation was permitted. When Conan Doyle had Holmes remark that the Diogenes "contains the most unsociable and unclubbable men in town," he may have been making a tongue-in-cheek joke about the Athenaeum, of which he was a long-standing member.

THE MOST DIFFICULT CRIME TO TRACK IS THE ONE WHICH IS PURPOSELESS
THE NAVAL TREATY (1893)

IN CONTEXT

TYPE
Short story

FIRST PUBLICATION
UK: October 1893
US: October 1893

COLLECTION
***The Memoirs of Sherlock Holmes*, 1894**

CHARACTERS
Percy Phelps Clerk in the Foreign Office.

Lord Holdhurst Foreign Minister and Phelps's uncle.

Annie Harrison Phelps's fiancée and nurse.

Joseph Harrison Brother of Annie.

Mr. and Mrs. Tangey Foreign Office commissionaire and his wife.

Charles Gorot Phelps's colleague at the Foreign Office.

Mr. Forbes Scotland Yard detective.

A t the start of this story, Watson receives a letter from his former schoolmate Percy Phelps, who is bedridden at his family home, Briarbrae, in Woking. Phelps is suffering from "brain fever" caused by a distressing event: he believes his career is possibly ruined, and he is requesting the help of Holmes. Conan Doyle is particularly fond of using the now-archaic term "brain fever" to refer to nervous illness, and appears in several Holmes stories, including "The Adventure of the Copper Beeches" (pp.98–101), "The Crooked Man" (pp.132–33), and "The Musgrave Ritual" (pp.120–25).

At Briarbrae. Watson and Holmes meet Joseph Harrison, the brother of Phelps's fiancée, Annie. In a ground-floor room, where in fact Joseph has been staying until recently, the delicate patient, Phelps, outlines his predicament from the sofa. As with "The Adventure of the Engineer's Thumb" (pp.90–3), this scene is reminiscent of Sigmund Freud's "couch" consultations that would soon become a fashionable treatment for nervous complaints.

Brain fever

Of the five short stories in which "brain fever" appears, three are in the *Memoirs*. It's unclear why Conan Doyle returned to the condition so frequently during the composition of this collection of stories. However, in each case apart from "The Naval Treaty" its victims are women; if Conan Doyle is implying that "weaker" women are more susceptible, perhaps it is Phelps's apparent feebleness that helps him to fit into that category. Either way, caused by acute anxiety and stress, the ailment was typically associated with the faint-hearted and formed a precursor to the similar late 19th-century complaint of "hysteria"—also conventionally associated with women, and considered spurious by some. Victorian readers would have been familiar with the term as part of a whole lexicon devoted to the gray area surrounding our gray matter. Today, "brain fever" is sometimes employed to refer to certain symptoms of meningitis and encephalitis, but it has mostly fallen out of use.

The British Foreign Office sat at the heart of the Empire in Victorian Britain. It was a place of complex diplomacy and political maneuvering, and a prize target for international espionage.

The series of events

Almost 10 weeks previously, Percy Phelps's uncle—the Foreign Minister Lord Holdhurst—entrusted his nephew with hand-copying a secret treaty between Britain and Italy. To contemporary readers this would have been thrillingly up to date: the "Triple Alliance" between Germany, Austria–Hungary, and Italy, in 1882, was a key part of the system of allegiances that would lead to World War I, and there was indeed a secret agreement between Italy and Britain in 1887.

It was clear to Phelps that the French or Russian embassies would pay handsomely for such classified information, so, as instructed by Holdhurst, he waited until his colleagues had all left work before carrying out the task. Feeling sleepy, Phelps rang the bell for some coffee and, to his surprise, it was the commissionaire's wife, Mrs. Tangey, who took his order. When the coffee failed to arrive, Phelps went to discover the cause of the delay and found Mr. Tangey, the commissionaire, asleep at the front entrance with the kettle boiling over—and no sign of Mrs. Tangey.

Suddenly, the bell rang from the office Phelps had been working in. Panicked at the thought of someone being in the same room as the top-secret document, he dashed upstairs to discover that it had disappeared. Phelps realized the thief must have entered via the side door; he had used the main staircase and so would have seen him or her entering the building.

A policeman on duty outside the Foreign Office saw only one person, whose description fitted that of Mrs. Tangey, leave via the side door. Despite the commissionaire's claim that his wife's integrity was beyond reproach, Phelps chased her home. He and a Scotland Yard detective named Forbes questioned her about the document and she was searched, but nothing was found. Unsure what to do, Phelps made his way home, having missed the train he was supposed to have caught earlier with Joseph Harrison.

An impossible situation

Several stories above ground level and with no possible hiding places, Phelps's office provides no clues. There were no footprints at the scene of the crime (even though it was a wet night) and no evidence that someone had been smoking there, which disappoints Holmes since stray ash at a crime scene often provides his first clue (in *A Study in Scarlet*, (pp.36–45) he mentions making "a special study of cigar ashes"). The description of Phelps's workplace fits the real Foreign Office—a grand classical building completed in the 1860s by the architect George Gilbert Scott. (Scott's own grandson, Giles, was to design London's red telephone booth—almost as much as an icon of the city as Holmes himself).

A conspiracy?

To learn more about the case, Holmes and Watson visit detective Forbes, who is distinctly unfriendly. He does reveal that Mrs. Tangey is of bad character, being a drinker with money problems, and that he suspects she knows something about the crime, although he has no proof. Other less likely suspects »

A cold hand seemed to close round my heart. Someone, then, was in that room where my precious treaty lay upon the table.
Percy Phelps

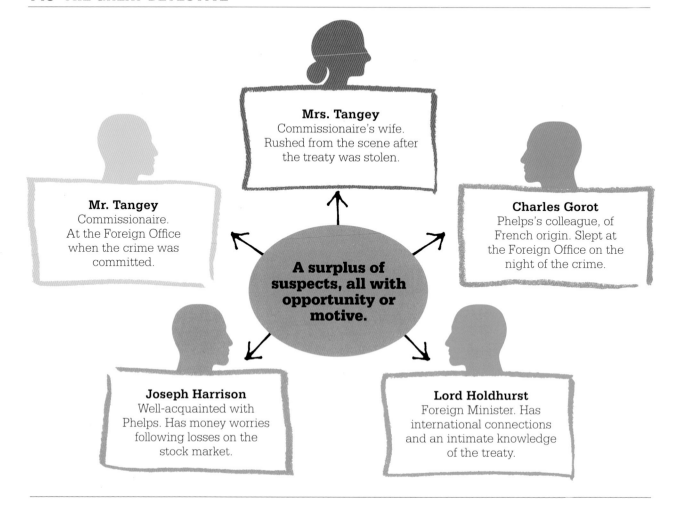

Mrs. Tangey
Commissionaire's wife.
Rushed from the scene after
the treaty was stolen.

Mr. Tangey
Commissionaire.
At the Foreign Office
when the crime was
committed.

Charles Gorot
Phelps's colleague, of
French origin. Slept at
the Foreign Office on the
night of the crime.

**A surplus of
suspects, all with
opportunity or
motive.**

Joseph Harrison
Well-acquainted with
Phelps. Has money worries
following losses on the
stock market.

Lord Holdhurst
Foreign Minister. Has
international connections
and an intimate knowledge
of the treaty.

are the commissionaire himself and Phelps's colleague, Charles Gorot, whose French name has aroused suspicion, since it suggests a motive for passing the treaty to the French government. The fact that Gorot is a name "of Huguenot extraction" is relevant here, although unexplained in the story. The Huguenots were persecuted French Protestants who took refuge in England from the late 17th century, so it is unlikely that Gorot would maintain much allegiance to France. In any case, the hapless Forbes has amassed no real evidence against anyone.

On Downing Street, Lord Holdhurst tells Holmes that the treaty could not yet have fallen into Russian or French hands, since there would already have been dire consequences as a result—and as yet nothing has occurred. When Holmes remarks that the document may not have been passed on due to the thief succumbing to a "sudden illness," Holdhurst seems to suspect his nephew, suggesting that it might be "an attack of brain fever, for example?"

After a nighttime intruder then tries to break into Phelps's room at Briarbrae, Phelps begins to wonder whether there is some kind of real conspiracy against him. Holmes suggests Phelps come to London with him and Watson for the night, but at the last minute Holmes tells

them that he has no intention of catching the train and is instead going to stay in Woking to "clear up" a few points.

At 221B Baker Street the next morning, Holmes returns bedraggled and wounded, but at the breakfast table he takes a theatrical relish in revealing, hidden under a plate cover, the original treaty. He then explains that after leaving Phelps and Watson the night before, he returned covertly to Briarbrae. There he had caught Joseph Harrison making his way into Phelps's room, lifting a floorboard and trying to leave with the treaty, which he had hidden there during his earlier occupancy of the room.

> I begin to believe that I am the unconscious centre of some monstrous conspiracy, and that my life is aimed at as well as my honour.
> **Percy Phelps**

Case analysis

The main difficulty in this case lies in a surplus of evidence. As Holmes says, "What was vital was overlaid and hidden by what was irrelevant." Mrs. Tangey's dubious character is a good example of this, and the treaty's great importance is also misleading: the reader assumes that the theft of the document was planned with a clear political aim in mind, yet the haste with which Harrison steals the document in fact suggests a purely opportunistic crime. It is only at the end of the story that Harrison's losses on the stock market, and therefore a motive for the crime, are revealed.

Many Holmesian scholars are dissatisfied with some of the details in this story, such as the extraordinary coincidence that Harrison enters the room precisely while Phelps is checking on the coffee, the fact that he decides to act so suddenly, and that he is not spotted leaving the building by the policeman. Also under scrutiny is the inexplicable fact that the treaty had to be hand-copied, given that mechanical methods of duplication already existed. Critics have even suggested that Harrison and Mrs. Tangey must have been in league with one another, but Conan Doyle offered as little subsequent comment on this theory as Holmes himself does within the narrative.

Enlightenment man

Of interest in this story are hints about Holmes's own world view. While discussing the crime with Phelps, Holmes digresses to briefly speculate on the nature of religion, saying, "Our highest assurance of the goodness of Providence seems to me to rest in the flowers." This comment—which Holmes refers to as a "deduction"—is inspired by his observation of a beautiful moss rose, and perhaps hints at a religious faith of his own. Holmes's idealistic comments carry through to his and Watson's train journey back to London. From the elevated section of railroad between Clapham Junction and Waterloo, he points out the "brick islands" of the Board Schools, ecstatically calling them "Beacons of the future! …Capsules, with hundreds of bright little seeds in each, out of which will spring the wiser, better England of the future." Established after the Education Act of 1870, these were the first schools to be funded by taxpayers.

The overtly liberal perspective here—perhaps a reflection of Conan Doyle's own opinions—tallies with an implicit criticism of a nepotistic Foreign Office. The word "nepotism" is derived from the Latin for nephew, which has particular resonance in this story. After all, Phelps owes his job to his uncle's prominent position, and the chaos of this case begins after Holdhurst entrusts his nephew with such a valuable document. The criticism also reflects political shifts in Britain: although William Gladstone's Liberal government was in power when "The Naval Treaty" was published in 1893, the story's 1889 setting would imply that Conan Doyle was leveling his criticism at the 3rd Marquess of Salisbury's previous Conservative administration. ■

Holmes frequently makes theatrical gestures, especially when proving his powers of deduction. Here, in Paget's illustration for *The Strand Magazine*, he reveals the stolen treaty over breakfast.

DANGER IS PART OF MY TRADE

THE FINAL PROBLEM (1893)

IN CONTEXT

TYPE
Short story

FIRST PUBLICATION
UK: December 1893
US: December 1893

COLLECTION
The Memoirs of Sherlock Holmes, 1894

CHARACTERS
Professor Moriarty
Mathematics professor turned criminal genius; Holmes's archenemy and nemesis.

Mycroft Holmes Elder brother of Sherlock Holmes.

Peter Steiler Landlord of the Englischer Hof hotel in Meiringen.

Of all the Holmes tales written by Conan Doyle, none caused as much of a stir as "The Final Problem." Most significantly, of course, it tells of Holmes's untimely death, but it also features the infamous villain Professor Moriarty (pp.28–9)—the most brilliant of all criminal masterminds and Holmes's nemesis.

When the story was published in *The Strand Magazine*, the reaction was consternation, shock, even outrage. Letter after letter of protest arrived on the desks of the *Strand* and Conan Doyle, with one woman famously beginning her note to the author with, "You brute!" In London, black armbands were

> I alone know the absolute truth of the matter, and I am satisfied that the time has come when no good purpose is to be served by its suppression.
> **Dr. Watson**

worn and the circulation of the *Strand* dropped so substantially that it almost closed down (see p.324).

Justifiable homicide
Conan Doyle was taken aback by his readers' extreme reaction. Later he defended himself by saying, "It was not murder, but justifiable homicide in self-defence, since, if I had not killed him, he would certainly have killed me." He had long felt that Holmes was taking up too much of his life, and churning out story after story to deadline was a demanding task that took precious time away from his serious literary work. Also, by 1893, both Conan Doyle's father Charles and his wife Louise were seriously ill. Charles died in October, and that same month Louise was diagnosed with tuberculosis and given just a few months to live—although in the end she survived for another 13 years (see pp.14–21).

This lantern slide made in 1895 captures Victoria Station much as it would have looked to Holmes and Watson as they made their escape to mainland Europe, via Canterbury.

It was while Conan Doyle and Louise were vacationing in the Alps in August 1893 that the author made the decision to kill off Holmes. "He is becoming such a burden to me," he told a friend, "that it makes my life unbearable." It was there, in the Swiss Alps, that he found the perfect location for a fittingly dramatic finale: the spectacular Reichenbach Falls. When he had finished writing the story, Conan Doyle wrote in his notebook simply: "Killed Holmes."

The hunter hunted
In most of the other stories, Holmes is the hunter, sniffing out clues and finally cornering his quarry. However, in "The Final Problem" it is Holmes himself who is the prey, pursued relentlessly by the evil genius Moriarty. The entire tale is a chase in which Holmes must use his great skill not for his usual deductions, but instead to avoid capture. As Watson says, it is now as if Holmes himself were the criminal.

Watson engages us in the tragedy of Holmes's death right from the start, opening with, "It is with a heavy heart that I take up my pen to write these the last words in which I shall ever record the singular gifts by which my friend Mr. Sherlock Holmes was distinguished." He says he has already stopped writing about Holmes and is only telling this story now because Moriarty's brother, Colonel James Moriarty, is spreading false rumors, and he wants to set the record straight.

The last battle
The ground has already been laid for Holmes's final disappearance from the world. He is no longer needed by society, or by Watson, in the way that he once was. Watson is not the disoriented young man who first met Holmes in *A Study in Scarlet* (pp.36–45); he is now married, with an established medical practice. The two no longer have the intimate relationship they once enjoyed, and see each other rarely. As for »

A criminal mind

In his creation of Moriarty, Conan Doyle was influenced by the theories of 19th-century Italian criminologist Cesar Lombroso (pp.310–15). Lombroso believed that some people inherit an irredeemably criminal nature, and that their nasty tendencies are evident in their appearance. Conan Doyle gave Moriarty all the benefits of nurture so as to emphasize the overwhelming effects of nature: Moriarty was born into privilege and became a mathematics prodigy and later a university professor, but his diabolical "hereditary tendencies" were ultimately destined to control him. Conan Doyle would use these same presuppositions to create Colonel Moran 10 years later, in "The Empty House." For Moriarty, the inherited criminal tendency is particularly dangerous because it is allied to a brilliant brain. His high-domed forehead is a feature he shares with the similarly clever Holmes (and his brother Mycroft), but Moriarty is likened to a lizard or a snake, a sign of the evil behind his genius.

Holmes himself, he has successfully foiled the plans of many dangerous criminals. "I have not lived wholly in vain," he declares prophetically; "the air of London is the sweeter for my presence." But before he departs, there is one last villain to defeat—Moriarty, the greatest of them all.

One April evening in 1891, Watson is surprised by a visit from a clearly alarmed Holmes. When Watson asks what he is afraid of, Holmes answers, "Of air-guns." As we later learn in "The Adventure of the Empty House" (pp.162–67), this is the silent, deadly weapon used by Moriarty's marksman,

If I could beat that man, if I could free society of him, I should feel that my own career had reached its summit.
Sherlock Holmes

Colonel Moran. Holmes knows that he is in danger, and invites Watson to come with him on a trip to the Continent. Realizing that Watson needs to know more, Holmes begins to tell him about Moriarty.

The Napoleon of crime

With a stroke of genius, Conan Doyle explains why Moriarty has not appeared in earlier tales. "Ay, there's the genius and the wonder of the thing!" Holmes cries. "The man pervades London, and no one has heard of him." Moriarty presides over a vast criminal network, pulling all the strings, and yet with the skill of a master chess player, he completely avoids being linked to it. He has such safeguards against being identified or having any crime proved against him that the police are never able to bring him to trial, even though hundreds of crimes—forgeries, robberies, and murders—have been committed at his bidding.

Watson and Holmes, played by David Burke (in his last appearance as Watson) and Jeremy Brett, are pictured here in the 1985 television adaptation of "The Final Problem."

Conan Doyle based Moriarty on a real master criminal named Adam Worth (see p.29), whom he had heard about from William Pinkerton, the head of the American Pinkerton detective agency. At the time Conan Doyle was writing, Worth was languishing in a Belgian jail for a petty crime, where his true identity as the head of the world's greatest organized crime network was unknown to local authorities. American-born Worth was indeed

a criminal mastermind who ruled the roost in London, posing as a respectable art lover and racing man. The police could never pin anything on him and dubbed him "the Napoleon of crime." In deference to Worth, Conan Doyle adopted this same nickname for Moriarty.

The dark side of Holmes

Adam Worth provided the bones for Moriarty, but Conan Doyle's character is a complex figure. Moriarty is Holmes's terrible mirror image—a distorted reflection of the great detective's remarkable power. When Holmes describes Moriarty as "a genius, a philosopher, an abstract thinker," he could easily be talking about himself. Holmes creates a chilling picture of how Moriarty operates. "He sits motionless, like a spider in the centre of its web, but that web has a thousand radiations, and he knows well every quiver of each of them." This sounds remarkably similar to Watson's description of Holmes in "The Cardboard Box" (pp.110–11): the detective "loved to lie in the very centre of five millions of people, with his filaments stretching out and running through them, responsive to every little rumour or suspicion of unsolved crime."

The dark alter ego, sometimes called *doppelgänger*, is a classic feature of Gothic fiction. It emerges in stories such as Mary Shelley's *Frankenstein* (1818), Oscar Wilde's *The Picture of Dorian Gray* (1891), and Robert Louis Stevenson's *Strange Case of Dr. Jekyll and Mr. Hyde* (1886). Moriarty is the Mr Hyde to Holmes's Dr. Jekyll. And, just as Jekyll and Hyde are one and the same, so Holmes is much more intertwined with Moriarty than he would care to admit. In order to solve crimes, Holmes has to think like a criminal, and he becomes, »

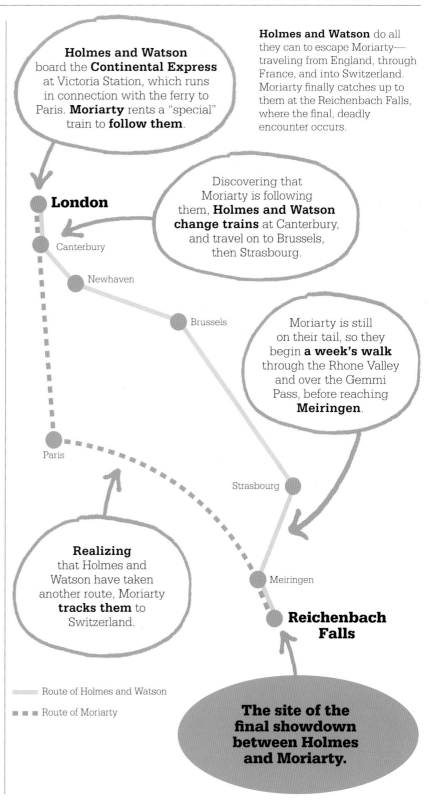

Holmes and Watson board the **Continental Express** at Victoria Station, which runs in connection with the ferry to Paris. **Moriarty** rents a "special" train to **follow them**.

Holmes and Watson do all they can to escape Moriarty—traveling from England, through France, and into Switzerland. Moriarty finally catches up to them at the Reichenbach Falls, where the final, deadly encounter occurs.

Discovering that Moriarty is following them, **Holmes and Watson change trains** at Canterbury, and travel on to Brussels, then Strasbourg.

Moriarty is still on their tail, so they begin **a week's walk** through the Rhone Valley and over the Gemmi Pass, before reaching **Meiringen**.

Realizing that Holmes and Watson have taken another route, Moriarty **tracks them** to Switzerland.

London
Canterbury
Newhaven
Brussels
Paris
Strasbourg
Meiringen
Reichenbach Falls

Route of Holmes and Watson
Route of Moriarty

The site of the final showdown between Holmes and Moriarty.

to some extent, tainted by the association. Indeed, as Holmes says to Watson of Moriarty, "My horror at his crimes was lost in my admiration at his skill."

Mortal combat

Holmes tells Watson of his struggle to bring Moriarty to justice as though they are two great warriors doing battle: "Never have I risen to such a height, and never have I been so hard pressed by an opponent. He cut deep, and yet I just undercut him." Holmes always enjoys the thrill of the chase, and this is the most exciting chase of his career. He remarks that he could happily retire, feeling his great work is done, if he could only bring the genius Moriarty down. Like a top athlete, he wants to go out on a high after winning the greatest contest of his career.

The crucial moment of the battle is now approaching, Holmes tells Watson. On the forthcoming Monday, the police will be able to move in and round up Moriarty's entire criminal network, provided he can stay out of Moriarty's clutches until then—since he will provide the key evidence that will convict Moriarty.

…you are now playing a double-handed game with me against the cleverest rogue and the most powerful syndicate of criminals in London.
Sherlock Holmes

However, the "Napoleon of crime" is thrilled by the challenge, too. With his customary chilling bravado, Moriarty has visited Holmes at 221B Baker Street that very morning, to get a good look at his adversary and to give him one last chance to back down. "If you are clever enough to bring destruction upon me," Moriarty warned him, "rest assured that I shall do as much to you."

Holmes is not to be cowed, in spite of several attempts being made on his life throughout the day. He gives Watson strict instructions to

meet him at Victoria Station the following morning, being careful not to be followed, and then leaves by climbing over the back garden wall.

The chase begins

Watson follows Holmes's instructions precisely, taking a brougham cab to the station that he later discovers was driven by a disguised Mycroft Holmes. As he settles into the first-class carriage reserved for himself and Holmes, he is irritated to find himself joined by an elderly Italian priest. The reader may be one step ahead of the doctor here—the priest is, of course, Holmes in disguise. Unmasked, Holmes informs Watson that members of Moriarty's gang had set fire to his rooms in 221B the previous evening, but that little damage was done. As the train pulls out of the station, Moriarty appears on the platform, angrily trying to stop the train. Watson breathes a sigh of relief when the train speeds away, but Holmes knows that Moriarty won't be stopped so easily. He guesses that he will likely rent a "special" (one-car) train to pursue them. But he has a plan: they will give him the slip by getting off the train at

The Reichenbach Falls

Situated in the Swiss Bernese Oberland region, the Reichenbach Falls were well known long before Conan Doyle's time. Dropping a total of 820 ft (250 m) in a series of torrents, the waterfalls are among the most spectacular in Europe. They were painted by the English Romanticist J. M. W. Turner in the early 1800s, but it is their role in "The Final Problem" for which they are best known today. Tens of thousands of Holmes fans trek to the site every year to see where Moriarty met his doom. There is a

funicular railroad to take them there from the nearby town of Meiringen, where there is also a Holmes museum. Many fans dress as characters from the Holmes stories and reenact the struggle, even sending dummy bodies plunging into the depths. On the cliff face is a plaque marking the spot of the great struggle between Holmes and Moriarty. The path on which the pair wrestled was then right beside the falls, but over the years it has crumbled away, and today it ends around 330 ft (100 m) short of the falls.

Holmes's deerstalker tumbles into the gorge as he and Moriarty struggle on the edge of its precipice, in this illustration by Sidney Paget originally published in *The Strand Magazine*.

Canterbury and detouring to Newhaven. The ploy works, and they see Moriarty's train roaring by as they hide behind a stack of luggage on a platform at Canterbury Station.

After reaching Strasbourg via Brussels, they learn that the police have arrested Moriarty's gang, but Moriarty has escaped. Holmes knows his enemy will now be set on revenge. Holmes and Watson decide to continue traveling, hoping to stay one step ahead of their pursuer. After a week's walking in the Alps, they arrive in the Swiss town of Meiringen. At the advice of the hotel landlord, Peter Steiler, they make a trip to the spectacular Reichenbach Falls, where "the torrent… plunges into a tremendous abyss, from which the spray rolls up like the smoke from a burning house." As they leave the waterfalls, a boy approaches Watson with a letter, ostensibly from Steiler, asking him to return and tend to an English woman who is dying of tuberculosis. Holmes realizes at once that it is a hoax, but says nothing, clearly feeling the time has come for his final combat with Moriarty.

The final moment
When Watson reaches the hotel, he finds that there is no sick woman awaiting his attentions. Realizing the trick, he rushes back to the Reichenbach Falls, but he finds only Holmes's Alpine-stock (walking stick), leaning against the rock. Two sets of footprints lead to a precipice above a deep chasm into which the water plunges, and there are no returning footprints.

The plowed-up soil and torn branches and ferns at the edge of the path show that there has been a fight beside the chasm.

Watson sees something gleaming from the top of a boulder, and finds Holmes's silver cigarette case. As he picks it up, out flutters a note from Holmes, which Moriarty had allowed him to write before their battle. The note reveals that Holmes is prepared to die in order to rid the world of Moriarty. The detective has written that "no possible conclusion to [my career] could be more congenial to me than this." The note ends by asking Watson to inform the police that the papers that will convict Moriarty's gang are with his brother Mycroft for safekeeping.

When Watson and the police search the scene, they find unmistakable signs that the two men tussled on the brink, then fell, presumably to their deaths. Watson thinks it is all over, and he has lost the man "I shall ever regard as the best and the wisest man whom I have ever known"—but of course he is wrong. For Watson, Holmes does return in "The Empty House," which reveals he did not perish at Reichenbach after all. The public, however, had to wait nearly a decade before he was seen again in *The Hound of the Baskervilles* (pp.152–61)—set before his apparent death—and in the meantime fans had to live with the devastating belief that the great detective was no more. ∎

A LEGEN

RETURN

Conan Doyle **travels to Egypt** and publishes *The Stark Munro Letters*, a fictionalized autobiography.

Conan Doyle publishes **Uncle Bernac**—another historical novel set in the **Napoleonic wars**. Bram Stoker publishes **Dracula**.

Conan Doyle's **Round the Fire Stories** begin appearing in *The Strand Magazine*.

Conan Doyle unsuccessfully runs as a **parliamentary candidate** for Edinburgh.

1895

MAY 1897

JUN 1898

1900

FEB 1896

JUN 1897

NOV 1899

MAR 1900

Event in the lives of Holmes and Watson

Conan Doyle publishes **The Exploits of Brigadier Gerard**.

Queen Victoria celebrates her **Diamond Jubilee** at age 78.

The play **Sherlock Holmes**, starring **William Gillette**, opens in **New York**.

Conan Doyle publishes **The Green Flag and Other Stories of War and Sport** as a collection.

IN THIS CHAPTER

Bram Stoker, author of *Dracula* and a distant cousin of Conan Doyle, was the business manager of London's Lyceum Theatre when *Sherlock Holmes, or The Strange Case of Miss Faulkner* moved there from New York in 1901. The play, which had been approved by Conan Doyle, was based largely on the existing novels and short stories, but gave Holmes an unlikely love interest in the eponymous "Miss Faulkner."

From stage to page

The play was a sellout, and its success was enough to convince Conan Doyle that there was still a public appetite for the detective. So, while the play was still on, he wrote *The Hound of the Baskervilles*. When the novel began its serialization in *The Strand Magazine* in August

1901, lines of people extended from newsstands across the country. The story sees Holmes back at the height of his powers, solving the mystery of a "giant hound" in western England. It is a curious fact that while the Holmes in this tale remains resolutely worldly, rejecting out of hand the idea that the grisly dog is supernatural, in these same years Conan Doyle was evidently reflecting on matters of faith—his semiautobiographical novel, *The Stark Munro Letters*, documents his rejection of Roman Catholicism and foreshadows his later interest in spiritualism. At this time, he was also writing his patriotic histories of the Boer War, based partly on the period he had spent in an army hospital unit in South Africa (where Sir Henry Baskerville made his money). He was knighted for this

Queen Victoria dies at age 81; **Edward VII** becomes king.

Conan Doyle publishes *The War in South Africa: Its Cause and Conduct.*

Holmes retires to the South Downs (see "The Lion's Mane," pp.278–83).

The stories later collected as **The Return of Sherlock Holmes** begin to appear in *The Strand Magazine*.

JAN 1901   **JAN 1902**   **1903**   **SEP 1905**

AUG 1901   **AUG 1902**   **MAR 1905**

Conan Doyle's **The Hound of the Baskervilles** is serialized in *The Strand Magazine*. It is published as a novel the following year.

Conan Doyle is **given a knighthood** for his writings on the **Boer War**.

Conan Doyle publishes **The Return of Sherlock Holmes**.

---

work by Edward VII in 1902—the king himself numbered among Holmes's fans and was as eager as anybody to hear more of his exploits.

An emotional reunion

The events in *The Hound of the Baskervilles* predate Holmes's apparent death in "The Final Problem," and so did not resurrect the detective as fans had hoped. Holmes's return from the dead in October 1903, in the short story "The Empty House," provoked an emotional response from fans. Watson, too, was overjoyed at the news, swiftly selling his practice to move back into 221B Baker Street. Watson later discovers that the practice was bought by a relative of Holmes, revealing—with wonderful understatement on Conan Doyle's part—that the feeling was mutual.

Perhaps the use of a waxwork decoy model of Holmes in "The Empty House" was Conan Doyle's wry comment on the fame that his detective had garnered by this point. Yet he did not shy away from satisfying his readers, making sure that *The Return of Sherlock Holmes* ran the gamut of his hero's talents. "The Dancing Men" features the most fiendish coded message in the canon, while the use of fingerprinting in "The Norwood Builder" was radical for its time. And Holmes's skill for disguise underpins both "Charles Augustus Milverton" and "The Empty House."

Exclusive company

These stories also often see Holmes hobnobbing with a high-society crowd. In "The Golden Pince-Nez," there is a tantalizing reference to

his having been admitted into the French "Legion of Honour" after he had apprehended "the Boulevard Assassin." Likewise, two of Conan Doyle's own favorite tales, "The Priory School" and "The Second Stain," see Holmes dealing with some highly illustrious personae. Yet Conan Doyle's aristocrats are not necessarily painted with affection. Lord Holdernesse is deeply implicated in the drama of "The Priory School," and Sir Eustace Bracknell in "The Abbey Grange" is notable for his violence and alcoholism. The well-to-do "Norwood Builder" Jonas Oldacre, meanwhile, is an out-and-out fiend. As in *The Hound of the Baskervilles*, the tales in this collection often play out in controlled, out-of-town environments, away from the chaos of London. ∎

THERE IS NOTHING MORE STIMULATING THAN A CASE WHERE EVERYTHING GOES AGAINST YOU

THE HOUND OF THE BASKERVILLES (1902)

IN CONTEXT

TYPE
Novel

FIRST PUBLICATION
UK: *The Strand Magazine*, August 1901

NOVEL PUBLICATION
George Newnes, March 1902

CHARACTERS
Sir Charles Baskerville
Squire of Baskerville Hall, recently deceased.

Sir Henry Baskerville
Inheritor of the Baskerville estate, arrived from Canada.

Sir Hugo Baskerville
Ancestor of Sir Henry.

Dr. James Mortimer Family friend of the Baskervilles and executor of Sir Charles's will.

Jack Stapleton Neighbor of the Baskervilles; a naturalist.

Beryl Stapleton
Costa Rican beauty.

John Barrymore
Butler at Baskerville Hall.

Eliza Barrymore
John's wife, and housekeeper at Baskerville Hall.

Selden Eliza's brother, an escaped convict.

Inspector Lestrade
Scotland Yard detective.

Chapters 1 & 2
Dr. Mortimer comes to 221B Baker Street and relates the legend of Sir Hugo Baskerville and the hound.

Chapter 4
Sir Henry receives a warning note and has a boot stolen from his hotel.

Chapter 6
At Baskerville Hall, Watson meets the suspicious servants, the Barrymores, and learns that an escaped convict is on the loose.

Chapter 3
Sir Henry Baskerville arrives in London; a huge, glowing hound is seen on the moor.

Chapter 5
Holmes sends Watson to Dartmoor with Sir Henry, who has inherited Baskerville Hall.

On a fall day in 1889, a Dr. Mortimer of Dartmoor calls at 221B Baker Street. He produces a manuscript, dated 1742, from which he recounts the story of how a curse was placed on the Baskerville family of Devonshire. The dastardly Sir Hugo Baskerville made a pact with "the Powers of Evil" and was subsequently chased down and torn to shreds by a "hell-hound" on the moor. The document warns his descendants to avoid the moor at night on pain of a similar fate. Now, Mortimer's friend and the latest squire of Baskerville Hall,

Sir Charles, has died of heart failure after fleeing from what paw prints suggest was a "gigantic hound," and his next of kin, Sir Henry, is arriving to from Canada inherit the estate.

At his London hotel, Sir Henry receives a note that reads: "as you value your life or your reason keep away from the moor." Holmes sends Watson to Dartmoor with Sir Henry and Dr. Mortimer, claiming that he is too busy to go himself. Watson finds Baskerville Hall "a place of shadow and gloom." On the "forbidding" moor, he meets a local naturalist, Jack Stapleton,

Chapter 9
Watson discovers that the escaped convict is Mrs. Barrymore's brother, hiding on the moor.

Chapter 12
Holmes and Watson discover that the convict has died after fleeing the hound.

Chapter 14
Stapleton releases the hound on Sir Henry; it is shot by Holmes and Watson. Stapleton flees into the mire and is sucked to his death.

Chapters 7 & 8
Watson meets Stapleton, hears the howl of a hound, and sees Barrymore signaling with a candle to somebody on the moor.

Chapters 10 & 11
Watson further investigates the local people, then discovers Holmes in a hideout on the moor.

Chapter 13
Holmes points out the likeness of Stapleton to Sir Hugo.

Chapter 15
Back in 221B Baker Street, Holmes sums up the case for Watson.

and the two see a pony sucked into the bog. As Jack departs, his sister arrives, and warns Watson to leave.

Sir Henry and Watson catch Barrymore, the butler, signaling at night to someone on the moor, and discover that he and his wife are taking food, and Sir Henry's old clothes, to Mrs. Barrymore's brother Selden, an escaped convict. While looking for the criminal, Watson and Sir Henry spot someone hiding out on the moor—who turns out to be none other than Sherlock Holmes. The detective has been spying on Stapleton, who he

suspects has a shady past. As night falls, baying and screams signal the convict's death. Seeing a portrait of Sir Hugo on the wall of the hall, Holmes notices a striking similarity to Stapleton.

When Sir Henry begins walking home from the Stapleton residence across the moor, a fog descends and the hound appears—a fearsome beast with fire bursting from its mouth and eyes. Just as it is about to tear Sir Henry's throat out, Holmes and Watson shoot it dead. The dog has been coated with phosphorus to look fiery. Stapleton, the man who is

behind the hound's murderous attempts on the life of both Sir Charles and Sir Henry, is sucked to his death trying to escape across the mire. Lestrade finds Stapleton's sister Beryl gagged and bound, and it becomes clear that she is actually his wife. She was the author of the warning note sent to Sir Henry in London, and has been tied up in the house as she refused to take part in Sir Henry's murder. It is revealed that Jack Stapleton was an unknown nephew of Sir Charles who planned to inherit the Baskerville fortune by murdering his relatives. ∎

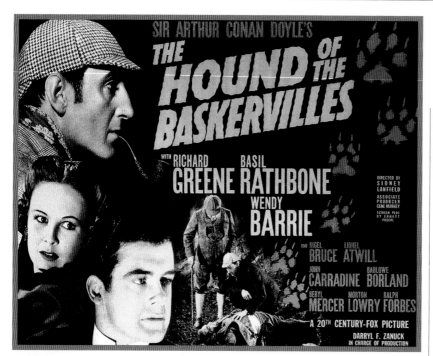

The eponymous 1939 movie is the best-known and perhaps most successful cinematic adaptation of the novel. Basil Rathbone and Nigel Bruce played Holmes and Watson in 13 more films.

When Conan Doyle killed off Holmes in "The Final Problem" (pp.142–47) in 1893, he was taken aback by the strength of feeling it incurred: fans reacted as if he had killed a real person. The author was also aware of how lucrative the Holmes franchise had been—and could be again. And so he eventually relented and incorporated Holmes into a supernatural horror story that he

It's an ugly business, Watson, an ugly, dangerous business and the more I see of it the less I like it.
Sherlock Holmes

was already working on: *The Hound of the Baskervilles*. It is something of a cliché that every major crime writer since has had to think twice about killing off a hero they've grown tired of. As comebacks go, *The Hound of the Baskervilles* (actually a prequel), is a mightily impressive and memorable one. Not only did it see the dramatic reintroduction of Conan Doyle's most famous literary creation, but it was also to become the most famous of all Holmes's adventures.

Imagining the hound
The first appearance of *The Hound of the Baskervilles* was in August 1901, when it was published in nine monthly installments in the great detective's spiritual home, *The Strand Magazine*. Once again the installments were graced with illustrations by Sidney Paget, who used a more detailed wash style than he had previously. However, like many subsequent film-makers,

he discovered that no image of the hound could do justice to the hellish creature conjured by Conan Doyle in the mind of the reader: "…there stood a foul thing, a great, black beast, shaped like a hound, yet larger than any hound that ever mortal eye has rested upon."

Unsurprisingly, Holmes's reappearance was a phenomenal success in both Britain and the US. Newnes initially produced 25,000 copies of the collected installments as a novel, but the print run was soon extended for readers in the colonies, and the US edition was published with a print run of 70,000. Noting the remarkable interest in the book, the US magazine *Collier's Weekly* made a favorable offer to Conan Doyle for further stories featuring the great detective. As a result, it was in *Collier's*, not the *Strand*, that subsequent Holmes stories were first published. Meanwhile, *The Hound of the Baskervilles* has become one of the truly great supernatural myths in literature. The book has been translated into almost every major language; adapted—with varying degrees of success—more than 20 times for cinema and television; and the story still remains fully embedded in the public imagination.

Holmes the masterful
The novel begins in a pleasingly familiar fashion. At 221B Baker Street, Holmes demonstrates to Watson his genius for scientific observation and deduction by analyzing Mortimer's walking stick in his typically masterful

style. But it is not long before the fantastical legend of the Baskerville hound intrudes into their ordered, rational, modern world. It sets Holmes and Watson off on a quest to track down a fabulous beast—reminiscent of those in medieval literature—a genre in which Conan Doyle was well versed.

Supernatural or natural

In later life, Conan Doyle displayed a personal—and, to many, a gullible—belief in the supernatural. Just after World War I, as he was mourning the deaths of both his son Kingsley and his brother Innes, Conan Doyle was famously duped by doctored photographs created by two Yorkshire schoolgirls, purporting to show fairies in their backyard (p.20). In 1901, however, through the cool, calm reasoning of Holmes, he gives the supernatural pretty short shrift. From the start, Holmes grasps the essential fact

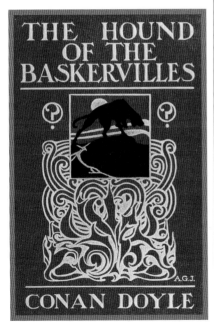

The cover of the first edition of the novel was adorned with a woodcut by British artist and illustrator Alfred Garth Jones (1872–1955).

Keep your revolver near you night and day, and never relax your precautions.
Sherlock Holmes

about the hound. The paw prints found at the scene of Sir Charles's death were real: therefore the hound must be a flesh-and-blood animal, and not a specter. This is confirmed to Holmes when one of Sir Henry's new boots is stolen from his London hotel room, only to be returned and another, older, boot taken. Crucially, Holmes does not reveal the meaning until the end of the story: the boot was stolen so that the hound would have a scent to follow, but the new boot, being as yet unworn, did not carry Sir Henry's scent, so the thief put it back and stole an old one instead.

Another key clue that Holmes discovers early on in the story, but keeps to himself until its very end, is the faint scent of white jasmine on the warning note sent to Sir Henry. Holmes knows that only one of the handful of neighbors living within a few miles of Baskerville Hall could have sent the message. When he detects the scent, he realizes the source must be a woman and his suspicions fall on Stapleton, whose "sister" might have written the note.

Down in Dartmoor

The details of the case established, the reader accompanies Watson, Mortimer, and Sir Henry to »

An inspirational acquaintance

In 1901, Conan Doyle played golf in Cromer, Norfolk, with a journalist acquaintance named Bertram Fletcher Robinson (1870–1907)— "Bobbles" to his friends— and subsequently stayed at Robinson's home in South Devon, where the journalist had a coachman called Baskerville. Bundled up against the cold, the pair would stroll across the lonely moors, Robinson regaling Conan Doyle all the while with myriad local legends. Together they came up with the basic idea for *The Hound of the Baskervilles*, and in a footnote at the beginning of the first installment of the book in *The Strand Magazine*, Conan Doyle wrote: "This story owes its inception to my friend, Mr. Fletcher Robinson, who has helped me both in the general plot and in the local details." Robinson himself, while he did accrue a share of the royalties, was always modest about the extent of his contribution. Whatever that was, it is clear that the finished *Hound of the Baskervilles* is overwhelmingly the handiwork of Sherlock Holmes's creator.

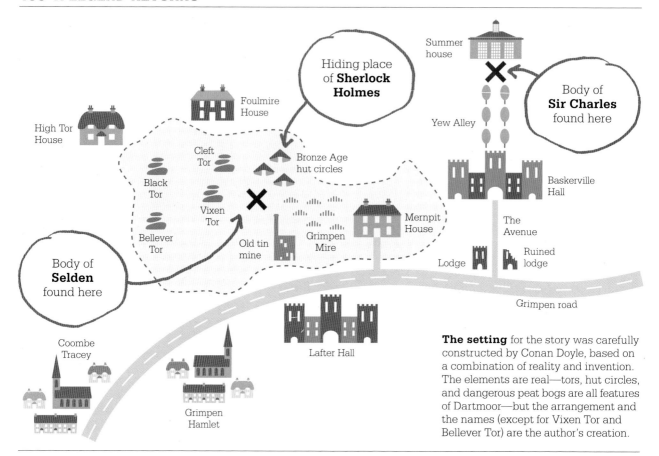

Hiding place of **Sherlock Holmes**

Summer house

Body of **Sir Charles** found here

Yew Alley

Foulmire House

High Tor House

Cleft Tor

Bronze Age hut circles

Baskerville Hall

Black Tor

Vixen Tor

Mernpit House

The Avenue

Bellever Tor

Old tin mine

Grimpen Mire

Lodge

Ruined lodge

Body of **Selden** found here

Grimpen road

Coombe Tracey

Lafter Hall

Grimpen Hamlet

The setting for the story was carefully constructed by Conan Doyle, based on a combination of reality and invention. The elements are real—tors, hut circles, and dangerous peat bogs are all features of Dartmoor—but the arrangement and the names (except for Vixen Tor and Bellever Tor) are the author's creation.

Dartmoor to face what is still an unknown enemy. Once there, the wonderfully sinister atmosphere of the moor and mire evoked by Conan Doyle, and the dramatic events that unfold, combine to deepen the sense of dread in the reader's mind (never mind Mortimer's) that the hound might really be supernatural—until Holmes's reappearance sees reason triumph over superstition.

The detective is actually conspicuously absent for a large part of the narrative, but this is not a misstep on Conan Doyle's part, for Holmes's absence only builds a sense of anticipation in the reader, particularly since much time is now spent describing events, without the usual excitement of seeing the detective's skills in action. When the reader discovers that Holmes

has in fact been secretly on the scene all the time, the ploy is retrospectively all the more pleasing.

The doctor may not have the genius of the detective but he is, as Holmes puts it, "a man of action,"

> They all agreed that it was a huge creature, luminous, ghastly, and spectral.
> **Dr. Mortimer**

whose "instinct is always to do something energetic." Certainly, in Dartmoor Watson is energetic, confronting Barrymore head on, bluntly interviewing local people, ambushing the stranger hiding out on the moor—who turns out to be Holmes—and charging recklessly after Selden, a convicted murderer.

Telling the story

Watson's account of his adventures on Dartmoor comprises a mixture of recollection, written reports sent back to 221B (from where, unknown to the good doctor, they are then sent all the way back to Holmes in his Dartmoor hideout), and detailed diary entries. This gives *The Hound of the Baskervilles* an episodic feel that is unusual in the Holmes canon. Rather than

A group of prisoners and their guards pass through the main gate of Dartmoor Prison, Princetown, in 1906. Built for prisoners of the Napoleonic Wars (1803–1815), the jail later housed murderers like Selden.

being punctuated with climactic moments of suspense and horror, as in most other Holmes stories, the narrative builds, with an insistent and increasing tempo, in a series of disparate and provocative scenes. This endows the narrative with a persuasive authenticity, making it easier for the reader to suspend disbelief in the face of the rather unlikely happenings that occur. But above all, the tale gives the reader Dartmoor, the unseen but eerily baying hound, and a deliciously sinister villain.

A worthy setting

Conan Doyle draws so vivid a picture of Dartmoor, with its bleak moorland, Neolithic ruins, craggy tors, twisting paths and streams, lonely dwellings, and fog-shrouded, menacing mire, that it almost becomes a character in its own right. Looming over it all is the very real Princetown Prison. As Holmes observes, it is a worthy setting for such a dark tale. Says Watson of his first glimpse of the moor from the train, "Over the green squares of the fields and the low curve of a wood there rose in the distance a gray, melancholy hill, with a strange jagged summit, dim and vague in the distance, like some fantastic landscape in a dream." Later, he describes Dartmoor as "… this most God-forsaken corner of the world. The longer one stays here the more does the spirit of the moor sink into one's soul…". Like the local "peasants," Sir Charles believed the legend of the hound, and nothing could induce him to go out on the moor at night. Watson and Sir Henry are made of sterner stuff, but even they are shaken to the core when they are out on the moor at night looking for Selden and suddenly hear the hound baying. "It came with the wind through the silence of the night," Watson reports, "a long, deep mutter, then a rising howl, and »

The hound of Hell

Myths from many countries refer to black hounds that are the servants of the devil, and a group of these sinister creatures is said to inhabit Dartmoor. The Wisht Hounds ("wisht" is an old word for "eerie") are creatures of Satan and able to fly after their quarry. They are led by a devil figure, Dewer, often identified with an evil 17th-century squire, Richard Cabell of Buckfastleigh. Cabell is variously said to have kidnapped maidens, been a vampire, and murdered his wife.

When he died in 1677, villagers buried him under a heavy stone inside a solid tomb. Some say the Wisht Hounds chased him to his death, and gather every night to howl around his tomb. Others say his headless ghost leads the Wisht Hounds on their rides over the moors.

In the story, Stapleton creates the Baskerville Hound by buying a bloodhound/mastiff cross from a London dealer—Ross and Mangles on Fulham Road—and keeps the huge animal half-starved and chained in the ruins of a miner's cottage.

then the sad moan in which it died away." Watson never once believes the hound is supernatural, but Sir Henry's faith is not so unshakeable. As he tells the doctor, "…it was one thing to laugh about it in London, and it is another to stand out here in the darkness of the moor and to hear such a cry as that."

The Baskerville line

Like his uncle Sir Charles, Sir Henry is of necessity a sympathetic character, for Conan Doyle wants the reader to be concerned for his safety. The two are a far cry from their ancestor Sir Hugo, who rode roughshod over the local peasants

Grimspound was one of the Dartmoor sites visited in 1901 by Conan Doyle and Bertram Fletcher Robinson, while researching the novel's grim setting.

and had his wicked, drunken way with kidnapped maidens. Sir Charles originally made his fortune in South Africa, and he donated generously to both local and county charities, according to a report in the fictional *Devon County Chronicle*. Sir Henry's years in Canada have evidently given him a similarly democratic outlook, for he is determined to build on the work his uncle did in the community.

Very different is the other Baskerville nephew, Jack Stapleton, the secret only child of Sir Charles's youngest brother, Rodger. "The black sheep of the family" and the "very image" of Sir Hugo, according to Mortimer, Rodger's deviant activity had made England "too hot to hold him" and he fled to South America. There, unknown to his English relatives, he had

married and had a son, Jack. The younger Stapleton stole some money and left for England with Beryl, a Costa Rican beauty, under the name Vandeleur. They settled in Yorkshire, where they founded a private school, but it soon sank "from disrepute into infamy," says Holmes, until they found it prudent to change their names once again and, disguising themselves this time as a naturalist and his dutiful sister, moved to Dartmoor. Here Stapleton learned of the legend of the hound and hatched his dastardly plot, forcing Beryl to be his reluctant accomplice.

Masterly creations

The human agency behind the real hound, Stapleton is one of the best villains in the canon. From the start, Holmes realizes he is dealing

with a criminal almost as brilliant as himself. Paraphrasing Sir Walter Scott, he tells Watson: "this time we have got a foeman who is worthy of our steel." In London, when a disguised Stapleton hires a cab to follow Sir Henry and Mortimer, he at once spots Holmes and Watson trailing the pair on foot, and gets away. Knowing that Holmes will trace and interview the cabbie, he cheekily tells the man, "It might interest you to know that you have been driving Mr. Sherlock Holmes." When the cabbie then duly informs Holmes of this, the detective bursts out laughing. "I feel a foil as quick and supple as my own," he says, quoting Laertes in *Hamlet.*

Holmes knows his only chance is to fool the "wary and cunning" naturalist into dropping his guard. He sends Watson on alone to Baskerville Hall, announcing, "I've been checkmated in London, I can only wish you better luck in Devonshire." In order to allay his adversary's suspicions, Holmes knows it is essential that everyone thinks he is staying in the capital.

That Stapleton may be slightly unhinged as well as brilliant is evident when, during Watson's first encounter with him on the moor, he suddenly sets off into the mire

A stone hound guards the entrance to Hayford Hall in South Devon, believed by many Sherlockians to be the model for Baskerville Hall.

in manic, "zigzag" pursuit of, appropriately enough, a Cyclopides, or skipper, butterfly, so named for its rapid, darting flight (Conan Doyle knew his butterflies). Later, Watson sees Stapleton confront Sir Henry over his courting of Beryl, Sir Henry being unaware she is the naturalist's wife. "He was running wildly towards them, his absurd net dangling behind him," reports Watson. "He gesticulated and almost danced with excitement in front of the lovers." Afterwards, a confused Sir Henry asks Watson, "Did he ever strike you as being crazy[?]… you can take it from me that either he or I ought to be in a strait-jacket."

When Holmes first spots the uncanny resemblance between the butterfly collector and the portrait of Sir Hugo, he exclaims, "We have him, Watson, we have him… A pin, a cork, and a card, and we add him to the Baker Street collection!", at which the great

detective bursts out laughing once more—an event that, as Watson notes, always bodes ill for someone.

And indeed, in classic detective-story tradition, Holmes ultimately triumphs over Stapleton, one of his greatest-ever opponents. After a lengthy period of chaos, his success definitively restores order to Dartmoor.

A sense of place

Holmes, his Baker Street rooms, and the bustle of London are all inseparably linked in the reader's mind, but with *The Hound of the Baskervilles,* the great detective is indelibly connected to Dartmoor too. As Watson unknowingly says of him, in an iconic image, when describing the stranger hiding out on the moor, "He stood with his legs a little separated, his arms folded, his head bowed, as if he were brooding over that enormous wilderness of peat and granite which lay before him. He might have been the very spirit of that terrible place." As the man who hunts Stapleton down, Sherlock Holmes—so often likened by Watson to a bloodhound in their adventures together—is arguably the real hound of the Baskervilles. ■

It is something to have touched bottom anywhere in this bog in which we are floundering.
Dr. Watson

I am not sure that of all the five hundred cases of capital importance which I have handled there is one which cuts so deep.
Sherlock Holmes

THIS EMPTY HOUSE IS MY TREE, AND YOU ARE MY TIGER

THE ADVENTURE OF THE EMPTY HOUSE (1903)

IN CONTEXT

TYPE
Short story

FIRST PUBLICATION
US: September 1903
UK: October 1903

COLLECTION
***The Return of Sherlock Holmes*, 1905**

CHARACTERS
Honourable Ronald Adair Second son of the Earl of Maynooth.

Lady Maynooth Ronald's mother.

Hilda Maynooth Ronald's sister.

Edith Woodley Ronald's former fiancée.

Colonel Sebastian Moran Ronald's card partner.

Inspector Lestrade Scotland Yard detective.

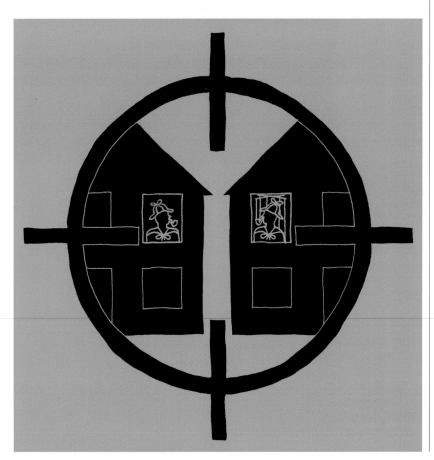

This story sees the dramatic resurrection of Sherlock Holmes, after his apparent death at the Reichenbach Falls in Switzerland, killed along with his nemesis, Moriarty, in "The Final Problem" (pp.142–47).

It is sometimes said that Conan Doyle was forced to bring Holmes back to life by public pressure. If that was the case, it took him a whole decade to yield. Given that that pressure is likely to have diminished rather than increased over the 10-year period, it seems more likely that Conan Doyle was swayed by the substantial financial deal being offered by the successful American periodical *Collier's*

The royal baccarat scandal

The card game in "The Adventure of the Empty House" was very likely based on the royal baccarat scandal ("the Tranby Croft affair") of 1890. A group of aristocrats and ex-army officers attended a house party at Tranby Croft in Yorkshire in order to play baccarat, an illegal gambling game. One of the party was the future King Edward VII. While playing, one of the guests, Sir William Gordon-Cumming, was accused of cheating. Like Moran, Gordon-Cumming was a decorated army officer. He agreed to never play cards again in return for the guests' silence. But when rumors began to circulate, Gordon-Cumming decided to sue his accusers for slander. Prince Edward was obliged to appear in court as a witness— the first time a royal prince had appeared in court for hundreds of years—and the story made headline news in Britain. Conan Doyle had met Prince Edward just a year before writing "The Empty House." One of Adair's card-playing associates is called Lord Balmoral (the name of the Queen's Scottish estate), linking him unmistakably to the prince.

Weekly. Therefore, the news of Holmes's amazing return reached the US one month before it arrived in the UK, when the story was published in *The Strand Magazine.*

By the time Conan Doyle wrote "The Adventure of the Empty House," it was the start of the 20th century and Queen Victoria had been dead for two years, yet he chose to set Holmes's return in 1894, firmly in the Victorian era, and only three years after Holmes's disappearance.

Murder on Park Lane

The story opens with Watson relating the strange murder of the Honorable Ronald Adair. He explains that the whole of London society was aghast at the killing of the young aristocrat, but Watson has taken a special interest in the case because he feels that the peculiar circumstances of Adair's death were of the kind that would have appealed to his late friend Holmes. The doctor misses his friend's company, and is keenly aware of the loss of Holmes's unique crime-solving abilities to the wider community. Adair was the second son of the Earl of Maynooth, the governor of an Australian colony, and lived with his mother and sister on London's exclusive Park Lane. A pleasant young man, he had no obvious enemies, and his only vice was that of playing cards. He was a member of several card clubs, and typically played whist, but apparently never gambled beyond his means. Just a few weeks ago, he had won £420 playing with his regular partner, Colonel Sebastian Moran.

On the evening of his murder, Adair returned home at 10pm and retired to his upstairs sitting room.

All day I turned these facts over in my mind, endeavouring to hit upon some theory which could reconcile them all.
Dr. Watson

When his mother, Lady Maynooth, came home later with his sister Hilda, she found his door locked from the inside. Failing to rouse him, she had the door forced open and discovered him dead— part of his head blown off by an expanding bullet.

The locked room mystery

There was no sign of a murder weapon in the room, nor any indication that anyone other than Adair had entered. Outside the window was a drop of at least 20 feet, and the flowerbed below showed no sign of disturbance. A brilliant marksman might have fired through the open window from the street, but no one outside on the busy Park Lane had heard the sound of a shot.

On the table at which the dead man was sitting were neat piles of money, and a sheet of paper with names and figures, suggesting Adair had been adding up his winnings and losses at cards. The sums were all modest, however, and so there seems to have been neither motive nor means for the young man's murder. Watson is mystified. At this stage, it seems »

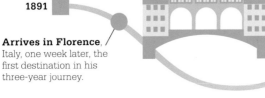

At **Reichenbach Falls** in Switzerland, Holmes apparently falls to his death, locked in a **fatal struggle** with his archenemy **Moriarty**.

1891

Arrives in Florence, Italy, one week later, the first destination in his three-year journey.

Poses as Norwegian explorer Sigerson, and publishes accounts of his adventures.

Travels in Tibet for two years, and spends time in the capital city Lhasa, where he meets the "head lama" (the Dalai Lama).

During the "Great Hiatus," as his three-year disappearance is called, Holmes certainly does not rest on his laurels. Among other adventures, he travels to Tibet, enters the holy city of Islam, and becomes a secret agent for the British government.

---

that Watson has set up the reader for a classic "locked room mystery" and is inviting the reader to solve the puzzle. However, the narrative then takes a different, and far more dramatic, twist, and soon the Park Lane mystery is all but forgotten.

The old bibliophile

Watson is standing outside Adair's house on Park Lane, attempting to think like Holmes, and "to find that line of least resistance which my poor friend had declared to be the starting-point of every investigation." Turning, he accidentally knocks a selection of books from the grasp of a hunched old man—clearly a collector of rare or unusual works— who happens to be standing nearby. Watson picks them up and tries to apologize, but the old man runs off angrily. Watson reaches home soon after, only for his maid to show in the very same old book collector to visit him.

> Holmes!…
> Is it really you?
> Can it indeed be
> that you are alive?
> **Dr. Watson**

The wizened old man apologizes for his earlier brusqueness and suggests that Watson might need some books to fill a space on his shelves. Watson turns around briefly to look at the shelf, and when he turns back he sees Sherlock Holmes in front of him, smiling. Out of sheer shock, Watson faints to the ground for the first time in his life.

When the doctor comes to, he sees a concerned Holmes bending over him, deeply concerned. "I owe you a thousand apologies," he says. "I had no idea that you would be so affected." Watson is overjoyed to see the dear friend he thought dead, and quickly recovers. It is a measure, perhaps, of the depth and trust in their friendship that Watson shows no resentment for the detective's deception; he simply wants to know how on earth Holmes escaped from the Reichenbach Falls.

Holmes cheats death

It transpires that Holmes knew already that Moriarty was after him when Watson was lured back to the hotel by the fake message in "The Final Problem." There, on the narrow path above the waterfalls, Holmes and Moriarty encountered each other. Moriarty gave Holmes a brief respite to write the farewell note Watson found later, before

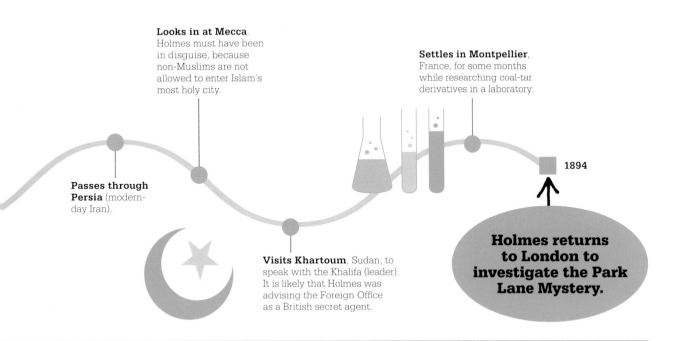

Looks in at Mecca.
Holmes must have been in disguise, because non-Muslims are not allowed to enter Islam's most holy city.

Settles in Montpellier,
France, for some months while researching coal-tar derivatives in a laboratory.

1894

Passes through Persia (modern-day Iran).

Visits Khartoum, Sudan, to speak with the Khalifa (leader). It is likely that Holmes was advising the Foreign Office as a British secret agent.

Holmes returns to London to investigate the Park Lane Mystery.

launching himself at Holmes. However, Holmes evaded him with a move from the Japanese martial art baritsu, and Moriarty slipped over the precipice to his doom. While the term "baritsu" does not exist, Conan Doyle was probably thinking of "bartitsu," a martial art devised by British mining engineer Edward Barton-Wright (1860–1951). Barton-Wright had learned jujitsu in Japan, and combined it with other disciplines, including boxing, to create a new self-defense method that he named after himself.

Holmes explains that, as he watched Moriarty fall, he realized how useful it would be for everyone to think that he too had perished. There were at least three other dangerous men who wanted to kill him, and if they believed he was dead, they might become careless, which would enable him to track down and destroy them. Holmes therefore decided to fake his own

death. With difficulty, he climbed the steep, rocky wall and hid on a ledge, while Watson and the local police examined the two footprints that led to the edge of the precipice, and reached the conclusion that Holmes had fallen into the deep chasm along with Moriarty.

The Great Hiatus
However, just when Holmes thought he was out of danger, a huge rock tumbled past him. He looked up the cliff to see one of Moriarty's associates above, trying to kill him.

Holmes escaped, of course, knowing that everyone, bar the rock-hurler, thought him dead. For the next three years, a period Holmesians call the "Great Hiatus," Holmes traveled the world. He relied on his brother Mycroft, his only confidant, to supply him with money and look after the 221B Baker Street lodgings. Conan Doyle gives the reader such a wealth of intriguing hints about what Holmes was up to in those three years »

Jeremy Brett plays the great detective in a 1986 television adaptation of "The Empty House." Here he encounters Watson while disguised as an elderly bookseller.

HUNTLEY & PALMERS
BISCUITS.

Reading & London.

Hunting tigers was a popular pastime for the British Raj in India, and was seen as a badge of British manhood, superiority, and mastery.

that there is enough to fill a whole series of adventure books. Holmes tells Watson that after first going to Florence, Italy, he then spent three years traveling the world. He even posed as a Norwegian explorer called Sigerson—a character probably inspired by the Swedish explorer Sven Hedin, who traveled widely in Central Asia in the 1890s. Holmes mentions several places in Asia—all British imperial hot spots—and implies that he was working as a secret agent for the British government. Despite the story's historic Victorian setting, Conan Doyle also wove up-to-the-minute global issues into Holmes's travels.

Both Lhasa and Persia were focuses of the "Great Game"—the name introduced to the British public in Rudyard Kipling's 1901 novel *Kim* to describe the long Cold War–like rivalry between

the UK and Russia for dominance in Central Asia. Before he met Holmes, Watson had served as a medical officer in the British army in one of the main conflicts in the rivalry, the Second Afghan War (1878–1880). The references Holmes makes to his time in Lhasa surely relate to the spying, exploration, and intrigue in the build-up to the British army's march into Tibet in December 1903, led by Lieutenant Colonel Francis Younghusband (1863–1942).

Holmes claims to have visited Khartoum, Sudan too—another imperial trouble spot. It was the scene of the defeat of British forces (led by General Charles Gordon) in 1885 by the Mahdiyah—the Sudanese Islamist rebellion. Gordon's portrait hangs on the wall at 221B, and Conan Doyle himself traveled with the British army to Sudan in 1897, as a journalist, before the decisive Battle of Omdurman. There is no doubt that if Holmes was working in such a dangerous region, he

would have done so undercover, making the most of his mastery of disguise.

The house with a view

His undercover work complete, Holmes settled down to conduct chemical experiments in Montpellier, France (see p.165). It was here that he heard of the Adair murder, news that finally brought him back to London. Holmes guesses that the murderer is Moran—the man who hurled rocks at him at Reichenbach—and this is his chance to finally flush him out.

It is a dangerous game, however. To catch Moran, Holmes must first become a target. He has been back in Watson's life for only a short while before he is again taking his friend on a perilous mission. After tracing a circuitous route through obscure back streets in London, Holmes leads Watson to the back door of an empty house and inside.

Watson is amazed to see that the house fronts on to Baker Street and gives a clear view of their old lodgings. To his even greater astonishment, he can see Holmes himself silhouetted in the lighted upstairs window. Holmes explains

This commemorative coin was issued in 1994 to celebrate the 100th anniversary of Holmes's return. The engraving shows Holmes and Watson overpowering Moran.

> I think you want a little unofficial help. Three undetected murders in one year won't do, Lestrade.
> **Sherlock Holmes**

that it is a wax decoy, and that Mrs. Hudson, now recovered from the shock of his return, is moving it around so it appears more lifelike.

After several hours waiting in darkness, they hear someone enter the house in which they are hiding. They shrink into the shadows and watch as an elderly gentleman in evening dress stealthily converts a cane into a rifle (the cane gun was a stylish but deadly accessory for Victorian gentlemen), carefully aims it out of the front window, and fires it, hitting the waxwork model of Holmes in 221B. Holmes and Watson grapple the man to the ground and Holmes then blows a whistle, summoning Inspector Lestrade and two other policemen, who quickly take hold of the prisoner. It seems Scotland Yard were also in on Holmes's plans.

The murderer revealed

With the blinds drawn and the lamps lit, Holmes introduces their captive as Colonel Moran, ex-British army marksman and tiger-hunter in India: "the best heavy-game shot that our Eastern Empire has ever produced."

"You cunning, cunning fiend!" Moran snarls, but Holmes responds that he is surprised a seasoned

shikari (Urdu for hunter) could fall for the old decoy trick. Incensed, Moran challenges Lestrade to name the charges against him. Lestrade answers with "the attempted murder of Mr Sherlock Holmes," but Holmes has other ideas. He knows that Moran's cane is the remarkable airgun made for Moriarty by a blind German mechanic called von Herder. (The choice of a German maker for this fiendishly ingenious weapon reflects a growing concern at the time of writing over the threat posed by German expansionism and military technology.) Holmes goes on to explain that what makes von Herder's airgun so remarkable is that it fires more or less silently, and has been adapted to shoot expanding revolver bullets. Thus Lestrade realizes that he has unwittingly caught the man all of London is looking for: the murderer of Adair. Moran shot Adair with his unique airgun through the open window of Adair's second-floor sitting room.

The cheat accused

With Moran in safe hands, Watson and Holmes withdraw to 221B, where Holmes explains that he had

been unable to move against Moran earlier without exposing and endangering himself. However, Adair's card-playing link to Moran, and the unique nature of his death, made it plain that the murderer was Moran—and that this was Holmes's opportunity to move against him.

When Watson asks why Moran killed Adair, Holmes says that he does not know for certain, but that he supposes Adair had realized that he and Moran had been winning only because Moran had been cheating. Adair must have threatened to expose him if he did not promise to stop playing cards, but Moran's livelihood depended on gambling, and so he killed Adair to keep him quiet. At the time of the murder, Adair was probably trying to work out how much to repay the players they had cheated.

After Holmes has put his theory to Watson, he asks his friend, with unusual deference, "Will it pass?" And Watson replies, "I have no doubt you have hit upon the truth." Behind this simple exchange lies a touching relief that the two friends are reunited at last, reinforcing the feeling that Holmes's long absence is truly forgiven. ■

Colonel Sebastian Moran

Like Moriarty, Colonel Sebastian Moran is a man who seemed to have everything going for him before he became a criminal. He was educated at Eton and Oxford, then embarked on a military career, during which he fought with distinction in the Second Afghan War (1870–1880), and became a marksman and tiger-hunter in India. But Moran suddenly changed, turning into the man Holmes describes as "the second most dangerous man in London" (after Moriarty).

Holmes's explanation is that Moran is the inevitable product of an evil strand in his ancestors, and Watson describes his appearance as conforming to the "criminal type." Conan Doyle seemed to embrace this popular explanation of aberrant behavior in earlier stories, but here Watson responds to Holmes's theory by noting, "It is surely rather fanciful"— an acknowledgement, perhaps, that by 1903, the theory was no longer so widely supported.

ALL MY INSTINCTS ARE ONE WAY, AND ALL THE FACTS ARE THE OTHER

THE ADVENTURE OF THE NORWOOD BUILDER (1903)

IN CONTEXT

TYPE
Short story

FIRST PUBLICATION
US: October 1903
UK: November 1903

COLLECTION
The Return of Sherlock Holmes, 1905

CHARACTERS
John Hector McFarlane
Young solicitor who seeks Holmes's help.

Jonas Oldacre Wealthy master builder, believed to have been murdered.

Mrs. McFarlane John McFarlane's mother.

Inspector Lestrade Scotland Yard detective.

Holmes is lamenting how dull London has become since the demise of "the foul spider" Moriarty when action arrives at 221B Baker Street in the form of a "wild-eyed and frantic" young solicitor, John Hector McFarlane. He is being hunted by the police, suspected of having murdered a prosperous builder, Jonas Oldacre, in his villa in suburban Norwood—a setting familiar to Conan Doyle, who lived in the area between 1891 and 1894. Inspector Lestrade then arrives to make the arrest, but first agrees to let McFarlane tell his story.

An unexpected inheritance
McFarlane explains that the day before, Oldacre had come to his office with a draft will. McFarlane was stunned to read that he had been made the sole beneficiary in spite of never having met the man.

Holmes displays his deductive skills to McFarlane

McFarlane's **untidy attire** suggests he dresses himself.

He is carrying a **sheaf of legal papers**.

"you are a bachelor, a solicitor, a Freemason, and an asthmatic."

His watch has a **recognizable charm**.

He **breathes heavily** as he enters Baker Street.

At Oldacre's request, he later visited him at his home to finalize the will, before being shown out by Oldacre. Yet the next day police were alerted to evidence suggesting that Oldacre had been murdered, and his body dragged outside, and then burned. Lestrade, typically bull-headed, is sure that McFarlane is guilty of the crime. But to the reader, Holmes's analysis is more compelling. Holmes deduces that Oldacre only drafted the will on his way to the solicitor's, on the train from Norwood Junction to London Bridge. The one passage of tidy writing, Holmes suggests, was made at a single station stop, the untidy passages as the train was moving, and the almost illegible passages as it passed over points. Holmes also queries why McFarlane would murder his new benefactor. And if he had, why then seek out Holmes, the one man who can be counted on to find the murderer?

Smoking out the truth

Yet the crime scene also points to McFarlane's guilt, and the next day when police find McFarlane's bloody thumbprint on Oldacre's wall, Lestrade is triumphant. But Holmes can barely contain his glee—from previous observations, he knows the print was not there the day before. A brief scout around is all he needs before indulging his flair for a theatrical "reveal."

When Holmes orchestrates a false fire alarm, Oldacre suddenly bursts out from behind a hidden door. As Holmes deduced, the builder had installed a secret room within the walls. Oldacre turns out to be an embittered former suitor of McFarlane's mother, and the intent of his entire plot was to destroy the life of his lost love's son. "It was a masterpiece of villainy," remarks Holmes, "...But he had not that supreme gift of the artist, the knowledge of when to stop." Oldacre had crept out at night and made the print using a wax impression of McFarlane's thumb, taken from a seal—a play on a new technique in criminal detection.

All this drama increases the impact of Holmes's mischievous nobility in the final moments: while the humbled Lestrade bubbles over with praise, Holmes still insists on handing him all the credit. Even if the case's high stakes—McFarlane would have faced the death penalty if found guilty—make Oldacre's malice verge on implausible, they ensure that Lestrade is suitably abject before the superior analyst. ∎

Fingerprinting

Although fingerprinting had been used in colonial India since 1897, it was not until 1901 that it became a staple of British criminal investigations, when the practice was imported to Britain by an officer who had trained in Bengal. Both these dates come after the 1894 setting of "The Adventure of the Norwood Builder," so Oldacre and Lestrade would both have been ahead of their time. Conan Doyle himself had probably been familiar with the idea for quite a while: the anthropologist Francis Galton's book *Finger Prints*, which was first published in 1892, had proved that each person's fingerprints were unique. This work had built on that of a surgeon named Henry Faulds, whose 1880 article in the scientific journal *Nature* described identifying a thief by means of greasy thumbprints left on a glass. To Faulds, fingerprinting was as reliable as photography, and it seems likely that Conan Doyle, as a medical man, would have read his work and seen its potential early on.

I HAVE THE THREADS OF THIS AFFAIR ALL IN MY HAND

THE ADVENTURE OF THE DANCING MEN (1903)

IN CONTEXT

TYPE
Short story

FIRST PUBLICATION
UK: December 1903
US: December 1903

COLLECTION
***The Return of
Sherlock Holmes***, 1905

CHARACTERS
Hilton Cubitt Squire of
Riding Thorpe Manor, Norfolk.

Elsie Cubitt Hilton's wife,
née Elsie Patrick.

Inspector Martin Policeman
from the Norfolk Constabulary.

Abe Slaney
Chicago gangster.

Wilson Hargreave Member
of the New York Police Bureau.

C onan Doyle had the idea
for, and partly wrote, "The
Adventure of the Dancing
Men" while staying at the Hill
House Hotel in Happisburgh, near
the town of North Walsham, on the
Norfolk coast. He wrote to Herbert
Greenhough Smith, editor of *The
Strand Magazine*, on May 14, 1903,
saying it was "a strong bloody story."
Indeed he placed it third in his
12 favorite Holmes stories because
of "the originality of the plot."

"The Dancing Men" explores
two of Conan Doyle's favorite
themes: a respectable person's
secret and disreputable past
finally catching up with them;
and American organized crime.

Every problem becomes very childish when once it is explained to you. Here is an unexplained one.
Sherlock Holmes

Both feature in the first-ever Holmes adventure, *A Study in Scarlet* (pp.36–45), as well as "The Five Orange Pips" (pp.74–9) and "The Red Circle" (pp.226–39).

Powers of reasoning
Holmes's astounding ability at logical reasoning comes to the fore in "The Dancing Men." He demonstrates it even before the story is underway. One evening at 221B Baker Street, in the summer of 1898, Holmes is brewing up a "particularly malodorous product" in an experiment when he suddenly announces, "So, Watson… you

do not propose to invest in South African securities?" Watson is astonished at his deductions, but Holmes puts his test tube to one side and lists what he calls the missing links of a "very simple chain." Constructing this "series of inferences" has been but a warm-up for the detective, and he now turns his attentions to another, much more complex case.

Mystery in Norfolk
The real puzzle begins as Holmes hands Watson a page torn from a notebook that features a series of 15 hieroglyphic-like doodles of matchstick men in various poses—the "dancing men" of the story's title. Watson reacts immediately: "Why, Holmes, it is a child's drawing," he says. But Holmes is already sure that there is more to this message than first appears.

The sender of the doodles is Mr. Hilton Cubitt, a simple country squire of Riding Thorpe Manor near North Walsham in east Norfolk. He arrives at 221B to tell his story to Holmes. "He was a fine creature, this man of the old English soil," says Watson, "simple, straight, and gentle, with his »

19th-century ciphers
Holmes's method of deciphering the cryptogram was inspired by Edgar Allen Poe's short story "The Gold Bug" (1843). Graphic-based secret languages were popular among gypsies, secret societies, and gangs in the late 19th century, especially in the US. By the mid-19th century, more impregnable ciphers had been developed, including "flattening" frequency analysis (by shifting letters or numbers to complicate the code), or secret "keys" that were needed by both

the sender and the recipient. The invention of the telegraph and Morse code opened the way to reducing coded messages to numerals or a series of binary symbols (commonly 0 and 1), creating a more complex code. The "Playfair Cipher," invented in 1854, encrypted pairs of letters or numbers rather than single characters, making the code much more difficult to crack using frequency analysis, and unbreakable unless the recipient knew the "key." This cipher was used extensively by the military well into the 20th century.

Holmes deduces Watson's investment decision

Watson returned from the club with **chalk** on his **left finger and thumb**.

He always puts **chalk on his fingers** to steady his **billiard cue**.

Watson only ever plays **billiards** with **Thurston**.

Thurston gave him a month to **decide** whether to **invest** in some **South African property**.

Watson's **checkbook** is **locked** in Holmes's drawer and the doctor has **not asked** for the **key**.

Watson does not plan to invest in South African gold fields.

North Walsham (pictured) is an old market town north of Norwich. The fictional Riding Thorpe is thought to be a combination of Ridlington and Edingthorpe villages in Norfolk.

great, earnest blue eyes and broad, comely face. His love for his wife and his trust in her shone in his features."

Cubitt explains that a year earlier, while visiting London for Queen Victoria's Diamond Jubilee celebrations (which took place in 1897), he met and fell in love with a lonely young American lady, Elsie Patrick, who was staying in the same boarding house as him. Elsie had candidly told him that she "had some very disagreeable associations" in her life, but would not go into any detail. Cubitt is

extremely proud of his old family's reputation in Norfolk and its "unsullied honour," and Elsie, deeply respecting that reputation, gave him the chance to break off the engagement. But Cubitt was not put off, telling Holmes, "If you saw her and knew her it would help you to understand." Cubitt promised never to ask her about her past, and within a month they were married; for the following year they lived in wedded bliss at his Norfolk home.

Everything changed

One day Elsie received a letter from America, at the mere sight of which she turned "deadly white." After reading it, she threw it on the fire, so Cubitt has no idea what was in it, but from that moment

she has gone about in obvious dread of someone or something. She has not said what that person or thing might be, and Cubitt, keeping his word, has not asked. "She would do better to trust me," he tells Holmes. "She would find that I was her best friend." Like many of Holmes's provincial clients who have not traveled beyond their comfortable borders, Cubitt is stolid and naïve, and is incapable of even imagining the sort of peril she might be in.

Then one night a number of "dancing" figures were scrawled in chalk on a downstairs window-sill of their house. Cubitt had the drawings washed off, but, when he mentioned them to Elsie, he was surprised at how seriously she took the matter. She begged him to show her any more similar drawings, should they appear. Sure enough, a week later on the sundial in the garden he found the piece of paper he had since sent to Holmes—and when he showed it to Elsie, "she dropped in a dead faint." Since then, Cubitt says, "she has looked like a woman in a dream, half dazed, and with terror always lurking in her eyes." Neither Cubitt nor Watson can

Our presence is most urgently needed… for it is a singular and a dangerous web in which our simple Norfolk squire is entangled.
Sherlock Holmes

This is the final message that Elsie receives from the mysterious cryptographer. Each "dancing man" represents a different letter, and Holmes begins by using frequency analysis, but he needs all of the messages before he can decipher the entire code.

The **most common letter** in the alphabet is "**e**," so the **most common figure** must stand for that letter.

The **flags** occur intermittently on different figures; they must mark the **ends of words**.

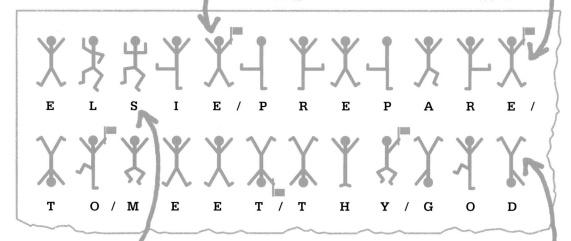

E L S I E / P R E P A R E /

T O / M E E T / T H Y / G O D

Cubitt's wife is named **Elsie**, and as the codes are being **sent to her** it is likely **her name will appear**.

Using the **previous codes**, Holmes **gradually** identifies each letter until this **final, fateful message** is revealed.

see it, but to Holmes the carefully defined matchstick men, some in the same poses, others bearing flags, are clearly a code—though he needs more samples if he is to crack it. He tells Cubitt to go home to Norfolk, and to keep him informed of any fresh developments.

Holmes the masterful

Two weeks later, a tired and worried Cubitt returns to Baker Street with three more coded messages that have been left outside his property, messages that he says are killing his wife "by inches." On the night the third message was left, he had stayed up and seen a "dark, creeping figure"

in the garden, but just as he was about to rush out with his revolver, Elsie had held him back, clinging to him desperately. For whatever reason, she did not want him to go outside. Evidently she knew who was out there, and that it was someone or something she did not want her husband to be involved in.

Holmes remains professional and calm until Cubitt leaves his lodgings, when he cannot contain his excitement any longer and throws himself into deciphering the messages. For two hours the great detective scribbles away, oblivious to Watson's presence. Finally, he springs from his chair with a cry of triumph—he has

cracked the code. He sends a telegram to an unknown person, and tells Watson they must wait for a reply before doing anything else. Meanwhile, Holmes receives a new coded message from Cubitt. On reading it, and then receiving the reply to his telegram, Holmes "suddenly sprang to his feet with an exclamation of surprise and dismay." He wants to rush at once to Norfolk, but the last train has left, and they must wait until morning.

Death in the study

When Holmes and Watson finally arrive at North Walsham the next morning, they are met off the train by the stationmaster with the » grim news that Mrs. Cubitt has apparently shot her husband dead, then turned the gun on herself, leaving her seriously wounded. Holmes's worst fears have been realized.

At Riding Thorpe Manor, with Inspector Martin of the local constabulary for an audience, the great detective conducts a thorough examination of the scene of the crime, and characteristically applies his forensic and reasoning skills to try to make sense of the tragic shootings. Initially the local police inspector is eager "to assert his own position," says Watson, but he is soon, "overcome with admiration and ready to follow without question wherever Holmes led."

Cubitt and his wife were found in the study. The maid and the cook, sleeping upstairs, heard "an explosion," then a second bang a minute later. Rushing downstairs, they found the passage and the study full of smoke, the window of the room shut from the inside, and a candle still burning on the table. They summoned the local doctor.

The Secret Weapon (1943) is credited as being an adaptation of "The Dancing Men." In fact, it is based on a number of Holmes stories, and the only element taken from this tale is the cryptic code.

Cubitt's pistol is still in the room, "two barrels of which had been emptied"—and Holmes points dramatically to a third bullet hole in the window sash. "By George!" cries the inspector. "How ever did you see that?" Holmes replies: "Because I looked for it." He has deduced from the smoke in the passage "that the window had been open at the time of the tragedy," and that a third person must have been involved—Cubitt had shot at whoever was outside the window, hitting the sash. This unknown person had fired the shot that killed Cubitt almost simultaneously, so that the two shots sounded like one "explosion" to the cook and the maid. Elsie had then shut the

window before shooting herself. Outside the window, the flowers are trampled and the soft soil is full of footprints. Holmes hunts around "like a retriever after a wounded bird." Then, with a similar cry of triumph to the one he made when he cracked the code, he finds a third cartridge ejected by another revolver. All the inspector can do is look on in "intense amazement at the rapid and masterful progress of Holmes's investigation."

The deciphered code has already given Holmes the third party's name and address. Pretending to be Elsie, he uses the dancing men code to construct a note intended for one Abe Slaney. Holmes asks Cubitt's stable boy to deliver the note to nearby Elrige's Farm. Only then does he confide in Watson and the inspector.

Breaking the code
Holmes explains how he deciphered the messages, once he realized it was a simple substitution cipher: each "dance" pose represented a letter of the alphabet (see p.173). The first message—"am here Abe Slaney"—revealed that a man by that name was in the area; the second—"at Elrige's"—gave his location at this nearby farm; and the third—"come Elsie"—summoned her to him. However, after Elsie responded "never," using the same code, the fourth and final message told her to "prepare to meet thy God."

After deciphering the third message, Holmes had sent a telegram to his friend, Wilson Hargreave, in the New York Police, asking if an Abe Slaney was known to them; the reply that he received, that Abe Slaney was "the most dangerous crook in Chicago," left Holmes anxious and ready to catch a train to Norfolk.

Abe Slaney

One of several American criminals to feature in Conan Doyle's work, Abe Slaney is a driven man who is obsessed with Elsie. "I tell you, there was never a man in this world loved a woman more than I loved her," he tells Holmes. The depth of his love is never in doubt, and when he is told that Elsie has been injured he declares, "I may have threatened her – God forgive me! – but I would not have touched a hair of her pretty head... If Elsie dies, I care nothing what becomes of me." When Holmes tells him Elsie is suspected of Cubitt's murder, he readily owns up to killing him himself.

What may have started as passionate love has become a sense of entitlement, as Elsie was pledged to him long ago. How much say Elsie had in that is never revealed. They were engaged before she left the US, and Slaney is convinced she would have married him had he gone straight. Unable to accept her decision to leave him and start a new life without him, his passion becomes a dangerous and tragic obsession.

All is explained

Soon enough, Abe Slaney, "a tall, handsome, swarthy fellow, clad in a suit of grey flannel, with a Panama hat, a bristling black beard, and a great, aggressive hooked nose" is striding up the path to Riding Thorpe Manor, flourishing a cane. The moment he enters the house, Holmes has a pistol to his head and Martin puts him in handcuffs. Slaney readily admits to killing Cubitt, but says it was in self-defense, because Cubitt fired first. He is genuinely grief-stricken to hear that Elsie is seriously injured, and explains that he had only threatened her out of anger, for he loved her and always had. They had grown up together in Chicago, and were members of a gang, of which Elsie's father was the leader. They had invented the code, deliberately making it look "like a child's scrawl" so that no one outside the gang would even realize it was a code, never mind be able to decipher it. Elsie "couldn't stand the business," and ran away to start a new life. Slaney wrote to Elsie after her marriage to Cubitt, but when she did not reply, he came to England to find her: "Who was this Englishman that he should come between us? I tell you that I had the first right to her, and that I was only claiming my own," he cries. The story ends with Slaney being condemned to death at the Norwich assizes, but his sentence is changed to penal servitude "in consideration of mitigating circumstances, and the certainty that Hilton Cubitt had fired the first shot." Elsie recovers, and devotes her life "to the care of the poor and to the administration of her husband's estate."

I am fairly familiar with all forms of secret writings, and am myself the author of a trifling monograph upon the subject, in which I analyze one hundred and sixty separate ciphers.
Sherlock Holmes

A tale of passion

Conan Doyle draws a striking contrast between the characters of Cubitt and Slaney. Cubitt is an old-fashioned figure representing the traditional British values of honor, loyalty, and decency, while the American Slaney is a brash gangster from the other side of the Atlantic, with his own firm, if somewhat warped, ideas about love and honor.

This is a tale of heated and hidden passions, where Holmes's rational logic leads the story, but he fails his client. In "The Adventure of the Dancing Men," Conan Doyle seems poised between the naturalism and social realism of 19th-century writers like Gustave Flaubert, Fyodor Dostoyevsky, Émile Zola, and Thomas Hardy on the one hand, and the sensationalism of his 20th-century successors such as Agatha Christie and Edgar Wallace on the other. Holmes, perhaps like Conan Doyle himself, is less interested in Slaney's thwarted passion, the intriguing nature of the triangular relationship, and the eventual, fateful, criminal outcome, than the logical problem of the cryptic code, and how to solve it. ∎

SHE THINKS SHE DOES NOT KNOW THE MAN; I AM CONVINCED SHE DOES

THE ADVENTURE OF THE SOLITARY CYCLIST (1904)

IN CONTEXT

TYPE
Short story

FIRST PUBLICATION
US: December 1903
UK: January 1904

COLLECTION
***The Return of Sherlock Holmes*, 1905**

CHARACTERS
Violet Smith Cyclist and music teacher.

Bob Carruthers Former prospector in South Africa, and widower with a daughter.

Jack Woodley Ruffian, recently returned from South Africa.

Mr. Williamson Disgraced former clergyman.

Cyril Morton Violet's fiancé and electrical engineer.

This tale opens with Watson telling the reader about Holmes's professional success, and ponders the difficulty in deciding which of his hundreds of cases should be presented to the public. Watson concludes that he will give "preference to those cases which derive their interest not so much from the brutality of the crime as from the ingenuity and dramatic quality of their solution." "The Adventure of the Solitary Cyclist" is certainly dramatic— with guns brandished and shots fired—and Holmes is at his most chivalrous and physical as he rescues the damsel in distress.

The mysterious stalker
It is April 1895 and Violet Smith arrives at 221B Baker Street. She is a beautiful, upright young woman, who is devoted to both her widowed mother and her fiancé, Cyril Morton. Holmes immediately identifies Violet as being an avid cyclist (from the roughening of the side of her sole

One of Holmes's many skills is boxing, which he puts to use when defending himself against a drunken Woodley. "It was a straight left against a slogging ruffian," he tells Watson.

caused by the friction of the pedal) and a musician (from her "spatulate finger-end").

She had recently responded to a newspaper advertisement from two men—Woodley and Carruthers— who claim to have known her uncle Ralph in South Africa. They told her of Ralph's death, and said that he had asked them both to tend to the needs of his relations. Woodley, she said, kept "making eyes" at her, but she found him "odious" and repellent. Carruthers, a widower, offered her a live-in job as a music tutor to his daughter at a remote house near Farnham. Since the position was

In Edwardian times, women cyclists were considered independent, modern, and daring. Cycling really emancipated women, because for the first time they could travel without male supervision.

well paid, and he seemed kind, she accepted. Each weekend, Violet cycles to Farnham station to take a train to see her mother but has noticed that she is always followed, at a distance, by another lone cyclist. Unnerved by her silent stalker, she is seeking advice from Holmes.

Uncovering the plot

Watson is sent to investigate but, predictably, Holmes is disappointed by his meager observations, which do little more than confirm the girl's story. So Holmes goes to Farnham himself, where he makes "discreet inquiries" at the local pub. There, he becomes embroiled in a brawl with Woodley, who wants to know why Holmes is snooping into his affairs.

A dramatic denouement ensues when Watson and Holmes conceal themselves on the country lane. For safety, Violet has begun traveling by dog-cart, but as it draws near they see it is empty. Violet has been abducted, and her stalker is cycling fast behind. The stalker turns out to be Carruthers in disguise, but he is desperately looking for Violet and

entreats Holmes to help him "save" her. Alerted by Violet's screams, they find her, gagged and faint, and learn she has been forcibly married to Woodley by Mr. Williamson—a notorious defrocked priest.

At the heart of this crime is, of course, money. Carruthers and Woodley, who knew each other from South Africa, were aware that Violet was about to inherit a fortune from her uncle, and devised a plot to

entrap her, enlisting Williamson's help. The plan was for Woodley to marry her and for Carruthers to have a share in the "plunder." The plan misfired when Carruthers fell in love with Violet and became her protector, cycling behind her each week to Farnham station in case of an attack by Woodley.

Carruthers is horrified Woodley has succeeded in marrying Violet, and shoots him in rage—Woodley is injured but survives. Holmes asserts that Mr. Williamson's right to conduct a marriage ceremony is questionable and that no forced marriage would be legally valid.

The dramatic conclusion, with a swooning girl, two brutal rogues, and an unscrupulous clergyman, forms a classic tableau of Gothic storytelling. And in spite of the fact that the heroine is an independent individual, she still needs saving from "the worst fate that can befall a woman" by the knight in shining armor—Sherlock Holmes. ∎

Fortune-seeking in South Africa

The wealth that fuels the crime in this story was generated in South Africa, which became a magnet for fortune-seekers in the late 19th century. In 1866, a child of a Dutch farmer found a diamond measuring 22 carats near the Vaal River. The next year, huge diamond deposits were discovered in Kimberley, and in 1884 the world's largest gold deposits were discovered in Witwatersrand. As news of the vast mineral wealth spread, thousands of immigrants from

all over the world made their way to the Transvaal. The huge influx of prospectors, laborers, and entrepreneurs had a huge impact on the region, leading to the foundation of cities—Johannesburg grew out of a mining camp named Langlaagte—and the development of a transportation infrastructure, such as improved roads and rails. Prospectors who became super-wealthy (as was the case with Violet Smith's uncle) were known as "randlords."

A CRIMINAL WHO WAS CAPABLE OF SUCH A THOUGHT IS A MAN WHOM I SHOULD BE PROUD TO DO BUSINESS WITH

THE ADVENTURE OF THE PRIORY SCHOOL (1904)

IN CONTEXT

TYPE
Short story

FIRST PUBLICATION
US: January 1904
UK: February 1904

COLLECTION
***The Return of
Sherlock Holmes*, 1905**

CHARACTERS
Dr. Thorneycroft Huxtable
Head of the Priory School.

Lord Arthur Saltire
Missing student.

Duke of Holdernesse
Arthur's father.

James Wilder Duke of
Holdernesse's secretary.

Heidegger German master
at the Priory School.

Reuben Hayes Landlord of
the nearby Fighting Cock Inn.

Collapsing onto a rug at 221B Baker Street, schoolmaster Dr. Thorneycroft Huxtable cuts an absurd figure. His calling card bears a welter of academic qualifications, and his "majestic figure" is as cumbersome as his unwieldy name. It is with this undignified entrance that this scholarly adventure begins.

Watson examines the supine figure and diagnoses exhaustion. Meanwhile, Holmes reaches into the man's pocket and pulls out a round-trip train ticket from Mackleton in northern England— it seems Huxtable has indeed traveled far. (In the original manuscript, the story was set in

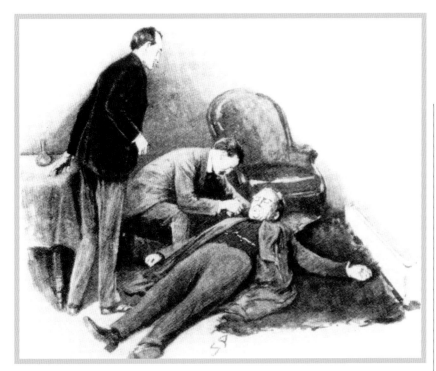

An exhausted Huxtable collapses at 221B Baker Street, where Watson describes him as "a sorely stricken man who lay before us." Illustrated for *The Strand Magazine* by Sidney Paget.

details suggest a planned escape. The school roll call has revealed that the German master, Heidegger, is also missing. Although there is no apparent connection between the student and master, there are obvious signs of the latter's rapid descent from his second floor window, which faces the same way as Saltire's, using the ivy outside. Heidegger's bicycle is also missing.

Saltire had not had any visitors before he vanished, although he had received a letter, which he took with him. Huxtable adds that the boy was apparently happy at school, but that his home life is unbalanced. His parents, the Duke and his wife, have recently separated, and she has moved to France. The Duke's secretary, James Wilder, has let Huxtable know that the boy prefers the company of his mother to that of his stiff and formal father. Could it be possible that he has fled to France to be with her? »

We have had some dramatic entrances and exits upon our small stage at Baker Street, but I cannot recollect anything more sudden and startling than the first appearance of Thorneycroft Huxtable.
Dr. Watson

the real-life village of Castleton, Derbyshire, which Conan Doyle changed to the fictional Mackleton, Hallamshire, in the printed edition.)

Huxtable eventually recovers enough to request a glass of milk and a cookie and, after this quaint refreshment, proceeds to explain his purpose. Although he is a rather comic figure, Huxtable's mission is serious. He is the principal of a highly exclusive preparatory school called the Priory, which educates the sons of the British aristocracy, and his newest and most well-connected pupil, young Lord Arthur Saltire, has gone missing. Holmes leaps to his feet to look up Saltire's father, the Duke of Holdernesse, in his "encyclopaedia of reference," and exclaims that he is "one of the greatest subjects of the Crown!"

Although Conan Doyle doesn't specify, the encyclopaedia Holmes is reading from is probably *Burke's Landed Gentry*, an index of Britain's noble families, produced in 1826 by

genealogist John Burke, which is still used as an active register today. Throughout the story, the action rings with the importance of the British aristocracy; its power, but also its vulnerability. The Duke may be rich, but this wealth has put his son at risk of abduction, and like many aristocratic families, he lives in fear of social scandal should the family name ever be tarnished.

Locked room mystery

The immediate facts of the case provide a compelling variation on the "locked room mystery." Saltire disappeared during the night from his second-floor room at the Priory, which is situated behind another, occupied by two notoriously light-sleeping students. There are no footprints below his open window, and no sign of intruders. He was dressed in his school suit of gray trousers and black Eton jacket—an allusion to Britain's elite public school, Eton College. All of these

The allure of cash

This mysterious web is sufficiently seductive for Holmes to abandon the other two cases he claims to be busy with. Either that, or he's been uncharacteristically seduced by the handsome reward offered by the Duke—£5,000 for the return of his son, and a further £1,000 for the names of his abductors. "I think we shall accompany Dr. Huxtable back to the North of England," Holmes decides, after being told about this generous offer—and even before hearing all the facts.

That same evening, Holmes and Watson arrive at the Priory, and find the Duke and Wilder already there. Wilder upbraids Huxtable severely for summoning Holmes, although his apparent concern that the case will cause a scandal begins to sound more like fear over what Holmes will learn. As for the austere Duke, it is unclear whether his reticence is due to aristocratic reserve or something more suspicious—with his booming "dinner gong" voice, he submits to Holmes's involvement in the case but offers little assistance.

In this first encounter with the men, Conan Doyle turns Wilder's caginess and the Duke's unease

After following his cycle tracks, Holmes and Watson discover the body of Heidegger, illustrated here by Sidney Paget in *The Strand Magazine*.

to dramatic effect, weaving the case's characters into an atmosphere of intrigue. It also gives Holmes an occasion to indulge in his love of play-acting. When Wilder pointedly suggests that Holmes should depart, he counters by making his visit sound like a simple vacation. "This Northern air is invigorating and pleasant. I propose to spend a few days upon your moors, and to occupy my mind as best I may." In truth,

he is planning to explore the moors not for the air but to find the missing boy, Lord Saltire.

Later that evening, Holmes and Watson pore over a map of the area. A main road runs across the front of the Priory, and on the fateful night, a police constable who had coincidentally been posted at its eastern end had seen nothing. A similar incident at the nearby Red Bull Inn conveniently rules out late-night fugitives at that end. To the south, the land is impassable by bicycle, while to the north a copse gives way to the rolling Low Gill Moor, eventually leading to the Duke's home, Holdernesse Hall. As Holmes concludes that this moor should be their focus, Huxtable joins them, brandishing Saltire's blue cricket cap in his hand. It has been found in a caravan of gypsies who left the moor on Tuesday, showing that this is indeed the place to search.

On the right track

A major aspect of the case hinges on Holmes's ability to read tracks. Venturing onto the moor, they find bicycle tire marks. In keeping with his usual precision, Holmes claims to have an expert knowledge of bicycle tracks, and states that these tires have been patched and do not match the tread on Heidegger's bike.

This is a fairly convincing deduction, but Holmes's logic that the bicycle's direction of travel (away from the school) can be seen by the heavier rear tire's tracks periodically overlaying those of the front tire is misleading—in fact, this would offer no clue to the direction of travel. Conan Doyle often argued that accuracy was unimportant next to dramatic effect, but later admitted in his memoirs that some illogical plot details had generated questions from fans all over the

The Duke of Holdernesse

The Duke of Holdernesse's name may have alluded to the original location of the Priory, written in the manuscript as Castleton in Derbyshire. Holderness is the name of a large area in the east of Yorkshire, not far from this county. Scholarly attempts to match the Duke with a real person have proved more fruitless than most, and this has led some Holmesians to attribute this lack of information to Watson's masterful smudging of delicate facts.

The Holdernesse whom Watson describes in the story is a cold, aloof figure, with a flaming red beard, "a drawn, thin face, and a nose which was grotesquely curved and long." This is quite appropriate, perhaps, for one of the most decorated noblemen in Britain—a Knight of the Garter, a Privy Councillor, a Lord Lieutenant, and more—but not exactly consistent with the secretly weak-hearted romantic that the case's true history reveals him to be.

> A bicycle, certainly, but not THE bicycle… I am familiar with forty-two different impressions left by tyres.
> **Sherlock Holmes**

world. These troublesome tire tracks were a case in point, and Conan Doyle even went as far as to conduct his own experiments to prove his idea: "I had so many remonstrances upon this point, varying from pity to anger, that I took out my bicycle and tried. I had imagined that the observations of the way in which the track of the hind wheel overlaid the track of the front one when the machine was not running dead straight would show the direction. I found that my correspondents were right and I was wrong, for this would be the same whichever way the cycle was moving. On the other hand the real solution was much simpler, for on an undulating moor the wheels make a much deeper impression uphill and a more shallow one downhill, so Holmes was justified of his wisdom after all."

A gruesome discovery

As the pair scour the moor, they find the distinctively narrow tread of Heidegger's Palmer tires, soon

Granada Television's adaptation in 1987, starring Jeremy Brett, was filmed at Chatsworth House in Derbyshire, just a few miles away from Castleton, where the story was originally set.

followed by the gruesome discovery of the German master's lifeless body, his head brutally smashed. Heidegger is wearing a nightshirt and is without socks, indicating a hasty exit from the school, in pursuit of Saltire. The violent death suggests it was committed by a strong adult, who was presumably with Saltire. Heidegger, an expert cyclist, had cycled five miles to reach that point, so Saltire and his companion must have had some means of travel. However, there are no other bicycle tracks, or even footprints, around the body—just cattle hoofprints.

It is at the Fighting Cock, a nearby inn, that Holmes puts in a second dramatic turn, feigning a sprained ankle as an excuse to borrow a bicycle from the sour, bad-tempered innkeeper. Alas,

Reuben Hayes has the manners of a criminal, but no bicycle, only horses. It is not until Holmes spots the stable and the smithy that he makes a sudden deduction. He notes that while there were cow hoofprints all around the bicycle tracks and the body on the moor, neither he nor Watson have seen a single cow. Furthermore, the tracks indicated distinctly un-cowlike movements—"it is a remarkable cow which walks, canters, and gallops"—remarks Holmes. He then investigates the horses in Hayes's stable and surmises that they have been freshly shod—in old shoes.

Hereditary scandals

As the pair leave the Fighting Cock, the Duke's secretary speeds past on a bicycle, heading for »

Holmes studies a map of the area around the Priory school and Holdernesse Hall, to deduce where Saltire and Heidegger may have gone. The bicycle tracks on the moor provide him with useful clues.

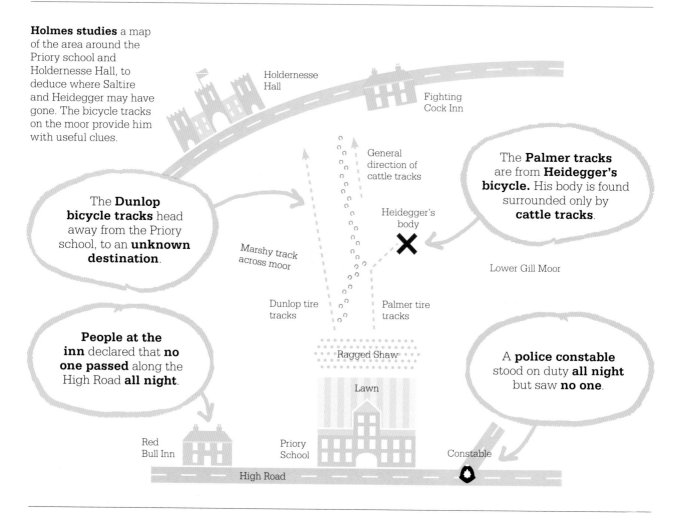

Holdernesse Hall

Fighting Cock Inn

General direction of cattle tracks

Heidegger's body

The **Palmer tracks** are from **Heidegger's bicycle.** His body is found surrounded only by **cattle tracks**.

The **Dunlop bicycle tracks** head away from the Priory school, to an **unknown destination**.

Marshy track across moor

Lower Gill Moor

Dunlop tire tracks

Palmer tire tracks

People at the inn declared that **no one passed** along the High Road **all night**.

Ragged Shaw

Lawn

A **police constable** stood on duty **all night** but saw **no one**.

Red Bull Inn

Priory School

Constable

High Road

the inn. Upon closer inspection, Wilder's patched bicycle tire matches that which Holmes first identified from the set of tracks on the moor, and his unexpected appearance at the inn is the first sign that a plan is falling apart. After peering into a window at the inn, Holmes declares the case closed—he now has his answers.

At Holdernesse Hall the next morning, Holmes reveals the name of his suspect, and accuses the Duke of knowing exactly where his son is. Quite apart from Holmes's extraordinary abruptness with the nobleman, the real revelation here is that the Duke admits that Wilder is

his first-born son—the illegitimate result of an earlier love affair—who has no hope of ever inheriting his father's wealth or title. The Duke now assumes a sympathetic character: for all his concern with propriety, he has brought Wilder up himself after the death of his beloved.

The real villain turns out to be the nervous and shifty Wilder. Since discovering his parentage, he has been holding the Duke to ransom with the threat of scandal. His plot to abduct Holdernesse's rightful heir, the young Lord Saltire, hiding him at the Fighting Cock Inn in order to blackmail his father,

had been the culmination of a lifetime's hatred toward his half-brother and an intense bitterness at the injustice of his lost inheritance.

The letter that Saltire received had been from his father; however, Wilder had added a note purporting to be from Saltire's mother, asking him to meet a man with a horse that evening, who would take him to meet her. This man was Hayes, employed by Wilder, and he and Saltire set off on horseback. Unknown to Saltire, however, he had been spotted leaving the school by Heidegger, who duly followed him by bicycle, concerned for the boy's well-being. As the school master caught up with the fleeing pair, Hayes struck him with a stick and killed him. Heidegger's death was unplanned, a result of Hayes's desperation and brutality.

Justice is served

The Duke reveals that he had learned of the plot after the discovery of Heidegger's body, but he had "yielded—as I have always yielded" to Wilder's plea for him to "keep his secret for three days longer" to allow Hayes to escape. Fearing that Hayes's capture would expose his eldest son's involvement, the Duke felt he had no alternative but to acquiesce.

There is certainly an interesting moral situation here, and Holmes himself points out its muddiness. The Duke's extraordinary sympathy toward Wilder and Hayes seems hard to credit, and even a little irrational. He allowed time for Hayes to make his escape, and has graciously tried to clear up the mess of his first son's sordid machinations. In doing so, however, he has not only conspired to aid a murderer's evasion of justice, but has also left his younger son, and precious heir, in the hands of a known, violent killer.

Holmes has little sympathy for the Duke's cold, remote way of conducting family relationships, saying, "To humour your guilty elder son, you have exposed your innocent younger son to imminent and unnecessary danger." He insists that the young Saltire be brought from the inn immediately, and suggests that Wilder be sent away. Holmes suggests that the Duke attempt a reconciliation with his wife not that his illegitimate son is gone.

Yet if Holmes's dressing-down of Holdernesse runs counter to the story's sycophantic attitude toward the Duke and nobility, his willingness to accept the Duke's money and hush up both the nobleman's involvement and his relationship to Wilder (who is set to depart for Australia) only seems to confirm it. It seems easy to forget that an innocent teacher has been brutally murdered, and the Duke's none-too-subtle trick of quietly doubling Holmes's payoff, which he duly accepts, marks an ignobly neat transition from reward to bribe.

Holmes's final question about the peculiar horseshoes might seem like a return to his usual interest in

> I must take the view, your Grace, that when a man embarks upon a crime, he is morally guilty of any other crime which may spring from it.
> **Sherlock Holmes**

technical details above all else. Shaped like cows' hooves, the horseshoes turn out to be family relics from "the marauding Barons of Holdernesse in the Middle Ages," designed to throw pursuers off their trail. It is thought that similar tricks were really used during the English Civil War. Yet the detective declares the crafty ironwork to be only the "second most interesting object that I have seen in the North"— clearly, his hefty, dubious check takes first place. ∎

The rules of succession

"Primogeniture" is the practice by which land and titles are left to the eldest son within a family. In Britain, this has meant that power and land ownership have always been a male prerogative. Regardless of whether he was the first-born, an illegitimate son, born out of wedlock, had no right to inherit his father's estate. Even today, many historic aristocratic families still follow the rules of primogeniture. However, by the turn of the 21st century, most remaining monarchies, including Britain's, had established gender-blind succession, which means

that a princess with a claim to the throne will no longer be usurped by a younger brother.

In Conan Doyle's time, the principle of "entail" also meant that it was illegal to break up or sell landed estates, so they remained in the hands of a small, powerful minority. Along with primogeniture, entail was a relic of medieval feudalism— in France, entailment was one of the first things to be overturned after the 1789 revolution. It was abolished in Britain by the Law of Property Act of 1925, after which many estates were sold.

ONE SHOULD ALWAYS LOOK FOR A POSSIBLE ALTERNATIVE, AND PROVIDE AGAINST IT

THE ADVENTURE OF BLACK PETER (1904)

IN CONTEXT

TYPE
Short story

FIRST PUBLICATION
US: February 1904
UK: March 1904

COLLECTION
The Return of Sherlock Holmes, 1905

CHARACTERS
Captain Peter Carey ("Black Peter")
Retired whaling captain.

John Hopley Neligan
Banker's young son.

Patrick Cairns Whale harpooner who once served under Peter Carey.

Stanley Hopkins
Young police inspector.

Holmes deduces the identity of the murderer

Whoever impaled the victim had **amazing strength**.

He drank **rum and water**, a sailor's favorite.

"All these pointed to a seaman, and one who had been a whaler."

He had **great skill** in the use of the **harpoon**.

He carried a **seal-skin tobacco pouch**, suggesting a life at sea.

Set in 1895, Conan Doyle's "The Adventure of Black Peter" is an atmospheric story of the murder of a brutal retired whaling captain. Its rich authenticity comes in part from the author's personal experiences. As a young medical student, he spent seven months as surgeon on a whaling ship, the *Hope*, as it hunted in the Arctic. As Conan Doyle wrote later, he "came of age

at 80 degrees north latitude," amid the ice floes and flailing whales. The whalers themselves were a tough breed, and Conan Doyle would have gotten to know hard men like Black Peter only too well.

The tale opens with Holmes returning to his and Watson's lodgings with a harpoon tucked under his arm. Holmes reveals that he has been at the butcher shop, trying to spear a pig carcass with

> ...if I killed Black Peter, the law should give me thanks, for I saved them the price of a hempen rope.
> **Patrick Cairns**

a single strike and singularly failing. Watson, familiar with such extraordinary behavior, concludes that Holmes is engaged in an investigation. In fact, Holmes is conducting a forensic experiment that is itself far ahead of its time—a controlled test of the effectiveness of a murder weapon. Tests such as this are now standard practice for a forensics team undertaking a murder investigation, but Holmes, it seems, was a (fictional) pioneer.

Inspector baffled

Holmes and Watson are soon joined by the young police inspector, Stanley Hopkins, a great admirer of Holmes. It seems that Hopkins has been investigating the same case—the gruesome murder of retired whaler Peter Carey. He has had little success and is seeking Holmes's help.

Carey, commonly known as "Black Peter," was a cruel man, loathed and feared by all who knew him. He slept away from his house in a hut, which was arranged like a ship's cabin, and it was there he was found murdered—pinned to the wall, "like a beetle on a card," with a harpoon that had passed all the way through his body. The only clues Hopkins has found are a

tobacco pouch with the initials "P.C." inscribed on it (which is strange, since Peter Carey rarely smoked), and a notebook carrying the initials "J.H.N."and filled with details about the stock exchange.

A double arrest

Hopkins, Holmes, and Watson arrive at Black Peter's cabin in the Sussex countryside and discover that someone has tried to break in. They lie in wait the following night and catch the would-be burglar—a frail young man called John Hopley Neligan (J.H.N.). Neligan explains that he was looking for some securities he believes Black Peter obtained by murdering his banker father. Convinced he has found his killer, Hopkins arrests Neligan.

However, knowing from his experiments that this "anaemic youth" would not have had the strength to harpoon Black Peter, Holmes continues his investigation. As "Captain Basil", Holmes advertises for a harpooner for a whaling trip. One of three applicants is Patrick Cairns, a hard-as-nails harpooner who once crewed on Black Peter's ship, The Sea Unicorn. Cairns's initials are also P.C., and Holmes—sure he has his man—handcuffs him. Cairns admits he killed Black Peter, but insists it was in self-defense. He says that he went to Black Peter to demand money for keeping quiet about the murder of Neligan's father, which he had witnessed years earlier. As Cairns is led away, Hopkins is full of admiration for Holmes's success in identifying the real killer.

The tale ends on a note of mystery, with Holmes telling Hopkins that if he is needed for the trial, his address and that of Watson will be "somewhere in Norway"—leaving the reader to speculate on what the next adventure will be. ∎

19th-century whaling

Throughout the first half of the 19th century, whale blubber was the main source of oil for the lamps that lit the world's homes. Whaling became big business, and the British whaling ports of Whitby and Dundee (where Black Peter's ship The Sea Unicorn was registered) boomed. Across the Atlantic, New Bedford, Massachusetts, was soon dubbed "the city that lit the world."

Life aboard a "whaler" was perilous and tough, as Herman Melville's great novel Moby Dick (1851) makes clear. Many whalers never made it home, yet the financial rewards were tempting enough to make countless men take the risk. Every February, whalers sailed north to make the most of the brief Arctic summer. By 1895, though, the industry was in decline as kerosene from mineral oil supplanted whale oil for lamps. Strong-armed harpooners, like Patrick Cairns, became increasingly rare, as more whalers used the new harpoon guns to kill their prey with brutal efficiency and little skill.

BY JOVE, WATSON; I'VE GOT IT!

THE ADVENTURE OF CHARLES AUGUSTUS MILVERTON (1904)

IN CONTEXT

TYPE
Short story

FIRST PUBLICATION
UK: April 1904
US: April 1904

COLLECTION
***The Return of Sherlock Holmes*, 1905**

CHARACTERS
Charles Augustus Milverton Professional blackmailer.

Lady Eva Brackwell Beautiful former debutante.

Earl of Dovercourt Lady Eva's fiancé.

Agatha Milverton's housemaid.

Anonymous lady Widow of one of Milverton's victims.

Inspector Lestrade Scotland Yard detective.

The eponymous villain of this story is a professional blackmailer who Holmes considers more despicable than any murderer he has ever known. Conan Doyle's inspiration for the character was Charles Augustus Howell, an art dealer and alleged blackmailer nicknamed "The Owl," who died in London under strange circumstances, with his throat cut and a coin shoved into his mouth— a symbol of revenge on someone guilty of slander.

The debutante in distress

Charles Augustus Milverton makes his living by blackmailing wealthy people with incriminating letters acquired from disloyal servants and lovers. His latest victim is "the most beautiful debutante of last season," Lady Eva Brackwell, who hires Sherlock Holmes to negotiate the return of some "imprudent," "sprightly" letters, which threaten her engagement to an earl. As a debutante, Lady Eva would have been formally presented to the

queen at a "coming-out ceremony," before attending a full "season" of various social events with a view to securing a favorable marriage. The besmirching of her good name would mean the permanent ruin of her reputation, so the letters could have potentially dire consequences. When Milverton demands £7,000, Holmes offers him £2,000—but the blackmailer won't budge. He wants to make "a severe example" of Lady Eva, leaving Holmes determined to retrieve the letters.

In an arguably ill-conceived plot device, Conan Doyle then has Holmes, usually a gentleman, behave with uncharacteristic

Charles Augustus Howell (1840–1890) as drawn by Frederick Sandys in 1882, eight years before his macabre murder.

> I think there are certain crimes which the law cannot touch, and which therefore, to some extent, justify private revenge.
> **Sherlock Holmes**

caddishness by becoming falsely engaged to Milverton's maid, Agatha, in order to learn the layout of the blackmailer's house and details of his habits. "Surely you have gone too far?" cries Watson. Holmes replies: "You must play your cards as best you can when such a stake is on the table." While he adds that he has a rival suitor who will no doubt step in the moment he is off the scene, clearly, to Holmes, the feelings and reputation of a maid count for less than those of a lady.

Holmes tells Watson that they must break into Milverton's house and steal the compromising letters from his safe, which the two agree is a "morally justifiable, though technically criminal" act. Holmes has a sense of natural order, seeking to right wrongs, even if it means breaking the law. As a private detective he feels he can do this when he judges that the ends justify the means.

Defying the law
Holmes and Watson break into Milverton's house at night and witness a meeting between the blackmailer and a woman purporting to be the maid of a certain countess, offering to sell

compromising letters. But very soon she reveals her true identity as the widow of one of Milverton's victims, before committing the most violent act by a woman in the Holmes canon, pumping Milverton's body full of bullets. Held back by Holmes, Watson realizes "that justice had overtaken a villain." Holmes burns all of Milverton's blackmail papers before they beat a hasty retreat.

The following morning, Inspector Lestrade visits Holmes to tell him that two burglars were seen fleeing the scene. Holmes mischievously suggests that the appearance of one

The widow pours "bullet after bullet into Milverton's shrinking body," as Paget shows in *The Strand Magazine*.

of the felons "might be a description of Watson." When he has had his fun, he declines to help Lestrade with the case, explaining, "my sympathies are with the criminals." In a final twist, Holmes sees a photograph of Milverton's killer in a shop window. But when Watson also recognizes her, Holmes puts a finger to his lips. Once again, his moral compass steers him away from adhering to the letter of the law. ∎

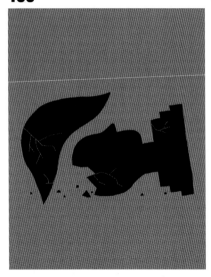

THERE IS A CERTAIN METHOD IN THE GENTLEMAN'S ECCENTRIC PROCEEDINGS
THE ADVENTURE OF THE SIX NAPOLEONS (1904)

IN CONTEXT

TYPE
Short story

FIRST PUBLICATION
US: April 1904
UK: May 1904

COLLECTION
The Return of Sherlock Holmes, 1905

CHARACTERS
Inspector Lestrade
Scotland Yard inspector.

Morse Hudson Shop owner who buys three busts.

Horace Harker
Elderly journalist.

Beppo Italian craftsman.

Manager of Gelder & Co.
Beppo's former manager.

Pietro Venucci Powerful mafioso of Neapolitan descent.

Josiah Brown
Owner of the fifth bust.

Mr. Sandeford Former owner of the bust sold to Holmes.

This adventure opens with a warm scene between Sherlock Holmes and Inspector Lestrade that reflects how their relationship has grown over their years of working together. Now a regular at 221B Baker Street, Lestrade keeps Holmes in touch with activities at Scotland Yard.

A case of insanity
The case surrounds the bizarre theft and apparently wanton destruction of three plaster-cast busts of Napoleon; one at a shop in Kennington owned by Morse Hudson (who, according to some Holmesians, is the estranged husband of landlady Mrs. Hudson), and two others at nearby addresses in south London. Lestrade's idea that the thief could be a "criminal or lunatic," and possibly a "local fanatic," perhaps stems from the area's close proximity to Bedlam, the notorious insane asylum—now London's Imperial War Museum. In any case, this theory serves Holmes well. When a fourth bust is stolen from the home of Horace Harker, a journalist in Kensington, and a man is found murdered on the front steps,

The science of phrenology

In the 1800s, many people became convinced that a person's psychology could be determined from the shape of their brain—and, therefore, their skull. Known as "phrenology" (meaning "study of the mind"), the subject has since been debunked as a pseudoscience. But the idea that the brain could be "anatomized" into segments, each of which had some bearing on an individual's personality, was in keeping with the Victorian spirit of scientific progress and taxonomy: if the brain is the "organ of the mind," then it would seem logical that its shape reflects a person's mental life. By the mid-19th century, the Italian criminologist Cesare Lombroso introduced this idea to the study of crime, writing a series of books on the supposed cranial peculiarities of gamblers, fraudsters, and all manner of dastardly types. Conan Doyle himself studied medicine at The Edinburgh Phrenological Society.

> It is undoubtedly queer, and I know that you have a taste for all that is out of the common.
> **Inspector Lestrade**

Holmes's false hint to the resident journalist about "a dangerous homicidal lunatic, with Napoleonic delusions" is reported in the evening papers. Chuckling over the reports later on, Holmes remarks, "The Press, Watson, is a most valuable institution, if you only know how to use it."

Holmes is on the case

It is clear that Holmes has a plan: while these reports are designed to mislead the criminal and make him think that Holmes is clueless, in fact he has two major leads. One is a photograph carried by the murder victim, depicting "an alert, sharp-featured simian man, with thick eyebrows and a very peculiar projection of the lower part of the face, like the muzzle of a baboon." This description accords with phrenological theories about criminals' physical appearance.

The other clue of interest to Holmes is that before smashing the fourth bust, the thief had mysteriously carried it from the house to a better-lit place farther down the street, even though he risked being seen while doing so. If this was merely an act of destruction, why did the thief need to do it in the light?

Italian connections

In typical Scotland Yard fashion, Lestrade focuses only on the murder and the break-ins. Unlike Holmes, he doesn't see that the Napoleon busts are the key to the case. Holmes traces the busts back to the workshop where they were made in Stepney—a district that was described as "vicious, semi-criminal" by social researcher and philanthropist Charles Booth, and characterized by Conan Doyle as a place where "tenement houses swelter and reek with the outcasts of Europe." Here Holmes discovers that the photographed man is Beppo, an Italian former employee, who had been jailed the year before for knifing a man in the street, at around the same time the busts were made. At 221B that evening, Lestrade identifies the murder victim as Pietro Venucci, a mafioso from London's squalid Italian underworld. Now interested in the busts, Lestrade's new theory is that Venucci was sent to kill the bust-smasher, in some kind of mafioso vendetta. However, Holmes knows better, and offers him a bet that they will catch the villain that night at the Chiswick home of Josiah Brown, who purchased one of the two remaining busts out of the six the workshop had produced.

A smashing climax

Beppo is duly arrested at Brown's house and Lestrade sees the case as closed, until Holmes offers to explain the full facts the following evening at 221B. Purchasing the last Napoleon bust from its new owner for a seemingly generous £10, he promptly smashes it, thus revealing that hidden inside is the priceless "black pearl of the Borgias," the most famous pearl in the world, which had previously been stolen from an Italian hotel room.

Holmes cannot claim all the glory, since Lestrade's work was vital for this theatrical climax. Holmes realized what was afoot when he learned the name of the murder victim, Venucci. Remembering the theft of that pearl the year before, he recalled that the suspect, a hotel maid, had the same surname. She had passed the stolen pearl on to her brother, who had been stabbed and robbed by Beppo during a street fight. Before his arrest for the stabbing, Beppo had hidden the pearl inside an unfinished bust at the workshop. Venucci had been looking for Beppo when he stabbed him outside Harker's house.

Lestrade's heartfelt praise—"at Scotland Yard… we are very proud of you"—elicits a rare glimpse into Holmes's sensitive side, and Watson observes how "he was more nearly moved by the softer human emotions than I had ever seen him." ∎

Inspired by "The Six Napoleons," *The Pearl of Death* was a 1944 movie starring Basil Rathbone and Nigel Bruce, in their ninth outing on screen as Holmes and Watson.

LET US HEAR THE SUSPICIONS. I WILL LOOK AFTER THE PROOFS

THE ADVENTURE OF THE THREE STUDENTS (1904)

IN CONTEXT

TYPE
Short story

FIRST PUBLICATION
UK: June 1904
US: September 1904

COLLECTION
The Return of
***Sherlock Holmes*, 1905**

CHARACTERS
Hilton Soames Professor at
St. Luke's College.

Bannister Soames's
loyal servant.

Daulat Ras Reserved and
industrious student from India.

Giles Gilchrist Athletic
and hard-working student.

Miles McLaren Brilliant
but wayward student.

Despite all of his journeys around the country, and his intrepid meanderings through Tibet and the Middle East during the "Great Hiatus" (pp.164–65), Holmes is never entirely comfortable away from 221B Baker Street. Whenever possible, he is eager to wrap up a case in time to catch the last train back to London, and even on supposedly therapeutic trips out of the city, as in "The Adventure of the Devil's Foot" (pp.240–45), he pines for the excitement of the Big Smoke.

Well, Watson, what do you think of it?… Quite a little parlour game— sort of three-card trick, is it not? There are your three men. It must be one of them.
Sherlock Holmes

In "The Adventure of The Three Students," Holmes and Watson are undertaking research in an unnamed university city, where the doctor notes that "my friend's temper had not improved since he had been deprived of the congenial surroundings of Baker Street." Fortunately, Holmes is always distracted by the prospect of a case, and an acquaintance, Hilton Soames, provides just the thing.

The trio of suspects
Soames, a university professor, had been checking a passage of ancient Greek text for unseen translation printed in an exam paper for a lucrative scholarship, when someone entered his office while he was out and copied part of it. The exam is the next day, and unless the culprit can be found it will have to be canceled—to the embarrassment of the college. Once again, in his capacity as a private operator, and with a reputation for discretion, Holmes is ideally placed to investigate the delicate matter.

The perpetrator had accessed Soames's office when his servant, Bannister, accidentally left his keys in the door. Suspicion then immediately falls on the three students who live in the same building as Soames's office. All three students use the staircase next to it, and are all about to take the exam. There are reasons to suspect each of the three students: McLaren has had a previous brush with scandal, Ras is quiet and elusive, and Gilchrist is apparently honest but short of money, giving him the most obvious motive.

Examining the clues

On inspecting the scene, Holmes's first clue is suggested by some wooden shavings that allow him to discern the make and length of the miscreant's pencil. He then deduces from the way that the papers are strewn around the room that the culprit was almost caught in the act. More mysterious, however, is the "small ball of black dough or clay, with specks of something which looks like sawdust in it."

The key to the solution lies at the athletics track. Holmes turns up at the college early the next morning brandishing three little clay pyramids. He reveals them to be lumps of earth from the long-jump pit that had fallen from the spiked soles of track shoes. Faced

with this evidence, the athlete, Gilchrist, owns up, claiming that he had already decided to do so prior to Holmes's involvement.

Redemption overseas

Bannister, the servant, has also played a significant role. Upon first discovering Gilchrist's crime, he hid a pair of gloves that he knew would implicate the young man. It then transpires that Bannister was once in the employ of Gilchrist's father, and has been motivated by loyalty. It also appears that the trusty manservant has already had a chance to set his former young master on the straight and narrow. In the tradition of James Ryder in "The Adventure of the Blue Carbuncle" (pp.82–3) and James Wilder in "The Adventure of the Priory School" (pp.178–83), Gilchrist accepts exile rather than publicly disgracing himself and his college. Most top universities at this time still had strong religious backgrounds, and dishonorable behavior by one student would reflect on the whole institution.

Gilchrist announces that he intends to accept a commission with the Rhodesian police, an

The culprit confesses to Holmes, as illustrated by Paget in *The Strand Magazine*. He had, however, already decided to admit his guilt to Soames.

adventurous but respectable job, in what would at the time have been a rapidly changing part of Southern Africa, and one that would take him far away from the ivory towers of academia. ∎

Universities in the Victorian age

In the Victorian era, attending university was still largely the preserve of wealthy young men, and usually meant receiving a education in subjects such as Latin and ancient Greek. While other subjects, such as medicine, were taught, undergraduates did not have access to the wide range of disciplines available today. Neither did they have access to the number of universities that exist now. For the Victorian scholar, choice was dominated by the ancient institutions of Oxford, Cambridge, and the old Scottish universities, along with some

more recent additions, such as Durham and the University of London colleges. Women could sometimes attend universities, although they were not allowed to receive degrees until 1878, when University College London started to award them.

Change came at the turn of the twentieth century, when "red-brick" universities sprang up in industrial cities, including Manchester, Birmingham, Bristol, and Leeds. With subjects such as engineering, there was a clear move toward more practical education.

SURELY MY DEDUCTIONS ARE SIMPLICITY ITSELF
THE ADVENTURE OF THE GOLDEN PINCE-NEZ (1904)

IN CONTEXT

TYPE
Short story

FIRST PUBLICATION
UK: July 1904
US: October 1904

COLLECTION
***The Return of Sherlock Holmes*, 1905**

CHARACTERS
Stanley Hopkins Young police detective.

Professor Coram Elderly professor and invalid.

Willoughby Smith Young researcher working for Professor Coram.

Anna Former Russian revolutionary.

Mrs. Marker Professor Coram's housekeeper.

Susan Tarlton Professor Coram's maid.

Mortimer Professor Coram's gardener and army pensioner.

This case shows Holmes at the height of his deductive powers, brilliantly piecing together the truth behind a baffling murder. Just a few easily overlooked clues are enough to lead him straight to the culprit. However, while the eager young police detective Stanley Hopkins, who is investigating the case, tries to apply Holmes's forensic methods at the crime scene, he is left watching open-mouthed as the detective shows just how it should be done.

A midnight visitor
Holmes and Watson are quietly at work at 221B Baker Street on a dark and stormy winter's night in 1894. Watson notes how, even in the heart of London, a tempestuous night such as this is a reminder of the elemental power and wildness of nature. So often in the Holmes tales, the danger is lurking deep in the untamed darkness of the countryside beyond London—perhaps a reminder that the constant vigilance of Holmes's reason is needed to keep the dark forces of chaos at bay.

Each man is focusing on his own area of interest: Watson is reading a medical treatise, and

Holmes is studying a palimpsest, a very old document often made of parchment, from which the original writing has been erased so that it can be used again. However, a discerning eye, such as Holmes's, can sometimes decipher the original, hidden text, beneath the overlay of the new; and his analysis of the palimpsest can be seen as a metaphor for his criminal detection methods.

Holmes and Watson's evening is suddenly interrupted by the arrival of Police Inspector Hopkins, who is seeking Holmes's help with a murder that has taken place earlier that day.

What did you do, Hopkins, after you had made certain that you had made certain of nothing?
Sherlock Holmes

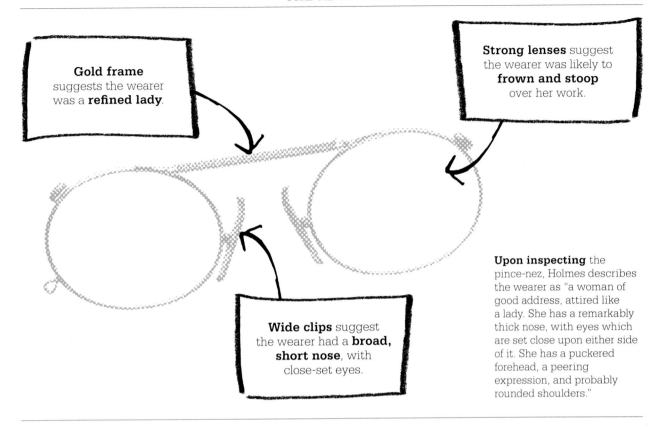

Gold frame suggests the wearer was a **refined lady**.

Strong lenses suggest the wearer was likely to **frown and stoop** over her work.

Wide clips suggest the wearer had a **broad, short nose**, with close-set eyes.

Upon inspecting the pince-nez, Holmes describes the wearer as "a woman of good address, attired like a lady. She has a remarkably thick nose, with eyes which are set close upon either side of it. She has a puckered forehead, a peering expression, and probably rounded shoulders."

The Yoxley murder

Willoughby Smith, a young man working as a researcher for the elderly, bed-bound Professor Coram in Yoxley Old Place—a secluded house in the Kent countryside—has been murdered in the professor's study, stabbed in the neck with a paper knife taken from the desk. His dying words uttered to the maid who found him—"The professor—it was she"—indicate the murderer was female (Professor Coram being a man). Nothing has been stolen, no member of the household has seen or heard anything, and there appears to be no motive. Hopkins's search indicated that the murderer's only escape route would have been via the garden, but he found no footprints.

At this point Hopkins reveals that the victim was found clutching a golden pince-nez (glasses that are kept in place only by pinching the bridge of the nose), which the detective has brought with him. He says Smith had clearly grabbed them from the assassin at the time of the murder, as he did not wear glasses. While pince-nez were widely worn in the 1890s, Holmes is confident that this pair will yield valuable clues. Clearly relishing this chance to show off his powers to his young disciple, Holmes examines them closely, then jots down a full physical description of the wearer, including the key fact that she is incredibly nearsighted and so should be easy to track down—all deduced before he has even visited the crime scene.

On the path

The following morning, Holmes travels down to Yoxley Old Place with Watson and Hopkins. It is here that Holmes makes his most brilliant deductions, although he keeps them to himself until the dramatic denouement of the case.

On arriving at the garden of Yoxley Old Place, Holmes carefully inspects the path. Hopkins then reiterates that when he examined it the previous day, there had been no visible footprints, yet now there were signs of someone having trodden on the narrow grass border alongside it. Hopkins assumes someone had walked on that instead of the footpath in order to avoid leaving a track. When Holmes asks whether Hopkins is sure that the murderer must have left the house the same way she entered, Hopkins says she must certainly have done so, since there is no other way out. Holmes seems unconvinced—but the reader has yet to learn why. »

On examining the professor's study, Holmes immediately notices a new scratch near the lock on a bureau, and deduces that the murderer was trying to break into it when Smith interrupted her. Holmes then considers her escape route. There are two options—either the way she came, or along a corridor that leads into the professor's bedroom.

Holmes, Watson, and Hopkins visit the professor. While Holmes chain-smokes the professor's Egyptian cigarettes, they discuss the possible causes of Smith's death, which the professor says he believes was suicide. Holmes then departs, saying he will return that afternoon to report back on the case. When asked by his companions whether he has any clues, Holmes's enigmatic response is that "the cigarettes will show me."

> It would be difficult to name any articles which afford a finer field for inference than a pair of glasses.
> **Sherlock Holmes**

The Russian in hiding

Holmes returns to the professor's room at the specified time, and after "mistakenly" dropping the box of cigarettes offered to him and picking all the stray cigarettes off the floor, he announces that he has solved the mystery, much to everyone's amazement. He immediately identifies a bookcase with a secret closet as the place where the assassin has concealed herself. Realizing the game is up, the murderer—who is exactly as Holmes has described her—emerges, and tells her story. She confesses that she had entered the house to recover some crucial personal documents, but was caught in the act by Smith, and killed him accidentally while trying to escape. Fleeing down the wrong corridor in panic, she ended up in the professor's bedroom—and he, although surprised to see her, then hid her from the police.

It turns out that the woman is the professor's Russian wife, Anna. Years earlier, the couple were involved in a revolutionary

---

Stanley Hopkins's sketch of the crime scene

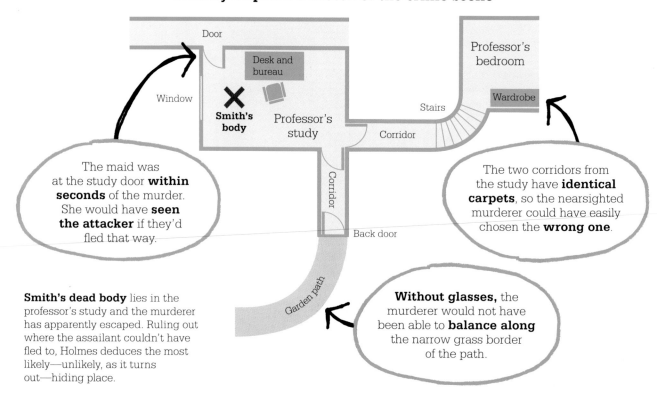

The maid was at the study door **within seconds** of the murder. She would have **seen the attacker** if they'd fled that way.

The two corridors from the study have **identical carpets**, so the nearsighted murderer could have easily chosen the **wrong one**.

Without glasses, the murderer would not have been able to **balance along** the narrow grass border of the path.

Smith's dead body lies in the professor's study and the murderer has apparently escaped. Ruling out where the assailant couldn't have fled to, Holmes deduces the most likely—unlikely, as it turns out—hiding place.

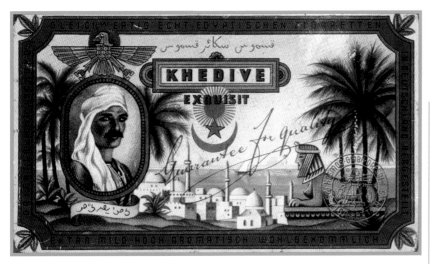

Egyptian cigarettes, as smoked by Professor Coram, were the height of fashion in Victorian society. British and American companies copied Egyptian motifs, hence today's Camel brand.

movement in their homeland, but their activities were uncovered by the authorities and in order to save his own life, the professor betrayed Anna and their comrades, and fled to England. Many of the group were jailed, including Anna's close friend Alexis, who was innocent of any wrongdoing and had written many letters dissuading his comrades from the path of violence. The professor had discovered these letters, which may have prevented Alexis's conviction, but he withheld them, prompting Anna to take matters into her own hands and try to steal them.

Having explained her noble quest to save her friend, Anna falls on to the bed and dies, having taken poison before she revealed herself. The story's ending is tragic, but the case has been solved, and Holmes has the documents that may ensure Alexis's freedom.

The detective's summary
What is remarkable about this case is the speed at which Holmes succeeds in solving it: barely 14 hours had passed since Hopkins's arrival in Baker Street. In few other adventures do we see Holmes working so swiftly to solve a crime from just the slimmest of clues.

As always, the secret to Holmes's success is in his observation of details that others have overlooked. He tells his stunned companions how he reached his conclusions. First, the style and fit of the pince-nez found at the crime scene enabled him to create a detailed image of the wearer (see p.193). Second, on examining the garden path, he realized that the murderer—half-blind without her glasses—could not possibly have made her escape down a narrow strip of grass without making a false step, so she must have still been in the

house. Third, the fact that the two corridors were both covered in coconut matting meant it was likely that someone with poor eyesight might have taken the wrong corridor, ending up in the professor's room. And finally, Holmes's brilliant ploy with the cigarette ash: noticing a clear space in front of the bookcase, he had dropped ash over the floor. When he returned in the afternoon, the ash had been stepped in, revealing that the "prisoner" had come out of her hiding place.

These and various other details missed by Hopkins yielded their secrets to Holmes's piercing eye. He knows it is crucial not to let the truth escape just because it is unexpected. "A simple case," Holmes says, "yet, in some ways, an instructive one." He clearly expects Hopkins to have learned from it— and feels sufficiently satisfied to congratulate him on bringing his case to a successful conclusion. ∎

Russian revolutionaries

Russia's Czar Alexander II was a reformer who freed the serfs in 1861, but many thought it was a ruse and that autocratic rule would go on as before. Young intellectuals, in particular, came to believe that the only way to achieve true freedom was through violent revolution.

Alexander II survived one assassination attempt in 1879, only to be killed two years later in St. Petersburg. After his death, the stakes were raised even higher. The secret police

(*Okhrana*) cracked down on young revolutionary groups like the one Anna and Professor Coram were involved in, and pogroms were launched against Jews, who were thought to have been involved in the Czar's assassination. The revolutionaries fought back with bomb plots and terrorism. One group, the Nihilists, became known throughout Europe for their willingness to use violence to bring about the political change they felt was essential.

WHEN A MAN IS LOST IT IS MY DUTY TO ASCERTAIN HIS FATE

THE ADVENTURE OF THE MISSING THREE-QUARTER (1904)

IN CONTEXT

TYPE
Short story

FIRST PUBLICATION
UK: August 1904
US: November 1904

COLLECTION
The Return of
Sherlock Holmes, 1905

CHARACTERS
Cyril Overton Skipper of
the Cambridge University
rugby team.

Godfrey Staunton
Missing "three-quarter,"
Cambridge's star rugby player.

Lord Mount-James
Godfrey's miserly uncle.

Dr. Leslie Armstrong
Friend of Godfrey.

I n a plot device deployed in only a few Holmes stories, no actual crime is involved in "The Adventure of the Missing Three-Quarter." However, this fact comes to light at the end of the tale, in which Holmes investigates the mysterious disappearance of a talented Cambridge rugby player.

First impressions

While investigating the case, Holmes and Watson encounter two extraordinary—and contrasting—characters. The first, the missing man's uncle and his only living relative, Lord Mount-James, is one of the richest men in England but

You live in a
different world to me,
Mr. Overton—a sweeter
and healthier one.
Sherlock Holmes

also a mean-spirited miser who is spectacularly uninterested in his nephew's whereabouts. The second, Dr. Leslie Armstrong, is a "grim, ascetic, self-contained, formidable" figure who is deeply suspicious of Holmes, regarding him as a meddler in search of a scandal. Bad-tempered and defensive, his unprovoked hostility toward Holmes seems likely to be masking criminality. Holmes even goes so far as to say that he has not "seen a man who, if he turns his talents that way, was more calculated to fill the gap left by the illustrious Moriarty." In fact he could not be more wrong.

London to Cambridge

In addition to exploring how appearances can be disturbingly deceptive—how it is imperative to penetrate beneath the surface to find true motivation—this story explores the dangers of idleness. It opens on a gloomy morning in February when Holmes has little to do and is deeply bored. Watson is alarmed because he fears that the understimulated Holmes could relapse into his former drug addiction, the "fiend" that "was not dead but sleeping."

First played in 1872, and continuing to today, the Varsity Match is a hotly contested annual game of rugby union between the universities of Cambridge and Oxford.

The client is Cyril Overton, captain of the Cambridge University rugby team. His star player, Godfrey Staunton, a "three-quarter," has gone missing just days before he is due to play in an important match against Oxford University. Holmes searches Staunton's London hotel room, where he discovers part of a telegram message imprinted on blotting paper, then charms a post office clerk into revealing the telegram's destination.

This leads him to the recalcitrant Dr. Armstrong in Cambridge. A cat-and-mouse game then ensues, with Holmes being led a merry dance as he tries to trail the doctor's carriage, while his quarry becomes more and more incensed by the pursuit.

One morning, two days into their quest, Watson is panicked when he sees Holmes holding a syringe. In fact, the detective has just used it to squirt aniseed on the carriage wheels so they leave a scent trail for a sniffer dog, Pompey.

The dog duly leads Holmes and Watson to a remote cottage where they find Staunton weeping over his wife, who has just died of tuberculosis. He had married her secretly and kept her hidden in the knowledge that his uncaring uncle, Lord Mount-James, would be enraged by her humble birth. Armstrong had been treating her illness, and turns out to be the kindest of men—deeply loyal and protective of his friend, Staunton.

Conan Doyle himself was only too familiar with the horrors of tuberculosis. His first wife, Louise, was diagnosed with the disease in 1893, succumbing to it in 1906.

No crime has been committed, but Staunton has suffered a tragic loss. Holmes insists that he will do his utmost to keep the truth from the papers. He and Dr. Armstrong have misjudged each other, and their gaining of mutual respect is the true climax of the story. ∎

Sniffer dogs

Bloodhounds have been used to track outlaws since the Middle Ages; in Scotland, they were known as "slough hounds," the origin of the word "sleuth."

In 1869, following a public outcry about the failure of the Metropolitan Police to capture Jack the Ripper (p.312), the police commissioner, Sir Charles Warren, had two bloodhounds trained to perform tracking tests and hunt for the serial killer. The investigation proved unsuccessful, however, as Warren was bitten and both dogs ran away.

In his hunt for Godfrey Staunton, Holmes is, fortunately, much more successful. Pompey is a drag hound. This breed of dog is generally a cross between a foxhound and a beagle, and is trained to follow the trail of a scent (often made up of aniseed oils) either laid or "dragged" over a course. The Cambridge University Drag began in 1855, and today is the only pack of drag hounds in England still run by students. Certainly Holmes would have had no difficulty in locating a dog such as Pompey in Cambridge at the time.

THE GAME IS AFOOT

THE ADVENTURE OF THE ABBEY GRANGE (1904)

IN CONTEXT

TYPE
Short story

FIRST PUBLICATION
UK: September 1904
US: December 1904

COLLECTION
***The Return of Sherlock Holmes*, 1905**

CHARACTERS
Stanley Hopkins Young police inspector.

Sir Eustace Brackenstall Wealthy man and owner of the Abbey Grange.

Lady Brackenstall (née Mary Fraser) Sir Eustace's Australian wife.

Theresa Wright Lady Brackenstall's maid.

Jack Croker Sailor and Lady Brackenstall's admirer.

Frequently in the canon, Holmes's sense of justice is at odds with legal convention—in "The Boscombe Valley Mystery" (pp.70–73), for example, the detective sympathizes with the murderer because he was being blackmailed, and agrees to keep his crime a secret because he is an old man who is dying, and will soon have to answer "at a higher court than the Assizes."

In "The Adventure of the Abbey Grange," Holmes goes even further, allowing a healthy young killer to walk free. "Once or twice in my career," he tells Watson, "I feel that

Like this grand house in Hampshire, Abbey Grange is a mansion built "in the fashion of Palladio." Palladian design was popular in 18th-century Europe.

I have done more real harm by my discovery of the criminal than ever he had done by his crime. I have learned caution now, and I had rather play tricks with the law of England than with my own conscience." Watson, in turn, readily colludes with his friend's morally dubious stance.

"The Abbey Grange" is notable, too, for tackling the dilemma of women trapped in abusive marriages: in this case with a husband who is a violent drunkard. Conan Doyle had had firsthand experience of alcoholism, for his own father, Charles, was a weak-willed alcoholic; he addresses the subject in several Holmes stories as well as in other works, including his short story "The Japanned Box".

Holmes is summoned

"The Abbey Grange" begins early one bitterly cold winter morning in 1897. Holmes rouses Watson: they have been summoned by Inspector Hopkins to Abbey Grange—a Palladian mansion in Marsham, near Chislehurst, Kent—for what looks like a promising murder case.

On the train, Holmes indulges in some lighthearted criticism of Watson who, he claims, has a fatal habit of looking at everything with the eyes of a sensationalist storyteller, skating over the finer points. Watson's grumpy riposte is that Holmes should try writing up his cases himself. Holmes assures his companion that he intends to do so in his old age. He claims that he will one day

A change had come over Holmes's manner. He had lost his listless expression, and again I saw an alert light of interest in his keen, deep-set eyes.
Dr. Watson

write a textbook that will "focus the whole art of detection into one volume."

They are met at the doorway of Abbey Grange by Inspector Hopkins, who fills them in briefly on what has happened. The murder victim turns out to be Sir Eustace Brackenstall, "one of the richest men in Kent," who is thought to have been killed when three burglars attacked him with a poker. Hopkins assumes from the descriptions given by Lady Brackenstall (and verified by her maid) that the attackers are the notorious Randall gang, who "did a job at Sydenham a fortnight ago," rashly claiming that they did it "beyond all doubt."

The Brackenstall victims

Hopkins then introduces them to Lady Brackenstall—originally Mary Fraser from Adelaide, Australia. She is blonde, blue-eyed, and beautiful. "Seldom have I seen so graceful a figure, so womanly a presence, and so beautiful a face," gushes Watson. She has a wound over one eye, along with two "vivid red spots" on one of her arms, which, she tells Holmes, have nothing to do with the events of the previous evening. However, the nature of these marks soon becomes clear when she explains that her husband of about a year was a "confirmed drunkard" who beat her up regularly and—we later learn—once doused her dog in gasoline and set it on fire. She has clearly been trapped in an abusive and desperately unhappy relationship.

She proceeds to tell her version of the events that occurred the previous evening. Around bedtime, on finding the dining-room window open, she was confronted by three burglars, who punched her in the eye and threw her to the ground, knocking her out. She awoke to

find they had torn down the bell-rope, using it to tie her to a chair, and gagged her. Sir Eustace must have heard noises, as he burst into the room brandishing his "favourite blackthorn cudgel." However, one of the burglars struck him down with a poker taken from the grate. He fell and never moved again. She passed out once more, and when she came to, saw that the men had picked up the silver from the sideboard. They were talking in whispers and each of them had a glass of wine in their hand, poured from a nearby bottle. When they finally left, she managed to free herself and raise the alarm.

Holmes has misgivings

The case seems to be clear-cut, and Holmes and Watson leave for London, and yet Holmes is plagued by doubts. Why would the Randall gang risk carrying out another burglary in the same area again »

Murdered with a single blow from a fire poker, Sir Eustace Brackenstall—seen here in an illustration from *The Strand Magazine*—is not the helpless victim that he first appears.

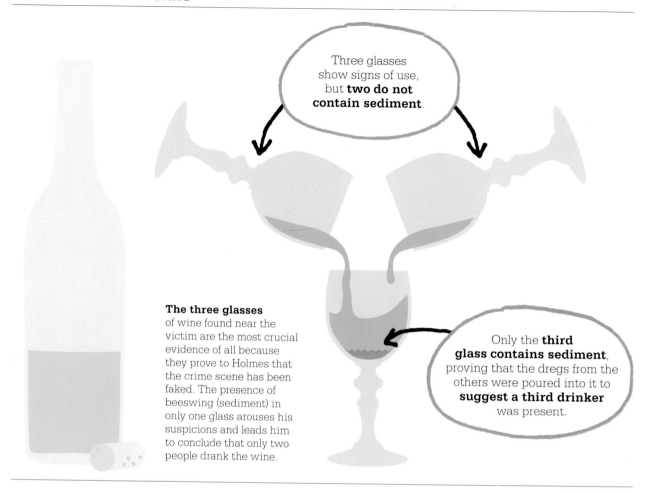

Three glasses show signs of use, but **two do not contain sediment**.

The three glasses of wine found near the victim are the most crucial evidence of all because they prove to Holmes that the crime scene has been faked. The presence of beeswing (sediment) in only one glass arouses his suspicions and leads him to conclude that only two people drank the wine.

Only the **third glass contains sediment**, proving that the dregs from the others were poured into it to **suggest a third drinker** was present.

so soon? Why murder Sir Eustace rather than simply overpower him, as the three of them could easily have done? Why steal so little? Why hit Lady Brackenstall to stop her screaming, as she would only scream more? And why did only one of the three wine glasses contain sediment? Holmes suspects that only two people drank the wine, but then poured the dregs into a third glass to give the impression three people had shared it. He decides to return and investigate further.

Holmes investigates

Holmes locks himself in the dining room and, in the words of Watson, devotes himself "to one of those minute and laborious investigations" for which he is famous. Two hours later, he concludes that someone had not torn down the bell-rope, which would have rung the bell and alerted the servants, but instead climbed onto the mantelpiece and cut it cleanly with a knife. To do so, they had to be exceptionally tall—taller even than Holmes. And, from a bloodstain found on the chair where Lady Brackenstall was tied, he deduces that she was placed there after her husband's death.

Establishing the truth

Lady Brackenstall has told a pack of lies, but after hearing from her austere but devoted maid Theresa the full extent of the abuse she has suffered at the hands of her husband, Holmes challenges her gently to tell him the truth. However, she maintains her story.

On leaving the Grange with Watson, Holmes stares at an unfrozen pond and scribbles a note for Hopkins, then suggests they visit the London shipping office of the Adelaide–Southampton line. From the real killer's obvious agility, and the knots used to tie up Lady Brackenstall, Holmes has surmised that the culprit is a sailor, and most likely someone she met when she sailed to England. Sure enough, Holmes ascertains that one of the ship's officers, Jack Croker, who lives in Sydenham, has not made the return passage. Hopkins, meanwhile, learns that the Randall gang has been arrested in New York, and therefore could not have committed the Abbey Grange "burglary." Guided by Holmes's note, he also finds the "stolen" silver at the bottom of the pond. Confused as to why the thieves had thrown away their haul, he does not take the hint when Holmes suggests it was put there "for a blind" to mislead people.

The case is resolved

Summoned by Holmes, Croker arrives at 221B Baker Street, where he is persuaded to tell the truth. "Be frank with me, and we may do some good. Play tricks with me, and I'll crush you," Holmes tells him.

Tall, handsome, blond, blue-eyed, and young, Croker stands for everything Sir Eustace did not: "as fine a specimen of manhood" as ever stood before them, reckons Watson. He is chivalrous, too, explaining that he fell in love with Lady Brackenstall on board the ship but, being a mere sailor, could only admire her from afar, and be happy for her when she later made a "favourable" marriage. However, a chance encounter with the maid Theresa revealed the horrible truth about Lady Brackenstall's husband. He resolved to see her again and in due course she fell in love with him.

On the fateful night, the lovers were surprised by Sir Eustace, who rushed into the room, called his wife "the vilest name that a man could use to a woman," and struck her with his cudgel. This is the crux of the story—the moment when Sir Eustace transgressed all moral boundaries. Croker grabbed the poker and struck him down, then gave Lady Brackenstall some wine to relieve her shock and had some himself. Croker and Theresa then acted swiftly to fake the scene. After dumping the silver in the pond

to make it look as though a burglary had occurred, Croker departed, feeling he had done "a real good night's work."

Holmes plays judge

Satisfied with Croker's account, Holmes sympathizes with his actions and says he will delay telling Hopkins for 24 hours so that he can flee. Croker is outraged, and swears that he would never dream of leaving Lady Brackenstall to be arrested as an accomplice. Delighted by this response, Holmes elects himself judge, and Watson jury. They duly pronounce him "not guilty," and Holmes tells Croker to wait a year before claiming his beloved.

For Holmes, Captain Croker's killing of a wife-beating tyrant is a case of justifiable homicide. His feelings of protectiveness toward Lady Brackenstall are reinforced by his admiration for Croker's manly and unflinching loyalty. He has given Hopkins every chance to solve the case, and has insufficient faith that the law would acquit Croker. In this case, Holmes truly takes the law into his own hands. ∎

Inequality of divorce

It was once notoriously difficult for women in England to obtain a divorce, and Lady Brackenstall—trapped in a marriage to an abusive drunk—speaks with passion about the "monstrous laws" that prohibit her escape.

Before the mid-19th century, a full divorce was obtainable only through a Private Act of Parliament. In 1857, the Matrimonial Causes Act transferred divorce proceedings from Parliament to a civil court, but even then the grounds for divorce remained limited, and in practice it merely enshrined the double standard that existed between men and women. From 1857 to 1922, adultery was considered the sole ground for divorce. However, a husband's adultery had to be accompanied by one or more other transgressions: incest, cruelty, bigamy, sodomy, or desertion. This did not apply to a husband who petitioned for divorce because of his wife's adultery. Lady Brackenstall, therefore, confronted by great cruelty but evidently not adultery, was completely trapped.

I should not sit here smoking with you if I thought that you were a common criminal, you may be sure of that. Be frank with me and we may do some good. Play tricks with me, and I'll crush you.
Sherlock Holmes

IT IS A CAPITAL MISTAKE TO THEORIZE IN ADVANCE OF THE FACTS

THE ADVENTURE OF THE SECOND STAIN (1904)

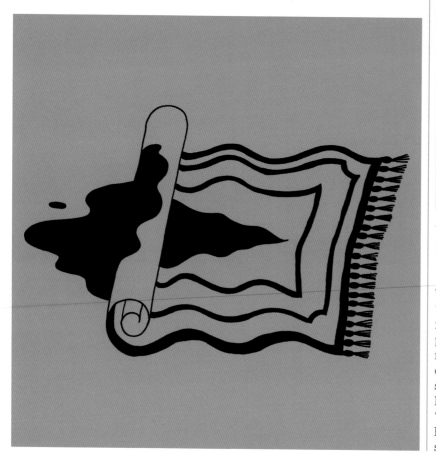

IN CONTEXT

TYPE
Short story

FIRST PUBLICATION
UK: December 1904
US: January 1905

COLLECTION
***The Return of Sherlock Holmes*, 1905**

CHARACTERS
Lord Bellinger
British Prime Minister.

Right Honourable Trelawney Hope Secretary for European Affairs.

Lady Hilda Trelawney Hope Wife of the Right Honourable Trelawney Hope.

Eduardo Lucas Spy (also known as Henri Fournaye).

Madame Fournaye Secret Parisian wife of Lucas.

John Mitton Lucas's valet.

Inspector Lestrade Scotland Yard inspector.

Constable MacPherson Guard of Lucas's house.

This story is the final case in *The Return of Sherlock Holmes*. Within the canon, Watson is both the chronicler and "publisher" of Holmes's cases, but immediately he makes excuses for publishing it, claiming that he had made a "promise" to his readers—even though there is no trace of such a contract in any story. To Holmes, now retired in Sussex, "notoriety has become hateful" and he clearly does not want any more stories published. But this might be because he no longer requires the advertising that Watson's stories once usefully provided. In any case, it is hard to disagree with Watson's point that the collection surely must end with "the most important international case which he has ever been called upon to handle".

Historical context

Owing to the importance of the case, Watson insists on being "somewhat vague in certain details." For instance, he never specifies in which year the story is set. There are references to a "Second Stain" in "The Naval Treaty" (pp.138–41) and "The Yellow Face" (pp.112–13) but these don't help to date the story, as they seem to allude to a different case entirely. However, the political situation described in this story, in which Britain holds the balance of power between a "double league" of European alliances, suggests that the story must be set in the early 1890s: in 1892, Russia and France joined forces as a counterweight to the "Triple Alliance" of Germany, Italy, and Austria-Hungary (see p.139). And if Holmes's Great Hiatus (see p.164–65) is factored in, then the date is probably 1894 at the earliest.

> The situation is desperate, but not hopeless.
> **Sherlock Holmes**

The British Prime Minister in this story, "the illustrious Lord Bellinger," bears clear similarities to the former real-life Liberal prime minister William Gladstone, who left office in March 1894. Certainly, Watson's descriptions and Sidney Paget's illustrations published in *The Strand Magazine* strongly resemble Gladstone.

Distinguished visitors

At the start of the story, the arrival of both the Prime Minister and his Secretary for European Affairs, the Right Honourable Trelawney Hope, provide a certain gravitas to the "humble room in Baker Street."

A document has gone missing from Trelawney Hope's home in Whitehall Terrace, Westminster—and its rediscovery is vital to national security. The paper has disappeared from a locked dispatch-box in Trelawney Hope's bedroom, and he claims it had definitely been there the previous evening, as he had seen it before dinner, and that he and his wife would certainly have known had someone entered their room and taken it in the middle of the night. Only two servants had access to the room: his valet and his wife's maid, but they are both trusted employees and would not have known that there was anything valuable in the box. Only the Cabinet, along with two or three departmental officials, knew about the letter, and even then only since the previous day.

The police have not been told, for fear of the document's contents being made public, and Bellinger and Trelawney Hope are reluctant to give Holmes any real details. Yet Holmes declares that unless he knows something of the document's contents, he is unable to help, and that any further discussion »

European politics

The unnamed hot-headed "foreign potentate" who wrote the missing letter might well have been based on Kaiser Wilhelm II (pictured), who had ruled Germany since 1888. In 1895, this belligerent figure wrote a letter to South African president Paul Kruger, offering his congratulations on the recent defeat of a raid supported by British interests (thus closely mirroring the "colonial" subject matter of the letter in the story). This was a rash thing to do, risking the inflammation of tensions that would erupt into the Boer War in 1899. Although this incident occurred after the story's suspected setting, it was well timed for its publication—by 1904 there were growing concerns about Germany's burgeoning militarism. The delicate balance of European alliances—Russia, France, and Britain against the "Triple Alliance" of Germany, Italy, and Austria-Hungary—was becoming increasingly tense, and would, within just ten years, result in one of the deadliest wars in history.

Lady Hilda

It is never revealed if the tale's second letter, which Lucas uses to try to blackmail Lady Hilda (pictured, played by Patricia Hodge), refers to a relationship between them, or to some other "impulsive" youthful liaison. What is clear is that Lady Hilda is the very picture of feminine grace and Victorian respectability. Her anguish at having potentially brought about the undoing of her husband's career, in a vain and desperate attempt to ward off the slightest blemish on her dignity, proves this eloquently, while at the same time demonstrating the social pressure on ladies of her rank to have flawless reputations. Lady Hilda also shows great fortitude and resolve when standing up to Holmes's interrogations. As Watson notes, she was indeed "grandly defiant" and "her courage was admirable."

In contrast, Madame Fournaye is the embodiment of a hysterical woman. When she finds Lady Hilda with her husband, she flies into a murderous rage, throwing Lady Hilda's composure and self-control into stark relief.

would be a waste of time. In such eminent company, this might seem rather abrupt, but it is easy to see his logic—how can he be expected to grasp his beloved "technical details" without a little information? The two statesmen finally agree.

An inflammatory letter

It turns out that the document is a provocative letter written by a hot-headed foreign leader, and containing material certain to agitate international relations. As Bellinger tells Holmes, "I do not hesitate to say that within a week of the publication of that letter this country would be involved in a great war." Holmes writes a name on a slip of paper—it is confirmed by the Premier as being that of the sender, yet the reader remains none the wiser. This secrecy is clearly directed more at the reader than at potential eavesdroppers and is a masterful piece of drama on Conan Doyle's part, keeping his readers tantalized. Bellinger states that publication of the letter would not be in the interests of the "foreign potentate" who first wrote it, but in the interests of his enemies. If the letter's contents became public, it would encourage a war between Britain and the potentate's own country, which would in turn create a power shift and thus assure the supremacy of the country that had stolen the letter (see box, p.203).

Holmes reasons that the letter must have been stolen between 7:30pm, when Trelawney Hope was at dinner, and 11:30pm, when his wife returned from the theater and they went up to bed. If nobody could have entered the second-floor room from outside, that leaves only the maid or the valet, in spite of their reliability. And from there, it was most likely taken to someone who might know what best to do

with it—one of many "international spies and secret agents" with whom Holmes is familiar.

Hot off the press

When the two grandees depart, Holmes smokes a characteristically meditative pipe and gives the case some thought. Considering that the letter does not yet appear to have been passed on, it then occurs to Holmes that the spy or secret agent who has stolen it might well be waiting for offers of money to come in, from Britain and the letter-writer's country, before handing it over to the highest bidder. He states that there are only three spies who would "be capable of playing so bold a game": Oberstein and La Rothière—both of whom reappear in the 1908 tale "The Adventure of the Bruce-Partington Plans" (pp.230–33)—and the popular socialite Eduardo Lucas.

Meanwhile, Watson reads in the papers about a "sensational" crime committed the previous evening. The story reports the death of the aforementioned Eduardo Lucas at his house in Godolphin Street, just around the corner from the European Secretary's house in Westminster. Holmes is amazed at the coincidence, and it forms a

It was with a sense of exultation that I realized how completely I had astonished him.
Dr. Watson

Holmes's amazement on learning of Lucas's murder is captured in this *Strand* illustration, as he snatches the paper from Watson's hands.

Holmes's amazement on learning of Lucas's murder is captured in this *Strand* illustration, as he snatches the paper from Watson's hands.

productive development in his deductions: Lucas was murdered between 10pm, when the valet went out, and 11:45pm, when a passing policeman found him stabbed in the heart with a dagger taken from his own mantelpiece.

Shortly afterward, the elegant Lady Hilda Trelawney Hope arrives at Baker Street, anxious to find out about the content and nature of the document that her husband has lost. Holmes refuses to divulge any details, but does agree that the loss of the document may have "terrible public consequences," and could endanger her husband's political career unless it is found. When Lady Hilda withdraws, Holmes expresses his famous bafflement at the "inscrutable" nature of women. However, he does remark on the fact that she clearly sat with the light behind her, in order that they could not see her expressions.

Slow progress

Over the next few days, Holmes is restless, and it seems that things are not going well with the case. From the papers, Watson learns that no suspects were apprehended for Lucas's murder except his valet John Mitton, who was promptly released because of insufficient evidence against him. There was no apparent motive for the murder, and none of Lucas's many valuable possessions had been removed.

However, on the fourth day, a telegram from Paris appears in the news—a Frenchwoman (of Creole extraction) who returned from London on Tuesday was declared insane, and there is evidence to suggest she was connected with the crime at Westminster. It then transpires that her husband, Henri Fournaye, was in fact the exact same man as Eduardo Lucas, who had been leading a double life in

Paris and London. Madame Fournaye has a history of violent attacks of jealousy, and although it is not clear what she was doing the night of Lucas's murder, she was seen behaving wildly at Charing Cross the following morning. With his characteristic eye for the case above all else, Holmes writes the incident off as "a trivial episode." In the meantime, he ruminates that during the days since the letter's loss there has been no related news, and points out that the only important thing that has happened "is that nothing has happened." This is both an expression of his frustration and a real insight, echoing the situation in "The Naval Treaty": it is likely that the letter has not yet reached dangerous hands, or something catastrophic would have occurred by now.

A mysterious stain

At Godolphin Street, Inspector Lestrade is convinced that the Paris police are right in suspecting Madame Fournaye. However, he then mysteriously summons »

> Only one important thing has happened in the last three days, and that is that nothing has happened.
> **Sherlock Holmes**

Holmes (Jeremy Brett), Watson (Edward Hardwicke) and Lestrade (Colin Jeavons) examine the rug in the 1986 ITV episode of "The Second Stain."

Holmes back to the crime scene. As it turns out, the police, convinced that their investigation is as good as over, had started clearing up the crime scene that morning, only to find something mysterious. The carpet, which had been stained with Lucas's blood at one corner, must have been moved shortly after he was murdered, as the location of the stain on the wooden floor does not correspond with the one on the carpet. When Holmes says it is clear that the carpet has been turned

around, there is an opportunity for some dry wit from the Scotland Yard inspector, who remarks, "The official police don't need you, Mr. Holmes, to tell them that the carpet must have been turned round." Still, he does want Holmes to explain who did it and why. Holmes suggests that Lestrade interrogates the officer who has been guarding the house, but while the inspector is busy in the other room, Holmes and Watson quickly search under the carpet for possible secret floor cavities, and discover a hinged compartment—which, disappointingly, is empty. Just as Lestrade returns, Holmes faultlessly resumes his former "languid," bored posture. It turns out

that Lestrade's guarding officer, Constable MacPherson, had indeed let in a visitor—a "very respectable, well-spoken young woman"—on the previous evening.

The penultimate act

When Lestrade announces to the shamed constable, "It's lucky for you, my man, that nothing is missing, or you would find yourself in Queer Street," there is a deep dramatic irony, since the reader, together with Holmes and Watson, knows with great certainty that something is indeed "missing" from the room, and that this disappearance is crucial to the case. It is also worth noting Conan Doyle's reference to "Queer Street" here—a colloquial expression that refers to Carey Street, where the bankruptcy courts were once located. Charles Dickens had used the expression to refer specifically to bankruptcy in *Our Mutual Friend* (1864), but its wider meaning of being in financial difficulty had already been employed in literature by Conan Doyle's friend Robert Louis Stevenson, in his novel *Strange Case of Dr. Jekyll and Mr. Hyde* (1886), when the upright Mr. Enfield remarks, "the more it looks like Queer Street, the less I ask."

The reader soon realizes that the "handsome" visiting woman was unquestionably Lady Hilda. And when Holmes holds up something to the stunned constable—which turns out to be Lady Hilda's face cut out of a portrait—Holmes declares, "Come, friend Watson, the curtain rings up for the last act."

Dramatic timing

Holmes and Watson head straight to Trelawney Hope's residence, where Holmes asks Lady Hilda to hand over the letter, reassuring her that her husband need not know of her involvement in the affair. After listening to Lady Hilda's various denials, Holmes threatens to inform her husband, who will be home in 15 minutes. Holmes plays a waiting game before Lady Hilda ultimately relents; she produces "a long, blue envelope" that contains the letter, then proceeds to tell her story.

Lucas had somehow come into the possession of a compromising letter that Lady Hilda had written before her marriage to Trelawney Hope. He was using it to blackmail her, saying he would show it to her husband unless she was prepared to exchange it for the document that was hidden in the dispatch-box. Lucas had heard about the letter through a spy in the Cabinet, and Lady Hilda had agreed to the deal in order to protect her dignity.

That fateful Monday night, while Lucas and Lady Hilda were exchanging letters, they had been surprised by the sudden arrival of Madame Fournaye, and Lucas had quickly thrust the political letter into a hiding place beneath the carpet. A violent scuffle broke out between the jealous, knife-wielding Madame Fournaye and Lucas. Lady Hilda fled the scene. It was not until the next morning that Lady Hilda learned of Lucas's murder, and having learned from Holmes the serious implications of the document's falling into the wrong hands, she then returned in secret to Lucas's house to retrieve the letter from its hiding place.

When Trelawney Hope and Lord Bellinger burst in, Holmes announces that he is convinced that the letter was not taken at all but surreptitiously returned to the dispatch-box. Bellinger is stunned to find it where Holmes suggests, and asks how the letter managed to be returned. To this Holmes roguishly remarks, "We also have our diplomatic secrets."

A nod to Dupin

Despite Holmes having solved the crime while preserving the dignity and reputation of Lady Hilda, there is a pronounced loose end here: although Holmes's own reputation for demonstrations of unorthodox

> I would not bring one shadow on his life, and this I know would break his noble heart.
> **Lady Hilda**

brilliance allows him to get away with the dramatic "re-appearing act" of the letter, his silence also means that the reader never finds out the identity of Lucas's Cabinet informant. More importantly, Lord Bellinger is left without so much as an inkling that such a spy exists.

Holmes's final moves in this case are, most likely, a play on Edgar Allan Poe's 1844 tale "The Purloined Letter," in which the loss of a vitally important note leaves the Paris police utterly flummoxed, before Poe's famous detective (the Chevalier C. Auguste Dupin) reveals that it had been in the thief's letter-rack the whole time. It is fitting that here, in a case purporting to be the last ever—and which concludes *The Return of Sherlock Holmes*—Conan Doyle should allude not only to one of Holmes's key sources, Dupin, but specifically to the last of the three tales in which Dupin appears. And the fact that this intricate story should turn so neatly on suggestion as well as deception—the letter's importance misleading both the ministers and the reader into believing that it must have traveled much farther afield than it really did—gives good justification for why Conan Doyle named it as one of his favorite cases. ∎

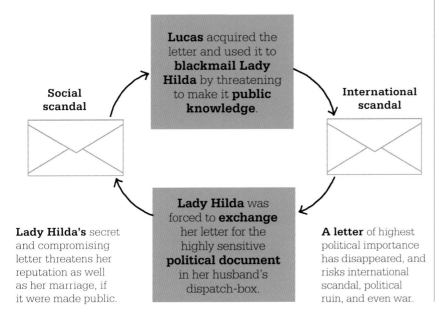

Social scandal

Lucas acquired the letter and used it to **blackmail Lady Hilda** by threatening to make it **public knowledge**.

International scandal

Lady Hilda was forced to **exchange** her letter for the highly sensitive **political document** in her husband's dispatch-box.

Lady Hilda's secret and compromising letter threatens her reputation as well as her marriage, if it were made public.

A letter of highest political importance has disappeared, and risks international scandal, political ruin, and even war.

HOLMES
A BOW

TAKES

Conan Doyle's *Sir Nigel* stories are serialized in *The Strand Magazine.*

DEC 1905

Conan Doyle publishes **"The Case of Mr. George Edalji"**—which leads to the **real-life subject's** exoneration from the charge of **cattle-maiming.**

1907

Sidney Paget, *The Strand Magazine* **illustrator** of Sherlock Holmes, dies at age 47.

JAN 1908

Edward VII dies at age 68, and **George V** becomes king.

MAY 1910

JUL 1906

Conan Doyle's **first wife**, Louise ("Touie"), dies from **tuberculosis.**

SEP 1907

Conan Doyle **marries** his "close friend," **Jean Leckie.**

SEP 1908

The stories later collected in *His Last Bow* start to appear in *The Strand Magazine.*

1912

Conan Doyle publishes his science fiction novel *The Lost World* (p.345).

Event in the lives of Holmes and Watson

IN THIS CHAPTER

NOVEL
The Valley of Fear, 1915

COLLECTION
His Last Bow, 1917
Wisteria Lodge
The Red Circle
The Bruce-Partington Plans
The Dying Detective
The Disappearance of Lady
  Frances Carfax
The Devil's Foot
His Last Bow

In the preface to the 1917 collection *His Last Bow*, Watson describes Holmes's retirement in England's South Downs, and yet the collection's final, eponymous tale has him returning to action as a secret agent on the eve of World War I. Chronologically, that story is also Holmes's final outing anywhere in the canon—the other stories in *His Last Bow* are set much earlier, while the action in *The Valley of Fear*, the final novel, occurs in 1888.

In the national interest

The tension in the tales of *His Last Bow* bears the imprint of the impending trauma of World War I. "The Bruce-Partington Plans"—a gripping tale of espionage set in 1895, featuring Holmes's brother Mycroft—is an early example of the "spy thriller" genre. Submarines,

which are key to this story, would not play a serious part in warfare until the start of World War II, in 1939. The story "His Last Bow" in which Holmes outsmarts the German spy Von Bork, is set two days before Britain declared war on Germany, after the latter's invasion of Belgium, and it is imbued with pathos and foreboding.

Belgium was elsewhere in Conan Doyle's thoughts, too. In 1909, influenced by the work of his friend Roger Casement, a human rights activist, he wrote against King Leopold II's exploitation of Africa in *The Crime of the Congo*; his later chronicles of the Western Front would be focused on the Belgian battlefields.

Conan Doyle's shift to support Irish Home Rule in late 1911 may also have been influenced by

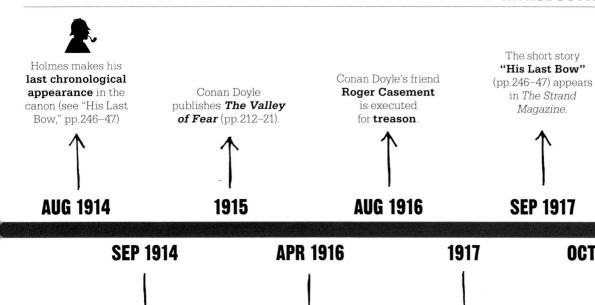

Holmes makes his **last chronological appearance** in the canon (see "His Last Bow," pp.246–47)

Conan Doyle publishes ***The Valley of Fear*** (pp.212–21).

Conan Doyle's friend **Roger Casement** is executed for **treason**.

The short story **"His Last Bow"** (pp.246–47) appears in *The Strand Magazine*.

AUG 1914

1915

AUG 1916

SEP 1917

SEP 1914

APR 1916

1917

OCT 1917

The Valley of Fear starts appearing in serialization in *The Strand Magazine*.

Conan Doyle's ***The British Campaign in France and Flanders 1914*** appears in *The Strand Magazine*.

Conan Doyle publishes accounts of the **1916 battles**, including the **Battle of the Somme**.

Conan Doyle publishes the collection ***His Last Bow***.

Casement, who was executed for treason in 1917. Despite the author's family roots, Ireland itself never features in the canon. Holmes impersonates a specifically Irish-American character in "His Last Bow," however, and *The Valley of Fear* features the "Scowrers," a secret criminal society based on the notorious "Molly Maguires," an Irish-American labor organization thought to have been responsible for terrorist acts in the coalfields of Pennsylvania and West Virginia.

Real-life detection
Conan Doyle considered his 1905–1906 "Sir Nigel" series, set during the Hundred Years' War of the 14th–15th century, to be his "high-water mark in literature." Most of Conan Doyle's work at this time was far more contemporary and

politically engaged—he made a second run for Parliament in 1906 and published the articles "The Case of Mr. George Edalji" and "The Case of Oscar Slater," interventions on behalf of two wrongfully convicted men of foreign origin whose cases he had investigated. In taking up their causes, Conan Doyle rose nobly above the racial prejudice of his day. On the other hand, Holmes stories such as "Wisteria Lodge" feature blatant ethnic stereotyping, while the deadly poison in "The Devil's Foot" associated Africa with horror, despair, and death.

A new age of crime
The advent of a harder, more violent era, complete with organized crime gangs, is reflected in the eight stories of *His Last Bow*. "The Red

Circle" contains a second reference to the Mafia (the first was in 1904's "The Six Napoleons"). And, like *The Valley of Fear*, the story features an undercover man from the real-life Pinkerton Detective Agency, the first US detective organization, which had been founded in 1850.

Elsewhere in the collection, Watson has to go it alone in Europe in "The Disappearance of Lady Frances Carfax," before Holmes reveals himself in the guise of a French laborer. In this story, the detective is fairly cynical about the doctor's detection skills, and in "The Dying Detective" he fools his friend into thinking that he has contracted a fatal disease. Yet when Holmes has a real brush with death, in "The Devil's Foot," it is Watson's quick-witted intervention that saves the day. ∎

A GREAT BRAIN
AND A HUGE ORGANIZATION HAVE BEEN TURNED TO THE
EXTINCTION OF ONE MAN

THE VALLEY OF FEAR (1915)

IN CONTEXT

TYPE
Novel

FIRST PUBLICATION
UK: *The Strand Magazine*, September 1914

NOVEL PUBLICATION
George H. Doran, February 1915

CHARACTERS
John "Jack" Douglas
Fearless, intelligent, and good-natured Irish-American living in Sussex. The entire plot hangs on his backstory and multiple identities.

Ivy Douglas John's beautiful, young second wife.

Inspector Alec MacDonald
Young Scottish Scotland Yard detective.

Fred Porlock Member of Moriarty's network, and informer for Holmes.

Cecil James Barker House-guest and wealthy English friend of John Douglas.

Ted Baldwin Member of the Scowrers who tries to assassinate Douglas.

Professor James Moriarty
Holmes's unseen archenemy, in cahoots with the Scowrers.

Ettie Shafter John's first wife, who he married in Pennsylvania.

Chapter 1
Holmes and Watson decipher a coded message from Fred Porlock, an agent of Moriarty. It reveals that a man called Douglas is in danger.

Chapter 3
The Sussex police begin to investigate the murder and then decide to call in Scotland Yard and Sherlock Holmes.

Chapter 5
Mrs. Douglas and Cecil Barker tell Holmes and MacDonald their version of events.

PART 1

Chapter 2
Inspector MacDonald arrives at 221B Baker Street and announces that John Douglas has been murdered. He is not convinced that Moriarty is involved.

Chapter 4
Holmes discovers that Douglas is somehow linked to America, and finds a single dumbbell in his room.

Chapter 6
Holmes is sure Barker and Mrs. Douglas have lied, and stresses the importance of the missing dumbbell.

Holmes receives a coded message from an informer working within Professor Moriarty's criminal network, about a man called Douglas who is in imminent danger. Inspector MacDonald of Scotland Yard then calls: John Douglas, an American, has been murdered at his home, Birlstone Manor, in Sussex. Holmes suggests that Moriarty is involved, but the inspector is not convinced.

Holmes, Watson, and MacDonald travel to Douglas's home. The victim has been shot in the face with a sawn-off shotgun. Curiously, his wedding ring is missing, and a card marked "V. V. 341" is beside the body. A houseguest, Cecil Barker, points out a bloody footprint, indicating that the killer escaped through the window and swam across the moat. Barker suspects the involvement of a secret society from Douglas's past—the dead man had told his wife Ivy, "I have been in the Valley of Fear. I am not out of it yet."

Holmes finds a dumbbell at the crime scene, noting that they come in pairs. He then matches Barker's slipper to the bloody footprint. Convinced that both Barker and

Chapter 7
Barker is trapped into revealing the truth about the murder. Douglas appears and tells his story.

Chapter 2
McMurdo finds work as a bookkeeper, and makes himself known to the leader of a gang called the "Scowrers."

Chapter 4
McMurdo and other Scowrers are on trial for the beating, but several "witnesses" provide alibis for them, and they are set free.

Chapter 6
McMurdo tells his fellow Scowrers that a Pinkerton agent called Birdy Edwards is after them, and volunteers to trap the man.

Epilogue
Holmes learns that Douglas/ McMurdo/Edwards has been lost overboard a ship, murdered by agents of Moriarty working with the Scowrers.

PART 2

Chapter 1
Twenty years earlier, John McMurdo travels by train from Chicago to Vermissa Valley, Pennsylvania, and finds lodgings.

Chapter 3
McMurdo is initiated into the Scowrers and helps them beat up a newspaper editor.

Chapter 5
McMurdo witnesses the gang members murder a mine manager.

Chapter 7
The trap set by McMurdo is actually for the Scowrers, and McMurdo reveals himself to be Birdy Edwards.

Ivy Douglas are lying, Holmes sets a trap, telling Barker the moat will be drained in the morning. Hiding nearby that night, Holmes, Watson, and MacDonald witness Barker fishing a bundle from the moat.

Caught in the act, Barker admits that the dead man was actually Douglas's would-be assassin, shot in a struggle. With his features obliterated, they dressed him in Douglas's clothes, and threw his clothes in the moat, weighed down by the missing dumbbell. Holmes then dramatically calls Douglas forth from a hidden room.

Douglas hands Watson a written testimony. His real name is Birdy Edwards and, 20 years ago, he had been a private detective with the famous American agency, Pinkerton's. Under the name of John McMurdo, he had infiltrated Lodge 341 of a secret society of murderers, the "Scowrers," a corrupt faction of Freemasonry in "the Vermissa Valley"—"V. V.", the Valley of Fear—in Pennsylvania. Edwards brought the gang to justice, but some of its members escaped, including the dead man, an old rival of his named Ted Baldwin.

Moriarty was commissioned by Edward's enemies to kill him. At Holmes's urging, Edwards and Ivy board a ship for South Africa, but off St. Helena (where Napoleon was exiled) Edwards is lost overboard. A note arrives for Holmes, which simply reads, "Dear me!"—a mocking use of one of Holmes's favorite expressions, in this and other stories. "There is a master hand here," says Holmes. "…You can tell an old master by the sweep of his brush. I can tell a Moriarty when I see one." The Napoleon of crime has indeed struck. ■

The fourth and final Sherlock Holmes novel may be a suitably resounding end to the great detective's exploits in the longer story form, but it also bears the signs of Conan Doyle's famous disenchantment with his creation. While Holmes aficionados may be disappointed that their hero is absent for half the narrative, the adventure is nonetheless an intriguing one, which cleverly channels real-life events in the US into a typically baffling English country house murder mystery.

Just like *The Hound of the Baskervilles* (pp.152–61) a decade earlier, *The Valley of Fear* also appeared in monthly instalments in *The Strand Magazine*. These prompted the usual enthusiastic response from Holmes fans, but ultimately the response to the novel was not the unqualified success that *The Hound of the Baskervilles* had been. Even its admirers would be unlikely to disagree that *The Valley of Fear* is a book of two halves: a slightly uneasy marriage of a detective puzzle and an espionage adventure. As in *A Study in Scarlet* (pp.36–45) and *The Sign of Four* (pp.46–55), the first section of the book details a crime, and the second relates the circumstances that set

We think in the CID that you have a wee bit of a bee in your bonnet over this Professor.
Inspector MacDonald

that crime in motion. *The Valley of Fear* has familiar themes too: namely a dark past abroad finally catching up with someone, and the deeds of an organized crime network in America. Conan Doyle had explored both of these ideas previously in several of his short stories, such as "The Five Orange Pips" (pp.74–9), and "The Adventure of the Red Circle" (pp.226–29). Such a deep fascination with organized crime in America was uncharacteristic of British writers of this period, apart from Edgar Wallace (1875–1932), who, unlike Conan Doyle, was no stranger to the far side of the Atlantic himself.

Holmes in fine form

The opening sections, dealing with Holmes's investigation and solving of the murder, are as adroitly put together as anything in the canon, and as complicated yet satisfying as ever. From the very start, Conan Doyle adopts a more humorous tone than usual, as Holmes frequently

In the US Civil War Pinkerton agents like these were employed as Abraham Lincoln's bodyguards. By the time of *The Valley of Fear* they were often being used as strike-breakers.

teases the doctor. The novel opens with the two men in conversation: "I am inclined to think—" begins Watson; "I should do so," interrupts Holmes, pointing out the doctor's language has inadvertently implied that he wasn't thinking at all.

The detective is in his element when he receives a coded message from a criminal informer, Fred Porlock. He identifies Porlock as an agent of his greatest adversary, Professor Moriarty, and compares the two men for Watson's benefit: "Picture to yourself the pilot-fish with the shark, the jackal with the lion—anything that is insignificant in companionship with what is formidable." He is clearly looking forward to the challenge ahead as he describes his archenemy in admiring tones: "The greatest schemer of all time... the controlling brain of the underworld." As Watson puts it, after several dull weeks, "here, at last, there was a fitting object for those remarkable powers which, like all special gifts, become irksome to their owner when they are not in use."

The teasing reveal

The highlight of any Holmes story—one that retains its charm despite its repeated use—is the moment at which Holmes theatrically reveals to Watson the reasoning behind a particularly baffling piece of deduction. This is always presented by Conan Doyle in delayed fashion, usually with Holmes first making some striking and apparently random statement, so that both Watson and the reader are eager to hear its justification. In *The Valley of Fear* this comes when Holmes announces at the breakfast table, "A great big, thumping, obtrusive, uncompromising lie—that's what meets us on the threshold... The whole story told by Barker is a lie. But Barker's story is corroborated by Mrs. Douglas... They are both lying and in a conspiracy."

At the time this statement is made, Conan Doyle has allowed us to connect some facts but not—inevitably—as cleverly or completely as Holmes. Our awareness that we are incapable of reaching the correct conclusion only confirms Holmes's almost supernatural abilities. For example, Barker says he heard the gunshot at 11:30 pm. The housekeeper says she heard what she thought was the sound of a door slamming half an hour earlier. But only Holmes makes the correct deduction: what she actually heard was the real gunshot.

The theatrics continue when Holmes asks Watson and the inspector to hide with him in the »

Deciphering the coded message

534 C2 13 127 36 31
4 17 21 41

DOUGLAS 109 293
5 37

BIRLSTONE

26 BIRLSTONE
9 127 171

Watson asks what can be done with a **cipher message without the cipher**, and Holmes turns this **absence into a clue**. As the author did not include the cipher (the volume to which the message refers) he surely anticipated that **Holmes owns a copy**. The book must therefore be a **common household title**. Its length and the number of columns suggest a reference work.

The **first number** in the cipher message, **534**, is likely to indicate a **page number**. If so, the book to which it refers is a long one.

Watson suggests that **C2** refers to "Chapter the Second," but as the **page is already known**, this must mean **Column Two**.

13 and all the subsequent numbers must refer to the placing of **individual words** on page 534 within Column Two.

The **words** in the message are **critical but too obscure** to appear in the column in question, so have been **written directly**.

The Bible is the first possible cipher, but there are too many different editions to be sure of a page number. Both **the dictionary and Bradshaw's** (a book of train timetables) are dismissed for their limited number of words, before Holmes alights on **Whitaker's Almanac** and tests his theory to find he is indeed correct.

In memory of
Sir Arthur Conan Doyle
1859 – 1930
a frequent visitor to Groombridge Place
Opened By
Mrs Georgina Doyle & Dame Jean Conan Doyle
1st July 1995

Groombridge Place is the moated manor house that Conan Doyle used as the model for Douglas's home, Birlstone Manor. Living at nearby Crowborough, the author was a frequent visitor.

bushes for several hours in the dark, refusing to tell them why. When MacDonald asks for an explanation, Holmes replies, "Watson insists that I am the dramatist in real life. Some touch of the artist wells up within me and calls insistently for a well-staged performance." Holmes's discovery is worth the wait: he has already found the bundle in the moat and put it back so Barker can be caught retrieving the evidence.

The most shocking reveal is yet to come. To the further astonishment of Watson and MacDonald, Holmes turns to Ivy Douglas, saying: "I should strongly recommend that you ask Mr. Douglas to tell us his own story." Thus the supposedly dead man emerges from his hiding place and hands Watson a bundle of papers that comprise a written account called "The Valley of Fear."

Back to reality

With the murder mystery solved, Conan Doyle embarks on a long flashback, just as he did in *A Study in Scarlet*. Once again, Holmes vanishes from the narrative, and now the reader relives Douglas's adventures among the "Scowrers" in America. Echoing Conan Doyle's earlier use of authentic legend in *The Hound of the Baskervilles*, the Scowrers were based on a real-life 19th century Irish-American secret society, the Molly Maguires (p.220). The Mollies were active in the Pennsylvania mining communities until a series of violent incidents resulted in 20 of their members being hanged. Much of the evidence against them was provided by a detective from the Pinkerton agency, James McParland—the model for John McMurdo. Conan Doyle heard about the Mollies and McParland from the American detective and writer William John Burns, who visited the author at his home in the village of Crowborough.

On completing the manuscript, Conan Doyle apologized to his publisher for providing lightweight reading material when World War I was looming large in everyone's thoughts—not least in those of the author himself. But *Strand* editor Herbert Greenhough Smith thought that the public needed some relief after the flood of war reports in the press, and an exciting diversion featuring the nation's favorite detective could be precisely the kind of escapism readers were looking for. He was right: sales of the magazine with the first installment were as buoyant as ever. War or no, readers had not lost their appetite for Holmes and Watson.

Conan Doyle was aware that moving Holmes offstage for a great part of the novel would not be to the taste of all his readers, but he defended the decision to his editor as a necessary one. Many fans, however, expressed their deep disappointment at the absence of Holmes. It is for this reason that, in spite of *The Valley of Fear*'s gritty storyline and cutting humor, it is among the least regarded of the Holmes novels, which also perhaps explains the relative dearth of film and television adaptations.

In all my experience I cannot recall any more singular and interesting study.
Sherlock Holmes

Love and hate

When Holmes and Watson go to Sussex to investigate Douglas's murder, they are put up at a local inn, the Westville Arms, and share what Watson describes as "a double-bedded room." This was apparently "the best that the little country inn could do for us," but it is not clear from Watson's description whether the room had one double or two single beds. Holmes has sometimes been portrayed as a repressed homosexual—in Billy Wilder's film *The Private Life of Sherlock Holmes* (1970) and (in the view of some fans) the BBC television adaptation *Sherlock* (2010–) for example—but Conan Doyle clearly depicts Holmes as an asexual ascetic. In *The Valley of Fear*, Holmes admits to Watson that he is "not a whole-souled admirer

The Strand Magazine was designed to appeal to a new white-collar, middle-brow audience, who typically traveled to and from work by train. The Holmes stories were just the ticket.

of womankind." The exception, of course, is Irene Adler in "A Scandal in Bohemia" (pp.56–61), whose more "male" qualities of intelligence and ingenuity earned her the detective's respect.

That Holmes adores Watson, and that the plainly heterosexual doctor returns the compliment, is not in doubt. Conan Doyle himself intended a platonic friendship, although his successors may—and do—speculate.

Arguably, Holmes has almost as strong a relationship with his archenemy, Professor Moriarty, as with Watson, but this is a love/hate affair. Holmes is horrified by his nemesis's criminality, but in thrall to the genius at work in his evil acts. The detective cannot help but reluctantly admire the professor's extraordinary genius—as he tells Watson, the professor possesses "a brain which might have made or marred the destiny of nations"— for it is the one intellect that matches his own. Of all his foes, therefore, Moriarty is the only one who »

James McParland

Birdy Edwards, one of the most unusual characters in the entire Holmes canon, was based on a real person, James McParland. Born in County Armagh, Ireland in 1843, he traveled to New York in 1867 and worked as a laborer and then a policeman before moving to Chicago, where he owned a liquor store. When that business was destroyed in the Great Chicago Fire of 1871, he became a private detective for the legendary Pinkerton's agency, founded in 1850 by Allan Pinkerton, a Scottish American.

McParland is best known for his success against the clandestine group, the "Molly Maguires," in the 1870s. Using the name James McKenna, he gained the confidence of the group, but was appalled when it used information he supplied in assassination attempts. He also became disenchanted with coal mine operators who wished to exterminate the Mollies. However, unlike his murdered fictional counterpart in *The Valley of Fear*, Birdy Edwards, James McParland died in bed, at the Mercy Hospital in Denver in 1919.

THE CIPHER AND THE MAN WHO SOLVED IT.

presents him with a true challenge, and vice versa. They are perfectly matched opponents, and it is almost as if the one cannot exist without the other. Yet, in the end one of them must, inevitably, lose. When Barker asks Holmes if "this king-devil" can ever be defeated, Holmes replies without his customary confidence: "I don't say that he can be beat. But you must give me time."

Holmes and Moriarty are the first crime-fighter and villain who can be seen as alter egos of one another. It was to become a popular double act whose descendants include James Bond and Blofeld, and Batman and the Joker. Like Holmes, Gotham's Dark Knight has also been called "The World's Greatest Detective."

Bad timing

The attention that modern crime writers apply to the chronologies of their stories might have alarmed the rather slack Conan Doyle; there is a prize error in *The Valley of Fear*. It is set before Moriarty's famous appearance in "The Final Problem," (pp.142–47) yet in that story Watson has apparently never heard of him.

> Moriarty rules with a rod of iron over his people. His discipline is tremendous. There is only one punishment in his code. It is death.
> **Sherlock Holmes**

Writer Anthony Horowitz (1955–) simply ignored this problem when he included Professor Moriarty in his Holmes pastiche *The House of Silk* (2011). And the glitch hardly matters, for "The Final Problem" represents the professor's only other appearance in the entire canon. That he is a solely unseen presence in *The Valley of Fear* makes him the perfect *eminence noir*, subtly manipulating events behind the scenes. Indeed, it could be argued that being off-stage is crucial in making him believable as Holmes's ultimate enemy.

The view from abroad

Throughout the Holmes stories, foreign lands are frequently portrayed as a source of evil and danger, sometimes in animal form, as in "The Adventure of the Speckled Band" (pp.84–9), or via a human agent. The "fear of the foreign" was a typical 19th century upper-middle-class English attitude, which (the Scottish) Conan Doyle was happy to exploit. The author's use of dangerous animals and blowpipe-wielding natives in the stories also shows him to be a product of his time and social class. Contemporary readers enjoyed these types of storylines and devices for their exoticism. The "exotic" may carry derogatory connotations today, but in Conan Doyle's time, it implied a rather more innocent curiosity in strange and unfamiliar things. However, if the reader has any doubts about Conan Doyle's morality, there is the vivid, overriding sense of his enduring humanity, expressed in the tolerance and empathy of Watson's character.

As for Americans, Conan Doyle clearly admired their vigor, yet he was also fascinated by their

The Molly Maguires

Conan Doyle based the Scowrers on a real group of labor agitators, the Molly Maguires. The Mollies, as they were known colloquially, were a 19th-century secret society that originated in Ireland but later also had dedicated memberships in Liverpool and Pennsylvania. There, the group instigated (sometimes violent) activism among coal miners of Irish-American descent in reaction to the inhuman working and living conditions, and the low wages imposed by the ruthless mining operators. Agrarian rebellion in Ireland was usually directed against property (destroying fences, plowing up converted croplands) and land agents, but in the US, violent beatings and even murders became commonplace occurrences.

In Pennsylvania, the secret organization is now regarded by historians as a violent group struggling against a corrupt institution. Some even argue that the Mollies did not really exist, but were created by the mine operators as a focus for destroying dissent. If that was the case, the authorities were largely successful.

> The clever forecast of coming events, the triumphant vindication of bold theories—are these not the pride and the justification of our life's work.
> **Sherlock Holmes**

excesses. The America he portrays in *The Valley of Fear* and elsewhere is a land of boundless opportunity, yet, at the same time, a hotbed of gangsters and corruption, the evil tentacles of which extend right across the Atlantic as far as London and even into quiet English country houses. McMurdo/Edwards finds the Vermissa Valley a grim place where "The terror is in the hearts of the people from the dusk to the dawn," but once his work there is done, he is able to assume a new identity and make his fortune in the California gold fields. Later, living as Douglas in Sussex, he becomes noted for his bravery, cheerfulness, generosity, and, most significantly, "democratic manners." Like Henry Baskerville in *The Hound of the Baskervilles*, his time in the New World has taught him not to be a snob. But even while Edwards' good qualities make him a popular figure in the village of Birfleet, the cutthroat gangsters he has left behind in the US are hunting him down in league with Moriarty.

The modern age beckons

The Valley of Fear is notable, in the Holmes canon, for looking nervously forward to the modern age and a different, edgier kind of crime fiction. It moves swiftly from the comfortable domestic setting of 221B Baker Street to a particularly gruesome and bloody murder and—most significantly—a depiction of a violent America riven with corruption and summary justice. In this it anticipates such hard-boiled American crime fiction as Dashiell Hammett's *Red Harvest* (1929). In the passages set in the US, and the novel's bleak ending, which is a marked contrast to the

The California Gold Rush of 1848 brought some 300,000 gold-seekers to the state. They collected the gold mostly by panning in the rivers. Some, like Douglas, made their fortunes.

humor of the opening, there is a sense of dark nihilism not found elsewhere in Conan Doyle's work. This seems very modern among the usual Victoriana, and can be seen to prefigure the 20th-century angst born of the mass slaughter witnessed in World War I. ∎

THE WHOLE INEXPLICABLE TANGLE SEEMED TO STRAIGHTEN OUT BEFORE ME

THE ADVENTURE OF WISTERIA LODGE (1908)

IN CONTEXT

TYPE
Short story

FIRST PUBLICATION
US: August 1908 (as "The Singular Experience of Mr. J. Scott Eccles")
UK: September 1908

COLLECTION
His Last Bow, 1917

CHARACTERS
John Scott Eccles
Respectable English bachelor.

Aloysius Garcia Young Spaniard living in Surrey.

Garcia's cook Chef at Wisteria Lodge.

Inspector Gregson
Scotland Yard policeman.

Inspector Baynes
Provincial policeman.

Don Murillo
Neighbor of Garcia.

Miss Burnet Governess at Henderson's house.

Lucas Henderson's secretary.

This story was originally published in *The Strand Magazine* under the title "A Reminiscence of Sherlock Holmes," and split into two halves: "The Singular Experience of Mr. John Eccles" and "The Tiger of San Pedro." Later editions compiled the full text under the title "The Adventure of Wisteria Lodge."

According to Watson, the case begins on a bleak day in March 1892, but this date is squarely within the so-called "Great Hiatus" (see pp.164–65), which fell between 1891 and 1894, and so either the doctor, or Conan Doyle, must have been mistaken.

Grotesquery and intrigue
The tale opens with Holmes receiving a telegram: "Have just had most incredible and grotesque experience. May I consult you?" He asks Watson how he would best

Released in 1928, this silent Jean Epstein film of "The Fall of the House of Usher" hints at the Gothic atmosphere also present in Wisteria Lodge.

define the word "grotesque," and to Watson's suggestions of "strange" and "remarkable," Holmes adds, "some underlying suggestion of the tragic and the terrible." He then retrospectively characterizes two of his past cases, "The Red-Headed League" (pp.62–67) and "The Five Orange Pips" (pp.74–79), as being more than a little grotesque. In this exchange, Conan Doyle is alluding to Edgar Allan Poe, a past master of the compulsively atmospheric short story, and author of *Tales of the Grotesque and Arabesque* (1840). Poe's fictional French detective, the Chevalier C. Auguste Dupin, was an acknowledged inspiration for Sherlock Holmes. This case, however, draws more parallels with Poe's earlier story "The Fall of the House of Usher" (1839), with its dark and sinister house, which is exactly what Conan Doyle's Wisteria Lodge turns out to be.

When the sender of the telegram, the highly respectable John Scott Eccles, reaches 221B Baker Street, he professes an antipathy to the business of private detection, but says he does not know where else to turn. This begins a coolness

My mind is like a racing engine, tearing itself to pieces because it is not connected up with the work for which it was built.
Sherlock Holmes

between Holmes and his client, which is contrasted with the sleuth's high opinion of Inspector Baynes, who arrives shortly after with the familiar Gregson of Scotland Yard. Against all convention, Baynes, from the local Surrey Constabulary, proves to be a worthy rival for Holmes, and his methods elicit respect and a proud twinkle in the eye of the great detective.

A bewildering dinner date

Eccles has come directly from Wisteria Lodge in Surrey, where he was an overnight guest of Aloysius Garcia—a young Spaniard with whom he had recently struck up a friendship. Eccles had not enjoyed the visit: he found Garcia's home rather disquieting, and the chain-smoking, nervous agitation displayed by his normally upbeat host had not helped. Garcia's mood had worsened on reading a note that his servant delivered to him during dinner, and Eccles was relieved to turn in for the night. But his reprieve was short-lived, for he was surprised to be woken at 1am by his host asking him if he had

The 1988 television adaption of "Wisteria Lodge," starring Jeremy Brett, differs from the original tale and sees the Tiger of San Pedro killed on a train while escaping Holmes.

rung the bell. Eccles said that he had not, and Garcia apologized for disturbing him.

Events had taken an even stranger turn the following morning. Eccles found the house deserted— there was no trace of Garcia, nor the surly servant who had served dinner, nor the gigantic cook who had prepared it. What he does not know is that Garcia was murdered in the early hours on the common near his home. A note found by Baynes on the dead man's body confirmed Eccles's presence at the lodge and explains the police's interest in him. Yet, satisfied by the Englishman's clear respectability, they soon eliminate him as a suspect.

Baynes then produces another note, the one delivered to Garcia during dinner—although he had thrown it on the fire, it got caught in the grating, where the inspector had spotted it. Holmes is impressed by »

The cryptic note found in the hearth at Wisteria Lodge at first confused Holmes, who thought that it referred to racing colors, and that it was written by a jealous husband. He later deduces that it details the layout of what must be a large house nearby, with each part of the note revealing an important aspect of the property.

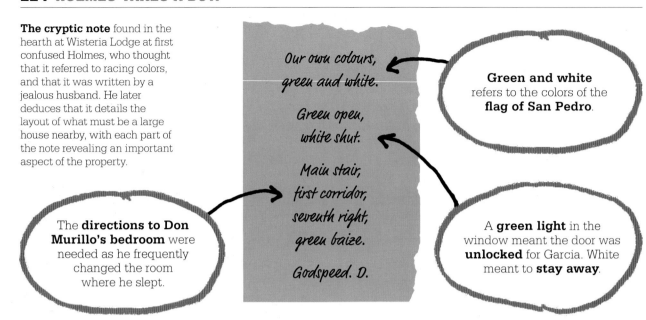

Our own colours, green and white.

Green open, white shut.

Main stair, first corridor, seventh right, green baize.

Godspeed. D.

Green and white refers to the colors of the **flag of San Pedro**.

The **directions to Don Murillo's bedroom** were needed as he frequently changed the room where he slept.

A **green light** in the window meant the door was **unlocked** for Garcia. White meant to **stay away**.

the policeman's sharp eye and his canny, Holmesian diagnosis that the handwriting in the note, a woman's, does not match the address on the reverse side. The note itself is cryptic, and at first Holmes is baffled. He later deduces that the first part must be a signal, and the second an appointment (see above); he also concludes that Garcia must have been heading for a large house near his own when he was killed, and decides to list such properties.

Alibi material

Holmes ponders the unnaturally sudden friendship between Eccles and Garcia, and wonders why the Spaniard's servants had fled. He concludes that while Eccles is "not a man likely to be congenial to a quick-witted Latin," he is nevertheless "the very type of conventional British respectability." That is, someone who might be counted on to provide an alibi.

That evening Holmes, Watson, and Baynes head to Wisteria Lodge, an old, tumbledown place looming "pitch-black against a slate-coloured sky." There, the constable on guard reports being spooked earlier by a huge, devilish figure at the window. Baynes also has some peculiar and grotesque things to show Holmes—a small shriveled humanoid figure on the kitchen sideboard; the limbs and body of a large white bird in the sink; a zinc pail full of blood; and a platter covered in pieces of charred bone.

Unexpected teamwork

From here on in, Holmes and Baynes indulge in some friendly competition, each man following his own leads, and the resolution of the case becomes an instance of perfect, if inadvertent, cooperation. When the "devil" who had startled the constable returns to Wisteria Lodge, he is found to be Garcia's cook, and Baynes charges him with murder. Holmes is certain the inspector has the wrong man, but it transpires that Baynes's move was straight out of the detective's own box of tricks: his false arrest of the cook later flushes out the real culprit, a wealthy local man called

"Henderson"—in fact a fugitive former Central American dictator named Don Murillo, who had been in hiding in Britain with his family.

Murillo, the notorious "Tiger of San Pedro," had led a brutal regime for over a decade, his name striking fear into the hearts of people across Central America, until he was deposed by a popular uprising and escaped to Europe, his ill-gotten fortune intact. Garcia, part of an organization set on bringing justice to this "lewd and

This fellow is a perfect savage, as strong as a cart-horse and as fierce as the devil.
Inspector Baynes

Described as looking like a hungry beast, the devilish appearance of the cook, illustrated by Arthur Twidle in *The Strand Magazine*, was a ploy by Conan Doyle to give the story a sense of horror.

bloodthirsty" tyrant, had indeed invited Eccles to his house to provide an alibi for the night he intended to kill Murillo.

The mysterious note found in the hearth at Wisteria Lodge had been written by "Miss Burnet," the governess in Murillo's household. Acting undercover, and secretly working with Garcia, she was in fact Signora Victor Durando, whose husband had been killed by Murillo in San Pedro. Her cryptic note was to explain that the coast was clear for Garcia to attack, and where in the house he could find the former tyrant. Unfortunately for them, however, Murillo's secretary, Lucas, had caught her writing the note, locked her away in a room, and addressed and sent the note himself—hence the different handwriting. He then intercepted Garcia on the common, killing him before he could fulfill his mission.

The tyrant escapes

From his appearance, Holmes had known only that Henderson—or Murillo—was "either a foreigner or has lived long in the tropics," but the presence of two foreign households in one sleepy Surrey village was enough to put him on alert. He had therefore hired Murillo's fired gardener, John Warner, to watch the house and to report back on developments. What he had not realized, however, was that Baynes was also on to Murillo's true identity. The two detectives' plans then converge when the tyrant, believing he is safe because the cook has been arrested, decides to escape by train, heading to the

station with Lucas and a heavily sedated Miss Burnet in tow. But Warner follows them, and when the governess manages to break free from her captors, the gardener rescues her and delivers her to Holmes. Baynes explains that he had a plainclothes policeman at the station all week, but it was Holmes's man who saved the day. When the governess recovers, she reveals the full story of Murillo and San Pedro's band of freedom fighters.

Although, ultimately, Murillo and Lucas manage to escape from Holmes and Baynes at the station,

Watson reports Murillo's murder in Madrid six months later—clearly at the hands of Garcia's organization. But what of the lurid remains in Garcia's kitchen, and of the "devil" that had frightened the constable? In fact the devil was merely Garcia's cook trying to collect his personal belongings, and the mention of his "savage" activities is a red herring, used to embellish the "grotesque" atmosphere. In fact, "Wisteria Lodge" is one of the earliest works of English literature to feature depictions of voodoo—religious rites practiced mainly in the West Indies. ■

DIFFERENT THREADS, BUT LEADING TO THE SAME TANGLE
THE ADVENTURE OF THE RED CIRCLE (1911)

IN CONTEXT

TYPE
Short story

FIRST PUBLICATION
UK: March 1911
US: April 1911

COLLECTION
***His Last Bow*, 1917**

CHARACTERS
Mrs. Warren Elderly
landlady of a boarding house.

Gennaro Lucca Young
Italian man who flees to
New York, then London.

Emilia Lucca Gennaro's wife.

Giuseppe Gorgiano Member
of the Neapolitan criminal
society, the Red Circle.

Inspector Tobias Gregson
Scotland Yard policeman.

Leverton American detective
with the Pinkerton Agency.

Originally published in two separate parts (apparently against Conan Doyle's wishes), "The Adventure of the Red Circle" has a double, interwoven narrative. In the first installment, Holmes is asked to investigate the eccentric and mystifying behavior of a reclusive lodger in a London boarding house; in the second, the plot dramatically escalates into a major international hunt for an infamous murderer and criminal gang leader who is wanted in both the US and Italy.

A reclusive lodger

Landlady Mrs. Warren approaches Holmes because she is concerned about her new lodger, who never leaves his rooms. Ten days earlier, the young, black-bearded man, who had spoken in good but accented English, had paid over and above the usual rate for two weeks' board, but with the strict condition that he be given a key to the house and on no account be disturbed. Since then, Mrs. Warren explains to Holmes, he has emerged only once, on the first night, when he left the house and returned without being seen.

As per his instructions, the lodger's meals are left on a tray outside his door, and if he requires anything else, he prints the word for it, in block capitals, on a piece of paper and leaves it for her.

The boarding house run by Mrs. Warren is on Great Orme Street, a fictional version of Great Ormond Street, which has many buildings in the Queen Anne style (pictured).

Holmes believes that the fact the lodger writes notes is an attempt to disguise a lack of proficiency in English, and as other clues come to light he deduces that the person now occupying the rooms is not the bearded man who had rented them, and that one lodger has been substituted for another.

The lodger regularly requests a copy of the *Daily Gazette* newspaper, and Holmes suspects that the bearded man may be sending messages to the lodger via the paper's personals column. Scanning through his collection of clippings, Holmes immediately comes across an advertisement posted just two days after the room was let: "Be patient. Will find some sure means of communication. Meanwhile, this column. G." Later postings seem to confirm that Holmes is on the right track and alert him to both a code and a nearby building—"a high red house with white stone facings"—from which "G" will signal messages.

At that very moment, a flustered Mrs. Warren arrives at Baker Street with a peculiar story: that morning her husband was abducted by unknown assailants as he left the house. After being driven around in a cab for an hour he was dumped, unharmed, on Hampstead Heath; Holmes guesses that the kidnappers had mistaken him for the lodger in the foggy morning light, and so he asks to see the lodger.

Warnings by candlelight

Holmes and Watson visit the house and, through the artful placing of a mirror opposite the door of the lodger's rooms, they manage to catch a glimpse of the substituted lodger; to their surprise, rather than seeing a man they observe a beautiful, dark-skinned young woman who seems very frightened.

Cracking the code

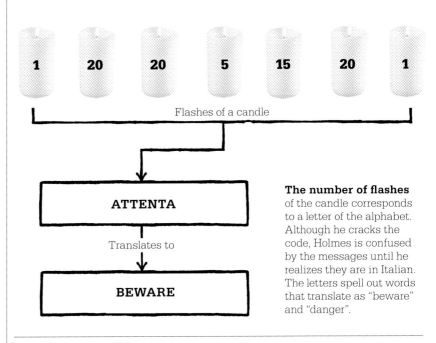

Flashes of a candle

ATTENTA

Translates to

BEWARE

The number of flashes of the candle corresponds to a letter of the alphabet. Although he cracks the code, Holmes is confused by the messages until he realizes they are in Italian. The letters spell out words that translate as "beware" and "danger".

That evening, Holmes and Watson position themselves at a window in the lodging house. They witness a candle flashing in the nearby house, which must be "G" sending coded messages to the lodger's room. The code makes no sense until Holmes realizes it is in Italian: *attenta* (beware) and *pericolo* (danger).

What is at the root of it all? Mrs Warren's whimsical problem enlarges somewhat and assumes a more sinister aspect as we proceed.
Sherlock Holmes

The final message is interrupted very suddenly. Alarmed, Holmes and Watson hurry down to the building in which "G" is located, and are amazed to find standing in its doorway Inspector Gregson of Scotland Yard, and Leverton— a detective with the Pinkerton Agency (a private detective firm established in the US in 1850, which also features in *The Valley of Fear*, pp.212–21). They are on the trail of Italian mobster Giuseppe Gorgiano—a notorious killer responsible for about 50 deaths.

Murder in the house

The men have traced Gorgiano to this building and have been lying in wait for him. Since they began their watch, three men have come out of the house, including one whose description fits that of Mrs. Warren's bearded lodger. However there is no sign of the killer himself. Holmes tells the police about the warning signals that were sent » from an upstairs window, and they assume that Gorgiano must have been attempting to alert his accomplices in London of the dangers.

Deciding to make an arrest, the policemen enter the house and Holmes and Watson follow. They locate the room from which the messages had been sent and find Gorgiano's dead body sprawled on the floor. The blade of a knife has been plunged into his throat, and at his side lie a dagger and a single black leather glove. Clearly there has been a fight, and the huge Italian has been felled. As the men survey the grisly scene, Holmes retrieves the candle and signals *vieni* (come) from the window.

Moments later, the mysterious female lodger arrives. When she sees Gorgiano's body, she reacts with joy and delight as she thinks that the police have killed him. However, on realizing that, in fact, her husband—"G" (Gennaro), the bearded man—is the murderer, she insists on telling the investigators the whole truth; she is confident that, given the dead man's heinous crimes, "there can be no judge in the world who would punish my

> My poor Gennaro…
> had joined a Neapolitan
> society, the Red Circle…
> The oaths and secrets of this
> brotherhood were frightful,
> but once within its rule no
> escape was possible.
> **Emilia Lucca**

husband for having killed him." The rest of the story, apart from a short epilogue, is related almost entirely through the lodger, who introduces herself as Emilia Lucca.

Emilia's tale
Emilia explains that she and her husband Gennaro emigrated to New York from Italy four years ago, fleeing both her father's disapproval of their relationship and Gennaro's naïve youthful involvement in a Neapolitan criminal society called

the Red Circle. For a while, the couple enjoyed a settled life: Gennaro was given a responsible job by a fellow Italian he had helped, and they bought a small house. But then Gennaro's past caught up with him: he was tracked down by a member of the Red Circle called Gorgiano – the "grotesque, gigantic and terrifying" thug who had first initiated him into the organization back in Italy. Once they had taken an oath of allegiance, the Red Circle's members were in the organization's grip for life.

After escaping the authorities in Italy, Gorgiano had settled down in New York, where he soon established a new branch of the Red Circle that funded its activities by blackmailing wealthy Italian-Americans, threatening violence if they did not cooperate. Gennaro's employer and benefactor (who was also his best friend) became a target of the organization, but he refused to give in to their demands, and so Gennaro was ordered, on pain of death, to dispose of him, having been given a disc with a red circle on it—"the mandate for murder." Of course, he had no intention of murdering his friend,

The Black Hand

The early-20th century saw a dramatic shift in the nature of organized crime as criminal networks began to emerge—particularly in New York, but also in London. From 1880 to 1910 nearly 500,000 Italians arrived in New York. They clustered in the same neighborhoods, living in overcrowded tenements. Regarded with suspicion by longer-established citizens, some Italians felt the only people who could protect them were the members of Italian-American criminal societies, who took law enforcement into their own hands.

Extortion and protection rackets became rife, practiced by gangs like *La Mano Nera* (the Black Hand, pictured). In 1908, the Italian Bank of Pasquale Pati & Son was blown up by a Black Hand bomb. This was not an attempted robbery but a warning to Pati, who had publicly stated he would not yield to the gang. A run on the bank after the bombing, and an attack on Pati's home, left him ruined. It may have been this event that gave Conan Doyle the inspiration for the Red Circle's threat to Gennaro's employer.

Holmes, Watson, and Inspector Hawkins (played by Jeremy Brett, Tom Chadbon, and Edward Hardwicke) investigate the mark of the Red Circle in the 1994 Granada television episode.

and after warning him of the Red Circle's orders and notifying the Italian and American police, Gennaro and Emilia escaped to London, with Gorgiano in pursuit.

Once there, Gennaro ensured Emilia's safety in Mrs. Warren's house, but it appeared that Gorgiano had closed in on him, ahead of the police. Fortunately, however, it seems that it was Gennaro who managed to strike the fatal blow.

An inconclusive ending
Conan Doyle does not reveal how Gennaro managed to dispatch his enemy—single-handedly, or aided by the two other men seen exiting the house. Neither does he say whether he is later apprehended by the police. Emilia's fate also goes unrevealed, with the tale wrapping up, rather abruptly, with Holmes

> Well, Watson, you have one more specimen of the tragic and grotesque to add to your collection.
> **Sherlock Holmes**

and Watson heading off to the opera. The last few pages introduce a rambling story that roams from Italy to New York to London, and some have suggested that Conan Doyle was unable to produce a satisfying ending because of the *Strand*'s scheduling and space constraints.

In spite of this, the story's build-up is intriguing. Throughout much of the tale, Holmes's own small investigation runs in parallel with the one headed by Scotland Yard and the Pinkerton detective agency—as Holmes observes, the two "different threads" lead "to the same tangle." And so, while the story begins in a familiar vein, with Holmes piecing together small clues, it becomes a drama about organized crime and intimidation within the US that seems in many ways far beyond the world of Holmes. ∎

THE LONDON CRIMINAL IS CERTAINLY A DULL FELLOW
THE ADVENTURE OF THE BRUCE-PARTINGTON PLANS (1908)

IN CONTEXT

TYPE
Short story

FIRST PUBLICATION
UK: December 1908
US: December 1908

COLLECTION
***His Last Bow*, 1917**

CHARACTERS
Mycroft Holmes Elder brother of Sherlock Holmes and influential government official.

Inspector Lestrade
Scotland Yard detective.

Arthur Cadogan West Junior clerk at Woolwich Arsenal.

Violet Westbury Arthur Cadogan West's fiancée.

Sir James Walter Official guardian of the papers.

Colonel Valentine Walter Sir James Walter's brother.

Sidney Johnson Senior clerk at Woolwich Arsenal.

Hugo Oberstein German spy.

The spy thriller was not yet a fully formed genre when "The Adventure of the Bruce-Partington Plans" was first published. It is now widely recognized as a forerunner of spy fiction.

The tale is concerned with national security—it was written as alliances shifted, rivalries intensified, and the threat of conflict loomed across Europe—and draws on the media story of that period. The notorious Dreyfus Affair, involving the false imprisonment of a French-Jewish army officer accused of espionage, had been resolved only two years before Conan Doyle wrote this tale. The political scandal had alerted society to the possibility of closely guarded military secrets finding their way into the wrong hands.

Conan Doyle had positioned Holmes as a spy hunter once before, in "The Adventure of the Second

Woolwich Arsenal in London was established in the 16th century for the manufacture and storage of weaponry. Its activities were so secretive that it didn't appear on London street maps.

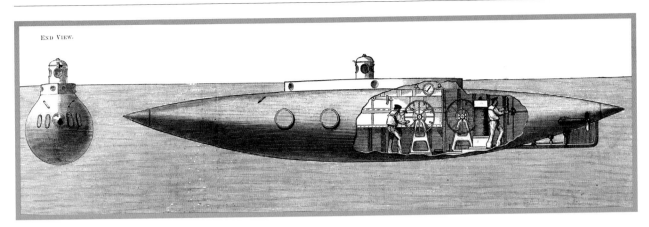

Stain" (pp.202–07). Continuing the theme of espionage, Holmes later acts as a double agent in "His Last Bow" (pp.246–47). Of these stories, "The Bruce-Partington Plans" brings the theme of government intrigue to life most vividly, thanks to the central role of Holmes's elder brother Mycroft, who features in only four stories in the canon and makes his final appearance here. In previous stories, Mycroft is known to Watson as a junior government official, but it is not until this story that Holmes finally reveals that his brother is in fact so important that "occasionally he *is* the British government."

A stolen military secret
It is late November 1895. A dense fog has hung over London for some days, and Holmes and Watson have been confined to their apartment. This fog is a running theme and an important narrative device throughout the story.

Mycroft arrives at Baker Street with Inspector Lestrade to ask for his brother's urgent assistance. Holmes is restless from inaction and eager for adventure, and agrees to help with the case.

The body of Arthur Cadogan West, a young clerk working at the Woolwich Arsenal (an armaments factory), has been found on the

Underground tracks just outside Aldgate station. His skull has been fractured, and he has a sheaf of top-secret government papers in his pocket. These were the Bruce-Partington Plans, concerning a revolutionary new submarine. Such vessels were not in use until World War I, but research and development was ongoing in the early years of the 20th century, so the story anticipates the critical role these covert naval vessels were to play in the coming decades. Work on Britain's E-class submarine was also in progress at the time, and the Bruce-Partington submarine may well have been a

The thief or the murderer could roam London on such a day as the tiger does the jungle, unseen until he pounces, and then evident only to his victim.
Sherlock Holmes

Submarines captured the public imagination in 1870 when Jules Verne published his novel *20,000 Leagues under the Sea*. The British Navy commissioned its first vessel in 1902.

code for this particular pioneering war vessel. The plans comprised 10 pages, but only seven are found on the clerk; three of the four most vital pages are missing. Mycroft urges his brother to find them as a matter of vital national security.

Piecing things together
As the story unfolds, it seems that the apparently steady and honest Cadogan West is in fact guilty of the crime. The plans were kept in a safe in a locked office next to the arsenal. Only two people had keys to this office—Sir James Walter, a prominent government scientist who is beyond reproach, and Sidney Johnson, the loyal senior clerk. However, Cadogan West worked alongside Johnson and had daily access to the plans. Holmes surmises that he could have had duplicate keys made as part of a plan to steal and sell the papers to a foreign agent for a large sum.

Holmes visits the spot where the clerk's body was found—a junction in the line—and learns that a passenger had heard a loud thud at around 11:40pm, but was »

**The final journey
of Cadogan West**

—— Alive
- - - - Dead

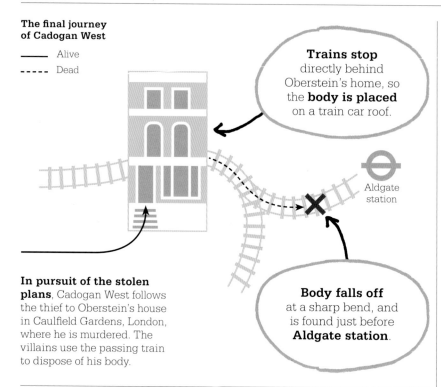

Trains stop directly behind Oberstein's home, so the **body is placed** on a train car roof.

Aldgate station

Body falls off at a sharp bend, and is found just before **Aldgate station**.

In pursuit of the stolen plans, Cadogan West follows the thief to Oberstein's house in Caulfield Gardens, London, where he is murdered. The villains use the passing train to dispose of his body.

agitated man boarding the 8:15pm train to London. Holmes is stumped, and says he cannot recall that he and Watson "have ever had a case which was more difficult to get at."

A clever conceit
Holmes asks his brother for a list of all the foreign agents in London. One of these, Hugo Oberstein, has just left town. This is the German spy's second appearance in the Holmes stories—he was one of the foremost agents in "The Second Stain" (pp.202–07)—but plays a more significant role in this story.

In his pursuit of moral justice—even at the expense of the law—Holmes persuades Watson to help him break into Oberstein's residence. The lodgings back onto an above-ground section of the Underground line near Gloucester Road station, at a junction where the trains often stop for several minutes. They soon notice scuffs and bloodstains on the window overlooking the line and conclude that Cadogan West's body was placed on the roof of a carriage from the window, which is immediately above where the train would have stopped. They also come across a series of coded messages in the

unable to see anything through the thick fog. Strangely, although the poor clerk's head had been crushed, there were no signs of violence in the train cars, nor any blood on the line. Holmes deduces that he must have been killed elsewhere, and that his body, which Holmes believes was placed on the train's roof, had fallen as the train turned the corner.

A round of calls
Holmes and Watson proceed to visit several people connected with the case. First, they go to the home of Sir James Walter, but to their surprise they discover that he has died that morning; his brother, Colonel Valentine Walter, informs them that the scandal of the missing papers was a "crushing blow" that killed him. Holmes wonders whether it is suicide—a "sign of self-reproach for the duty neglected"—but strangely, the reader never learns the cause of his death.

Next, they visit the murdered clerk's fiancée, Miss Violet Westbury, who tells them that she and Cadogan West had been on their way to the theater when he had inexplicably disappeared into the fog near his office at about 7:30pm. The two theater tickets found in his pocket would seem to corroborate her story. She says he would never sell a state secret, but does admit that he had seemed upset and said something about "foreign spies" and "traitors."

A visit to Sidney Johnson at the arsenal yields information that excites Holmes: outside the window of the office from which the papers were stolen is a bush with snapped-off branches; also, the shutters do not close fully, making it possible for someone outside to observe the activity inside the room. Finally, they speak with the railroad officer at Woolwich station, who remembers having seen a very

This must be serious, Watson. A death which has caused my brother to alter his habits can be no ordinary one.
Sherlock Holmes

I'm afraid… that all the queen's horses and all the queen's men cannot avail in this matter.
Sherlock Holmes

Daily Telegraph agony column, posted by "Pierrot," arranging to buy the Bruce-Partington plans from a mystery seller.

In an ingenious move, Holmes posts another "Pierrot" message in the paper, requesting to meet the unknown document thief that night at the agent's Caulfield Gardens apartment. The ruse works, and Colonel Valentine Walter arrives to find Holmes, Watson, Lestrade, and Mycroft waiting for him.

A satisfying conclusion

Colonel Walter confesses to the theft, explaining that he was in debt and motivated by the financial reward, and had copied his brother's keys to the office. Cadogan West, while out with his fiancée, had seen lights on in the office and had gone to investigate. He had then boarded the 8:15pm train to London in pursuit of the colonel, and followed him to Oberstein's lodgings where he met his unfortunate end.

Colonel Walter insists that the fatal blow to the young clerk's head was inflicted by Oberstein, who had taken three of the most important pages of the document, hoping the remaining seven would be enough to incriminate the clerk. Holmes persuades the colonel to write to the treacherous agent, who is now on the Continent, offering him the fourth vital page he needs to be able to build the submarine.

Oberstein takes the bait, returns to London, and is captured, and the missing pages from the Bruce-Partington plans are discovered in his trunk. Holmes's genius at solving the crime wins him an emerald tie pin from a "certain gracious lady"—Queen Victoria herself. Colonel Walter goes to prison and dies there. Oberstein serves 15 years—a light sentence for what was then a capital offense, prompting critics to suggest that he "bought" his life with more secrets.

Real-life crimes

The fog—so much a feature of Victorian London—plays a pivotal role in this story of conspiracy and deception. Its presence, as Holmes maintains at the story's opening, allows people to roam around unnoticed. The heavy shroud it casts over the city makes it possible for Cadogan West to follow Colonel Walter to Oberstein's house, and both enables Oberstein to place Cadogan West's body on the train, and allows it to fall unseen.

Over the years, experts have debated the extent to which real-life crimes inspired this Holmes tale. It has been suggested that the body of a young woman found in a London train tunnel gave Conan Doyle the idea for Cadogan West's end, and that the character of Colonel Walter is based on Frank Shackleton, brother of polar explorer Sir Ernest Shackleton and a prime suspect in the 1907 theft of the Irish Crown Jewels. Whether accurate or not, one thing is certain: Conan Doyle was a master at weaving real-life circumstances—from political scandals to the lead-up to war— into his intricately crafted fiction. ∎

The birth of the London Underground

As the population of London ballooned in the first half of the 19th century, it became increasingly difficult and time-consuming to cross the city along its busy streets. A group of engineering entrepreneurs came up with a radical vision of "trains in drains"—an underground system of passenger steam trains.

After years of investment, planning, and construction, the world's first underground railroad, the Metropolitan Line, opened in 1863. One of its stations was Holmes's local— Baker Street. The gas-lit wooden carriages carried 40,000 Londoners the 3-mile (5-km), 18-minute stretch on its first day. Detractors warned of the slippery slope to social equality as upper-class passengers were forced "to ride side by side with Billingsgate 'fish fags'." But the Underground network expanded rapidly and became largely responsible for the move of low-paid workers out of inner-city slums, the expansion of the suburbs, and the birth of commuting.

234

WELL, WATSON, WE SEEM TO HAVE FALLEN UPON EVIL DAYS
THE ADVENTURE OF THE DYING DETECTIVE (1913)

IN CONTEXT

TYPE
Short story

FIRST PUBLICATION
US: November 1913
UK: December 1913

COLLECTION
His Last Bow, 1917

CHARACTERS
Mrs. Hudson
Holmes's landlady.

Culverton Smith Planter and amateur microbiologist.

Inspector Morton
Scotland Yard detective.

Holmes often goes to great lengths to solve his cases, and in "The Adventure of the Dying Detective" he takes his dedication to the cause to a new level. Having been previously unable to prove a case of poisoning—and having provoked the wrath of the murderer in the meantime—Holmes prepares a cunning trap, while in the process coldly and calculatedly deceiving those who love him most into believing that he is dying.

Holmes at death's door
One foggy November day, a distressed Mrs. Hudson calls on Watson with devastating news: Holmes is at death's door. Poor Mrs. Hudson; Holmes, not content merely with swamping her house with acrid tobacco fumes, keeping wildly uncivilized hours, conducting "weird and often malodorous scientific experiments," and firing his revolver indoors—making him the "very worst tenant in London"—

The tools of Holmes's transformation

Belladonna is used by Holmes to imbue his eyes with "the brightness of fever."

Beeswax crusted around his mouth makes him look like he has not had food or water for days.

Vaseline applied across Holmes's forehead further embellishes his "ghastly face."

> The sick room was
> a gloomy spot, but it
> was that gaunt, wasted
> face staring at me from
> the bed which sent
> a chill to my heart.
> **Dr. Watson**

now adds extreme emotional manipulation to the catalog of indignities he has perpetrated on his landlady over the years.

A distraught Watson rushes to Holmes's bedside to find him rambling deliriously about oysters and apparently suffering from a highly contagious tropical disease he says he must have caught while "working on a case" among Chinese sailors at Rotherhithe docks. Not caring for his own safety, Watson wants to examine him, but Holmes insists he stay back, woundingly making reference to his "mediocre qualifications." Mysteriously, Holmes also sharply reprimands him when he is about to touch a small ivory box on the mantelpiece.

Holmes dispatches Watson, now bitterly hurt as well as distressed at the imminent death of his friend, to fetch the one man Holmes says can help him: Culverton Smith, a planter and amateur microbiologist visiting London from Sumatra. On his way out, Watson encounters a strangely excited Inspector Morton of Scotland Yard (described here as "an old acquaintance," but never explicitly encountered anywhere else in the canon).

A formidable foe

The ill-tempered Smith is small and frail, but with "menacing" eyes, and a "skull of enormous capacity." Clearly he is a mastermind from the same mold as Moriarty. Initially reluctant to receive Watson, he brightens up when he hears of Holmes's plight: "He is an amateur of crime, as I am of disease. For him the villain, for me the microbe." Smith agrees to call on Holmes.

Obeying Holmes's strict, cryptic instructions, Watson returns alone to 221B and hides behind his friend's bed. When Smith turns up, it is to gloat. Thinking he and Holmes are alone, he admits to sending the small ivory box, which he had booby-trapped with a deadly disease. He also confesses to murdering his nephew in a like manner to secure a "reversion"; that is, to get his hands on the young man's property. At Holmes's request, he turns the gaslight up, unwittingly signaling to Inspector Morton outside, who promptly arrives to make the arrest. With Watson as a witness to all that has been said, the game is up, and Holmes admits to deceiving his adversary as well as his friend.

The truth comes out

Holmes tries to soothe Watson by explaining that he could never have deceived him if he had let him get close—"Do you imagine that I have no respect for your medical talents?"—and that in turn Watson could never have fooled Smith without himself really believing that Holmes was dying. Having not eaten for three days, he suggests a restorative meal at one of their favorite establishments, Simpson's-in-the-Strand. That he has put Watson and Mrs. Hudson through the wringer does not seem to cross his mind. ∎

A deadly cosmetic

Holmes fooled Watson and Mrs. Hudson by dilating his pupils with belladonna, smearing beeswax around his mouth, and rubbing petroleum jelly on his forehead. The belladonna that Holmes uses would have come from *Atropa belladonna*, or deadly nightshade. Highly poisonous, belladonna's Latin name (which translates as "beautiful woman") derives from a habit common among Venetian ladies during the Renaissance of using the atropine from the plant to dilate their pupils. As a former ophthalmologist, Conan Doyle would have been well aware of its properties.

A sensational case took place in New York in 1893, when doctor Robert Buchanan was convicted of murdering his wife with morphine: he had also given her belladonna to disguise the characteristic narrowing of the pupils that would betray the presence of the drug. During the trial, the courtroom was subjected to a horrifying demonstration in which a cat was given a fatal dose of morphine, and then belladonna was applied to its eyes to show the effect.

WE SIMPLY CAN'T AFFORD TO WAIT FOR THE POLICE OR TO KEEP WITHIN THE FOUR CORNERS OF THE LAW
THE DISAPPEARANCE OF LADY FRANCES CARFAX (1911)

IN CONTEXT

TYPE
Short story

FIRST PUBLICATION
UK: December 1911
US: December 1911

COLLECTION
His Last Bow, 1917

CHARACTERS
Lady Frances Carfax
Noble lady of modest means.

Honourable Philip Green
Englishman who has made his fortune in South Africa.

Dr. Shlessinger Convalescent missionary recently returned from South America.

Mrs. Shlessinger
Missionary's wife.

Marie Devine Lady Frances Carfax's maid.

Jules Vibart Marie Devine's fiancé.

This case begins, as so many do, in the sitting room at 221B Baker Street, where Holmes divines Watson's recent activities from the splashes of mud seen on his left coat sleeve (which indicate that he shared a hansom cab that morning) and the way his boots have been tied differently than usual (by the boy at the Turkish baths). He teases the doctor about his extravagant bathing habits, asking, "Why the relaxing and expensive Turkish rather than the invigorating home-made article?" A little hypocritical of him, perhaps, given Watson's later claim in "The Adventure of the Illustrious Client" (pp.266–71) that "both Holmes and I had a weakness for the Turkish bath," but the detective nevertheless suggests a far superior form of therapy for his friend—a trip to Switzerland to undertake some preliminary research on a case.

Watson goes abroad
Lady Frances Carfax, the middle-aged, unmarried daughter of an earl, has gone missing. She was staying at a hotel in the town of Lausanne, but left very suddenly and has not been heard from since.

Lady Frances is not a wealthy woman, but she does own some unique and valuable items of jewelry, which she carries with her everywhere. Holmes is buried in another case, and says, half-joking, that "It is best that I should not leave the country. Scotland Yard feels lonely without me, and it causes an unhealthy excitement among the criminal classes." So Watson is dispatched as Holmes's representative, and the pair agree to keep in contact via telegram.

Conan Doyle himself was very fond of Switzerland, having first visited the country in 1893. He took his first wife Louise (or "Touie") on

Ah, what has happened to the Lady Frances? Is she alive or dead? There is our problem.
Sherlock Holmes

Holmes deduces Watson's movements that day

Watson is in the habit of **tying his boots** in a certain way, but today they are fastened with an **elaborate double bow**.

It is clear that he has **removed his boots**, and that **someone else** has later tied them.

It could only be either a **bootmaker**, or the boy at the **Turkish baths**.

It is **unlikely** to be the **bootmaker**, since Watson's boots are **nearly new**.

"Well, what remains? The bath."

Conan Doyle helped to popularize skiing, and correctly predicted that in the future people would flock to Switzerland to enjoy the skiing season.

an extended vacation to Davos in an attempt to alleviate the symptoms of her tuberculosis. While there, he became a very early exponent of skiing—a Norwegian sport that was almost unheard of in the Swiss Alps. But perhaps the greatest testament to his affection for the country was that, shortly after his first visit, he was inspired to use it as the location for Holmes's death in "The Final Problem" (pp.142–47).

A suspicious stranger

In Lausanne, Watson speaks with the fiancé of Marie Devine, Lady Carfax's maid, who reports that the noblewoman's abrupt departure came shortly after she was seen talking earnestly to a wild-looking, bearded Englishman. He also discovers that her next destination was the German town of Baden. Hot on her trail, he heads there, only to find that three weeks earlier, she had departed for London with

some new friends—Dr. Shlessinger, a charismatic missionary who was recovering from a disease he had contracted in South America, and his wife. "Like most lonely ladies, Lady Frances found her comfort and occupation in religion," Watson remarks on being told by the hotel manager that Lady Frances had helped Mrs. Shlessinger nurse the "convalescent saint." It also emerges that Marie Devine no longer works for Lady Carfax, and that the mysterious Englishman has been in Baden, inquiring after her whereabouts. By now Watson is convinced that this "sinister and unrelenting figure" is pursuing poor Lady Carfax from place to place, forcing her to flee in fear of him. In a telegram to Holmes, he boasts of how "rapidly and surely I had got down to the roots of the matter."

Watson then heads to France, in the hope of getting a lead from Marie Devine. He tracks her down

in Montpellier, and she confesses her own suspicions about the "fierce and terrible" bearded man; as the two talk, the man himself appears in the street outside. Watson accosts him, demanding to know what he has done with Lady Carfax. The man is amazed, and then furious, grabbing Watson by the throat: the doctor is saved only by the unexpected intervention of a local workman, who turns out to be Holmes, in disguise. The half-strangled Watson is then told mockingly by Holmes, "A very pretty hash you have made of it!… I cannot at the moment recall any possible blunder which you have omitted. The total effect of your proceeding has been to give the alarm everywhere and yet to » discover nothing." He lampoons his friend's investigative efforts before going on to trumpet his own superior findings in the case.

If Watson feels bitter about this, he is probably justified, since Holmes's treatment of him is even more insensitive than usual. It is not the first time he has sent Watson on ahead, following more discreetly himself, but unlike in *The Hound of the Baskervilles* (pp.152–61), in which Watson's presence as the apparent sole investigator serves a valuable purpose, Holmes's somewhat unsatisfactory explanation for his sudden appearance here is simply that he was able to get away from London after all. Holmes can be a mercurial creature, and there is clearly no sign of the occasionally humble and affectionate man who exclaims, in "The Adventure of the Devil's Foot" (pp.240–45), "Upon my word, Watson! I owe you both my thanks and an apology."

On the trail of a scoundrel
Watson's irascible assailant turns out to be the Honourable Philip Green—an English noble who has recently returned from living in

Well, there's nothing for it now but a direct frontal attack.
Sherlock Holmes

South Africa. He explains that he and Lady Frances had been sweethearts when they were young. However, as he had been a "wild youngster" and "she could not tolerate a shadow of coarseness," ultimately she rejected him. Now, many years later, he has made his fortune in South Africa and has been attempting to win her over.

Holmes is then provided with information which confirms that "Dr. Shlessinger" is in fact an extremely dangerous Australian criminal by the name of "Holy" Peters, who preys on "lonely ladies by playing upon their religious feelings," and that the vulnerable

Lady Frances is undoubtedly in grave danger. Together with Green, they return to London to continue the search. It proves fruitless until some distinctive ancestral jewelry turns up in a pawnshop. Green lies in wait there and before long, Peters's so-called wife returns with more of Lady Frances's inheritance; he follows her, first to an undertaker, and then to an address in South London. Ominously, as he watches the building, a coffin is delivered.

One funeral or two?
Inside the "dusty and moth-eaten" apartment, Holmes and Watson confront Peters, demanding to know what happened to Lady Frances. He claims that she had traveled to London with the couple before giving them the slip, leaving a few old-fashioned jewels behind to cover her bills. Although he has no warrant, Holmes announces that he wants to search the place, and while Peters's wife calls the police, he barges into a room off the hall. Inside is a coffin, and when Holmes lifts the lid he is astonished to find the wizened body of an old woman. Peters taunts him mercilessly: had he expected it to be Lady Carfax?

Chloroform

Widely used as an anesthetic during the Victorian period, chloroform—a colorless liquid, the vapors of which can cause unconsciousness—eventually fell out of favor in the early 20th century, when it was linked to heart complications. Although the image of a sinister kidnapper clapping a chloroform-soaked handkerchief over the mouth of his victim is a popular one in fiction, it is actually very difficult to incapacitate a non-consenting person with chloroform. It takes

at least five minutes, and a continuous supply needs to be administered thereafter. This did not stop people from trying, however, and there are many stories of criminals attempting to sedate their victims in this way. The notorious serial poisoner and (tenuous) Jack the Ripper suspect Dr. Thomas Neill Cream (pictured) is alleged to have used it in at least one of his murders, when in 1879 one of his patients (perhaps also his lover) was discovered dead of a chloroform overdose in an alleyway behind his clinic.

The corpse is that of his wife's old nurse, who they found, close to death, in the local workhouse and brought home with them; she is to be buried at 8am the next day. The police arrive and eject Holmes and Watson; they can do nothing more until a warrant is secured.

Back at Baker Street, Holmes spends a sleepless night relentlessly going over every detail of the case; then, the next morning, he suddenly realizes what is going on. "Quick, man, quick! It's life or death... I'll never forgive myself, never, if we are too late!" He and Watson race to Peters's house and arrive just as the casket is being carried out. Holmes demands that it is opened and inside, along with the old woman, they find Lady Frances, who has been heavily chloroformed. They are able to revive her, but in the confusion, the criminals slink away.

Unusually, Holmes's methods are fairly unsophisticated here. There are few illustrations of his analytical mind at work, and, save a timely inference drawn from one important clue (the admission by the undertaker's wife that the coffin "took longer, being out of the ordinary"—large enough for

> My night was haunted by the thought that somewhere a clue, a strange sentence, a curious observation, had come under my notice and had been too easily dismissed.
> **Sherlock Holmes**

two bodies), the results are reached mainly through patient surveillance and straightforward questioning.

An unwanted admirer?

Philip Green displays distinct similarities to Leon Sterndale in "The Devil's Foot." Both are big, bearded men with hot tempers who have lived for long periods in Africa and returned to Britain with an element of residual savagery and a propensity to take the law into their own hands. Most significantly, both men are frustrated lovers—a motivation that makes them at once gallant and potentially dangerous.

Modern readers may feel uneasy about Green's persistent stalking of Lady Frances, not to mention Holmes's apparent complicity. Although Green claims that she "loved me well enough to remain single all her sainted days just for my sake alone," the fact is that Lady Carfax has turned him down at least twice, even going to the extraordinary lengths of fleeing Lausanne and taking an elaborate route to Baden with the intention of throwing him off her trail. It is

Victorian workhouses, from one of which Peters takes the old lady, were set up to house and provide work for the poor, elderly, and infirm. Those living in workhouses faced tough conditions.

true that Conan Doyle's stronger female characters tend to be middle-class, such as Violet Hunter in "The Adventure of the Copper Beeches" (pp.98–101) or Irene Adler in "A Scandal in Bohemia" (pp.56–61), and Lady Carfax's propensity to be so easily duped seems to place her in the same category of credulous noblewomen as Violet de Merville in "The Illustrious Client" (pp.266–71). However, at no point do Holmes or Green consider the possibility that her independent lifestyle might be a conscious choice rather than an unhappy circumstance. Lady Frances's true feelings are not known, but there is something faintly alarming about the ending, as Green's heavy step is heard, and Holmes withdraws, leaving the semiconscious and defenseless spinster in the hands of "someone who has a better right to nurse this lady than we have." ∎

I HAVE SELDOM KNOWN A CASE WHICH AT FIRST SIGHT PRESENTED A MORE SINGULAR PROBLEM

THE ADVENTURE OF THE DEVIL'S FOOT (1910)

IN CONTEXT

TYPE
Short story

FIRST PUBLICATION
UK: December 1910
US: January 1911

COLLECTION
His Last Bow, 1917

CHARACTERS
Dr. Leon Sterndale
Lion-hunter and explorer.

Mortimer Tregennis
Bachelor lodging at the
local vicarage.

**Owen and George
Tregennis**
Mortimer's brothers.

Brenda Tregennis
Mortimer's sister.

Mr. Roundhay Local vicar.

Dr. Richards Local doctor.

Mrs. Porter Housekeeper
at Tredannick Wartha.

When asked by *The Strand Magazine* in 1927 to list his 12 favorite Holmes stories (see p.18), Conan Doyle commented laconically: "'The Devil's Foot' has points. It is grim and new. We will give it the ninth place." It is indeed a grim tale—one of Conan Doyle's most atmospheric and chilling, with a wild, sinister setting, and a horrific mystery at its heart that hints at the dark forces of the supernatural. To solve this case Holmes has to be at his most objective, ingenious, and daring.

In 1910, Conan Doyle and his second wife Jean went to Poldhu in Cornwall for a spring break, staying

The dramatic setting of Mounts Bay, Cornwall, has inspired writers and artists for centuries. This painting was made in 1909 by Canadian Elizabeth Forbes, who settled in Newlyn.

at the Poldhu Hotel. Jean was pregnant with their second son, Adrian, who was born just a few weeks before "The Adventure of the Devil's Foot" was published. This area of England was steeped in legends of witchcraft, and Conan Doyle evidently decided it was the perfect setting for "The Devil's Foot"; the story is also perhaps influenced by Conan Doyle's increasing interest in spiritualism.

Holmes on vacation
It is March 1897, and work has taken its toll on Holmes—he has been advised by an eminent Harley Street doctor to take a vacation, "on the threat of being permanently

disqualified from work." And so Holmes and Watson rent a cottage on the headland at Poldhu. It is a wonderfully atmospheric setting, overlooking "the whole sinister semicircle of Mounts Bay, that old deathtrap of sailing vessels, with its fringe of black cliffs and surge-swept reefs on which innumerable seamen have met their end."

Why not tell them of the Cornish horror—strangest case I have ever handled.
Sherlock Holmes

But it is the "sombre" rolling moors, ancient Cornish language, and prehistoric stone monuments that fascinate Holmes, as they did Conan Doyle. For a few days they enjoy a "simple life" of walks on the moors, while Holmes theorizes that the Cornish language developed from Chaldean, an Aramaic language brought over in the Bronze Age by Phoenician tin-traders. This idea, for which there is little evidence, was popular among antiquarians at the time.

Now and again during their wanderings outdoors, they catch sight of a famous local, "the great lion-hunter" Dr. Leon Sterndale, a giant of a man with grizzled hair and a white beard.

Madness and death
One morning, while Holmes and Watson are eating their breakfast, two men arrive: the local vicar, »

Mr. Roundhay, and his lodger, Mortimer Tregennis, a bachelor of independent means. Between them they have a terrible tale to tell.

The previous evening, Mortimer had been playing cards with his brothers, George and Owen, and his sister Brenda at Tredannick Wartha, their house on the moor. The three siblings live in the family home, while Mortimer lives locally. He had left them in good spirits just after 10pm, but while out on a walk the following morning, he met Dr. Richards, the local physician, rushing to the house in response to an urgent summons. There they found the three siblings still seated around the card table, just as Mortimer had left them. Brenda was dead and her brothers were both shrieking dementedly, "an expression of the utmost horror" on each of their faces. On entering the room, Dr. Richards himself almost

> There still lingered upon it something of that convulsion of horror which had been her last human emotion.
> **Dr. Watson**

fainted. Concluding his narrative, Mr. Roundhay tells Holmes, "In all England you are the one man we need." Despite orders for a peaceful vacation, Holmes is as thrilled by the mystery as "an old hound who hears the view-halloa." All Watson's hopes of a respite are dashed.

A visit to the scene
Accompanied by Mortimer, Holmes and Watson go to the house to investigate. On the way, they pass a coach taking Owen and George to the asylum. Watson glimpses a "horribly contorted, grinning face glaring out at us. Those staring eyes and gnashing teeth flashed past us like a dreadful vision."

Arriving at Tredannick Wartha, Holmes trips over a watering can, spilling its contents. An act of apparent clumsiness at the time, Holmes uses this to gauge a clear impression of Mortimer's footprint. From this he is able to trace Mortimer's tracks from the previous night and verify his claim that he had gone straight back to the vicarage. Once inside, Holmes and Watson see Brenda, once a great beauty, laid out on her bed. They learn that the housekeeper, Mrs. Porter, fainted on entering the room where her mistress had died. Examining the scene, Holmes finds it odd that a fire had been lit in such a small room on a spring evening. Mortimer explains the night had been "cold and damp."

Holmes laments there are simply too few clues: "To let the brain work without sufficient material is like racing an engine," he says. "It racks itself to pieces." He suggests a walk to Watson, to talk things over. Both agree that they can rule out any supernatural "diabolical intrusions into the affairs of men."

Murder at the vicarage
When they return to the cottage, Holmes and Watson are surprised to find the eminent Leon Sterndale

The Victorian fascination with drugs and madness informed contemporary fiction, such as R L Stevenson's *Strange Case of Dr. Jekyll and Mr. Hyde*, and this appeal continued into the 20th century.

Leon the lion-hunter

Dr. Leon Sterndale, lion-hunter and explorer, was already a somewhat dated figure in 1910. The image of the romantic adventurers that Conan Doyle had idolized in his youth was tarnished by the growing realization that white colonials had not behaved well toward native people in Africa. However, Conan Doyle admired the exploits of men like Richard Burton and John Speke who blazed trails into the African wilderness. Some Holmes scholars have suggested that Sterndale is based on English naturalist and explorer Charles Waterton (1782–1865, pictured), who once walked barefoot through the Amazon. His book *Wanderings in South America* (1825) inspired naturalists such as Charles Darwin and Alfred Wallace. But Sterndale is probably a mix of the great Victorian explorers. His name may have been inspired by Robert Sterndale, who wrote about big-game hunting in India in books like *Seonee* (1877)—the inspiration for Rudyard Kipling's *The Jungle Book* (1894).

waiting for them, eager to hear Holmes's suspicions about the tragedy. He claims he had been about to leave for Africa, but rushed back from Plymouth on receiving a telegram from the vicar with news of the tragedy, even though some of his luggage was already on board the ship. Holmes is unconvinced by the explanation that this loner chose to abandon his African trip due to his friendship with Owen, George, and Brenda, and refuses to give him any details. Sterndale leaves, Holmes following him in secret. Sterndale goes to the vicarage, looks around, then returns home.

There is a thread here which we have not yet grasped and which might lead us through the tangle.
Sherlock Holmes

The next day, Mr. Roundhay calls on Holmes and Watson in a state of deep agitation. "We are devil-ridden, Mr. Holmes! My poor parish is devil-ridden! Satan himself is loose in it!" Mortimer Tregennis has been found dead in his downstairs room, in a similar state to his sister.

They rush to the crime scene before anyone (including the police) can disturb it, and find Mortimer sitting dead in his chair, with the same look of horror on his face as had been on Brenda's. They also note the stuffy atmosphere in the room—a lamp is still "flaring and smoking" on the table. With this fresh lead, Holmes rushes around: "He was out on the lawn, in through the window, round the room, and up into the bedroom, for all the world like a dashing foxhound drawing a cover," notes Watson. Holmes examines the lamp and takes a sample of powder from it, leaving some for the police.

A dangerous experiment

Back at the cottage, Holmes once again becomes the experimental scientist, just as when Watson first met him in *A Study in Scarlet* (pp.36–45). With a lamp identical to the one in the room in which Mortimer was found, Holmes conducts a series of tests. He reveals that he has realized a connection between the lamp, the fire in the room at Tredannick Wartha, and the "horrible stuffiness" at both crime scenes. He reasons that something toxic must have been burning in both of the fateful incidents. To clinch this theory, he needs to test the powder retrieved from the lamp, and invites Watson to join his experiment. The loyal doctor does so willingly. Holmes puts the powder taken from the second crime scene on a burning lamp, and together they sit down to await its effect. Within moments, Watson is suffering from terrible hallucinations, but when he catches a glimpse of Holmes's face, "white, rigid, and drawn with horror," it rouses him enough to grab his friend and drag him outside into the garden, where they both lie gasping in relief in the open air. It has been a close call, and there follows an unusually touching moment that reveals the depth of their friendship. For an instant, the curtain is lifted, and each says what he truly feels, knowing they have »

Using a lamp similar to the one that burned in the vicarage, Holmes, here played by Jeremy Brett, experiments with the burning times of different oils.

escaped death by a hair's breadth. "I owe you both my thanks and an apology," says Holmes. "It was an unjustifiable experiment… I am really very sorry." Watson replies, "You know that it is my greatest joy and privilege to help you." Within seconds, however, Holmes is back to his usual sardonic self.

Medical experimentation
The idea of self-experimentation was very much a part of doctors' lives in the 19th century. Before the days of clinical trials for testing drugs and poisons, often the only way doctors could discover the effects of such chemicals was to experiment on themselves. There was an element of bravado about this, but also a sense of pushing at the frontiers of science. Conan Doyle himself tried the poison gelseminum (made from the root of yellow jasmine) while a medical student in Edinburgh, and wrote a paper for the *British Medical Journal* in 1879 about his observations. When Watson first meets Holmes, the detective is covered in scars from his own experiments. His drug habit may even have begun this way.

Nevertheless, to involve Watson in this experiment was, as Holmes admits, sheer madness, and they were lucky to escape with their lives, even if it confirmed how the deaths at Tredannick Wartha and the vicarage occurred. Holmes is now certain that Mortimer threw some of the powder on the fire as he left Tredannick Wartha, leaving the fumes to wreak their terrible effect

> At the very first whiff of it my brain and my imagination were beyond all control.
> **Dr. Watson**

on his siblings. He had admitted being in a bitter dispute with them over an inheritance, but had claimed "it was all forgiven and forgotten"—but as Holmes observes, "He is not a man whom I should judge to be of a particularly forgiving disposition."

Holmes knows all
Sterndale soon arrives, at Holmes's invitation. The great explorer is visibly bristling at the summons, but goes quiet when Holmes informs him that he knows he killed Mortimer. Holmes reveals that he had followed Sterndale home after their first meeting, and

Poisonous plants

The fictional devil's-foot root is reminiscent of the *Mandragora*, or mandrake, genus of plants, whose forked roots are said to look human, and supposedly "scream" when pulled up. Mandrakes contain poisonous hallucinogens and are a staple of European witchcraft. Witch doctors across the world use a variety of plants to induce hallucinations and even madness and death. A legendary teacher at Conan Doyle's medical school in Edinburgh, Robert Christison (1797–1882), nearly killed himself by eating part of a Calabar bean (left) sent from

tropical Africa by missionaries, only saving himself by drinking his shaving water and making himself sick. He was also known for firing blowpipes when lecturing on the South American plant poison curare. Explorer Charles Waterton (1782–1865) who, like Conan Doyle, went to school at Stonyhurst College, Lancashire, showed that a donkey poisoned by curare could be kept alive by artificial respiration until the effects wore off. This led Waterton, rightly, to conclude that the plant could be used as an anesthetic.

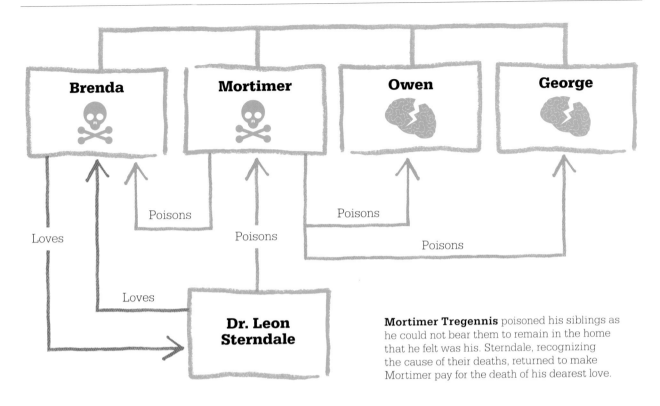

Brenda

Mortimer

Owen

George

Poisons

Poisons

Poisons

Loves

Loves

Poisons

Dr. Leon Sterndale

Mortimer Tregennis poisoned his siblings as he could not bear them to remain in the home that he felt was his. Sterndale, recognizing the cause of their deaths, returned to make Mortimer pay for the death of his dearest love.

then how a later investigation found gravel from his cottage on the lawn below Mortimer's bedroom window. From this Holmes concluded that Sterndale had gone to the vicarage early that morning and thrown gravel at the window to wake Mortimer. Sterndale had then shut him in the room with the burning lamp, while he stood outside on the lawn smoking a cigar and watching him die.

"You are the devil himself!" cries a stunned Sterndale to Holmes. He confesses what Holmes suspected all along—that he had been in love with Brenda for years, but had a long-estranged wife whom he was unable to divorce. Just a few weeks earlier, Sterndale had shown Mortimer some of his "African curiosities," among them a reddish-brown powder made from *Radix pedis diaboli*, or devil's-foot root, a secret "ordeal poison" used by

"medicine-men in certain districts of West Africa." Mortimer, upon learning of its deadly effects, had stolen some and used it to kill his siblings, thus making himself "sole guardian of their joint property." To avenge Brenda's murder, Sterndale, armed with a gun, forced Mortimer to sit in his chair and face the same hideous death. "In five minutes he died," the explorer tells Holmes. "My God! How he died!"

Remarkably, the detective sympathizes with Sterndale and, now that he knows the truth behind his motives, decides to let him go free. Holmes always leans in favor of acting fairly over the letter of the law, and is rarely concerned with legal process once he feels that justice has been done. He advises the great explorer to go and finish his work in Africa. After Sterndale leaves, Holmes tells Watson, "I have never loved, Watson, but if I did and

if the woman I loved had met such an end, I might act even as our lawless lion-hunter has done."

There is something so marked and poignant in Holmes's sympathy for Sterndale's predicament that it is hard to escape the idea that this could be Conan Doyle speaking from the heart. In 1897, the year in which "The Devil's Foot" is set, Conan Doyle had met and fallen in love with Jean Leckie. But his wife Louise (or "Touie") was very ill with tuberculosis, and rather than leave her at this time of crisis, he kept his affair quiet and looked after his wife until she died in 1906, without her ever knowing she had a rival. Conan Doyle finally married Jean in 1907. This decade of heartache meant that the author would know what star-crossed love felt like, and could only too well imagine Sterndale's agony of having his love suddenly snatched away from him. ∎

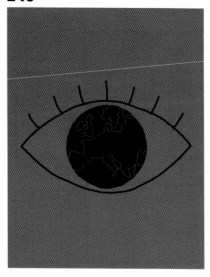

THERE'S AN EAST WIND COMING, WATSON

HIS LAST BOW (1917)

IN CONTEXT

TYPE
Short story

FIRST PUBLICATION
UK: September 1917
US: September 1917

COLLECTION
***His Last Bow*, 1917**

CHARACTERS
Von Bork Avid sportsman
and a German spy.

Martha Von Bork's servant.

Baron Von Herling Chief
Secretary of the German
legation to London.

Altamont Anti-British,
Irish American informant.

So great is Sherlock Holmes's popularity it is often forgotten that Conan Doyle received his knighthood for his role as a reporter in the Boer War rather than for the creation of the world's favorite detective. Indeed, the author could never quite escape Holmes. In his World War I account *A Visit to Three Fronts* (1916), Conan Doyle records being asked by a French officer whether Holmes was in the British

Using chloroform, Holmes subdues the German agent, Von Bork—shown here in a *Strand Magazine* illustration by Alfred Gilbert—before bundling him into the back of his car, set for London.

Army. "Mon général," replied Conan Doyle, "he is too old to serve." However, it is clear that he soon reconsidered this. Published in 1917, "His Last Bow" documents the now-retired detective's undercover military activities, and, chronologically, its 1914 setting features Holmes's final appearance anywhere in the canon. Originally, the story was subtitled "The War Service of Sherlock Holmes," but this was dropped from later editions.

It is also one of only two tales written in the third person, the other being "The Adventure of the Mazarin Stone" (pp.252–53), published four years later. This might have been an intentional decision by the chronicler, Watson; in "The Problem of Thor Bridge" (pp.254–57) he makes passing reference to cases in which he "was either not present or played so small a part that they could only be told as by a third person."

An ominous moment

The language of the opening lines, "It was nine o'clock at night upon the second of August—the most terrible August in the history of the world," is unusually ominous, and the doom-laden atmosphere can be explained by the date, for August 2, 1914 saw a war-bound Germany deliver its ultimatum to Belgium, overthrow Luxembourg, and sign a secret alliance with Turkey. Russia invaded Prussia that same day, and Britain declared war on Germany only two days later.

At his country house in England, Von Bork—a German spy—is in conversation with his superior, Baron Von Herling. In expectation of the approaching conflict, Von Bork is preparing to leave the country. Von Herling suggests this may not be necessary, since he feels England is unprepared for war and distracted by domestic troubles, particularly Ireland. Most of Von Bork's family and staff have already departed, leaving only his servant Martha, of whom Von Herling remarks contemptuously, "She might almost personify Britannia, with her complete self-absorption and general air of comfortable somnolence."

Deep undercover

After Von Herling leaves, Von Bork's star informer—an anti-British, Irish American man named Altamont—arrives to deliver what

> Stand with me here upon the terrace, for it may be the last quiet talk that we shall ever have.
> **Sherlock Holmes**

is supposed to be a stolen copy of the British Navy's secret signals. Von Bork boasts to Altamont about his safe, which is filled with secret intelligence. Its combination code, "August 1914," set four years earlier, indicates that the Germans had been plotting the beginning of the war for some time.

On opening the package containing the book, Von Bork is stunned to see a copy of *Practical Handbook of Bee Culture*, but before he can react, Altamont leaps up and knocks him out with

a chloroform-soaked rag. Thrillingly, it is then revealed that Altamont is none other than Holmes in disguise, whisked out of his beekeeping retirement two years earlier to scupper the troublesome German. As he and his "chauffeur," Watson, help themselves to Von Bork's wine, Holmes explains that Martha (whom some Holmesians believe is Mrs Hudson) was in on the secret, and he had spent two years undercover (including some time in the US) to prepare for his dealings with the spy. The similarities with Birdy Edwards in *The Valley of Fear* (pp.212–21), published a month later, are striking.

Holmes is notably even-handed with Von Bork when he wakes, characterizing his brand of patriotic benevolence perfectly. However, the tale ends with a note of warning, with the detective voicing Conan Doyle's own feelings about the menace of Germany: "There's an east wind coming… such a wind as never blew on England yet. It will be cold and bitter, Watson, and a good many of us may wither… But it's God's own wind none the less, and a cleaner, better, stronger land will lie in the sunshine when the storm has cleared." ∎

Wartime espionage

Contrary to public concern, there was little German espionage in Britain during World War I. Only 31 German spies were brought to trial, 11 of whom were executed at the Tower of London. In "His Last Bow," Von Herling implies that Germany had a hand in stirring up trouble in Ireland and inciting the suffragettes. While there is no evidence for the latter, German support of the Irish campaign for "home rule," to weaken British power, is well documented. A key figure was the Irishman Roger Casement (pictured), whose courting of German support led Germany to supply arms for the 1916 Easter Rising. Casement, who knew Conan Doyle and his writing, helped put an end to Belgium's ruthless colonial exploitation of the Congo. He was later denounced for homosexuality before being tried for high treason and executed by the British in 1916 as a *persona non grata*. Even Conan Doyle's intervention could not save him.

THE FIN

DEDUCT

AL
IONS

Conan Doyle publishes **The New Revelation**, and declares his belief in **spiritualism**.

↑

1918

Conan Doyle publishes **Danger! and Other Stories**; His son, **Kingsley, dies**, partly as a result of war wounds.

↑

DEC 1918

Conan Doyle's mother, **Mary, dies.**

↑

1921

The stories later collected in **The Case Book of Sherlock Holmes** begin to appear in *The Strand Magazine*.

↑

OCT 1921

NOV 1918

↓

Britain and Germany sign the armistice that **ends World War I**.

FEB 1919

↓

Conan Doyle's **brother, Innes, dies**, as a result of pneumonia contracted during the war.

MAY 1921

↓

Conan Doyle presents Holmes on stage again in a play, **The Crown Diamond**, which opens in Bristol.

1922

↓

Conan Doyle publishes **The Poems of Arthur Conan Doyle**.

IN THIS CHAPTER

COLLECTION
The Case Book of Sherlock Holmes, 1927
The Mazarin Stone
The Problem of Thor Bridge
The Creeping Man
The Sussex Vampire
The Three Garridebs
The Illustrious Client
The Three Gables
The Blanched Soldier
The Lion's Mane
The Retired Colourman
The Veiled Lodger
Shoscombe Old Place

Four years after the exploits which were recounted in the collection *His Last Bow*, Sherlock Holmes returned one last time in 1927's *The Case Book of Sherlock Holmes*. These 12 stories, which were written during the last decade of Conan Doyle's life, begin in 1921 with "The Mazarin Stone," an adaptation of Conan Doyle's single-act stage play *The Crown Diamond*, and culminated in "Shoscombe Old Place."

To the dark side
Compared with the earlier stories, those in the *Case Book* are darker, more violent, and tougher in theme, perhaps a reflection of what Conan Doyle called the "feverish days" in which they were written, and the widespread disillusionment in the aftermath of World War I. Holmes displays a range of more negative emotions, including fear and anger; he is also cynical and vengeful, and shows he is capable of misjudging a situation, and even of succumbing to defeat, as shown by the dispatch box full of unsolved cases seen in "The Problem of Thor Bridge." Holmes is also unprepared for the brave Kitty Winter, whose actions shock him in "The Illustrious Client."

Some critics have argued that these stories might not all be the work of Conan Doyle. They are certainly of varying quality, and often bleaker than his earlier tales, featuring themes such as mutilation ("The Illustrious Client" and "The Veiled Lodger") and even suicide ("The Problem of Thor Bridge"). In the climax of the violent tale "The Three Garridebs," Watson even gets shot.

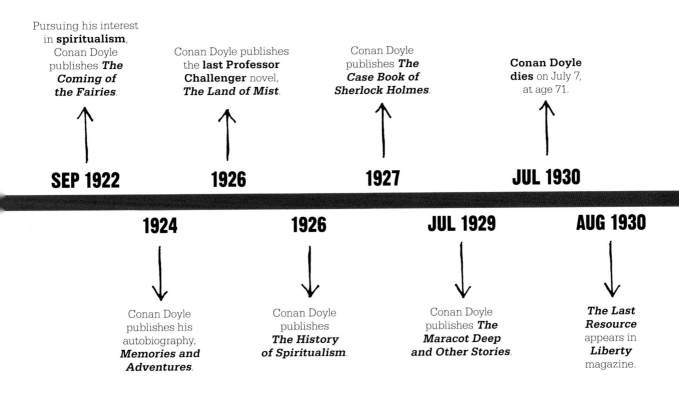

Pursuing his interest in **spiritualism**, Conan Doyle publishes *The Coming of the Fairies*.

SEP 1922

Conan Doyle publishes the **last Professor Challenger** novel, *The Land of Mist*.

1926

Conan Doyle publishes *The Case Book of Sherlock Holmes*.

1927

Conan Doyle dies on July 7, at age 71.

JUL 1930

1924

Conan Doyle publishes his autobiography, *Memories and Adventures*.

1926

Conan Doyle publishes *The History of Spiritualism*.

JUL 1929

Conan Doyle publishes *The Maracot Deep and Other Stories*.

AUG 1930

The Last Resource appears in *Liberty* magazine.

Two sides of the coin

Although Conan Doyle had accepted a knighthood in 1902, Holmes modestly turns one down in "The Three Garridebs." There are further divergences between the beliefs of the writer and his creation in these years: Conan Doyle's interest in spiritualism and clairvoyance were reaching their zenith. This was a result, in part, of the deaths of his beloved son during World War I, and Conan Doyle's brother, soon after, of pneumonia caught during the war.

By this time, Conan Doyle had become a fierce devotee of "the Spiritist conclusion," regularly taking part in séances and experiments with telepathy. His 1922 book *The Coming of the Fairies* defended two young girls who claimed to have photographed fairies (years later, they admitted their fraudulence). It is remarkable that, for all the strength of Conan Doyle's own beliefs in the paranormal, Holmes's remained as resolutely rational as ever—in particular, "The Sussex Vampire" demonstrates the detective's total rejection of supernatural theories: "No ghosts need apply."

A changing world

Apart from "The Lion's Mane," which is set in 1907, none of the action in the *Case Book* stories takes place any later than 1903—long before the 1914 setting of "His Last Bow," in which Holmes explicitly comments on the "changing age." Perhaps Conan Doyle preferred to keep the detective firmly rooted in the late Victorian and Edwardian era of his prime, sensing that even a skill set as uniquely effective as his might not be up to solving the complex moral and practical dilemmas of the early 20th century.

In the preface to this final collection of stories, Conan Doyle bids farewell to Holmes, adding his hope that he and Watson might, for a time, find a corner in that "fantastic limbo for the children of imagination." In the decades that followed, the creation that Conan Doyle regarded as "a lower stratum of literary achievement" went on to define the archetype of the brilliant but eccentric detective so common in modern crime fiction. Today, Holmes's popularity is undimmed, and the character continues to evolve, taking forms that his creator could never have imagined. All around the world, an ever-growing network of Holmesians are still held spellbound by his adventures, on both the page and the screen. ∎

THIS MAN HAS COME FOR HIS OWN PURPOSE, BUT HE MAY STAY FOR MINE
THE ADVENTURE OF THE MAZARIN STONE (1921)

IN CONTEXT

TYPE
Short story

FIRST PUBLICATION
UK: October 1921
US: November 1921

COLLECTION
***The Case Book of
Sherlock Holmes*, 1927**

CHARACTERS
Count Negretto Sylvius
Half-Italian nobleman and
master criminal.

Sam Merton Dimwitted
boxer; the count's accomplice.

Billy Holmes's streetwise
page boy.

Lord Cantlemere
One of Holmes's eminent
employers in the case.

This story is based on Conan
Doyle's short one-act play
The Crown Diamond (see
box), which was itself partially
derived from his earlier story "The
Adventure of the Empty House"
(pp.162–67), accounting for the
almost identical plot. It is also
notable for being one of only two
Holmes stories narrated in the third
person—alongside "His Last Bow"
(pp.246–47)—and for taking place
entirely in Holmes's sitting room.

A glittering prize
Holmes has been tasked by
the Prime Minister, the Home
Secretary, and a certain Lord

> You can't bluff me,
> Count Sylvius… You are
> absolute plate-glass. I see to
> the very back of your mind.
> **Sherlock Holmes**

Cantlemere with retrieving a stolen
Crown diamond worth £100,000,
a figure one hundred times more
than the Countess of Morcar's
stone in "The Adventure of the
Blue Carbuncle" (pp.82–3). Holmes
knows who the thieves are but
not where the stone is, so he has
allowed them to remain at large
despite the danger to himself. The
ringleader, the half-Italian Count
Negretto Sylvius, is a crack shot,
so Holmes has placed a wax dummy
of himself behind a curtain at the
front window to foil any attempts
to assassinate him. When the count
turns up at the front door, Holmes
sees a chance to resolve the case and
sends Watson to summon Scotland
Yard before receiving his visitor.

A familiar villain
Sylvius is a foreign incarnation of
big-game hunter Colonel Sebastian
Moran from "The Empty House,"
right down to the way Holmes
lectures both men on the parallels
between their form of hunting
and his own. Both villains favor
specially-engineered air rifles:
Moran's is made by "Von Herder,
the blind German mechanic," while
Sylvius's is the work of a similarly
Germanic-sounding gunsmith,

THE ADVENTURE OF THE MAZARIN STONE 253

> My old friend here will tell you that I have an impish habit of practical joking.
> **Sherlock Holmes**

"old Straubenzee." Admittedly, the count's preferred quarry is Algerian lions rather than Indian tigers, but Moran's mustache and large nose have found their way into Sylvius's appearance. He also has a "cruel, thin-lipped mouth," like the wicked Continental aristocrat, Baron Gruner, in the later story "The Adventure of the Illustrious Client" (pp.266–71).

Switch trick

Holmes offers to let Sylvius and his accomplice, Sam Merton, go free if they surrender the stone, and duly withdraws, ostensibly to play the violin in his bedroom. Thinking they are alone, Sylvius tells Merton

that he has the Mazarin stone on him—at which point the "dummy" dramatically springs to life, revolver in hand. Holmes has switched places with the wax figure via a secret door, and the violin music was courtesy of a gramophone. The thieves have been roundly outsmarted and are arrested.

In a familiar practical joke, Holmes then makes fun of the supercilious Lord Cantlemere by planting the diamond in his pocket while pretending to help him with his coat, and then mischievously accuses him of being its "receiver." In an instant, Lord Cantlemere switches from saying that he has never believed in Holmes, to congratulating him on his incredible skills: "We are greatly your debtors, Mr. Holmes… I withdraw any reflection I have made upon your amazing professional powers."

Pros and cons

The story recycles plot details to the extent that it feels like a pastiche of "The Empty House" by someone other than Conan Doyle. It is dialogue-heavy, and much of the speech, lifted straight from the

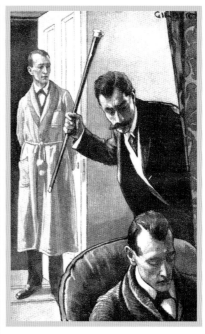

Count Sylvius, as illustrated by Alfred Gilbert in *The Strand Magazine*, prepares to attack the dummy but is instead greeted by Holmes's "cool, sardonic" voice in the doorway.

play, is hammy. The secret door is also a cliché. The story does, however, contain the occasional magnificent line, as when Holmes says, "I am a brain, Watson. The rest of me is a mere appendix." ∎

The Crown Diamond

The Crown Diamond: An Evening with Sherlock Holmes debuted at the Bristol Hippodrome in 1921, with Dennis Neilson-Terry as Holmes, Rex Vernon Taylour as Watson, and Norman Leyland as Moran (Taylour was soon replaced by Paul Ashwell due to a scandal involving a barmaid and a stolen watch). The play toured England following performances at the Coliseum in London (pictured). But as movies replaced such entertainments, the play was so forgotten that a copy found

among Conan Doyle's papers after his death was mistaken for an undiscovered work.

Conan Doyle was no stranger to writing for the stage. In 1899, *Sherlock Holmes*, a collaboration with playwright William Gillette (who played Holmes), opened at the Garrick, and was a huge hit. Other work included adaptations of his Napoleonic tales, a version of "The Speckled Band," and a joint venture with his friend J. M. Barrie on an operetta, *Jane Annie*, which was dismissed by George Bernard Shaw as an "outburst of tomfoolery."

I CAN DISCOVER FACTS, WATSON, BUT I CANNOT CHANGE THEM
THE PROBLEM OF THOR BRIDGE (1922)

IN CONTEXT

TYPE
Short story

FIRST PUBLICATION
UK: February 1922
US: February/March 1922

COLLECTION
***The Case Book of
Sherlock Holmes*, 1927**

CHARACTERS
Neil Gibson American
millionaire, gold magnate,
and former senator.

Mrs. Gibson
Neil's Brazilian wife.

Miss Grace Dunbar
Governess to the Gibsons'
two young children.

Sergeant Coventry
Local policeman.

The 50th story in the canon, "The Problem of Thor Bridge" begins with a revelation that has haunted avid Holmesians ever since, as Watson mentions the existence of a "travel-worn and battered tin dispatch-box" full of Holmes's untold cases. But this story gives fans of the great detective more than just teasers. Beyond the story itself, and the remarkable range of motivations displayed among its cast's principal players, it contains unusually rich insights into Holmes's character, prejudices, and even his fallibility.

A problem without
a solution may
interest the student,
but can hardly
fail to annoy the
casual reader.
Dr. Watson

No match for Holmes

The client is a ruthless American gold magnate and former senator named Neil Gibson, with a number of similarities to the real-life gold king and politician George Hearst (father of the famous newspaper baron William Randolph Hearst), which are surely too striking to be coincidental. Gibson's wife, a fiery Brazilian ("tropical by birth and tropical by nature"), has been found shot through the head on a stone bridge over a lake on Gibson's Hampshire estate, Thor Place. The Gibson children's governess, Grace Dunbar, who admits that she met Mrs. Gibson on the bridge, has been arrested. The dead woman was found clutching an incriminating note from Miss Dunbar, and a fired revolver was subsequently discovered in the governess's wardrobe.

Gibson is an unappealing character. His own estate manager calls him "an infernal villain," and Watson observes waspishly, "An Abraham Lincoln keyed to base uses instead of high ones would give some idea of the man." The millionaire wants Holmes to take the case in order to clear Miss Dunbar, but when he lies about being in love with her, Holmes sends him packing. Used to getting his own way, Gibson greets Holmes's refusal with angry threats, but Holmes is not remotely flustered, responding placidly, "Don't be noisy, Mr. Gibson." Holmes's delightful immunity to intimidation is one of his most appealing characteristics, and it is this same lack of deference to status or ego that causes him to needle his royal employer in "A Scandal in Bohemia" (pp.56–61) and to scoff at Baron Gruner's threats in "The Adventure of the Illustrious Client" (pp.266–71).

Eventually Gibson admits that he previously made unsuccessful advances toward the charismatic governess, which she rebuffed. She stayed in his household, however, because it seems she felt she could exert a positive influence on his character. Gibson is plainly under her benevolent spell, so Holmes takes the case for the sake of the governess rather than her employer.

A devilish crime

After visiting Thor Place with Watson, and inspecting the crime scene with the official investigator, Sergeant Coventry, Holmes then

interviews Miss Dunbar in her Winchester jail cell. She swears that the assignation at the bridge was proposed in a note from Mrs. Gibson herself, and that the letter she wrote in response merely confirmed the time and place. Miss Dunbar alleges that on arriving at the bridge, she was subjected to a tirade of bile from the jealous woman: "Never did I realize till that moment how this poor creature hated me... She poured her whole

The make of gun (or guns) owned by Holmes and Watson is the subject of great Holmesian debate. Some believe that Watson's revolver, which plays a vital role in this story, may have been either a Webley or an Adams (pictured).

wild fury out in burning and horrible words." She claims Mrs. Gibson then fled from the bridge.

The revolver in Miss Dunbar's wardrobe turns out to be one of a pair, but its match can not be found among Gibson's "formidable array of firearms of various shapes and sizes." British perceptions of gun-toting Americans have apparently not changed a great deal in the course of the past century, and Sergeant Coventry's observation that "these Americans are readier with pistols than our folk are" is echoed elsewhere in the canon in trigger-happy characters such as "Killer" Evans in "The Adventure of the Three Garridebs" (pp.262–65).

The breakthrough

The key to the case is a large, fresh chip in the bridge's parapet, a chip that appears to have come from a »

Crime scene reconstruction

Crime scene analysis and reconstruction was a relatively new but rapidly developing discipline during the 40 years Conan Doyle was writing the Holmes stories. Some elements of forensics – such as fingerprinting – were already in use by the turn of the 20th century, but the Victorians still relied largely on a flawed model of detection, in which theories were based first on testimony and motive, before corroborative physical evidence was sought.

In "A Scandal in Bohemia," however, Holmes warns against twisting facts to suit theories, and he was not alone in this belief. The criminalist Hans Gross wrote in 1898 that theories should be based on empirical physical evidence rather than testimony, and the criminologist Edward Oscar Heinrich held the belief that investigators needed to find out "what happened, where it happened and when it happened" before they could hope to find a suspect.

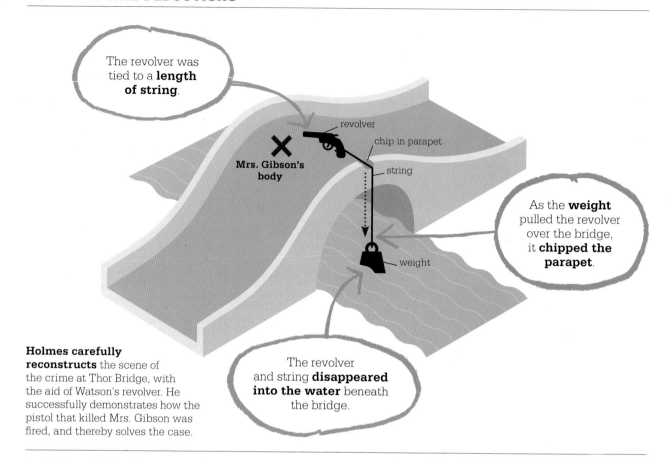

The revolver was tied to a **length of string**.

revolver

chip in parapet

Mrs. Gibson's body

string

As the **weight** pulled the revolver over the bridge, **it chipped the parapet**.

weight

The revolver and string **disappeared into the water** beneath the bridge.

Holmes carefully reconstructs the scene of the crime at Thor Bridge, with the aid of Watson's revolver. He successfully demonstrates how the pistol that killed Mrs. Gibson was fired, and thereby solves the case.

hard object hitting the stonework with great force. Holmes realizes its significance, and Watson's trusty revolver is once more pressed into service, as the crucial prop in a crime scene reconstruction. Holmes ties his gun to a length of string, and the other end of the string to a heavy stone, which he dangles over the bridge. Standing where Mrs. Gibson's body was found, he holds the gun to his head, then releases his grip. As the stone drags the revolver into the lake, the gun strikes the parapet, creating a chip identical to the one already there.

Holmes has proved that the case is not a murder, but a suicide cunningly contrived to implicate the unfortunate governess. Although the idea may seem fantastical, Conan Doyle was, in fact, inspired

by a real German case, reported by the Austrian criminalist Hans Gross in 1896, of a man who killed himself in just this manner, making it seem to be murder so as not to invalidate his life insurance policy, from which his family would benefit.

The power of love

Gibson has already admitted that, having long since fallen out of love with his wife, he began to have strong feelings for Miss Dunbar. Though there was no impropriety, he says, "There is no doubt that my wife was bitterly jealous." Mrs. Gibson was a passionate, primal South American (much like Mrs. Ferguson in "The Adventure of the Sussex Vampire," pp.260–61) and she was "crazy with hatred" toward her children's governess.

The story refers repeatedly to the difference between a "physical" relationship and a "mental" one, with the deep and intense, but chaste, intellectual bond between Gibson and Miss Dunbar being somehow more intimate than his former physical attraction and very real marriage to Mrs. Gibson. The governess speculates that Mrs. Gibson "loved so vividly in a physical sense that she could hardly understand the mental, and even spiritual, tie which held her husband to me," while Gibson himself grapples with this concept when he tries to explain that "there is a soul-jealousy that can be as frantic as any body-jealousy."

This question of physical versus spiritual love had at one time greatly occupied Conan Doyle's own mind.

Long before his first wife, Louise ("Touie") died in 1906, Conan Doyle had met and fallen in love with a beautiful woman, fourteen years his junior, named Jean Leckie. He always maintained that their relationship had remained platonic until they were married (following Touie's death), and it is difficult not to read overtones of his own life in the complicated love triangle of "The Problem of Thor Bridge." Alluding to the relationship with Leckie in a letter to his mother, Conan Doyle wrote, "there is a large side of my life which was unoccupied, but is no longer so."

Gibson evidently feels the same way, and he is ultimately offered a chance at achieving his creator's own happiness. The reader is left wondering whether he and Miss Dunbar will now get married, and whether she really will help him to "see past the dollars to something... more lasting."

A detached professional?

In "The Problem of Thor Bridge" Holmes's own behavior is complicated by his attitude toward his client, who seems to offend both his morals and his vanity. When first taking the case, Gibson asks him to name his price

> Every link is
> now in its place
> and the chain
> is complete.
> **Sherlock Holmes**

> Mr. Neil Gibson has learned something in that schoolroom of sorrow where our earthly lessons are taught.
> **Sherlock Holmes**

and think of his reputation: "If you pull this off every paper in England and America will be booming you. You'll be the talk of two continents." Holmes replies coldly that his fees are on a fixed scale, and that he prefers to work anonymously. These are rather contrary assertions for a man who has, for example, gleefully taken a large fee from the Duke of Holdernesse in "The Adventure of the Priory School" (pp.178–83). Possibly he is offended by the assumption that his motivations are so crude, or perhaps he simply wants some meaningful sacrifice from Gibson. While he enjoys prying riches from tightfisted Old World aristocrats, the American's money is inconsequential to Holmes because it is inconsequential to the client.

As Holmes explains, "it is the problem itself which attracts me," but if this desire to reduce human drama to a cerebral conundrum seems rather cold, it would appear that Holmes is more emotionally invested in the case than he will admit. He is genuinely sympathetic toward Miss Dunbar, and there is perceptible irritation in his voice when he snaps at Gibson, "Some of you rich men have to be taught that all the world cannot be bribed into condoning your offences."

A multifaceted hero

In this story, Conan Doyle depicts a much more layered Holmes than the detached superhero of earlier tales. Indeed, over the course of this and the other stories in *The Case Book of Sherlock Holmes*, the detective betrays cruder emotions, such as anger, fear, vengefulness, and cynicism, than previously, along with a capacity for misjudgment and even defeat. His injury in "The Illustrious Client," and the dispatch-box full of unsolved cases mentioned at the beginning of this story both imbue Holmes with a new and very human potential for failure. It may have been that Conan Doyle wanted to give his creation a more complex character, before consigning him to that "fantastic limbo for the children of imagination," as described in his preface to the *Case Book*. ∎

Holmes strikes the parapet of the bridge with his cane, as illustrated here by Alfred Gilbert in *The Strand Magazine*, and deduces that the chip was caused by a hard knock from above.

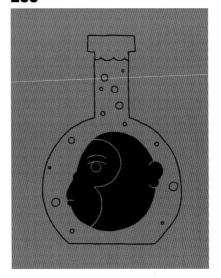

WHEN ONE TRIES TO RISE ABOVE NATURE ONE IS LIABLE TO FALL BELOW IT

THE ADVENTURE OF THE CREEPING MAN (1923)

IN CONTEXT

TYPE
Short story

FIRST PUBLICATION
UK: March 1923
US: March 1923

COLLECTION
The Case Book of Sherlock Holmes, 1927

CHARACTERS
Professor Presbury
Eminent physiologist at the University of Camford.

Trevor Bennett Professional assistant, lodger, and future son-in-law of the professor.

Edith Presbury
Daughter of the professor, and Bennett's fiancée.

H. Lowenstein
Prague-based physiologist.

A. Dorak Lowenstein's agent in London.

Jeremy Brett, Edward Hardwicke, and Colin Jeavons star as Holmes, Watson, and Lestrade, respectively, in this scene from the 1991 ITV adaptation of "The Creeping Man."

S et in 1903, shortly before Holmes's retirement, this story is prefaced with some interesting reflections from Watson about the role he has played in the great detective's brilliant career; the doctor fully acknowledges that his methodical and literal ways of thinking may be irritating, but considers that they have acted as a foil and a stimulant to Holmes's roving imagination.

A creepy case

The client in this case is Trevor Bennett, who is concerned about his employer, and presents Holmes

with a number of details about Professor Presbury, a 61-year-old widower. The professor has recently fallen passionately in love with a young woman in her twenties, but she rejected him because of his age. Presbury then took a mysterious trip to Prague, and has been in an uncharacteristically irascible and aggressive mood ever since. His once-devoted dog is now agitated by its master's presence, attacking him twice. Finally, the professor's terrified daughter has spotted him in the middle of the night, "creeping" around, animal-like, on his hands and knees, along the landing.

Brushing aside Watson's medical diagnosis of lumbago, Holmes suspects that something more interesting is afoot. Bennett has recorded that every nine days, the professor receives a package from a Bohemian dealer in London, which he will not let him open. The professor's fits of rage and vigor follow the arrival of the package, so Holmes concludes he is obtaining some sort of drug from Prague.

When, following the nine-day cycle, Holmes and Watson travel to meet the professor at his university, he is instantly overcome by an alarmingly violent rage; Holmes also observes that the man's knuckles are "thick and horny." One night, during a clandestine observation of the professor's movements, the duo watch in alarm as he squats on all fours, and then, with amazing agility, scales the ivy that grows on the side of his house. He is a sinister, terrifying apparition, "with his dressing-

> In all our adventures I do not know that I have ever seen a more strange sight.
> **Dr. Watson**

gown flapping on each side of him… like some huge bat…."
He then torments and taunts his chained wolfhound, until the animal breaks free and bites his master's throat. Bennett manages to calm the dog, and he and Watson dress the professor's injuries.

An unnatural solution

Holmes deduces that the professor, madly in love and conscious of his advanced years, has made contact with an experimental scientist in Prague, who has been sending him samples of a rejuvenating serum. They find a letter with a Prague postmark from an H. Lowenstein, which confirms that his "wondrous strengthgiving" serum is extracted from a black-faced langur, a kind of Himalayan climbing monkey. Lowenstein has been supplying it to the professor via a third party in London, a Mr. A. Dorak. Recklessly, the professor has attempted to manipulate nature, halt the aging process, and revive his waning powers. During the course of this dangerous experiment, however, he has taken on the characteristics of an aggressive primate. His own dog attacked him because its natural instincts alerted it to the danger.

The surreal spectacle of the professor's apelike behavior prompts Holmes to warn of the risks of scientific experimentation that distorts the "natural order." The story also explores the necessity of accepting that everything comes to an end—that youth disappears, and the more sedate pleasures of old age must be embraced. The advances of modern science may be enlisted to hold back the tide, but ultimately everyone shares the same fate. It is a lesson that Holmes must learn too, as he contemplates retiring to what he calls "that little farm of my dreams." ∎

Science fiction

In the late 19th and early 20th centuries, a number of writers were beginning to explore various speculative themes that were to become the preoccupations of later science fiction: time travel, lost worlds, utopianism, and ambitious scientists. The works of Jules Verne, H. G. Wells, and Edgar Rice Burroughs were to prove enduringly popular. Conan Doyle himself turned his talents to science fiction, writing a series of stories charting the adventures of Professor Challenger, who leads exhibitions into the unknown, discovers dinosaurs living deep in the South American rainforest, and wrestles with the imminent extinction of the Earth as it is threatened by poisonous ether from outer space.

"The Creeping Man", which was, in part, influenced by 1920s research into the rejuvenating effects of implanting monkey glands into humans, explores the consequences of reckless scientific experimentation. Presciently, it is also relevant to 21st-century fears about genetic mutation and eugenics.

THE WORLD IS BIG ENOUGH FOR US. NO GHOSTS NEED APPLY
THE ADVENTURE OF THE SUSSEX VAMPIRE (1924)

Love and betrayal within the Ferguson family

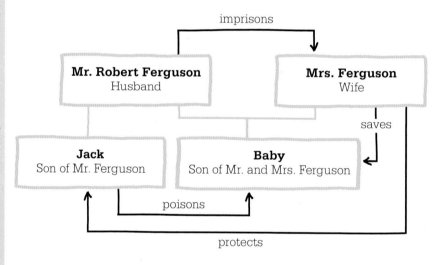

In contrast to Holmes's usually logical cases, "The Adventure of the Sussex Vampire" contains hints of the supernatural, similar to those in "The Adventure of the Creeping Man" (pp.258–59). A societal shift toward spirituality had begun in the late 19th century, and Charles Darwin's theory of evolution had shaken the religious foundations of society. People were searching for alternative meaning in their lives, and Conan Doyle became a great supporter of the Spiritualist movement. He was also a prominent member of the paranormal Ghost Club and an avid believer in an afterlife, telepathy, and even fairies.

Spiritualist journey
Conan Doyle's spiritualism has been attributed to the tragic deaths of his wife and son in the early 20th century; however, his interest began years before. "The American's Tale" (1880), a short story about a blood-sucking plant, reflects his early interest in the metaphysical; by

1924 when "The Adventure of the Sussex Vampire" was published, his spiritualism had become an obsession. Two years later, Conan Doyle published his pivotal work *The History of Spiritualism*.

A Peruvian vampire?

In "The Sussex Vampire," Robert Ferguson, a tea broker and father of two, asks Sherlock Holmes for help because he is convinced that his new Peruvian wife has been sucking the blood of their baby son. Although she is a devoted wife and mother, she was caught in this vampiric act by their nurse, who plucked up the courage to confide in her master.

Ferguson was in disbelief until he saw the baby's wounded neck and his mother's bloodied lips. His wife offered no explanation to her husband, but just gazed at him "with a sort of wild, despairing look in her eyes." She had also, inexplicably, twice beaten her crippled 15-year-old stepson, Jack—her husband's son from his previous marriage. Ferguson is appalled and beside himself with concern.

Holmes and Watson travel to Ferguson's Sussex home to confirm what Holmes has already deduced—that a vampire has not played any part in this strange case. Indeed, he says, "The idea of a vampire was to me absurd. Such things do not happen in criminal practice in England." Holmes, as the fictional standard-bearer for rationalism, is a clear-minded and reasoned forensic investigator who never falls for the illogical.

Once installed at Ferguson's decaying Tudor farmhouse, Holmes engages his powers of observation. He notices first that the central room of the house contains a collection of South American artifacts, including weapons. The second clue is a lame pet spaniel, which, his inquiries reveal, was suddenly semi-paralyzed by an unknown condition. The third clue is Jack's expression of intense jealousy and hatred when he watches Ferguson embrace his baby son.

Unraveling the mystery

Holmes soon announces that Ferguson's wife is entirely innocent and that the culprit, is in fact, Jack. The boy has taken poisoned darts from his stepmother's collection and shot them first at the dog, as a trial run, and later at the baby,

The original cover of *The Strand Magazine* that first featured "The Adventure of the Sussex Vampire." The short story was first serialized in the publication in January 1924.

attempting to kill his half-brother out of jealousy. Mrs. Ferguson saved her baby's life by sucking the poison from his neck, and beat her stepson for his wickedness. She did not reveal the reason behind these events for fear of breaking her husband's heart.

The tension between author and protagonist, spiritualist, and logician, runs throughout this story, and reflects the wider debate in society about spiritualism and rationalism, religion, and science, that was raging at the time.

In an ironic flourish at the end of the story, Mrs. Ferguson praises Holmes's intellect in supernatural terms: "this gentleman… seems to have powers of magic," she declares. It is as though Conan Doyle was proving that he could be true to the nature of his literary creation despite his own personal convictions regarding ghosts and spiritualism. ∎

Vampires in the Victorian era

From the ancient world to the 21st century, people have had a thirst for tales of blood-sucking vampires. Various supernatural, grotesque forms have been depicted in world culture, but it was the Victorians who made them human, albeit in a Gothic style. The most notable example in the literary genre is the 1897 novel *Dracula*, written by Conan Doyle's friend Bram Stoker.

Victorian writers and readers were fascinated by the pale, often fanged, undead. Their hypnotic powers and nocturnal habits pitted evil against the good nature of their victims, demonstrating both a *fin de siècle* decadence and the idea of betrayed innocence. At once sinister, inviting, shocking, and sensuous, Victorian vampires—male and female—can be seen as an articulation of suppressed homosexual and female sexual expression. Maternal and loving, Mrs. Ferguson certainly doesn't appear to fit the archetypal Victorian image of a vampire.

THERE IS SOME GUILTY SECRET IN THE ROOM

THE ADVENTURE OF THE THREE GARRIDEBS (1925)

IN CONTEXT

TYPE
Short story

FIRST PUBLICATION
US: October 1924
UK: January 1925

COLLECTION
***The Case Book of Sherlock Holmes*, 1927**

CHARACTERS
John Garrideb American lawyer from Kansas.

Nathan Garrideb Reclusive bachelor and dedicated collector of antiquities.

Alexander Hamilton Garrideb Wealthy, elderly American man.

I n his introduction to this tale, Watson states that the events it relates occurred in June 1902— he can clearly recollect the date because it was the month in which Holmes refused a knighthood "for services which may perhaps some day be described." He speculates about whether the "adventure" that follows is a comedy or a tragedy. Certainly, the story's ingenious plotting and flamboyant trickery incorporate some comic elements, but the consequences for the main protagonists are far from a laughing matter. For many readers, however, this is very much a story about the relationship between Holmes and Watson; in a life-threatening

Well, if you can lay your hand upon a Garrideb, there's money in it.
Sherlock Holmes

situation, the depth of Holmes's affection and respect for his friend and chronicler is finally revealed.

A mysterious legacy

The story begins with a visit from John Garrideb—an alert, bright-eyed American who says he is a counselor at law from Kansas. He tells an astonishing tale that relates to his unusual surname; he claims that he encountered just one other Garrideb in his home country— Alexander Hamilton Garrideb— a wealthy, elderly man who left a curious will: if John was able to find two other men with their surname, they would each inherit a part of his substantial estate. John left his practice to conduct a search, and he has now found and met with a Nathan Garrideb in London. In fact, against John's wishes, Nathan has already enlisted Holmes's help, and this is the reason for John's visit.

Holmes is deeply suspicious of this tale, and of John himself— the man implies that he is a recent arrival in London, yet his well-worn English clothes and smoothed-out American accent indicate that he has been in the country for some time. He is also defensive, quickly "ruffled" by Holmes, and clearly

This ITV adaptation, "The Mazarin Stone" (1994), combined that case with "The Three Garridebs" and starred Gavan O'Herlihy and Richard Caldicott.

angry that Nathan Garrideb considered it necessary to involve the detective. Nathan is easily located in the London telephone directory, which, in Holmes's day, would have been a relatively small volume: the first edition was only published in 1880, 22 years before this story took place, and listed only 248 names. Watson phones and makes an appointment to visit him.

Cabinets of curiosities

Nathan is a stooping, bearded man of around 60, who lives in a bachelor's apartment in a small street off Edgware Road; Watson notes that it is very close to the former site of the Tyburn gallows, a place of public execution for many centuries—an ominous observation that stirs a sense of danger. Holmes and Watson immediately like and trust this Garrideb, finding him "amiable, though eccentric." He is an avid collector of curiosities and antiquities, and his home is a veritable storehouse of treasures, ranging from ancient coins and fossilized bones to cases full of moths and butterflies. Studying and maintaining this eclectic personal museum is his abiding passion, and he admits that he rarely leaves the house. He is intrigued by the story of the Garrideb legacy and is so enthralled by the prospect of using his potential share—$5 million— to expand his collection, that he does not question its veracity.

At this point, John Garrideb arrives, brandishing a Birmingham newspaper in which the services of one Howard Garrideb—constructor of agricultural machinery—are advertised. John suggests that Nathan should travel by train to the city the following day, and explain the situation to the third Garrideb, who will likely be more receptive to a "Britisher"; the old man reluctantly agrees. Before leaving Nathan's home, Holmes and Watson obtain permission to view his collection while he is away. Holmes then informs Watson that John himself had placed the advertisement as part of a ruse to get Nathan out of his apartment; although he does not yet know why. »

Victorian collectors

When Nathan Garrideb says he wants to become "the Hans Sloane of my age," he is referring to British physician Hans Sloane (1660–1753; pictured), whose passion for collecting was ignited when he visited Jamaica and brought back some 800 species of plants and animals. Sloane's "cabinet of curiosities" grew over the years, and embraced objects from fields as diverse as botany, archaeology, ethnography, natural history, and geology. By the time of his death, Sloane had acquired around 71,000 items, which he bequeathed to the nation.

They became the foundation of the British Museum, which opened to the public in 1759. By the Victorian era, many of those who traveled to the farthest corners of the British Empire were also dedicated collectors, helping to stock the galleries of newly founded institutions such as London's Victoria & Albert Museum. However, the appetite for curiosities inevitably led to clever forgeries, and many amateur collectors were fooled by "authentic" treasures that had in fact been manufactured in Birmingham or Manchester.

The next day, Holmes conducts some investigations on his own, and returns in a somber mood. He warns Watson that they are up against a very hard case, and a dangerous one, too. He has paid a visit to Inspector Lestrade at Scotland Yard, and has found out that the lawyer John Garrideb is, in fact, a hardened Chicago-born criminal known as "Killer Evans." After murdering three men in the US and then breaking out of jail, he headed to London, where he has lived for the past ten years and where, in 1895, he shot and killed a fellow American named Rodger Prescott over a game of cards. The dead man drew his gun first, so Evans served a relatively light sentence of just over five years. Since his release, he has been under police watch, but so far, he has stayed out of trouble.

And there are still more revelations: after consulting the rental agent who manages Nathan Garrideb's apartment, Holmes learns that the previous tenant was a tall, dark, bearded man—a description that matches Rodger Prescott. The fact that the tenant disappeared suddenly lends weight to Holmes's theory that John Garrideb and Evans are one and the same man.

Holmes is now sure that "Killer Evans" invented the Garrideb story as an elaborate diversion, in order to gain access to the former home of the man he murdered—but to what end he has no idea. There is, he says, a guilty secret in the room, and this makes their imminent visit to Nathan's museum of curiosities a much riskier undertaking. Evans is known to carry a gun, so Holmes ensures that he and Watson are both fully armed. As always, the doctor

> You're not hurt, Watson? For God's sake, say that you are not hurt!
> **Sherlock Holmes**

accepts the dangers he may face with equanimity. He is determined to stand by, and support, his friend.

A close confrontation
The pair make their way to the empty apartment and conceal themselves in a closet in the main room, where they wait. As predicted, Evans arrives and breaks into the house. He makes a beeline for a table in the middle of the room, which he moves to reveal a trapdoor. Once he has descended through it, Holmes and Watson begin to creep stealthily toward the opening. A creaking floorboard alerts Evans to their presence, who emerges to find himself confronted by two pistols. Initially he is both bewildered and furious, but then he appears to give himself up: "I guess you have been one too many for me, Mr. Holmes. Saw through my game, I suppose, and played me for a sucker from the first." But this is just another diversionary tactic—moving quickly, Evans manages to fire two shots from his revolver, one of which grazes Watson's leg, before Holmes brings his gun crashing down on the man's head.

Evans's elaborate plot is then revealed. The man is a criminal. Beneath the trapdoor is a hidden

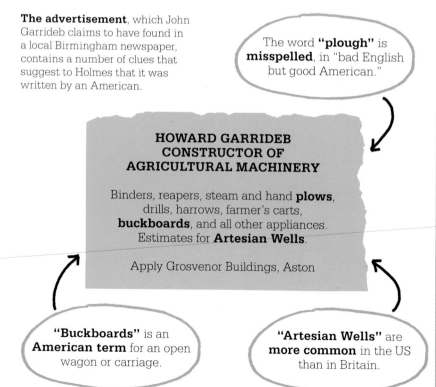

The advertisement, which John Garrideb claims to have found in a local Birmingham newspaper, contains a number of clues that suggest to Holmes that it was written by an American.

The word **"plough"** is **misspelled**, in "bad English but good American."

HOWARD GARRIDEB
CONSTRUCTOR OF
AGRICULTURAL MACHINERY

Binders, reapers, steam and hand **plows**, drills, harrows, farmer's carts, **buckboards**, and all other appliances. Estimates for **Artesian Wells**.

Apply Grosvenor Buildings, Aston

"Buckboards" is an **American term** for an open wagon or carriage.

"Artesian Wells" are **more common** in the US than in Britain.

room that contains a printing press, and Evans explains that the late Rodger Prescott was an expert counterfeiter—the most accomplished in London. Evans's quarry was the £200,000 in forged notes concealed in the hidden room. His story of the Garrideb inheritance is as counterfeit as the forged notes that lie beneath their feet. He had woven an elaborate web of lies so he could distract the gullible and preoccupied collector, whom he dismisses as a "crazy boob of a bug-hunter," and claim the wealth that lay just beneath his floorboards. Desperate to secure his freedom, Evans offers Holmes a share of the counterfeit booty, but the detective laughs in his face. Holmes hands the villain over to the police, and Evans finds himself back in jail for attempted murder.

Truth, lies, and loyalty

Nathan Garrideb's museum-style collection is a reflection of his single-minded passion for the past, and his desire to understand it.

His treasures—the reader is led to believe—are authentic, acquired from London's fine art auctioneers Sotheby's and Christies, and nothing gives him greater pleasure than studying and cataloging them. In contrast, "John Garrideb" is nothing but a fake—just a violent, greedy man who has utilized his intelligence for mere criminal gain. It seems strangely symbolic that underneath the lovingly assembled collection of an authentic seeker of knowledge lies the equipment of a criminal counterfeiter. Sadly, the news that his fabulous inheritance is mere fantasy sends Nathan Garrideb into a shock from which he never recovers, and he ultimately ends up living in a nursing home.

With its examination of truth and lies, authenticity and fakery, this story is also a tribute to the enduring friendship between Holmes and Watson. For all the banter and teasing, it is quite clear that Holmes feels genuine love for Watson and great respect for the unquestioning loyalty and bravery

Oxford University's Pitt Rivers Museum, founded in 1884, holds more than 500,000 objects gathered by Victorian collector General Pitt Rivers.

that his friend has displayed during their years together. His panic about the potential severity of Watson's injury, and his heartfelt concern for his friend, is very touching, and there is a rare moment of open emotion from the normally taciturn and cool detective when he turns furiously to Evans and declares, "If you had killed Watson you would not have got out of this room alive."

Watson, for his part, is clearly moved by Holmes's capacity for friendship here, saying, "It was worth a wound—it was worth many wounds—to know the depth of loyalty and love which lay behind that cold mask… For the one and only time I caught a glimpse of a great heart as well as of a great brain. All my years of humble but single-minded service culminated in that moment of revelation." ∎

SOME PEOPLE'S AFFABILITY IS MORE DEADLY THAN THE VIOLENCE OF COARSER SOULS

THE ADVENTURE OF THE ILLUSTRIOUS CLIENT (1925)

IN CONTEXT

TYPE
Short story

FIRST PUBLICATION
US: November 1924
UK: February 1925

COLLECTION
***The Case Book of Sherlock Holmes*, 1927**

CHARACTERS
Colonel Sir James Damery
High-society figure acting on behalf of an anonymous client.

Baron Adelbert Gruner
Austrian aristocrat and notorious violent womanizer.

Violet de Merville
Baron Gruner's fiancée.

Shinwell Johnson
Former criminal and associate of Holmes.

Kitty Winter Shunned former mistress of the baron.

Sir Leslie Oakshott Surgeon.

O ver ten years have passed since the events of this story took place, and Holmes has finally given Watson permission to write up the case, presumably because there is no longer a need to protect certain reputations. Watson claims the case is "in some ways, the supreme moment of my friend's career." However, readers might not entirely agree. It does not involve any particularly extraordinary deductions on Holmes's part, and the identity of the client remains undisclosed. The plot is also strikingly similar to the earlier Holmes tale "The Adventure of Charles Augustus Milverton" (pp.186–87). Nevertheless,

"The Adventure of the Illustrious Client" is a thrilling yarn that blends high-society glamour with the grit of London's criminal underworld. It also has one of the most compelling villains and most horrifically violent endings displayed anywhere in the entire Holmes canon.

A high-society visitor

Turkish baths were extremely popular among the well-to-do Victorians, and by the late 19th century, London was full of them. As Holmes and Watson enjoy a smoke in such an establishment on Northumberland Avenue (which runs between Trafalgar Square and the Embankment), Holmes takes out a note sent to him by a certain Colonel Sir James Damery, who has requested an audience with Holmes at Baker Street that day. Sir James's name is recognized by Watson as "a household word in society," and the Carlton Club in Pall Mall, where the note was written, was itself a well-known spot for high-ranking Conservative politicians and socialites in real life.

These high-society reference points suggest this case is likely to be one that will require the utmost discretion. Holmes himself notes that Damery has "a reputation for arranging delicate matters which are to be kept out of the papers"— that is, matters of social propriety. When Sir James arrives at 221B later that day, Watson describes

It is my business to follow the details of Continental crime.
Sherlock Holmes

his fastidiously well-turned-out figure, with top hat, frock coat, and varnished shoes. Sir James expresses his satisfaction at Watson's presence—a nod to the chronicler's own fame by this point.

An ill-advised match

Sir James then introduces his subject: the infamous Baron Albert Gruner, who he claims is the most dangerous man in Europe. Holmes immediately refers to Gruner as "the Austrian murderer"—clearly, both Holmes and Sir James are in agreement that (despite an official verdict to the contrary) the baron almost certainly murdered his ex-wife in Austria, and escaped prosecution only on technical grounds and due to "the suspicious death of a witness."

Sir James then declares that he is working on behalf of a man who wishes to remain anonymous—the "illustrious client" of the story title. Holmes is perturbed by this desire for secrecy and presses Sir James to reveal the client's identity, saying he is unable to commit to the case without knowing all the details. Damery remains resolute that he cannot disclose the client's name, but assures Holmes that "his motives are, to the last degree, honourable and chivalrous" and »

The connections of the mystery client

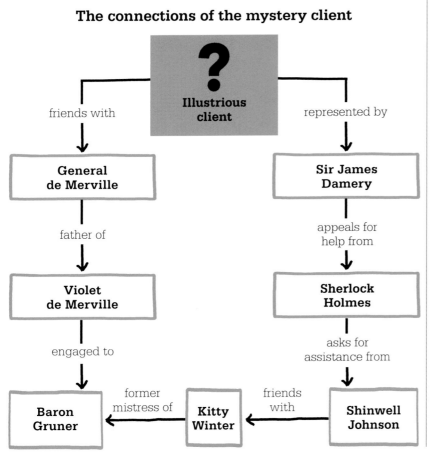

that Holmes will be proud to serve him. He begs Holmes to listen to all the facts before making a decision.

The baron, who is irresistible to women and frequently takes advantage of them, has recently become engaged to the wealthy and attractive Miss Violet de Merville, the daughter of a famous British general. Given the baron's violent and highly untrustworthy character, the match is sure to end in disaster for Violet. Holmes hears how deeply she has fallen for the handsome baron. "To say that she loves him hardly expresses it," says Damery. He says she is "obsessed" by Gruner, who has managed to convince her of his innocence in any wrongdoing to which his name is attached. General de Merville is extremely concerned about the engagement, as is the anonymous client, who has known Violet since she was very young.

After hearing the full story, Holmes agrees to take on the case. He asks whether there is any further information he needs to know about the baron, and learns that he is artistic and an avid collector of Chinese pottery and has even written a book on

I am accustomed to have mystery at one end of my cases, but to have it at both ends is too confusing.
Sherlock Holmes

the subject. Holmes observes that all great criminals have complex minds, citing the famous real-life Victorian villains Charles Peace—an inventor, violin virtuoso, and murderer—and "Wainwright," that is, Thomas Griffiths Wainewright, a talented artist, critic, and poisoner.

From the stars to the gutter

Holmes's first port of call is to contact his associate Shinwell Johnson—an ex-criminal who once served two jail terms but has since reformed. In creating this rather unlikely connection, Conan Doyle outlines the panorama of Victorian

society in one story—with the "famous" high-society figure of Sir Damery at one end, and the shadowy figure of Johnson, with his contacts in London's seedy criminal underworld, at the other.

Watson is not living at 221B at this point, but on Queen Anne Street. He meets the detective at Simpson's-in-the-Strand—a favorite dining establishment of Conan Doyle's in what was then one of London's busiest thoroughfares. It is there that Holmes gives a description of the baron, whom he had brazenly called upon earlier. Holmes had demanded that the baron call off the marriage, but Gruner responded with threats, alluding to another former detective who had been horribly crippled after inquiring into the baron's affairs. He also bragged that he has Violet de Merville in his thrall, and that, should Holmes call on her, she will not waver in her devotion to him.

Johnson tracks down a young working-class woman named Kitty Winter, who has suffered at the baron's hands as one of his many former mistresses—although the reader never finds out precisely how. She tells Holmes of a "beastly

Vitriol-throwing

Various descriptions of skin conditions in this story foreshadow the baron's disfigurement as a result of Kitty's throwing vitriol in his face. Watson describes Shinwell Johnson as "scorbutic," or scurvy-ridden, and "leprous," while Holmes reports how Violet received Kitty and him "like a Reverend Abbess receiving two rather leprous mendicants." Later on there are newspaper reports that claim Holmes is suffering from erysipelas—an infection that often manifests itself as a face rash.

Vitriol is better known today as sulfuric acid. As a common disinfectant, it was easy to get hold of, and Watson refers to another vitriol-throwing incident in "The Adventure of the Blue Carbuncle" (pp.82–83), but in reality the crime was actually relatively rare. In a letter to *The Times* in 1867, one man tells how his wife had vitriol thrown at her, but was saved from harm by the quantity of dresses and petticoats she was wearing. By the 20th century, regulations on the substance's sale meant that such attacks became even rarer.

The gentlemen's dining room at Simpson's-in-the-Strand, where Holmes and Watson dined. Women were forbidden to use this paneled, street-level dining room until 1986.

book" in which the baron records the truth of all his misdeeds. He keeps it in his inner study, secreted behind another room containing his "Chinese crockery," as she refers to his porcelain collection. Her own down-at-heel status, so far from that of Violet de Merville, is further evidence of the baron's indifferent womanizing. "This man collects women," Kitty tells Holmes, "and takes a pride in his collection, as some men collect moths or butterflies." She recalls two other murders that the baron laid claim to while she was his lover, and also describes to Holmes in detail the location of the baron's "inner study," where she believes his secret book is kept.

The next evening, at Simpson's again, Holmes tells Watson how he and Kitty visited the de Merville residence in upmarket Berkeley Square, Mayfair, which—in a show of his typical antipathy for houses of the wealthy—Holmes describes as "one of those awful gray London castles which would make a church seem frivolous." Holmes says that when he tried to dissuade Violet from marrying the baron, she accused him of being a mercenary, a paid agent: as far as she is concerned, he is the immoral one. Even the plain-speaking Kitty could not convince her, and the visit was a failure.

A murderous attack

Two days later, Watson is walking along the Strand when he sees a newspaper billboard announcing: "Murderous attack upon Sherlock Holmes." Both the experience, and Watson's stunned response, recall a moment in Conan Doyle's own life. In his 1924 autobiography, *Memories and Adventures*, the author reports how he learned of the death of his friend Robert Louis Stevenson: "I cannot forget the shock that it was to me when driving down the Strand in a hansom cab in 1896 I saw upon a yellow evening poster 'Death of Stevenson.' Some-thing seemed to have passed out of my world."

Holmes is not in fact dead, but he has been violently assaulted in an attack that took place that day on Regent Street. His assailants escaped through the Café Royal—as popular a haunt with writers as Simpson's, and, like Simpson's, still there to this day—into the grimy alleys of Soho, which at that time was still a poor, murky, and very overcrowded area. There is another »

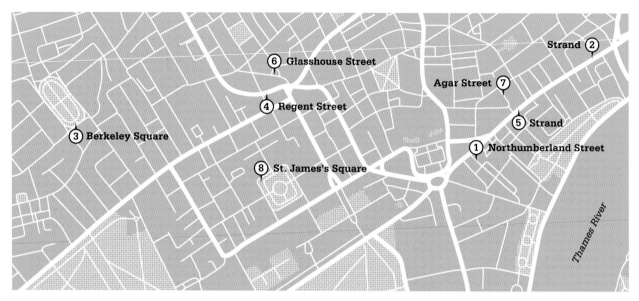

Throughout the story, Holmes and Watson visit real-life locations, most of which are concentrated in central London. Baker Street, where Holmes lives, is slightly north of the area shown on the map.

1. Northumberland Street: Holmes and Watson visit the Turkish baths.

2. Strand: Holmes and Watson dine at Simpson's restaurant.

3. Berkeley Square: Home of Violet de Merville.

4. Regent Street: Holmes is attacked outside Café Royal.

5. Strand: Watson learns of the attack on Holmes.

6. Glasshouse Street: Holmes's attackers make their escape.

7. Agar Street: Holmes is treated at Charing Cross Hospital, located here in the late 19th century.

8. St. James's Square: Watson studies ancient Chinese pottery at the London Library.

Stevenson link here. In Stevenson's story *Strange Case of Dr. Jekyll and Mr. Hyde* (1886), the whole mystery turns on Dr. Jekyll's grand residence having an incongruously "sordid" back door, leading onto a shadowy neighborhood—this is the door that

> I have my plans… They'll come to you for news. Put it on thick, Watson.
> **Sherlock Holmes**

his evil alter ego, Mr. Hyde, uses. Stevenson is thought to have based Dr. Jekyll's house on that of the eminent 18th-century Scottish scientist and surgeon John Hunter (1728–1793), whose own residence in Leicester Square was barely a stone's throw from the Café Royal, and would have backed onto the same seamy alleyways.

Holmes has a nasty head wound but will survive, thanks to the care of famous surgeon Leslie Oakshott. However, he asks Watson to greatly exaggerate his condition to all the press, and tell them he is dying so that anyone reading the papers will think he is off the case. However, when reports appear that the baron is soon to be traveling to America prior to the wedding, Holmes's hand is forced, since he knows that the baron will take the incriminating

book with him. With typical indifference to Watson's professional duties, Holmes tasks him with learning everything he can about Chinese pottery in just 24 hours. He then gives him a priceless Ming saucer (provided by the mysterious client), with the request that he try to sell it to the baron. At the time Holmes does not explain why, but it later becomes clear that he needs Watson to distract the baron so he can break into the inner study and find the book. Watson duly begins to memorize as much information on Chinese pottery as he is able.

Watson in the lion's den
Tension increases at the baron's luxurious residence as the highly suspicious host tests Watson, who is posing as Dr. Hill Barton, the ceramics expert, with excessively

tricky questions on the Emperor Shomu and the Northern Wei dynasty. Watson keeps his cool, but the baron quickly sees through his bluff, rightly guessing that Holmes has sent him, and is enraged. Just as he is about to attack Watson in fury, the baron is alerted to a noise from his inner study. Dashing inside, he finds Holmes, who escapes through a window. Baron Gruner chases him into the garden, but as he follows him Watson sees a woman's arm fly out from a bush and, Gruner utters "a horrible cry" and falls, clutching his face. Watson rushes to his aid but finds that his face is being eaten away by acid. The hand, as it turns out, was Kitty Winter's: Holmes had taken her with him to help locate the inner study but, acting of her own volition, she had seized a chance to take revenge on her past lover, and threw a measure of vitriol in his face (see box, p.268), making a mangled mess of the baron's once handsome features.

The wages of sin

Back at 221B, it is clear that Holmes and Watson have moral qualms over the violence dished out to the baron. Although he is a multiple murderer, the acid attack is perhaps

> It is his moral side, not his physical, which we have to destroy.
> **Sherlock Holmes**

disproportionately vicious. "The wages of sin, Watson—the wages of sin!" intones the clearly shaken Holmes, in an echo of the Book of Romans in the New Testament.

Thanks to Watson's keeping the baron talking for just long enough, Holmes is now in possession of the baron's "lust diary," which he stole from the inner study. This, Holmes believes, will finally open Violet's eyes and put a stop to the marriage. He is of the clear opinion that the baron's disfigurement alone would likely have the opposite effect as "she would love him the more as a disfigured martyr."

In Holmes's view, the state of being "madly in love" is equivalent to madness pure and simple, and indeed this story is peppered with references to women's irrationality. Early on, Kitty Winter declared her willingness to risk death in order to take revenge, saying it with an "intensity of hatred," Watson notes, "such as woman seldom and man never can attain." And Kitty's final, fateful deed plays out that reckless impulsiveness magnificently.

The day of judgment

Three days later, the marriage between Violet and Baron Gruner has been called off. Meanwhile, a newspaper reports that Kitty will be brought before the courts for her crime. There is also a nod toward a degree of benign corruption here: although Holmes risks prosecution for burglary, Watson feels sure that the eminence of their client will make the law "elastic."

Even at the end of the story, the reader never learns the identity of the client. When Watson realizes who it is, after seeing the "armorial bearings" on his carriage, Holmes silences him: "It is a loyal friend and a chivalrous gentleman. Let that now and forever be enough for us." ∎

The identity of the client

Conan Doyle's trick at the end of the tale is masterful: Holmes cuts Watson off immediately before he can blurt out the name of the "illustrious client" on whose behalf Sir James Damery has been acting. It may be that the "armorial bearings" (such as those pictured, above) on Damery's brougham coach, which Damery hastily tries to obscure with his overcoat, are in fact the royal coat of arms belonging to King Edward VII. Certainly, the fact that his driver is "cockaded," that is to say, carries a rosette or similarly vaunted badge on his uniform, suggests an extremely lofty eminence. The bait used for Baron Gruner in the form of the Chinese porcelain saucer provides yet more evidence for this argument—Holmes says a full set of such saucers would be "worth a king's ransom." Of course, the client might have been some other eminent and sympathetic friend of General de Merville—but for all of the debate of Holmesian scholars on the subject, the truth remains unknown.

I AM NOT THE LAW, BUT I REPRESENT JUSTICE SO FAR AS MY FEEBLE POWERS GO

THE ADVENTURE OF THE THREE GABLES (1926)

IN CONTEXT

TYPE
Short story

FIRST PUBLICATION
US: September 1926
UK: October 1926

COLLECTION
**The Case Book of
Sherlock Holmes, 1927**

CHARACTERS
Steve Dixie A prize fighter
hired to threaten Holmes.

Mrs. Mary Maberley
Elderly widow.

Douglas Maberley
Mrs. Maberley's late son.

Susan
Servant of Mrs. Maberley.

Mr. Sutro
Lawyer to Mrs. Maberley.

Isadora Klein
South American widow,
and former lover of Douglas.

Langdale Pike
London gossip-monger.

This story sees Holmes lock horns with one of the few truly formidable female characters in the canon. Unlike with Irene Adler in "A Scandal in Bohemia" (pp.56–61), Holmes stops short of expressing admiration for the "masterful" Isadora Klein, yet it is clear by the end of the tale that this *belle dame sans merci* has at least partially elicited Holmes's sympathies. Certainly he sees fit to resolve the matter himself, rather than turn to the law.

An unwelcome visitor
Holmes and Watson are at 221B Baker Street when they are accosted by a man described as a "huge negro," Steve Dixie—an aggressive member of a criminal gang, who warns Holmes not to interfere in any business in Harrow. As it turns out, Holmes has indeed been engaged on a case in this very area. Dixie is described by Watson with a casual racism common to the time, and Holmes, although under severe provocation, is uncharacteristically offensive to him. Dixie (a historical nickname for America's southern states) calls Holmes "Masser," a term that was often used by slaves in the US to address their masters.

He informs Holmes that he has been sent by Barney Stockdale, a senior member of the Spencer John gang. But Holmes believes that the entire gang has been hired by another, more formidable person.

A mystery buyer
Holmes and Watson travel directly to visit a new client—Mrs. Mary Maberley, a widow living at The Three Gables, a house in Harrow Weald—who needs Holmes's advice. Her son Douglas, formerly an attaché at the embassy in Rome, died recently, and she received a strange offer soon afterward. An agent, on behalf of a client, has asked to buy her house, its entire contents, and all of her personal effects. Holmes is instantly suspicious, surmising that the person must want something that is hidden inside the house.

The secret in the trunk
During the interview, Holmes unmasks Mrs. Maberley's servant, Susan, as another gang member. From this he concludes that the notorious gang is being employed to threaten the widow, and that the instigator must be someone who is familiar enough with the London underworld to employ Spencer John

> She was, of course, *the* celebrated beauty. There was never a woman to touch her.
> **Sherlock Holmes**

and his henchmen to intimidate Mrs. Maberley. After questioning Susan, Holmes suspects that the instigator may well be a wealthy woman, rather than a man. He then notices Douglas's trunk in the hall, recently arrived from Rome, and concludes it may contain the desired items, as the intimidation began just after his death, when the trunk arrived.

Surprisingly, Holmes suggests that Mrs. Maberley search the trunk rather than investigating it himself. For safety, he recommends that she invite her lawyer, Mr. Sutro, to stay the night. But the house is burgled that evening, the thieves targeting Douglas's trunk and stealing a manuscript. Just one page of 245 remains, and it is clearly the end of a lurid story of love and rejection; strangely, as Holmes notes, the tale shifts from the third person narrator to the first person toward its end. He is edging closer to solving the mystery, but has yet to discover who is behind it.

The final revelation

Holmes consults scurrilous gossip columnist Langdale Pike, who has an unrivaled knowledge of London society, for information. This leads him to the home of Isadora Klein—a beautiful, extremely wealthy South American widow and sexual adventuress. He learns that the stolen manuscript—now a charred pile of ash in her fireplace—was in fact Douglas's account of his doomed love affair with her. He had become "intolerable" when Isadora declined to marry him, and in a heartbroken rage he had decided to write and publish his manuscript in order to ruin her. She is now due to marry a young English lord and knows that the story would jeopardize her reputation and her quest for a British title. And so she enlisted

Isadora Klein, played here by Claudine Auger in the Granada TV series, is an exotic and uninhibited *femme fatale*, yet one whose wiles are wasted on Holmes.

the help of the Spencer John gang to obtain the compromising manuscript for herself.

Lesson learned

Unlike so many of the women Holmes encounters, Isadora is neither vulnerable, in thrall to a man, nor in any way dependent. In their final showdown, finding him "immune" to her seductive skills, she is honest about her reasons for soliciting the manuscript, claiming she had resorted to theft only when "everything else had failed." And while Holmes remains steadfastly disapproving, he clearly feels some sympathy for her predicament— perhaps Douglas's vengeful plan seemed too harsh a punishment for ending their love affair. Holmes extracts a promise from her to pay for Mrs. Maberley to travel around the world (a lifelong dream), warning Isadora of the dangers of her behavior: "You can't play with edged tools forever without cutting those dainty hands." ∎

Women in gangs

Women played their part in the underworld of Victorian London, and Isadora Klein and Susan's involvement with a gang was not unprecedented. A notorious all-female gang, known as the Forty Elephants, is thought to have operated in London from as early as the 18th century. This gang, headed by a "queen," was organized into cells and, from the 1870s to 1950s, ran an ambitious and highly successful shoplifting operation across London. The women would be equipped with specially designed clothing with hidden pockets, and in a prudish era they were often able to escape close physical scrutiny. They eventually became so well known in London that they were forced to branch out into other towns. In addition to shoplifting, they worked as housemaids in order to rob and blackmail their employers. The gang protected its territory, and trespassers were dispatched (sometimes violently); they also enjoyed the proceeds of their crimes, throwing glamorous parties.

I SEE NO MORE THAN YOU, BUT I HAVE TRAINED MYSELF TO NOTICE WHAT I SEE
THE ADVENTURE OF THE BLANCHED SOLDIER (1926)

IN CONTEXT

TYPE
Short story

FIRST PUBLICATION
US: October 1926
UK: November 1926

COLLECTION
***The Case Book of Sherlock Holmes*, 1927**

CHARACTERS
James M Dodd Ex-soldier.

Godfrey Emsworth
Ex-soldier and close friend
of James M Dodd.

Colonel Emsworth
Retired army officer and
Godfrey's father.

Mrs. Emsworth
Godfrey's mother.

Ralph and wife Emsworth
family's long-serving butler
and housekeeper, respectively.

Mr. Kent Godfrey's physician.

Sir James Saunders
Eminent dermatologist.

This story is unusual because it is narrated by Holmes, who explains that Watson—his usual chronicler—has "deserted him for a wife," leaving him to rise to the challenge of writing up a case himself. Holmes muses on his role as storyteller and realizes that, despite criticizing Watson for pandering to public

Like his characters, Emsworth and Dodd, Conan Doyle (above) also served in South Africa during the Boer War, working as a volunteer doctor in the Langman Field Hospital.

taste by including superficial and sensational details, he too must make the account entertaining for the reader. Holmes makes several references to Watson here: he applauds his good qualities, and comments somewhat sardonically that his perpetual ability to be surprised by Holmes's insights is one of his greatest strengths.

A visit from a soldier

The story begins in January 1903, with Holmes receiving a visit from a James M Dodd. Holmes instantly recognizes him as an ex-soldier, correctly identifying his regiment (Imperial Yeomanry, the Middlesex Corps) in a typical display of his powers of observation and deduction. Dodd is suitably impressed, confirming that he has indeed recently returned from South Africa, where he fought in the Boer War (1899–1902).

The discovery of gold in the Boer republic of Transvaal in 1886 made the area a potential threat to British colonial supremacy in South Africa, and so Britain sent troops there to defend its interests. Conan Doyle himself served in South Africa from March to June 1902 as a medical officer and was vocal in his defense

of the British cause there, opposing the many commentators who questioned the justness of the war.

Dodd needs Holmes's help with a puzzle concerning the fate of his old army friend Godfrey Emsworth, who was wounded in action and sent home. The pair had written to each other for a while, but then Emsworth fell silent, and Dodd has not heard from him for six months. Godfrey's father, Colonel Emsworth (a Crimean War hero), claims that his son is on a round-the-world voyage and will be away for a year, but Dodd is skeptical about this: surely his friend would never have embarked on such an adventure without telling him? Determined to root out the truth, Dodd persuaded Godfrey's mother to allow him to visit her at the family home, Old Tuxbury Park in Bedford.

A house of shadows

Immediately after arriving at the remote, rambling old mansion, Dodd was interrogated by Colonel Emsworth—an imposing and rather fierce man. Dodd's request for clarity on Godfrey's whereabouts was met with hostility, and the colonel hinted darkly that, for the family's sake, he should stop interfering. Later, over dinner, Godfrey's gentle, unassuming mother listened avidly to Dodd's recollection of his wartime experiences with her son, but the colonel showed no interest and seemed "morose and depressed." Dodd's suspicions were further roused during a conversation with Ralph, the family's ancient butler, who referred to his young master in the past tense. When Dodd asked

The Boer War was fought between Dutch settlers and the British in two African states, South African Republic and Orange Free State, over the control of gold and diamond mines.

outright if Godfrey was dead, the old man replied, ominously: "I wish to God he was!" before rushing off.

That night in his ground-floor bedroom, Dodd gazed out of the window and was astonished to see Godfrey's face—deathly white and ghostly, "as white as cheese"—pressed to the glass. Godfrey quickly leapt away from sight, but not before Dodd had detected "something furtive, something guilty" in his demeanor: a stark contrast to the forthright soldier he had known in South Africa. Dodd pursued his friend into the garden, but he soon became lost in the » darkness. However, Dodd was certain that he heard the sound of a door closing somewhere in the grounds and that Godfrey must have escaped into a hiding place.

The following morning, Dodd spotted a cottage in the garden; as he approached it, a sharply-dressed man came out of the door and locked it behind him. The pair exchanged pleasantries, but the man appeared rather guilty. Dodd waited until nightfall before sneaking back to the cottage. Peering through a crack in the shutter, he saw the same man and a second figure, who he was sure was Godfrey. At that moment, a furious Colonel Emsworth appeared and promptly threw him out of the house for "spying." This aggressive, threatening man, Dodd felt, was the source of all the lies and hostility he had encountered.

The truth is revealed
Holmes is confident he will have little difficulty in solving this "elementary" case, and a few days

When you have eliminated all which is impossible, then whatever remains, however improbable, must be the truth.
Sherlock Holmes

later he and Dodd set off to Bedford, accompanied by an elderly man whom Holmes introduces simply as an old friend. He cross-examines Dodd en route, confirming the dreadful whiteness of Godfrey's face—a fact that is seemingly of great significance to Holmes. When they arrive at the house, Holmes immediately observes a second revealing detail: Ralph, the butler,

is dressed in conventional servant's garb, but with the unusual addition of a pair of brown leather gloves. He instantly removes them on seeing the visitors, but Holmes's sharp nose detects a strong "tarry odour" emanating from them.

At this point, Holmes once again muses on his role as narrator, presenting himself as a guileless storyteller, in contrast to the more artful Watson. Somewhat facetiously he states that he has already shown his hand. Watson, he observes, would have concealed such significant details in the interests of creating a "meretricious finale."

The colonel is furious at their arrival, but when Holmes hands him a piece of paper on which he has written one word, which we later discover is "leprosy," he immediately relents. "How do you know?" he gasps, astonished. "It is my business to know things," Holmes replies.

Resignedly, the colonel takes his visitors to the cottage, where they meet Godfrey, whose handsome face has been marred by a number

To decipher the most likely explanation for why Godfrey is in hiding, Holmes uses his trademark method of "abductive reasoning" (see p.307). He uses the known facts to discount what is improbable and predict the most likely outcome.

Least likely → **Possible** → **Most likely**

Crime?
No reported crimes in the area, so unlikely.
Theory dismissed.

Insanity?
Lunatics could be kept at home, so again unlikely.
Theory dismissed.

Disease?
Would cause disfigurement and require segregation.
Strong hypothesis.

of white patches. He tells how, after he was shot in South Africa, he unknowingly sought refuge in a leper hospital. Back home, the marks appeared on his face and he concluded he had contracted the dreadful disease. Surely, Godfrey had reasoned, it would be better to live a life in quarantine with his family, two trusted servants, and a personal physician (Kent, the man Dodd had seen previously with his friend) rather than endure segregation? Holmes then reveals that his mystery companion is the eminent dermatologist Sir James Saunders, and suggests that Godfrey get a second opinion from him.

A process of elimination

In the meantime, Holmes explains to all present that he solved the case simply by using his trademark logical analysis. He identified three possible explanations for Godfrey's incarceration in an outbuilding on his father's estate. The first was that he was a criminal in hiding. He dismissed this because there had been no reports of unsolved crimes in the area, and it would be more logical to send a delinquent abroad. The second, albeit unlikely, possibility was that Godfrey was insane, and being kept under lock and key by a medical supervisor.

> He was deadly pale—
> never have I seen
> a man so white.
> **James M Dodd**

But why keep it secret? After all, at the time a lunatic could legally be kept at home under supervision. Once again, Holmes found he "could not get the theory to fit the facts."

The third—and the strongest—possibility was that Godfrey had contracted some kind of disease while in South Africa. At the time, leprosy was rife and so a likely candidate, and the associated stigma of leprosy fitted the premise of a man in hiding. Here, secrecy would be paramount—to ensure there would be no interference from the authorities. Not only was bleached skin symptomatic of leprosy, but Holmes's observation that the butler's gloves were impregnated with disinfectant confirmed his suspicions.

At this point, Sir Saunders, the dermatologist, returns with the welcome news that Godfrey does not have leprosy, but is suffering from "pseudo-leprosy," or ichthyosis, a curable skin infection. Godfrey's mother faints from the shock; with luck, her son will be able to live a normal life, rather than being concealed from society.

A positive outcome

This story cleverly misleads the reader at every turn. Dodd's honest, soldierly account portrays a sinister place presided over by the fearsome colonel. Holmes's revelations, however, neatly turn the tables, and we are presented with a loving father protecting his son from the stigma of a deadly disease he had caught while fighting for his country.

Some critics have suggested that leprosy is used metaphorically in "The Adventure of the Blanched Soldier," and that by letting Godfrey escape such a terrible fate, Conan Doyle was in fact defending Britain's colonial activities in South Africa. ∎

Leprosy

An infectious disease, leprosy starts by damaging small nerves in the skin's surface, leaving discolored patches. It can lead to disfigurement (pictured), severe disability, and blindness if left untreated. Leprosy has afflicted humans for millennia and was greatly feared and misunderstood: its victims were wrongly believed to be "unclean" and highly contagious, and systematically shunned as outcasts.

In the 19th century, leprosy was endemic in parts of the British Empire, and there was concern that colonialists and soldiers would contract the disease. *Mycobacterium leprae*, the bacteria that causes leprosy, was identified in 1873 in Norway, but the disease remained untreatable until the mid-20th century. In South Africa, the Leprosy Repression Act of 1892 established quarantine sites like the one Godfrey slept in. Today, the incidence of leprosy has decreased by 90 percent. It is now curable with multidrug therapy, but it still occurs in poorer parts of the world, particularly South Asia (especially India) and Brazil.

I AM AN OMNIVOROUS READER WITH A STRANGELY RETENTIVE MEMORY FOR TRIFLES

THE ADVENTURE OF THE LION'S MANE (1926)

IN CONTEXT

TYPE
Short story

FIRST PUBLICATION
US: November 1926
UK: December 1926

COLLECTION
***The Case Book of Sherlock Holmes*, 1927**

CHARACTERS
Harold Stackhurst
Headmaster of The Gables college, and friend of Holmes.

Fitzroy McPherson
Science master at The Gables.

Ian Murdoch
Mathematics master at The Gables.

Maud Bellamy
Young local beauty.

Tom and William Bellamy
Maud's father and brother.

Inspector Bardle
Sussex policeman.

This is one of Holmes's final cases, and one of only two in the canon to be narrated by Holmes rather than Watson; the other being "The Adventure of the Blanched Soldier" (pp.274–77). It is also the only story to feature an elderly Holmes living out his Sussex retirement.

Conan Doyle wrote this story hurriedly, almost as if he were anxious to be done with the character who had been such an important, and lucrative, part of his life for nearly 40 years. However, the author was pleased with the end result, and it was one of his favorite of all the Holmes stories.

The retired detective

In his introduction, Holmes informs the reader that he has retired. The man who was so much a part of the bustling metropolis of London has moved away to lead a quiet life on the Sussex coast, keeping bees and going for walks. He tells the reader, "I had given myself up entirely to that soothing life of Nature for which I had so often yearned during the long years spent amid the gloom of London." This does not sound like the tireless sleuth we have come to know in the previous stories. It is perhaps also surprising to learn that Holmes is now finding comfort in the quiet, because in earlier tales, such as "The Adventure of the Copper Beeches" (pp.98–101), he expresses a distinct horror of the countryside, fearing the isolation and the feeling that all kinds of criminal activities can take place without anyone finding out.

The missing link

Watson seems to have slipped out of Holmes's life: "an occasional week-end visit was the most that I ever saw of him." His presence is sorely missed, and this tale serves to illustrate the important role Watson plays in the other stories. With Watson as narrator, the reader

At 221B Baker Street, Holmes is busy and active: fueled by the London crime scene, he craves the most complex of mysteries, and finds solace in the crowded city.

In his retirement on the Sussex coast, Holmes's lifestyle is different: here he indulges in solitary walks, keeps bees, and rejoices in the countryside he once dreaded.

has a continual witness to the amazing feats of deduction that Holmes pulls off. As Watson is astounded, so too is the reader, creating a sense of both excitement and anticipation regarding what the detective will do next. However, because Holmes regards many of his deductions as commonplace and self-evident, when we see the sleuthing process from his point of view, his discoveries no longer seem quite so marvelous or even surprising. Holmes acknowledges this, saying in his introduction that while Watson would make much of "so wonderful a happening" he, Holmes, has to tell the tale in his "own plain way." The reader may also find Holmes's narration less charming than that of the often baffled Watson.

> At this period of my life the good Watson had passed almost beyond my ken.
> **Sherlock Holmes**

A mysterious death

This adventure begins in July 1907. The wind has finally abated after a severe gale and it is a beautiful summer morning. As Holmes takes a morning stroll along the cliff, he meets his friend Harold Stackhurst, headmaster of the local Gables college. Despite being a loner by nature, Holmes perhaps misses his comfortable friendship with Watson, and has found another companion. Holmes tells us that Stackhurst is the only man who "was on such terms with me that we could drop in on each other in the evenings without an invitation," evoking memories of Watson turning up unannounced at 221B.

Shortly after their meeting, the pair spot a young man they know. Wearing only trousers, a coat, »

Holmes looks into the lagoon, puzzling over McPherson's death. This illustration was included in the first publication of "The Lion's Mane" in *The Strand Magazine*.

sinister, aloof, strange character, and tells the reader that Murdoch had once thrown McPherson's dog through a plate glass window in a fit of temper. Murdoch is clearly a violent man—possibly with a grudge against McPherson. The reader's interest is piqued.

Holmes investigates

Murdoch is dispatched to summon the police from nearby Fulworth while Holmes begins his investigation. He sees signs that McPherson had fallen over several times as he ascended the cliff path. Down on the shore, Holmes sees some naked footprints that suggest McPherson had gone into the lagoon in which he was planning to swim. However, his towel is folded and dry, so the detective concludes that he could not have gone into the water. There is no one to be seen nearby and no other clues.

Holmes returns to the body to find the police have arrived. They discover a note in McPherson's pockets indicating an assignation: "I will be there, you may be sure— Maudie." When the police search McPherson's rooms, they find letters revealing a secret affair with local Fulworth beauty Maud Bellamy. It seems unlikely the two would arrange to meet in such a public place as the lagoon if they were trying to keep their affair secret. It then emerges that some Gables students would have gone to swim with McPherson had Murdoch not held them back in class. Holmes pointedly asks if it were "mere chance" that McPherson was alone, throwing the reader's suspicion on

and some unlaced canvas shoes, he staggers up the path and falls down in agony nearby. Holmes and Stackhurst rush to help him, but it is too late. The young man dies, uttering the words "the Lion's Mane" with his last breath.

As the coat falls from the dead man's bare shoulders, Holmes and Stackhurst see that his back is covered in long, bleeding lines "as though he had been terribly flogged by a thin wire scourge." Holmes

notes that "The instrument with which this punishment had been inflicted was clearly flexible," as the markings are curved around the young man's shoulders and ribs.

The dead man is Fitzroy McPherson, the science master at The Gables college. As Holmes and Stackhurst stand over the body, another familiar figure, Ian Murdoch, the mathematics master from the same establishment, arrives. Holmes describes him as a

In all my chronicles the reader will find no case which brought me so completely to the limit of my powers. Even my imagination could conceive no solution to the mystery.
Sherlock Holmes

Murdoch. Holmes and Stackhurst walk into Fulworth to talk to Maud Bellamy, but as they approach her house, they see Murdoch emerging. When he rudely refuses to divulge what he is doing there, Stackhurst fires him from the school.

Maud's secret

Holmes's admiring description of Maud is more what we would expect of Watson than the famously indifferent detective, as he notes "her perfect clear-cut face, with all

the soft freshness of the downlands in her delicate colouring." He learns that she and McPherson were engaged, but that they kept it a secret from both of their families to avoid upset. As we learn later, Murdoch has just told her that her fiancé is dead, and she is eager to offer Holmes any help that she can with the investigation, but can offer no real clues. It seems, however, that Murdoch was, and perhaps still is, in love with her. Suspicions are settling on the mathematics master, who, as Holmes notes, has taken the earliest opportunity to get away by provoking Stackhurst into firing him. He demands that Murdoch's rooms are searched.

Holmes's epiphany

Holmes goes home to ponder the mystery, and news then comes that McPherson's faithful Airedale terrier has been found dead at the lagoon where his master died, its little body contorted in agony. Holmes is at a loss what to think. There is something nagging at the back of his mind, however. He goes for a walk to the lagoon to clear his head, and on his return suddenly remembers what it was: "Like a

John George Wood, the author of *Out of Doors*, wrote several books. He was a parson-naturalist: a clergyman who viewed the study of natural science as part of his religious vocation.

flash, I remembered the thing I had so eagerly and vainly grasped." He reminds the reader how his brain is like a "crowded box-room" packed full of data, or "out-of-the-way knowledge," that might one day come in useful. This idea of the "box-room" (or "brain attic" as Holmes also describes it) dates back to the very first Holmes book (*A Study in Scarlet*, pp.36–45), and is a key image Conan Doyle uses to describe Holmes's way of thinking, which various psychologists have embraced. Russian-American psychologist Maria Konnikova, for instance, has adopted the "brain attic" metaphor as a useful way of understanding how humans store information, organize knowledge, and use it to devise strategies for clearer thinking and "mindfulness."

In this particular case, however, the reference to the "brain attic" merely serves to remind Holmes »

Ian Murdoch

The mathematics master, Ian Murdoch, is set up as the villain of the story. He is described as having "strange outlandish blood", as well as swarthy features, coal-black eyes, and a ferocious temper. In the Holmes tales, Conan Doyle often used the popular Victorian idea that a criminal type can be revealed in physical appearance (see p.188). Here, however, he is using this stereotype to mislead the reader into thinking Murdoch must be the murderer.

As a rival for Maud's attention, Murdoch is a natural suspect. However, Maud states clearly that he stepped aside as soon as he found out that she had chosen McPherson. And Stackhurst insists that Murdoch and McPherson had put the incident of the dog behind them and were now firm friends. Yet Holmes ignores these witness statements and continues to suspect Murdoch. It is strange that Holmes, who is generally so logical and rational, should be led astray by prejudice at this late stage in his career.

The sting in the tale

Holmes's source for this story (*Out of Doors*) was correct. A giant jellyfish called the lion's mane—the world's largest—really does exist. The biggest specimens have a bell up to 10 ft (3 m) wide, with tentacles that can extend 100 ft (30 m) or more. The lion's mane is found primarily in the North Atlantic, and grows especially big in cold Arctic waters. Small specimens are often seen on the south coast of England, but giant ones may appear occasionally, as explained in the story by the fact that the severe southwest gale could have carried it beyond its normal range.

The lion's mane's tentacles have thousands of stinging cells. These contain poisonous threads that unfold and launch themselves like harpoons into a victim's body. They leave large red welts or ridged zigzag lines in the skin, along the path of the jellyfish's lashing tentacles, just as Holmes describes. These stings can cause intense pain or, in very rare cases, death.

to look in his real attic, in which he finds a little "chocolate and silver" book, entitled *Out of Doors*. Written in 1874, this was in fact a genuine publication by a popular Victorian natural history writer at the time, John George Wood (1827–1889).

Delayed revelation

Having verified his suspicions by consulting his book, Holmes has, to all intents and purposes, solved the mystery of McPherson's death. But Conan Doyle sustains the story a little longer, tantalizing the reader by introducing a sequence of obstacles that prevent Holmes from revealing his great solution.

First comes Inspector Bardle, who Holmes describes as "a steady, solid, bovine man," to suggest that he is trustworthy but not especially intelligent. He asks for Holmes's opinion as to whether he should arrest Murdoch before the suspect leaves town. The fact that Murdoch is hot-tempered, has argued with McPherson in the past, is in love with Maud, and is preparing to leave Fulworth—combined with a lack of any other likely suspect—all indicate guilt to the inspector. But Holmes points out that Murdoch

has an alibi, and that the evidence against him is flimsy. The great detective also tells him that he has examined a photograph of McPherson's wounds, and teases the inspector—and the reader—with possible explanations for their strange nature. Then, just as he is about to explain the truth of the matter to him, Murdoch bursts in and delays the revelation further.

Murdoch is in a bad way. He is in terrible agony, branded with the same weals on his shoulder as

> The sufferer's breathing would stop for a time, his face would turn black, and then with loud gasps he would clap his hand to his heart, while his brow dropped beads of sweat.
> **Sherlock Holmes**

McPherson. After knocking back several large doses of brandy, he finally falls into an unconscious stupor. Stackhurst, who had met Murdoch on the cliff and followed him in to Holmes's house, pleads with Holmes to save them from this apparent curse.

Finally, Holmes relents. "We will see if we cannot deliver this murderer into your hands," he announces, leading the inspector and Stackhurst down to the lagoon on the shore. As Holmes scans the pool below, he yells triumphantly, "Cyanea! Behold the Lion's Mane!" and in the water all three men spot the tentacles and globular body of a giant jellyfish. Holmes spies a large boulder above the pool and, at his call to "end the murderer forever," between the three of them they roll the boulder into the pool to kill the jellyfish.

A natural killer

It seems there was no murder at all and that McPherson, his dog, and Murdoch were all victims of a natural hazard—the sting of the jellyfish *Cyanea capillata*, commonly known as the lion's mane. As Holmes shows his

> I often ventured to chaff you gentlemen of the police force, but *Cyanea capillata* very nearly avenged Scotland Yard.
> **Sherlock Holmes**

friends in his book *Out of Doors* when they get home, McPherson is not the first to encounter this dangerous giant jellyfish: author John George Woods explains how he had once had a close encounter with a lion's mane and was lucky to escape with his life. His book warns swimmers who see a tawny-colored membranous mass that resembles a lion's mane, "Let him beware, for this is the fearful stinger, *Cyanea capillata*."

The stings of these jellyfish are extremely painful, but rarely fatal. However, Conan Doyle is careful to stress that McPherson had a weak heart, and so it is entirely plausible that the stings could kill him, while Murdoch survives the attack.

Holmes on the wane?

In this story, Conan Doyle has employed a fascinating, real-life killer, and Inspector Bardle is full of admiration for the way Holmes has gotten to the bottom of the case. "I had read of you, but I never believed it. It's wonderful!" the

inspector cries. But as Holmes modestly admits, "I was slow at the outset—culpably slow," and certainly this is a tale that has not shown him at his most perceptive.

Holmes assumed from the start that McPherson's death was murder and that there was a human killer, possessing a flaying instrument, to track down. At first he suspected Murdoch of being the murderer, but this was based largely on the man's appearance and character rather than fact—the type of red herring that Watson might have fallen for.

Holmes was misled, he says, by McPherson's dry towel: it made him think that the dead man had never been in the lagoon, and claims that had he found him in the water the true cause would have been clear. However, the observant reader will

note that Holmes must have failed to spot that when McPherson died his hair was surely still wet, and that his clothes would certainly have been damp had he thrown them on without drying himself first. Also, when Holmes inspected the crime scene he somehow missed the huge jellyfish. But in spite of these slips, it is ultimately only Holmes who solves the puzzle.

Without Watson as Holmes's foil, Conan Doyle may have forfeited a little of the detective's brilliance to the plot. But any fears the reader may have that Holmes's powers are waning with age and retirement can be allayed: his dramatic undercover work in "His Last Bow" (pp.246–47), set seven years after "The Lion's Mane," shows Holmes at the height of his powers. ∎

Holmes's Sussex home, like these coast guard's cottages, looks across the channel, taking in a view of the chalk cliffs. One of Holmes's pleasures is walking the cliff path to the beach.

WE REACH. WE GRASP. AND WHAT IS LEFT IN OUR HANDS AT THE END? A SHADOW

THE ADVENTURE OF THE RETIRED COLOURMAN (1927)

Intricate web of involvement

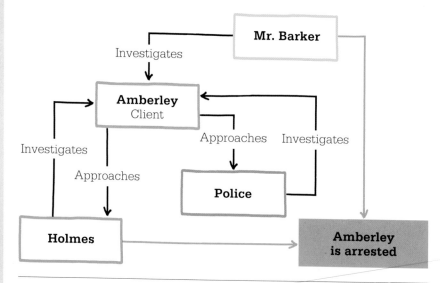

IN CONTEXT

TYPE
Short story

FIRST PUBLICATION
US: December 1926
UK: January 1927

COLLECTION
***The Case Book of Sherlock Holmes*, 1927**

CHARACTERS
Josiah Amberley Retired colorman (manufacturer of art materials).

Mrs. Amberley Josiah Amberley's young wife.

Dr. Ray Ernest Chess-playing companion of Josiah.

Mr. Barker Private investigator and Holmes's professional rival.

Mr. JC Elman Vicar of Little Purlington.

Inspector MacKinnon Smart young police officer.

After a recent first encounter with a new client, referred to him by Scotland Yard, Holmes is in a melancholy mood. The client, Josiah Amberley, is the "retired colourman" of the story's title, a former manufacturer of art materials and now a pathetic, broken creature, aged beyond his years, his face lined, his posture stooped, and his appearance unkempt.

Amberley claims that his young wife has been having an affair with his chess partner, Dr. Ray Ernest,

and now the pair have gone missing with his life savings. Watson is enlisted as Holmes's proxy and sent to Amberley's Lewisham home to investigate. This is an unusual, though not unique, procedure for Holmes, who tends to distrust and double-check Watson's investigative work, as in *The Hound of the Baskervilles* (pp.152–61). The report Watson writes shows him at his most creative, giving Holmes ample opportunity to call out his tendency to embroider and embellish the facts.

Holmes takes charge

Crucially, Watson observes that Amberley is painting a door and passageway in his house with a strong-smelling green paint. Watson also notices a tall, dark, mustached man who follows him when he leaves Amberley's house. This is enough to engage Holmes's suspicions. Holmes despatches Watson and Amberley on a wild-goose chase to Essex using a false telegram purporting to come from a vicar named Elman. With them out of the way, he establishes that Amberley's alibi for the night of his wife's disappearance (a theater trip) is false. Holmes then breaks into Amberley's house and discovers, behind the freshly painted door, a sealed chamber with a telltale gas inlet pipe—a perfect murder room. Amberley lured his wife and her suspected lover into the chamber and trapped them there, flooding the room with poisonous gas.

Joining forces

The mysterious dark man spotted by Watson turns out to be Holmes's rival, the private investigator Mr. Barker, who has been hired by Dr. Ernest's family. Unusually, the

> Burglary has always been an alternative profession had I cared to adopt it…
> **Sherlock Holmes**

two join forces, handing over the murderer to Inspector MacKinnon of Scotland Yard. Holmes instructs the inspector to look for conclusive evidence of the murder around the house, including in a disused well, and the bodies are duly discovered. The inspector shows his genuine respect for Holmes when he states, with admirable understatement, that "it's as workmanlike a job as I can remember."

Amberley's approach to the authorities, and latterly Holmes, was "Pure swank"—the murderer had complete confidence that he would not be outwitted by either the police or the renowned detective.

Motives and madness

Holmes observes that Amberley's mind was deranged by jealousy, and it is probably no coincidence that Amberley used green paint (the color associated with jealousy) to mask the smell of gas emanating from the murder chamber. Holmes sees the extreme cruelty of the murder as a sure sign of madness, and suggests that Amberley is more likely to end up in the Broadmoor asylum than on the gallows.

This story is lighter and more playful in tone than the melancholy of the opening would have the reader believe. Assigning Watson an investigative role inevitably leads to some witty banter between the two friends, as they contrast their abilities. Holmes is depicted at his enterprising best as a hyper-observant cat burglar, and the police are, as usual, left flat-footed. Although Holmes has solved the crime, he does not seek public recognition, and seemingly enjoys reading accounts of the case that credit the police with solving the mystery. However, he still suggests, in his wry way, that Watson make a record of the events, saying, "Some day the true story may be told." ∎

Broadmoor

As Holmes suggests, Amberley may plead "not guilty by reason of insanity" and be sentenced to a life of incarceration rather than hanging. During the 19th century, there was a growing awareness that mentally ill criminals required different treatment from common felons, and the Criminal Lunatics Act of 1800 allowed them to be detained indefinitely.

The Broadmoor Criminal Lunatic Asylum, in Crowthorne, Berkshire, opened its doors in 1863 and was the first custom-built institution for such cases. It was self-sufficient, with its own farmland and workshops operated by inmates. Men and women were segregated and underwent a routine of work, exercise, and rest. The hospital was managed by a medical superintendent and two doctors, and assisted by a staff of 100 non-medical attendants.

Today, Broadmoor still has "special hospital" status, but no longer treats women. Men who are a high risk to themselves, or to others, are treated at this high-security facility.

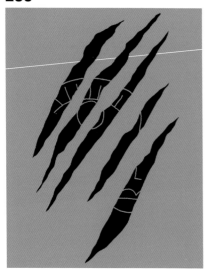

PATIENT SUFFERING IS IN ITSELF THE MOST PRECIOUS OF ALL LESSONS
THE ADVENTURE OF THE VEILED LODGER (1927)

IN CONTEXT

TYPE
Short story

FIRST PUBLICATION
US: January 1927
UK: February 1927

COLLECTION
The Case Book of
***Sherlock Holmes*, 1927**

CHARACTERS
Eugenia Ronder Former
circus performer.

Mr. Ronder Eugenia's late
husband, a circus showman.

Leonardo Circus strong
man and Eugenia's late lover.

Mrs. Merrilow Eugenia's
landlady, who approaches
Holmes on her behalf.

Unusually for a Holmes
story, this tragic tale of
love and revenge hinges
almost entirely on a confession
rather than any detection. Holmes
is not the analytical and deductive
genius in this case, but a priestlike
listener, whose role is simply to
provide compassion and absolution
to a spiritually tormented woman.

A woman with a past

In late 1896, Holmes is approached
by a landlady, Mrs. Merrilow, who is
worried about one of her tenants—
a peculiarly reclusive woman named
Eugenia Ronder, who wears a
permanent veil to hide her facial
deformities. She seems to be
"wasting away" and has been
crying out "Murder!" in her sleep.
The landlady has suggested that if
Eugenia has any secrets to divulge,
she should see a member of the
clergy, the police, or Sherlock
Holmes—and Eugenia chooses
to meet with the latter.

Holmes tells Watson he
remembers reading about the
case of Eugenia. She had worked
for the circus, and married the
lion tamer and proprietor of a

The traveling circus

The first circus in England was
started in 1768 by an ex-cavalry
officer named Philip Astley, and
was entirely focused on displays
of horsemanship. Increasingly,
bands of roving performers
roamed from town to town.
Gradually, tightrope walking,
acrobatics, and clowning were
introduced, and many circuses
advertised their arrival with an
impressive parade.

By the late 19th century, the
circus had become a truly great
and magnificent spectacle. The
American Barnum and Bailey
Circus, which toured Europe
from 1897 to 1902, thrilled its
audiences with trick riding,
juggling, and trapeze acts, as
well as human freak shows.
Another highlight was the
performing elephants, lions,
and other exotic creatures (by
then there was an international
trade in wild animals tamed
for circuses). Animals toured
with British circuses until
fairly recently, but today a legal
ban on their use is impending.

A fearless lion-tamer performing at L'Hippodrome in Paris in 1891. Theatrical and daring performances involving wild animals were typically among the most popular circus acts.

traveling "wild beast" show. One night, seven years previously, the lion had escaped and attacked Eugenia, mutilating her face and mauling her husband to death, crushing his head with its claws. However, the police investigation left many questions unanswered, and Holmes says that he found the eventual verdict of "death from misadventure" unsatisfactory.

The secret unveiled

Holmes and Watson arrive at Eugenia's lodgings, where she reveals her long-held secret. Her husband had been a violent drunk who inflicted physical and emotional humiliation on her, and was cruel toward both human and animal members of his troupe.

Leonardo, the show's strong man, was Ronder's polar opposite—attractive and confident. Eugenia fell in love with Leonardo, and soon they were plotting to rid themselves of her keeper. The smitten strong man created an ingenious weapon, a cudgel with five nails spaced to

resemble a lion's claw. One night, as Ronder went out to feed the lion, Leonardo felled his rival with a lacerating blow to the head.

In accordance with their plan, Eugenia freed the lion from its cage, hoping it would be blamed for her husband's death. But the beast leapt at her, sinking its teeth into her face, and Leonardo ran away in terror. After Eugenia was rescued, she kept quiet about Leonardo's role in Ronder's death; despite his desertion, she still loved him.

A life saved

Eugenia had lost her beauty, her lover, and her livelihood, and chose to disappear into obscurity. Recently, however, having learned of Leonardo's death, she had felt an urge to confess. Her testimony elicits great sympathy from Holmes. Astutely sensing that Eugenia is contemplating suicide, which was illegal at the time, he admonishes her: "Your life is not your own... Keep your hands off it." Two days later, Eugenia sends Holmes a bottle containing a deadly poison; the accompanying note indicates that she has chosen to live.

The story describes both a literal act of unveiling—Eugenia revealing her face to Holmes—and

No words can describe the framework of a face when the face itself is gone.
Dr. Watson

a symbolic one: lies being cast aside to reveal the truth. Ronder trapped his wife in a cage of his own devising, for his own pleasure; and when the lion destroyed her life, Eugenia crawled like a wounded animal into her own cage—the sequestered lodging house. In freeing the lion, Eugenia also liberated her murderous hatred of her husband, but with terrible, lifelong consequences.

At its heart, this story is about Eugenia's entrapment in an abusive marriage. The plight of women who were utterly powerless to change their fates was a theme common to many Holmes stories, including "The Adventure of the Abbey Grange" (pp.198–201). ∎

Triangle of abuse and betrayal

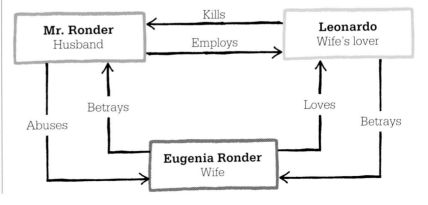

IT IS ONLY THE COLOURLESS, UNEVENTFUL CASE WHICH IS HOPELESS
THE ADVENTURE OF SHOSCOMBE OLD PLACE (1927)

IN CONTEXT

TYPE
Short story

FIRST PUBLICATION
US: March 1927
UK: April 1927

COLLECTION
***The Case Book of Sherlock Holmes*, 1927**

CHARACTERS
Sir Robert Norberton
Volatile master of Shoscombe Old Place.

Lady Beatrice Falder
Sir Robert's invalid sister.

John Mason Sir Robert's head trainer.

Mrs. Norlett Lady Beatrice's maid.

Mr. Norlett Mrs. Norlett's husband, an actor.

Stephens Sir Robert's butler.

Josiah Barnes Landlord of the Green Dragon inn.

Sandy Bain Jockey.

The very last of the 56 Sherlock Holmes short stories, "The Adventure of Shoscombe Old Place" was published three years before Conan Doyle died at the age of 71, and so it is a farewell to Holmes. The story begins by showing the great detective very much looking to the future as he exhibits his masterful grasp of forensic science. As the case unfolds, however, Holmes needs his powers of deduction far more than forensic science— essentially because there is no crime scene to speak of. The thrill of the tale hinges on the potential for a really nasty crime to have been committed.

Master of forensics
As the story opens, Holmes, with the aid of a microscope, identifies minute blobs of glue on a cap found beside a murdered policeman at St. Pancras station, a clue that strongly implicates a picture-frame maker who has denied the cap is his.

Holmes was at the forefront of his profession in using forensic science this way. A pioneer in the use of trace evidence such as shoe prints, minute marks and scratches, and traces of blood, mud, organic matter, and other particles such as glue, Holmes's technique emphasized the minute study of a crime scene to yield tiny clues. This method is now the centerpiece of modern forensic investigation.

It is no coincidence that the great real-life visionary of forensic science, Dr. Edmond Locard (1877– 1966), came to be known as the "Sherlock Holmes of France." Locard's cardinal rule was that "every contact leaves a trace." Known as "Locard's exchange principle," this simple statement—

Dr. Edmond Locard (1877–1966) was a pioneering French scientist who established the first police laboratory in 1910, although its work was not officially recognized until 1912.

The Derby Day (1856–1858) by William Powell Frith depicts a scene Sir Robert would have been familiar with. The work was so popular that the Royal Academy added a rail to control crowds.

which might have been made by Holmes himself—argues that every criminal brings something to a crime scene, and takes something away—however miniscule.

The facts of the case

Shortly after Holmes correctly identifies the blobs of glue, he receives a visit from John Mason, the head trainer at Shoscombe Old Place, a grand country estate in Berkshire. Mason is worried about the behavior of his master, the rakish Sir Robert Norberton. A notorious spendthrift, Sir Robert is in a deep financial hole. To clear his debts, he is relying on his prize racehorse, Shoscombe Prince, to win the prestigious upcoming Epsom Derby at falsely long odds (he has cleverly misled watching touts with the horse's much slower half-brother on morning gallops).

Mason is concerned about other recent events, however. Why have Sir Robert and his reclusive and invalid sister—to whom he has always been devoted—suddenly stopped meeting? Why has Sir Robert given away her beloved pet spaniel to the landlord of a local inn, the Green Dragon? Why does Sir Robert meet a mysterious person in the haunted family crypt under the old ruined chapel late at night? Where did the mummy's head and bones that Mason and Sir Robert's butler, Stephens, found in the crypt come from? And finally, why was there a charred fragment of human leg bone among the ashes from the central-heating furnace in the cellar under Lady Beatrice's room?

Fishing for clues

With that last grim question, Holmes is hooked. Have Sir Robert and an as yet unidentified accomplice murdered Lady Beatrice and burned her body? Pretending to be vacationing fishermen, Holmes and Watson check in to the Green Dragon inn, where the landlord, Josiah Barnes, warns them about Sir Robert. "He's the sort who strikes first and speaks afterwards," he says. Undeterred, they offer to take the landlord's spaniel, once owned by Lady Beatrice, for a walk, and head straight for Shoscombe Old Place, timing their arrival to coincide with her daily coach excursion. As the coach slows down by the gate of the estate, Holmes releases the dog. It dashes toward the coach enthusiastically, then suddenly starts barking furiously »

These are deep waters, Mr. Mason; deep and rather dirty.
Sherlock Holmes

> Sir Robert is a man
> of an honourable stock.
> But you do occasionally
> find a carrion crow among
> the eagles... He could not
> fly the country until he
> had realized his fortune
> **Sherlock Holmes**

at its occupants—supposedly Lady Beatrice and her maid, Mrs. Norlett. But from behind "Lady Beatrice's" shawls, Watson and Holmes hear a harsh man's voice shouting, "Drive on! Drive on!" As Holmes observes, "We have added one card to our hand, Watson, but it needs careful playing, all the same."

Later that evening, the pair visit the crypt. The bones Mason saw are gone; Holmes speculates they have been burned in the furnace, along with the rest of the skeleton. Just

as he discovers a recently opened coffin, the pair hear footsteps, and "a terrible figure, huge in stature and fierce in manner" appears from the shadows. It is Sir Robert, and he demands to know who they are and what they are doing there.

In a wonderfully Gothic moment, Holmes flings open the coffin, and Sir Robert reels back and cries out. The body of Lady Beatrice is revealed, "swathed in a sheet from head to foot, with dreadful, witch-like features, all nose and chin, projecting at one end, the dim glazed eyes staring from a discoloured and crumbling face." Sir Robert resolves to explain his actions, and invites Holmes and Watson to accompany him to the house for an explanation so that they can judge the matter for themselves.

The truth comes out

He tells them that, about a week earlier, Lady Beatrice had died of dropsy. As a result, he faced losing the house, the stables, and all the horses—including Shoscombe Prince—just weeks before the hoped-for Derby win that would pay off all his debts, because the entire

> It was my duty to bring
> the facts to light, and
> there I must leave it.
> As to the morality or
> decency of your conduct,
> it is not for me to
> express an opinion.
> **Sherlock Holmes**

Shoscombe estate, including the racehorse, was actually hers, and would therefore revert to her late husband's brother when her death was known. In desperation, Sir Robert had decided to conceal her death until the race had been run.

To make room for her body in the old coffin, he and his servant, Mr. Norlett, the maid's husband, first had to remove the mummified body of an ancestor, and burn it in the furnace. "There was no indignity or irreverence," he claims. He then explains that Norlett—"a small, rat-faced man with a disagreeably furtive face," and once an actor—agreed to impersonate Lady Beatrice. They gave away her spaniel because it kept yapping at the old well-house where they initially hid her body.

When Holmes calls his conduct "inexcusable," Sir Robert retorts, "It is easy to preach. Perhaps you would have felt differently if you had been in my position." Holmes— a man who on previous occasions has let killers walk free when he felt their actions were justified— is clearly not persuaded, and declares it a matter for the police.

The role of the coroner

The coroner's role in investigating the cause of sudden deaths was established as long ago as 1194, by the Normans—not out of concern for justice, but instead to ensure the right taxes were paid. A fine called "Murdrum" (from which the word "murder" comes) was imposed on any village where a dead body was found, on the assumption the victim was Norman and the killers Anglo-Saxon. In 1836, the first Births and Deaths Registration Act made reporting every birth and death a legal requirement. There were growing concerns, though, that it was too easy to get away with murder, especially by poison, and that inquests were far too costly a way to look into suspicious deaths. So in 1887 a new Coroners Act made it the coroner's role to discover the medical causes of any sudden, violent, or unnatural death. Lady Beatrice's sudden death could therefore well have come within the new coroner's remit.

As Holmes discovers, the reality of Sir Robert's life at Shoscombe Old Place is very different from how it first appears. The master of a large estate and owner of a prize-winning racehorse, he is, in fact, in grave danger of losing everything.

He lives with his **elderly, invalid sister**, Lady Beatrice Falder, to whom he is devoted.

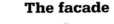

The facade

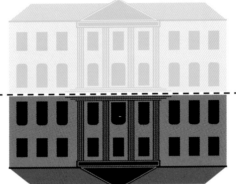

Sir Robert Norberton resides in **a grand country estate** in Berkshire.

His racehorse, Shoscombe Prince, is due to win his master **£80,000 in bets** in the Derby.

Sir Robert is **deep in debt** and threatened by **bankruptcy.**

Sir Robert **buries his sister's body** in the vacated coffin, swathed in a sheet.

The reality

Lady Beatrice is dead and Sir Robert must conceal her death until after the Derby.

To hide her body, Sir Robert removes and burns the **mummified remains** of an ancestor.

In Watson's words, the Shoscombe Old Place case ends "upon a happier note than Sir Robert's actions deserved." Given that the crime turns out to be so minor, the police take a lenient view and largely overlook it, simply rapping Sir Robert on the knuckles for failing to register the death of his sister immediately. Also, remarkably, Sir Robert's creditors agree to wait until after the race to be paid. And finally, Sir Robert's horse, Shoscombe Prince, wins the Derby, netting his owner £80,000 in bets, which allows Sir Robert to clear all of his debts and set himself up for life.

A career ends

Watson's description of the events in the crypt is unusually dramatic, reading like something from a horror story. He describes the appalling sight of Lady Beatrice's corpse, and the terrifying figure of the giant Sir Robert, in such Gothic detail that we are led to believe something appalling is going to happen. Instead, minutes later they are all sitting comfortably as Sir Robert tells a mundane story about a delay in reporting the death of an old invalid.

In "Shoscombe Old Place," Holmes uncovers not some terrible murder or dark cruelty, but instead a foolish and highly distasteful fraud perpetrated by a desperate, slightly unpleasant landowner— a fraud that the man in question also gets away with. It is something of an anticlimactic end to Holmes's career, and perhaps this is just what Conan Doyle intended. Watson begins the story with the remark, "He is one of those men who have overshot their true generation," and refers at the finish of the tale to "a career which has now outlived its shadows and promises to end in an honoured old age." In each instance he is talking about Sir Robert, but the descriptions could equally well apply to Holmes himself. ∎

THE WO
SHERLO
HOLMES

RLD OF
CK

The world of Sherlock Holmes, like the character himself, is a unique blend of popular myth and reality. In this final chapter, the detective and his era are explored from a range of perspectives, setting the context in which Conan Doyle lived, and also explaining the historical and social changes that influenced not only his life and those of his readers, but also that of his most famous creation. The enduring legacy of Holmes is also explored, in all its varied forms.

Myth, reality, and reason

The setting of late-Victorian London (pp.296–99) is central to Holmes's world, and is often thought of as a labyrinth of foggy backstreets in the notorious East End. However, this popular image is an inaccurate one. Conan Doyle's London had grand new buildings, fashionable shopping areas, broad gaslit thoroughfares, and affluent new suburbs. It was also at the heart of a communications revolution, with grand railroad termini, like Paddington and King's Cross, a national telegraph system, and a thriving popular press.

Holmes's London was one of contrasts. While steaming locomotives poured in and out of the great stations, and underground trains ferried commuters below the city's streets, wealthier citizens still traveled around the center by horse-drawn hansom cabs. Despite the wealth of the empire, the city was a place of crushing poverty, although this was never made apparent in Conan Doyle's canon.

Difference and tradition

London's population had increased from one to six million over the course of the 19th century. This influx of people, ideas, wealth, and cultures created a melting pot of complexity and social change (pp.300–05). The sheer scale of the city, the largest in the world at that time, generated fears of a lawless underclass, mainly squashed into

> [London] is the biggest aggregation of human life—the most complete compendium of the world.
> **Henry James**
> Novelist (1843–1916)

the overcrowded eastern districts. In spite of this, Holmes's cases feature characters mainly from the mid- to upper echelons of society, mirroring Conan Doyle's audience. Conan Doyle drew on social tensions and prevalent racial, gender, and class stereotypes in order to add fear, excitement, and zest to his tales. For all of Holmes's "bohemian" sensibilities, Baker Street is painted as a white, male, middle-class world that would sometimes seem bigoted by today's standards. Foreigners are criminals, and women are mainly victims or innocent pawns in the stories.

Crime and detection

Holmes was, metaphorically, the progeny of two men, having been inspired by Edgar Allan Poe's character C. Auguste Dupin, and Conan Doyle's former professor Joseph Bell. Both of these forebears excelled in the science of deductive reasoning, or ratiocination, which became the very heart of Holmes's science of detection (pp.306–09). The term's history is explored, from its roots in Greek philosophy, through to the Enlightenment ideals of the 17th century, and on to the importance of Charles Darwin's theories in his *On the Origin of Species* (1859).

Ratiocination was central to the burgeoning science of crime deduction (pp.310–15), which Conan Doyle reflected in the canon, as the concepts of forensics and criminology became established terms. Holmes's own contributions to the realm of forensic science, with his monographs on tobacco ash, typewriters, tattoos, and many other subjects, can be seen as part of a wider, pioneering spirit in the development of crime fighting.

The taste for crime

The success of Holmes compared to Conan Doyle's other characters can partly be attributed to the changing society. The growth of cities and increasing class divisions had led to a fear of crime and a hunger for justice, which the popular press, including the "penny dreadfuls," was more than happy to encourage. Just as the science of crime solving was growing at this time, so too was crime fiction (pp.316–23). The roots of the genre can be traced back to writers like Edgar Allan Poe, Wilkie Collins, and even Charles Dickens, as well as to contemporaries of Conan Doyle, including G. K. Chesterton and E. W. Hornung. The 20th century saw the rise of hard-boiled detective fiction, and the dominance of female crime writers such as Agatha Christie, P. D. James, and Ruth Rendell. Today, crime fiction (notably Scandinavian) is as popular as ever, and many of today's authors have taken inspiration from Holmes's legacy.

Fame and legacy

An important aspect of Holmes is how popular the character and his adventures were, and how quickly they captured the public's imagination. Conan Doyle's first Holmes novel, *A Study in Scarlet* (1887), may initially have gone unnoticed when first published, but his short stories, serialized by *The Strand Magazine*, created the phenomenon that endures to this day, with fan clubs and societies around the world (pp.324–27).

Just as Holmes inspired many literary interpretations, he was also an early star of stage and screen (pp.328–35). Many great actors have played the role of Sherlock Holmes, including Eille Norwood, Basil Rathbone, Jeremy Brett, and Benedict Cumberbatch.

A selection of Holmes's most important depictions is provided (pp.336–39)—from his early stage appearance in William Gillette's 1899 play, *Sherlock Holmes*, to the latest movie release, *Mr. Holmes* (2015), starring Sir Ian McKellan.

There are also countless and varied literary appropriations of Holmes (pp.340–43), from the early parodies, through to the sustained creation of the canon's many "untold cases," along with complete reimaginings and the current trend for "fan fiction".

Conan Doyle also wrote many novels and stories beyond the Holmes canon (pp.344–45). Here, his penchant for historical fiction, religious and political commentary, and spiritualist speculation—the "better things" that led him to temporarily kill off his most famous creation—is clearly demonstrated. Yet Holmes still remains his most enduring creation; a man who, in the words of writer Vincent Starrett, "Never lived and so can never die." ∎

Sherlock Holmes is a real character who is above reality; a person living in a distinct place and at a distinct period.
Richard Lancelyn Green
Author and Critic (1953–2004)

WHAT DO YOU SAY TO A RAMBLE THROUGH LONDON?

THE VICTORIAN WORLD

For many modern readers, the stories of Sherlock Holmes seem to provide a quintessential fictional depiction of Victorian Britain. The detective dresses as a late 19th-century English gentleman; he travels in horse-drawn hansom cabs through streets illuminated by gaslight; and his clients are often (but not always) moneyed members of the Victorian middle class, whose prosperity and status had increased as a result of industrialization and the expansion of Britain's imperial power. However, this is only half the story.

Holmes in context

It is misleading to classify Holmes and his creator as only "Victorians": while many of the stories are set in the 1880s and 1890s—toward the end of Queen Victoria's reign (1837–1901)—over half were written in the early 20th century, and are imbued with a more modern perspective.

Conan Doyle was born in 1859 and died in 1930, so 42 years of his life were spent as one of Queen Victoria's subjects, during a period of great innovation, expansion, and rapid change. He also lived through the Edwardian era, World War I,

and much of the interwar period, and witnessed a number of seismic cultural, economic, political, and technological developments, many of which make an appearance in the stories. As a result, Holmes and Watson's "Victorian" world is very different from the one portrayed in other novels of the era, such as Dickens's classic tale *A Christmas Carol*, published almost 50 years earlier in 1843. Holmes's own Christmas outing, "The Adventure of the Blue Carbuncle" (pp.82–3), is set in a far more cosmopolitan London than that of Dickens's day.

The London Fog

Conan Doyle's descriptions of the notorious fogs that afflicted London during the 19th century are not as frequent or as florid as those of Charles Dickens or Robert Louis Stevenson, but when Watson remarks in "The Five Orange Pips" (pp.74–9) that "the sun was shining with a subdued brightness through the dim veil which hangs over the great city," perhaps he is implying that their presence is a given. The thick, yellowish-brown "pea soupers" were a toxic combination of pollution from heavy industry, meteorological peculiarities, and

thousands of coal fires, and they posed a health hazard for many Londoners. At their worst, they caused a huge number of deaths; most of the victims were those with respiratory problems, the very young, and the elderly. However, a more commonplace nuisance was the floating smuts of soot, which soiled clothes and soft furnishings alike. When, in "The Norwood Builder" (pp.168–69), John McFarlane dresses in a "light summer overcoat" on a blisteringly hot day, he is most likely attempting to protect his clothes from the dirt in the air.

Conan Doyle's life coincided with the zenith of the British Empire during the reign of Victoria (pictured), and Holmes represents, and offers an alternative to, Victorian and imperial values.

By the time Conan Doyle was born, many of the events and individuals that have come to characterize the Victorian age were already old news: the Great Exhibition of 1851 had come and gone, the Crimean War (1853–1856) was over, and the engineer Isambard Kingdom Brunel (1806–1859), who had revolutionized the way in which trade and travel were conducted, was nearing death.

From a literary perspective, Conan Doyle's birth date was closer to that of F. Scott Fitzgerald (1896) and Ernest Hemingway (1899), two of the most influential American novelists of the early 20th century, than it was to that of Alfred Tennyson (1809), Elizabeth Gaskell (1810), and Charles Dickens (1812), three giants of Victorian writing; and the last Holmes story was published in 1927—almost 90 years after Victoria came to the throne.

[Holmes] began his adventures in the very heart of the later Victorian era, carried it through the all-too-short reign of Edward, and has managed to hold his own little niche even in these feverish days.
Arthur Conan Doyle
The Case Book of Sherlock Holmes

Urbanization and suburbia
Despite his frequent forays into the leafy counties that surround London (and occasionally farther afield), Holmes is a creature of the great metropolis, one of millions drawn to what Watson famously describes in the first novel, *A Study in Scarlet* (pp.36–45), as "that great cesspool into which all the loungers and idlers of the Empire are irresistibly drained." During the 1800s, the proportion of the British population living in cities rose from 20 percent to almost 80 percent, and by Holmes's time, London was the most populous city on Earth.

The Industrial Revolution and the subsequent rise in urbanization brought prosperity to many, but also buried countless others in crushing poverty. The working poor rarely appear in the Holmes stories, but the striking effect that their living conditions have on the city's character does not escape Watson's notice: as he and Holmes travel across London in "The Adventure of the Six Napoleons" (pp.188–89)—from super-rich Kensington in the west to impoverished Stepney in the East End—he watches as the scenery turns from chic and sleek to wretchedly sordid and deprived.

In the late 1800s, those who could afford to began to migrate to the relative peace of London's new suburbs—a trend that is noted in *The Sign of Four* (pp.46–55) as Holmes and Watson's cab races away from Baker Street in the city's center, past "interminable lines of new, staring brick buildings—the monster tentacles which the giant city was throwing out into the country." This is also reflected in the appearance of suburbs as locations in the stories, including the South London areas of Norwood (site of Jonas Oldacre's home in "The Adventure of the Norwood Builder" (pp.168–69) and of Conan »

Hansom cabs were famously safe, navigating street corners and traffic with ease. Holmes had other dangers in mind when he advised taking "neither the first nor the second which may present itself."

Doyle's London home); Brixton (home to Scotland Yard inspector Stanley Hopkins, who appears in several cases); and Streatham (home of the banker Alexander Holder in "The Adventure of the Beryl Coronet," pp.96–7).

Mass transit

The trend for suburban living gave rise to a modern phenomenon: the commuter. In "The Red-Headed League" (pp.62–7) Holmes and Watson both observe "one of the main arteries which conveyed the traffic of the City to the north and west," and the doctor remarks on the "immense stream of commerce flowing in a double tide inward and outward, while the footpaths were black with the hurrying swarm of pedestrians."

The emergence of the daily commute from home to work was a direct result of the development of London's transportation system in the Victorian era. In the early 1800s, people had to live close to their place of work, but by Holmes's time the city was crisscrossed by an extensive transportation network of omnibuses, boats, and trains.

The Metropolitan Railway—the first of several subterranean train lines that would later become the London Underground—opened in 1863, although when Watson and Holmes took it from Baker Street to Aldersgate (modern-day Barbican) in "The Red-Headed League," it would still have been hauled by steam engines. Above ground, too, the city's inhabitants had seen an explosion in rail travel (almost all of London's modern-day mainline rail stations opened during the 19th century). Holmes made excellent use of the network: various train companies ran different lines and stations, and the detective caught

trains out of London Bridge, Euston, Paddington, Victoria, Waterloo, Charing Cross, and King's Cross, traveling as far north as the Peak District in Derbyshire, as well as southwest to Devon and Cornwall.

Perhaps the most frequent Holmesian mode of transportation, though, was the iconic hansom cab. Pulled by a single horse, and with the driver sitting high up on a sprung seat behind his passengers, these two-seater carriages were ubiquitous, fast, and fairly cheap. They were first patented in the 1830s, and thousands of them plied the London streets until motorized taxis began to appear in the first

Numerous events, technological milestones, and inventions of historic significance took place in Britain within Holmes's presumed lifetime.

1860 Horse-drawn trams appear on London's streets.

1876 Invention of the telephone.

1854 Possible birth date of Holmes.

1855 First daily newspaper, *The Daily Telegraph*, is published.

1863 World's first underground train line opens in London.

1880 The first British homes are lit by electricity.

decade of the 20th century. A more comfortable but slower alternative was the larger four-wheeler (or "growler"), which was more like a conventional enclosed carriage.

Age of Empire

By the time of Queen Victoria's death, the soldiers of the British Empire had fought alongside or against many foreign powers—invariably over colonial disputes. This imperial and international environment led Conan Doyle to populate Holmes's world with exotic foreign caricatures, such as the lascar (sailor from the Indian subcontinent) in "The Man with the Twisted Lip" (pp.80–1) and the blowpipe-toting Andaman islander in *The Sign of Four*, and also with returning colonial adventurers, usually corrupted by their time overseas, such as Dr. Grimesby Roylott in "The Adventure of the Speckled Band" (pp.84–9).

Crimes and conflicts originating in other countries (particularly in North America) frequently found their way into Holmes's Victorian England, and it seems only fair that Conan Doyle, in turn, allowed one of Holmes's most famous episodes to take place abroad, when "The Final Problem" (pp.142–47) reaches its climax in alpine Switzerland. The Victorians' innumerable wars also flooded London with a steady stream of former military men, who feature in various Holmes stories, such as *A Study in Scarlet,* "The Naval Treaty" (pp.138–41), and "The Adventure of the Blanched Soldier" (pp.274–77). The most significant of these ex-soldiers, of course, is Holmes's great friend and chronicler, Dr. John Watson, who fought in the Second Afghan War (1878–1880), one of three conflicts in which Britain, from a base in India, attempted to extend its control over Afghanistan, and to oppose Russia's influence there.

A multi-era hero

Despite the Victorian setting of many of the stories, they often show 20th-century attitudes, and are sometimes used as a voice for their creator. For instance, when Holmes rails against the callous American millionaire Neil Gibson in "The Problem of Thor Bridge" (pp.254–57), his sentiments reflect growing tension between Britain and America. He also often displays anti-German feeling, which was prevalent at the time. Nowhere is this more blatant than in the cartoonishly patriotic events of "His Last Bow" (pp.246–47). Published in 1917, during World War I, the story features a German agent who chortles with his boss about the "docile, simple folk" of Britain, before being effortlessly outwitted by a sexagenarian Holmes. (This story also touches on Anglo-Irish relations, with Irish Home Rule a live issue throughout Holmes's era.)

So while Holmes may be a Victorian by background, the stories have a palpable sense of progress and modernity. His is a sophisticated world that features many of the wonders of the age, including telegrams, gramophones, scientific detection methods, vastly improved national and international travel, and even that definitive emblem of the 20th century, the motor car. Conan Doyle himself was one of the first car owners, buying one before he knew how to drive and signing up to take part in an international car rally; like his fictional character, the author was in many ways an adventurer and a pioneer. ∎

> *I have every hope that the light of truth is breaking through.*
> **Sherlock Holmes**
> **"The Problem of Thor Bridge"**

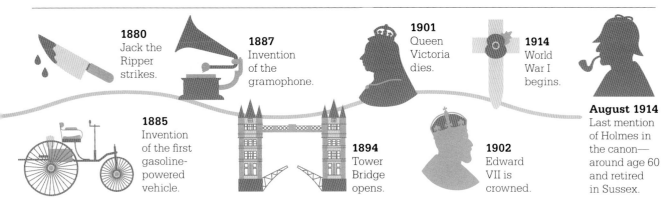

1880 Jack the Ripper strikes.

1885 Invention of the first gasoline-powered vehicle.

1887 Invention of the gramophone.

1894 Tower Bridge opens.

1901 Queen Victoria dies.

1902 Edward VII is crowned.

1914 World War I begins.

August 1914 Last mention of Holmes in the canon—around age 60 and retired in Sussex.

THERE IS NOTHING SO UNNATURAL AS THE COMMONPLACE

SHERLOCK AND SOCIETY

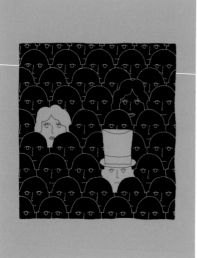

Given the popularity of the Sherlock Holmes stories, Conan Doyle's readers may be forgiven for treating the canon as a legitimate document of Victorian life. However, society in Holmes's fictional world did not always correspond to reality.

At first glance, it may seem that the stories simply reflect typical late-Victorian attitudes. Dig a little deeper, however, and the depiction of society is more complex—one that was informed by Conan Doyle's own views and values and is, by turns, both conventional and radical.

The social spectrum

Considering that they deal with crime and criminals, it seems likely that the Holmes stories would shed light on the social and economic disparities that existed in Britain at the turn of the 19th century. However, social status is treated ambiguously throughout the canon.

In 1889 (two years after Holmes first appeared in *A Study in Scarlet*, pp.36–45), social researcher Charles Booth published the first volume of his so-called "poverty maps" of London to illustrate the deplorable living conditions in much of the city.

In these plans, each of the capital's streets was color-coded according to eight categories of social class, based on income. Yellow streets denoted "Upper-middle and Upper classes. Wealthy," while black streets demarcated the cramped dwellings of the "Lowest Class. Vicious, semi-criminal." The map showed that more than a third of Londoners were living in poverty. Booth's classification of London's poor as "vicious, semi-criminal" might seem shocking today, but in Holmes's day, poverty and crime were often spoken of in the same breath—an association reinforced by the English word "villain," which originally referred to a low-born, rustic person, or a serf, but has since evolved to signify someone who is involved in illegal activities.

In "The Red-Headed League" (pp.62–7), Holmes makes a declaration that appears to reflect the exploratory spirit of social reformers such as Booth—"it is a hobby of mine to have an exact knowledge of London." Yet, as the literary critic Franco Moretti has pointed out, there is almost no overlap between the poor districts on Booth's map and where crimes occur in the Holmes stories.

Social explorers

In Charles Dickens's novels, crime is shown as the inevitable result of injustice—poverty and squalor rubbing up against luxury and excess. Crime in the Holmes stories, by contrast, is often the work of "professional" criminals, usually upper-class dilettantes or opportunists. This difference may derive from the two writers' wildly divergent familiarity with London.

Dickens's journeys through the city's poorest districts provided him with firsthand source material for depicting the slums and their inhabitants. These trips laid the groundwork for social explorers such as the American writer Jack London and, later, George Orwell.

Conan Doyle, however, rarely went out of his way to visit the places he described, and often worked from out-of-date maps. The London of his tales has a genteel sheen, its wealthy districts counterbalanced by the far-flung reaches of the British Empire, rather than the squalid working-class quarter a few miles east of Baker Street.

The contrast between leisured high society and bustling metropolis in Holmes's world is clearly seen in James Tissot's 1876 painting of upper-class passengers cruising on the Thames.

This was a conscious choice by Conan Doyle, as he was writing his stories for a bourgeois audience (even if they did attract readers from across society). After *A Study in Scarlet* and *The Sign of Four* (pp.46–55), in which the bulk of the action takes place in the "unfashionable" suburbs of South London, Holmes's exploits are set mostly in the capital's wealthier districts or in "the smiling and beautiful countryside" of southeast of England. It makes perfect sense, too, that on Booth's map, Baker Street is marked red for "Middle Class. Well-To-Do."

A class act

The shift in the setting of the Holmes stories after *The Sign of Four* resulted in a surge in their popularity. Correspondingly, the

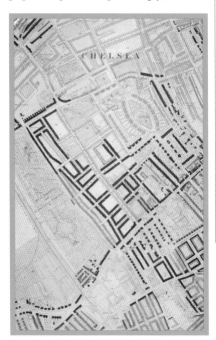

Section 41 of Charles Booth's map of London poverty covers Fulham and Chelsea. The different colors denote levels of wealth. Many of Holmes's cases are set in affluent red or yellow areas.

characters (both victims and villains) tended to be well-off. Grand personae—such as Lord Bellinger in "The Adventure of the Second Stain" (pp.202–07)—added a dose of glamour. Similarly, Holmes's great rival, Moriarty, is described as "an aristocrat of crime," a designation intended to add to his esteem.

It seems neither Holmes nor his audience had much interest in the lower classes. Although he takes on a few working class clients, such as the governess Violet Smith in "The Adventure of the Solitary Cyclist" (pp.176–77), he most relishes the intellectual puzzles brought to him by the middle and upper classes.

Nevertheless, Holmes succeeds in moving effortlessly through all levels of society, employing local street urchins as the "Baker Street Irregulars" and donning disguises with the skill of a stage actor. He also has an uncanny ability to determine the class of anyone he encounters, based solely on outward

appearance. In spite of his class awareness, however, Holmes's own background—as an educated descendant of country squires—is barely mentioned in the stories; within the context of the tales, it is only his intellect and skill that matter. In this, Holmes embodies the entrepreneurial spirit of 19th-century modernity, revealed in his declaration that "I have taken to living by my wits" in "The Musgrave Ritual" (pp.120–25). As the critic Iain Pears has claimed, this might make Holmes the archetypal "Victorian New Man... a meritocrat, living solely off his brains." »

I found that [Holmes] had many acquaintances, and those in the most different classes of society.
Dr. Watson
A Study in Scarlet

In the time of the Holmes stories, the London docklands were thriving. A link between the capital and the far-flung colonies, all kinds of foreign influences entered England through the docks.

so it is perhaps surprising that it is referred to in only a few cases (for example *The Sign of Four* and "The Adventure of the Six Napoleons," pp.188–89). However, Britain's status as the preeminent colonial superpower is the hinge on which many stories turn. Many Britons felt that the Empire had a duty to spread "enlightened values" around the world, just as in the stories Holmes is tasked with defending Britain from insidious foreign influences. Throughout the canon, it is often the "otherness" of strangers from distant territories or curious foreign objects that injects an element of the sinisterly exotic into the orderly imperial metropolis.

For example, characters who originate from, or have lived at some point in, the British colonies frequently have a criminal history, which, when dredged up, shatters all perceived respectability. Convict transportation to Australia figures prominently in "The *Gloria Scott*" (pp.116–19), while the wealthy landowner John Turner's previous

Indeed, Holmes seems to care little about the hierarchical strictures of the society in which he lives. He is no slavish adherent to class deference, concerning himself with the details of a problem, not the individuals involved, explicitly stating in "The Adventure of the Noble Bachelor" (pp.94–5) that "the status of my client is a matter of less moment to me than the interest of his case." This attitude even sees him making jokes at the expense of the upper classes. For example, in "A Scandal in Bohemia" (pp.56–61), he repeatedly undermines the status of his royal client.

Holmes also occasionally shows a tendency toward the progressive. His celebration of the new state-run schools as "Beacons of the future!" reveals his support for a measured and planned type of social reform. This perspective mirrors Conan Doyle's own liberal outlook. The author included a veiled criticism of the Conservative government led by the Marquess of Salisbury in "The Naval Treaty" (pp.138–41). Yet to characterize Holmes

as a model of the burgeoning British middle class would be excessive. He also has a string of louche, patrician attitudes, including an haughty disdain for the "imbecile" policemen he works alongside. His cocaine use and violin playing all fit the mold of dandyish bohemianism, while his famed satisfaction with finding solutions for the pleasure of it (rather than for any attached fee), reflects the contemporary cult of "art for art's sake." It is hardly surprising to learn that *The Sign of Four* was commissioned around the same dinner table as Oscar Wilde's classic novel of *fin de siècle* aestheticism and decadence, *The Picture of Dorian Gray* (1891).

Colonial souvenirs

At the turn of the 19th century, London's riverside East End dockyards were a major point of entry and exit for ships and people from all over the world. Integral to Britain's trade with its overseas empire, the area was also a hotbed of crime and vice of every kind,

London, that great cesspool into which all the loungers and idlers of the Empire are irresistibly drained.
Dr. Watson
A Study in Scarlet

involvement with an Australian criminal gang forms the basis of "The Boscombe Valley Mystery" (pp.70–3). These hidden histories can provide the key to unlocking the secret power plays that bind former colonials: just as John Turner is blackmailed by a tenant who once witnessed his past wrongdoing, in "The *Gloria Scott*", the haggard Hudson has a morbid authority over Victor Trevor due to his role in a mutiny many years before.

Some objects and creatures also symbolize the corruption that lies beyond England's shores. For instance, the swamp adder that is retrieved from Calcutta by Dr. Grimesby Roylott in "The Adventure of the Speckled Band" (pp.84–9) is employed as a murder weapon. Roylott himself also embodies a set of malevolent qualities—principally a proclivity to violence—apparently intensified during his time in India (a stark contrast with Holmes's cool, "English" rationality).

The role of race

On one of the few occasions he does visit London's docklands, Holmes exploits a subtler foreign danger by pretending to contract

> Violence of temper approaching to mania... had, I believe, been intensified by his long residence in the tropics.
> **Helen Stoner**
> **"The Adventure of the Speckled Band"**

"a coolie disease from Sumatra" in "The Adventure of the Dying Detective" (pp.234–35). An island in the Indonesian archipelago, Sumatra had been part of the Dutch empire. "Coolie" originally meant a locally-hired, unskilled Asian labourer, but by the 19th century it had, like villian, become a derogatory term; unlike villain it has almost completely vanished from use in the west today.

More pointed racial language and stereotypes appear elsewhere in the canon. The black boxer Steve Dixie in "The Adventure

of the Three Gables" (pp.272–73) is cruelly derided by Holmes, and specifically for his appearance. The Andaman Islander Tonga in *The Sign of Four*, a "pygmy," is consistently called "little Tonga". Much of the sinister atmosphere in "The Adventure of Wisteria Lodge" (pp.222–25), meanwhile, is derived from the voodoo practices of Aloysius Garcia's Haitian cook. In addition to this broadbrush caricature, the chef is described as "a huge and hideous mulatto, with yellowish features of a pronounced negroid type."

In other stories, black people are often called "devils" or "fiends," language that was not uncommon at the time. The profound but invalid belief in the supremacy of white British culture at that time had even taught people to associate dark skin with inferiority and repellent cultural practices.

However, while Conan Doyle was not particularly concerned with subverting the era's prevailing prejudices, his depiction of race is nuanced. His sympathetic portrait of a mixed-race relationship in "The Yellow Face" (pp.112–13) is a definite rejection of contemporary attitudes. »

Heroism and masculinity

Britain's overseas colonies and territories were once so numerous, and scattered so widely around the globe, that the empire was said to be one "on which the sun never sets." But by the late 19th century, the sun was setting on the very concept of imperialism. It is no wonder that, as a whole world of political and financial power was perched on one small island's precarious authority, anxieties about decline were rife among the British people.

Feminist critics have argued that, against this backdrop, stories such as Conan Doyle's actively

promoted an ideal of heroic, masculine culture to provide a sense of stability in turbulent times. In *The Madwoman in the Attic* (1979), Sandra Gilbert and Susan Gubar pointedly included the "detective story" and the Boys' Own genre in a tradition "from which women have almost always been excluded."

According to this view, Holmes, with his simple virtues of clinical reason and heroic bravery, represents a willful nostalgia for the patriarchal, imperial order, governed by white male rationality.

The male bond

Conan Doyle's use of a detective and a separate narrator (a technique lifted straight from the stories of Edgar Allan Poe) meant that a crime's solution could be slowly unraveled and turned into a story.

It also means that the friendship between detective and narrator had to be sustained at all costs, which explains the convenient death of Watson's wife, Mary Morstan, and the doctor's return to 221B Baker Street, for example. Likewise, any marriage or romantic relationship for Holmes himself would have spelled disaster for the stories.

The fraternal bond between Holmes and Watson has a strong literary heritage, stretching from Robinson Crusoe and Friday, to Tom Sawyer and Huckleberry Finn. This kind of male relationship is often seen in "boys' fiction." Indeed, one of Conan Doyle's literary role models, the British novelist H. Rider Haggard, had Allan Quatermain, the narrator of the high adventure story *King Solomon's Mines* (1885), dedicate the book "To all the big and little boys who read it."

As some critics have pointed out, Robert Baden-Powell's *Scouting for Boys*, published in 1908, set out an imprint of English "manliness" for the 20th century. In his section on "tracking," the British war hero and founder of the Boy Scouts specifically referenced both "The Greek Interpreter" (pp.136–37) and "The Resident Patient" (pp.134–35), and recommended that scout leaders read the tales to their troops.

A man's world

Unlike his brother Mycroft, Sherlock is not a member of one of London's private gentleman's clubs, yet 221B Baker Street often seems to be an equally male-dominated arena— a haven from which troublesome questions about gender roles have been conveniently excised. Yet, for all that, Holmes is, at times, required to think about women.

The attitude of the detective (and his creator) toward females is shifting and contradictory, but largely a product of typical male Victorian thought. Although Holmes does not seem to rate female mental faculties, he often goes out of his way to help women and release them from suspicion. Female characters also tend to occupy a peripheral position in the stories, and are rarely granted much to say, even when a plot turns on their involvement. They most often appear as clients in need of male aid, or as helpless victims of crime.

Holmes is often described by Watson as a pure, emotionless "reasoning machine": in "A Scandal in Bohemia", he remarks that "as a lover he would have placed himself in a false position. He never spoke of the softer passions, save with a gibe and a sneer." Therefore, Irene Adler, the "adventuress" who outsmarts Holmes in that story, had to be a truly exceptional female. Always described by Holmes as "*the* woman," she is bold, quick-witted, and American—free from the "old world" of European social conventions and able to set her own standards.

Apart from Adler, there are a few exceptions to the sidelined female: the proactive Isadora Klein

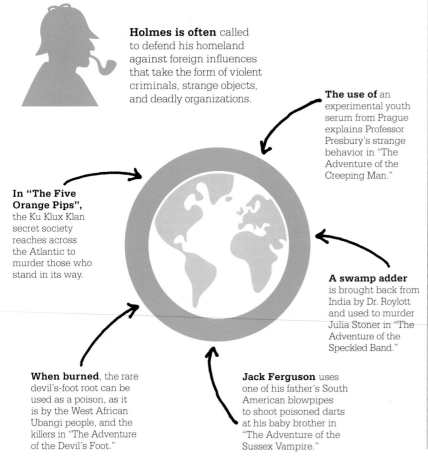

Holmes is often called to defend his homeland against foreign influences that take the form of violent criminals, strange objects, and deadly organizations.

The use of an experimental youth serum from Prague explains Professor Presbury's strange behavior in "The Adventure of the Creeping Man."

In "The Five Orange Pips", the Ku Klux Klan secret society reaches across the Atlantic to murder those who stand in its way.

A swamp adder is brought back from India by Dr. Roylott and used to murder Julia Stoner in "The Adventure of the Speckled Band."

When burned, the rare devil's-foot root can be used as a poison, as it is by the West African Ubangi people, and the killers in "The Adventure of the Devil's Foot."

Jack Ferguson uses one of his father's South American blowpipes to shoot poisoned darts at his baby brother in "The Adventure of the Sussex Vampire."

Conan Doyle was writing at a time when suffragettes were protesting for equal voting rights for women, but the movement was never mentioned in the Holmes stories.

in "The Three Gables" is one; Miss Burnet in "Wisteria Lodge" is another. However, neither of these women are heroic. Klein is a classic femme fatale, while Burnet's dogged pursuit of retribution fulfills the stereotype of the embittered woman.

When women are more active in the Holmes stories, their decisions can be disastrous. Lady Trelawney Hope in "The Second Stain" is both beautiful and reasonable, but it is her interference in matters of state that constitute the story's central crime, and Holmes's intervention is essential in order to bring about a return to peaceful, patriarchal order. Similarly, if Sophy Kratides had not succumbed to the charms of the villainous Harold Latimer in "The Greek Interpreter," her brother might not have been killed.

There are plenty of these less-than-flattering examples of late-Victorian womanhood. Female characters can be hysterical and vindictive, like Sarah Cushing in "The Cardboard Box" (pp.110–11); simple and meek, like Sarah's sister

Women are naturally secretive, and they like to do their own secreting.
Sherlock Holmes
"A Scandal in Bohemia"

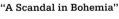

Susan; vengeful and scheming, like Mrs. Gibson in "The Problem of Thor Bridge" (pp.254–57); or icy and aloof, like Violet de Merville in "The Illustrious Client" (pp.266–71).

Given how peripheral female characters are in the canon, it can be easy to forget that the stories were published at a time when women were challenging their lower status. But although there was increasing female education and social mobility, most women remained subordinate. In his way, Conan Doyle helped to highlight this injustice by writing stories such as "The Adventure of the Abbey Grange" (pp.198–201) – which depicts an abusive marriage – in order to illustrate the situations in which women could be trapped.

However, the author's motto, "Steel true, blade straight," was redolent of the "manliness" and "unaffectedness" that he most admired in his fellow men. In his memoir, *Memories and Adventures* (1923), he casually mentions that "it is notorious that though ladies greatly improve the appearance of a feast they usually detract from the quality of the talk." However, he

ascribed this to men changing their conversation in order to suit the situation, rather than any specific foolishness on the part of women— if anything, he meant it as a slight on contemporary social strictures.

A rounded portrait?

In all, it is clear that Conan Doyle's treatment of contemporary class, race, and gender issues is far from straightforward. The social scene he depicts drew on the shifting sands of an increasingly fragmented society. Britain was facing huge upheaval as a result of rapid industrialization, population growth, and urbanization. Conan Doyle's depiction of society reflects this changing world, and suggests a conflict between his own liberal views and the prevailing conservative values of the time.

Although Holmes is white, male, middle-class, and resolutely Victorian, his complexity and contradictions still resonate with a modern audience. The stories remain captivating today, even in a society that would be unrecognizable to their creator. ∎

I HAVE A TURN BOTH FOR OBSERVATION AND FOR DEDUCTION

THE ART OF DEDUCTION

The term "ratiocination" is often used to describe the methodology employed by Sherlock Holmes in his work as a consulting detective. Derived from the Latin *ratiocinari*—"to calculate or deliberate"—it follows a process of step-by-step reasoning that begins with observation and the collection of evidence available, leading to an informed deduction and, therefore, a logical conclusion.

According to the Oxford English Dictionary, the term "ratiocination" was first used in Western Europe, which saw the birth of rationalism, a philosophy, which holds that reason is the main source and test of knowledge, rather than experience or divine revelation. Holmes is a direct descendant of this tradition, using his powers of rational, reasoned observation and deduction to help his clients and solve the many crimes that the police—who are hampered by the constraints of standard "procedures"—often find baffling.

The influence of Aristotle

However, the roots of ratiocination lie much farther back in history, originating in the writings of the ancient Greek philosopher and natural scientist Aristotle (384–322 BCE). A pupil of Plato, Aristotle soon rejected the central tenets of Platonic thought (which held that the observed or natural world was a mere approximation of an ideal, ethereal world), and promoted the science of reaching

Aristotle, depicted here in this Roman marble bust based on a Greek original, identified logic for the first time as a separate discipline and can be called the founder of ratiocination.

conclusions (often theoretical ones) simply by observing the characteristics of the natural world.

Aristotle applied his research across a broad spectrum of topics, from physics, mathematics, astronomy, botany, and biology to ethics, the arts, and even politics. He effectively created the first coherent system of Western philosophical thought, turning each of these subjects into academic "disciplines" in their own right. Underlying Aristotle's approach was the importance of logic, based on reasoning and derived from observation, physical evidence, empirical experiment, and general knowledge—in short, ratiocination.

The deductive and empirical process that Aristotle outlined later became central to the scientific studies of the English Franciscan friar Roger Bacon (1214–*c.* 1292), as well as a host of other so-called "natural philosophers" over the subsequent centuries. Observation of natural phenomena, often down to its minutiae, lay at the heart of almost all their investigations. Many were aided by contemporary inventions such as the magnifying glass, the thermometer, the telescope, and

Forms of reasoning

Deduction
Often found in classic detective fiction and requiring **incontrovertible** facts, this formulaic type of reasoning involves the following argument: if the **premises** are true, then the **conclusion** must also be true.

Induction
Induction is a form of reasoning based on **assumptions** and commonly utilized by Watson and the police in the Holmes stories. It requires a **conclusion** to follow from a premise with **probability** only, rather than necessity.

Abduction
Also called an "argument to the best explanation," abduction is a **form of reasoning** often used by Holmes when faced with a **variety of explanations** for a particular occurrence. As shown below, he uses the method of abduction to help him decide which explanation **best fits the evidence**.

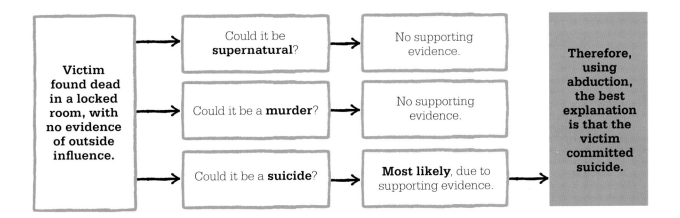

Victim found dead in a locked room, with no evidence of outside influence.

Could it be **supernatural**? → No supporting evidence.

Could it be a **murder**? → No supporting evidence.

Could it be a **suicide**? → **Most likely**, due to supporting evidence.

Therefore, using abduction, the best explanation is that the victim committed suicide.

---

the microscope, all of which permitted them to delve ever deeper into their respective observations and discoveries; Holmes also uses these tools.

The science of deduction
By the time Conan Doyle began writing the Holmes stories in the 1880s, Aristotelian thought and the philosopher's demonstrations of empirical logic had become central to most educational and scientific systems in Western culture. Ratiocination defines Holmes's principal approach to a problem—that is, deduction based on the evidence available;

however, Holmes also uses variants of detection and logical thought that often place him several steps ahead of the regular, plodding, do-it-by-the-book police investigators.

"Inductive" reasoning, for example, is a technique used in mathematics and chemistry (in which Holmes was trained), whereby a theoretical inference might be reached based purely upon the particular circumstances of an experiment or situation that itself stands outside "received" knowledge. While Holmes does take this approach, it is also often colored by his perception of the protagonists involved. In *The Valley*

of *Fear* (pp.212–21), for example, Holmes finally reduces the mystery to an inevitable conclusion through a process of weighing up possible solutions alongside his perception of the protagonists' characters.

However, more often Holmes uses "abductive" reasoning—quite literally the removal of a person or, in Holmes's case, an idea, from the potential scenario of a crime, thereby leaving the theoretical question "What if…?". He uses this to good effect in "The Man with the Twisted Lip" (pp.80–1), when he "abducts" that Neville St. Clair, who has apparently disappeared, in fact never left the room that he was »

"DUPIN STEPPED TO THE CARD-RACK AND TOOK THE LETTER."

Edgar Allan Poe, whose fictional detective Dupin is shown here in this illustration from "The Purloined Letter" (1844), was an early proponent of ratiocination in his stories.

and often projecting himself into the mind of the criminal before reaching a damning conclusion. Subsequent writers, such as Wilkie Collins and even Charles Dickens, picked up on this theme, although not with the ferocious enthusiasm of Conan Doyle who, through the character of Holmes, strengthened the concept of ratiocination in his absolute reduction of logic to an essential conclusion.

A well-stocked brain attic

Conan Doyle's presentation of his detective as a fundamentally scientific individual and a pioneer of forensic crime-solving methods (Watson first meets Holmes when the latter is a medical research chemist at St. Bartholomew's Hospital in London) is telling—it is a scenario that provides the key to most of the Holmes mysteries.

However, in the first Holmes novel, *A Study in Scarlet* (pp.36–45), Conan Doyle sets some interesting limitations on the great intellectual powers of his eccentric and brilliant sleuth. As he gets to know his enigmatic new companion, Watson notes that Holmes is astonishingly selective in what he chooses to learn: he knows nothing about literature, philosophy, astronomy, or politics, yet has a deep understanding of chemistry, an encyclopedic knowledge of "sensational literature" (accounts of criminal cases), and a "practical knowledge" of British law. Holmes brushes this implied criticism aside, stating that he is only interested in that which will prove useful to him in his work. "I consider that a man's

last seen entering. All that is found in the room are his clothes and an old beggar man. In asking the question, "What if he never left?" Holmes can abduct that the beggar man is, in fact, St. Clair in disguise.

The deployment of the method of ratiocination in crime-solving was not invented by Conan Doyle— he was building on a fictional tradition that originated in the

"murder mystery" tales created by the American writer Edgar Allan Poe (1809–1849), whose interests stretched from contemporary science to cryptanalysis (the study of ciphers)and the supernatural. Poe published a trio of short stories featuring the detective C Auguste Dupin. In all three tales, Dupin uses the devices of ratiocination to solve murders, observing the evidence

brain originally is like a little empty attic, and you have to stock it with such furniture as you choose," he tells Watson. He is careful to fill his own "brain attic" with facts and information that he can draw on to make his deductions and solve cases—at the expense of other things he considers superfluous, even fundamental truths about science and the universe. "There comes a time when for every addition of knowledge you forget something you knew before," Holmes explains.

"The observance of trifles"
Further revelations about Holmes's methodology are gradually revealed over the ensuing 40 years, in the stories that follow *A Study in Scarlet*. Conan Doyle focuses on the small, detailed, but outstanding and often overlooked features of a crime, which provide Holmes with the key to many apparently unsolvable riddles, much to the astonishment of Watson. It is not only cold, hard logic but also Holmes's highly developed eye for detail that enables him to solve crimes: "I can never bring you to realize the importance of sleeves,

In questions of science, the authority of a thousand is not worth the humble reasoning of a single individual.
Galileo Galilei
(1564–1642)

the suggestiveness of thumb-nails, or the great issues that may hang from a bootlace," he remarks in "A Case of Identity" (pp.68–9).

Equally significant is Holmes's shrewd, encyclopedic knowledge of seemingly arcane data: the impressions left by a carriage, bicycle tires, or footprints; the myriad types of tobacco ash found at a scene in an era when almost every man smoked; the tiny clues offered up by dirt and dust particles—all of which provide extra information for him when solving cases. Holmes

regularly consults his obsessively compiled "great book," into which he pastes daily clippings of the agony columns (personal advertisements) of popular newspapers. These were often used as a means of disguised or coded communication and, according to Holmes, were "the most valuable hunting ground that ever was given to the student of the unusual."

A lasting impact
The Holmes stories incorporate several historic developments: a flood of new research was rapidly entering into everyday life and the popular consciousness—which the detective eagerly exploits— while police practices were also gradually becoming more scientific and rigorous. An entirely new way of looking at the human personality, psychoanalysis, was also becoming popular, although it is difficult to prove the extent to which Sigmund Freud's work influenced Conan Doyle's writing. However, it was with Holmes's methods of deduction that Conan Doyle introduced a new scientific rigor to the mystery story that would impact crime writing for over a century to come. ∎

Darwin and ratiocination

Charles Darwin's groundbreaking book *On the Origin of Species* (1859), perhaps the most influential scientific treatise of the 19th century, used ratiocination to devastating effect. In this detailed publication, Darwin (1809–1882) propounded his concepts of a theory of natural selection, the "survival of the fittest," and from there to his general theory of evolution. A prime example of Aristotelian logic and deduction, the work sparked global debate and sold out on publication day.

Many of Darwin's crucial premises were derived from seemingly arcane and very small clues—accumulated over many years from his studies of fossils, geology, and animal and bird behavior. His conclusions often flew in the face of received knowledge, tradition, and prejudice. In Conan Doyle's Sherlock Holmes stories, the great detective stands squarely within this tradition, although he has to move quickly to track down the perpetrators of crime.

THERE IS NOTHING LIKE FIRST-HAND EVIDENCE

CRIMINOLOGY AND FORENSIC SCIENCE

Criminology and forensic science as we know them emerged in the 19th century, and had become well-established in criminal investigations by the turn of the 20th century. However, their origins lay in the 18th century, when there was great scientific progress in the fields of chemistry, physics, botany, zoology, geology, and anatomy. This increase in scientific knowledge led to a more rational, non-speculative, evidence-based approach to solving crimes, and opened up a wider field of possibilities for the police. Conan Doyle made Sherlock Holmes a pioneer of forensic analysis and the use of reasoning, and as a detective working in the 19th century he was in many ways ahead of his time.

The main contributors to the development of criminology as a science were German psychologist and neuroanatomist Franz Josef Gall (1758–1828) and the Italian

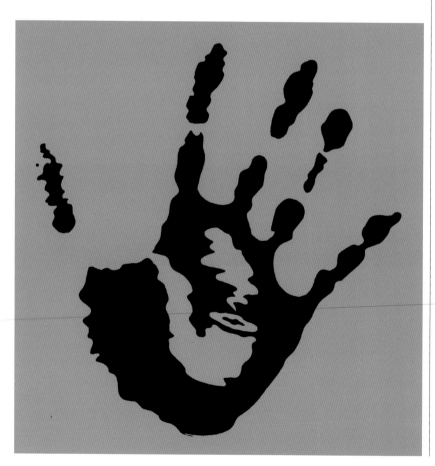

Reformer and politician Sir Robert Peel (1788–1850) created the first British police force. The policemen were called peelers or bobbies (after Peel's nickname "Bob"), a term still in use today.

The Watch House in London's Covent Garden was built in 1729. In 1829, the newly formed Metropolitan Police took it over as headquarters of F Division, controlled by Superintendent Thomas.

consultation with Vidocq. It would be many years later that the burgeoning population of the US saw the creation of the Bureau of Investigation in 1908 and its cross-state federal remit, the Federal Bureau of Investigation (FBI), which was introduced in 1935 under its first director, J. Edgar Hoover. The aim of these policing institutions was to centralize information-gathering and intelligence distribution on a national and even transnational basis. The International Criminal Police Organization (Interpol) was another French innovation, created in 1923 to share and disseminate information around the world.

In addition to a new style of policing, a different dimension of detection and crime resolution became necessary, using a range of new techniques and methodologies. The principal steps forward in this area during the 19th century (of which Conan Doyle was well aware) fell into three main categories: the gathering of intelligence, especially concerning the activities of the »

sociologists Cesare Beccaria (1738–1794) and Cesare Lombroso (1835–1909). Beccaria published *On Crimes and Punishments* (1764), in which he argued that crime was an endemic trait of human nature; Lombroso rejected this idea, claiming that psychological, social, and inherited conditions predisposed a person toward criminal tendencies.

Urban expansion and crime
Rapid population growth and urbanization at the end of the 18th century—especially in London, Manchester, Liverpool, Edinburgh, and Glasgow, as well as many other industrial cities across Europe (particularly Paris)—presented new social challenges. Urban expansion created dense populations within which crimes could be concealed easily and criminals could move around unnoticed in the crowds. This meant that policing, crime control, and solving or resolving

criminal cases of forgery, assault, burglary, homicide, and organized gang crime became pressing issues. Previously, crimes had been dealt with on a largely local basis, within small communities, based on local knowledge and relatively simple information-gathering. However, this often involved rumor, hearsay, or prejudice—hence, in part, the so-called "witch trials" of the 16th and 17th centuries, in which local scores were settled by invidious accusations.

The first professional police forces set up to investigate crimes came into existence in the early 19th century. In 1812, Eugène François Vidocq (see p.317), a former criminal, established the *Sûreté Nationale* in Paris; it was a modest but ambitious operation that recruited other reformed criminals to its staff. In 1829, Robert Peel set up the Metropolitan Police Service, based at Scotland Yard in Whitehall, London, in

> Police are the public and the public are the police.
Sir Robert Peel
"Principles of Policing" (1829)

"underground" classes; the collection and collation of details and characteristics of criminal "types" (phrenology and anthropometry); and the scientific analysis of forensic material gathered at the scene of the crime—unique datasets such as fingerprints, photographic files, and traces of blood types. A fourth important element was the development of a range of new infrastructure systems: the popular press, railroads, an efficient postal service, and high-speed communications, especially the telegraph—all of which Holmes exploits extensively in solving the enigmas that confront him.

Intelligence-gathering

Since the late 16th and early 17th centuries, the accumulation of evidence against "suspects" was largely a matter driven by concerns of national security, especially in non-Catholic Reformist countries, worried by the threat of Catholic subversion—for instance, when there were plots in England to assassinate Queen Elizabeth I (the Babington Plot, 1585) and blow up Parliament and King James I

By the aid of phrenology, we have obtained a tolerably clear view... of the mind.
George Combe
Constitution of Man **(1828)**

(the Gunpowder Plot, 1605). This perceived danger led to a culture of "observation" and the incipient invasion of personal privacy. The system also relied on the interception of messages, and blackmailing and torturing possible suspects or their associates. Other countries, including Spain, France, Russia, the Habsburg Empire, and other European states, developed "secret police" forces whose sole purpose was information-gathering.

By the beginning of the 19th century, police forces across Europe had become extremely adept at compiling damning dossiers on

thousands of individuals deemed suspicious for one reason or another. Franz Kafka's novel *The Trial* (1925) is just one example of many that exemplify the sense of paranoia created by the state's intrusion on personal liberty and privacy. On the other hand, the collection and collation of information from a wide variety of sources has undoubtedly prevented a huge number of criminal acts. Holmes sits somewhere in the middle of this conundrum: while preferring to rely on his personal observations, he equally does not eschew using intelligence and information from international police forces to help in his investigations.

The practice of phrenology

The classification of human "types" based on class, social background, and physical characteristics—founded on supposedly scientific methods dating back to the ancient Greek scientist Galen—began with the development of phrenology (p.188) in Germany in the early 19th century. Franz Josef Gall claimed that the size and shape of the skull revealed the intelligence, personality, and moral faculties of the subject, and would

Jack the Ripper

In 1888, London was shocked by the brutal serial murders of at least five East End prostitutes. Although forensic evidence was collected and examined, the techniques available to Scotland Yard at this time were basic, and forensic investigation was not an established procedure, so they focused on identifying and interviewing a large number of suspects. Police surgeon Dr. Thomas Bond used his knowledge of the victim autopsies to create one of the

earliest "criminal profiles" of the murderer. Scotland Yard was reluctant to share details of its investigations with the press, since it was afraid of revealing its methods to the murderer himself. Faced with a lack of information, journalists resorted to sensationalized, speculative reports, and criticized the methods of the police force. This critical press, coupled with the unsolved murders, had a negative impact on the reputation of Scotland Yard. The murders remain unsolved to this day, but there are many theories as to the killer's identity.

A phrenologist is seen here trying to assess a boy's future by measuring the bumps on his head. Although not based on fact, this practice became popular in the early 19th century.

therefore be useful in categorizing criminal types. Gall also produced "brain maps," which divided the brain into 27 "organs" ranging from areas responsible for the sense of taste and smell to those provoking criminal urges.

These brain maps proved hugely popular, and by 1820 the Edinburgh Phrenological Society was set up by one of Gall's disciples, George Combe, and his physician brother Andrew. Although the society was disbanded in 1870, the museum remained open until 1886. Conan Doyle would have been aware of the Society's work and would probably have visited while he was studying medicine in Edinburgh. He incorporated these "criminal traits" in many of his male villains, describing them as being huge, bearded, and swarthy with a low brow—for example in "The Adventure of the Six Napoleons" (pp.188–89), "The Adventure of the Blue Carbuncle" (pp.82–3), and "The Adventure of the Speckled Band" (pp.84–9).

This dubious pseudoscience persisted for well over a century, and was used to provide simplistic evaluations of racial hegemony. The Nazis were enthusiastic phrenologists, and SS commander Heinrich Himmler (1900–1945) amassed a collection of skulls that he used to demonstrate his arguments concerning racial superiority and criminality.

Anthropometry

The basic tenets of phrenology were taken several steps further by the French criminologist Alphonse

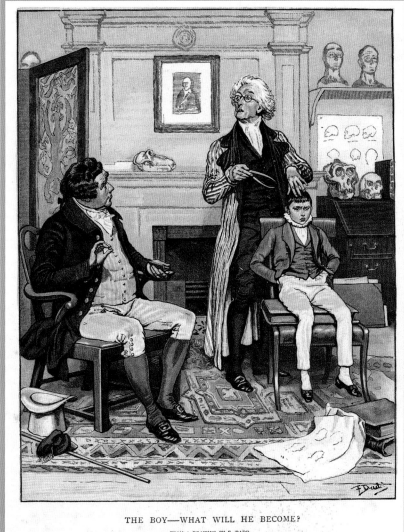

THE BOY—WHAT WILL HE BECOME?
FROM A DRAWING BY F. DADD.

Bertillon (1853–1914), who developed the "science" of anthropometry. Bertillon carefully measured anatomical details (length of the neck, arms, legs, feet, and so on), of known or suspected criminals, subjecting them to humiliating physical analysis. His victims were also photographed—mainly at the time to analyze rather than to record their facial features, although this later formed the basis of the "mugshot" archives central to criminal archives today.

Handwriting analysis

Bertillon also developed another specialty—handwriting analysis. Started by French priest Jean-Hippolyte Michon, the "science" of graphology (p.127) was based on the theory that a person's handwriting is unique and reflects a range of underlying psychological characteristics. However, handwriting can be imitated and forged, faked or misidentified, so handwriting analysis is not reliable and has since been discredited. »

The use of photography to record known criminals dates back to the 1840s. In 1871, a law was passed in the UK requiring that anyone arrested for a crime must be photographed.

as criminal records, mugshots, and fingerprints was still in its infancy, although he included them in his works—for instance, the use of fingerprinting to help solve the mystery in "The Adventure of the Norwood Builder" (pp.168–69). The problem of how this information would be managed and disseminated, however, was a challenge for the future.

Blood typing
The classifying of blood samples into types A, B, and O was first codified by Austrian biologist Karl Landsteiner (1868–1943) in 1900, but research in the area began in the 1870s. Identification of the fourth blood type, AB, was published in 1902. Conan Doyle would have been aware of these advances in forensic analysis, which served as narrative inspiration. For example, in the first Holmes tale, *A Study in Scarlet* (pp.36–45), Holmes declares to Watson that he has successfully invented "the Sherlock Holmes' test"—an "infallible test for blood stains," old or new, which can result

Why, man, it is the most practical medico-legal discovery for years.
Sherlock Holmes
A Study in Scarlet

In an infamous case of 1894, Alfred Dreyfus, a French artillery officer of Jewish descent, was incorrectly convicted of treason. Bertillon's identification of his handwriting was used as critical evidence in his conviction. Dreyfus was not exonerated until 1906.

Holmes is an expert at analyzing handwriting, as seen in "The Reigate Squire" (pp.126–31), in which he identifies the murderers from a handwritten note. At the time of its publication (1893), graphology was little known in Britain, and for many readers this would have been the first they had heard of it.

Fingerprints and datasets
One accurate early method of crime scene investigation (CSI) was the recognition of the unique genetic quality of fingerprints. In 1892,

Argentinian police officer Juan Vucetich proved the guilt of a murderer from the bloody hand stains she had left at the scene of a murder that irrefutably confirmed her presence at the crime scene. The idea was taken up by various police agencies, such as in Calcutta, India, where the first fingerprint-recording bureau was set up in 1897 by Sir Edward Richard Henry. Although fingerprint recording for identification was rejected at first by London's Metropolitan Police in 1886, the system was adopted by the New York Civil Service Commission in 1901 and, within a decade, had become recognized internationally as an essential tool in criminal identification and detection.

At the time that Conan Doyle began writing the Holmes stories, the accumulation of datasets such

Dr. Hawley Harvey Crippen

The notorious case of wife-murderer Dr. Crippen combined a number of factors worthy of Holmes's ingenuity. Dr. Crippen, an American homeopath, lived in London with his wife, Cora, but in 1908 began an affair with Ethel Le Neve. In January 1910, Cora disappeared, and in July Crippen and his lover fled, boarding a boat to Canada. Scotland Yard's Inspector Dew ordered a further look at Crippen's home, and human remains were found under the basement floor. Pathologist Bernard Spilsbury found traces of the toxic drug hyoscine in the remains, and identified some scar tissue as being consistent with an operation that Cora had undergone. Crippen and Ethel were arrested on arrival in Canada. Crippen was tried, found guilty, and hanged, while Ethel was acquitted. Forensic pathology played a key role in Crippen's conviction. However, further DNA tests made a century on have confirmed that the remains were not Cora Crippen's, and were of a male. His identity, whether Crippen killed him, and what happened to Cora, remain a mystery.

in identification of the criminal. The significance of this test is immense, as he tells a bewildered Watson. "Had this test been invented, there are hundreds of men now walking the earth who would long ago have paid the penalty of their crimes."

Forensic pathology

The science of forensic pathology (determining the cause of death by studying a corpse) was clearly of interest to Conan Doyle. It was a rapidly developing science. The practitioners at the turn of the 19th century were usually referred to as "medical examiners" or "police surgeons." During Conan Doyle's (and Holmes's) career there were a number of high-profile cases in Britain that involved the work of forensic pathologists, such as Sir Bernard Spilsbury (1877–1947), whose work and analysis brought many notorious murderers to the gallows, including Dr. Hawley Harvey Crippen.

Britain's foremost forensic scientist and pioneering pathologist Sir Bernard Spilsbury performed thousands of autopsies on both murder victims and criminals.

A taste for crime

From the beginning of the 19th century, there was a newsprint-buying public baying for sensational details of crimes. Conan Doyle not only fed this appetite, but also built on sociological theories such as those propounded by Gall, Beccaria, Lombroso, and others concerning the causes of crime. Conan Doyle was, after all, a doctor, and well aware of scholarly medical publications. He wrote the Holmes tales during a fascinating and rapidly developing period in criminology, which bridged the gap between the speculative and the scientifically based forensic pathology. As well as having a highly logical, analytical mind, Conan Doyle's awareness of many theories and discoveries allowed him to keep ahead of the public's knowledge, enabling him to constantly astound his audience with Holmes's ingenuity. ∎

YOU KNOW MY METHODS. APPLY THEM

CRIME WRITING AND DETECTIVE FICTION

Villains have always existed in literature, appearing in the works of Homer and the Bible to Chaucer, Shakespeare, and beyond. Yet until relatively recently, it was either natural justice or fate that determined the villain's eventual downfall—detectives, like Holmes, simply did not exist.

The origins of crime fiction

In the late 18th century, most European novels fell into two groups: social comedies and Gothic romances. It was from the latter genre that crime fiction eventually emerged. Early proponents of the form included the Marquis de Sade (1740–1814), who portrayed vicious criminals in the 1780s and 1790s with considerable relish, while Matthew Lewis wrote populist Gothic mysteries, such as *The Monk* (1796). Some novels, such as Pierre Choderlos de Laclos's *Les Liaisons Dangereuses* (1782), even crossed the boundaries between these two categories. But while criminal activity features in all of these stories, there are no detectives to solve the crimes.

However, in the first half of the 19th century, crime writing began to move in a different direction. The US poet, critic, and novelist

It is, I admit, mere imagination, but how often is imagination the mother of truth?
Sherlock Holmes
The Valley of Fear

Jean-Pierre Fossard, regarded as one of the great Parisian criminals, was captured by Eugène François Vidocq on December 31, 1813, while he was in charge of the *Sûreté Nationale*.

Edgar Allan Poe (1809–1849) and his French contemporaries Honoré de Balzac (1799–1850), Victor Hugo (1802–1885), Alexandre Dumas (1802–1870), and Émile Gaboriau (1832–1873) defined the concept of the dogged detective and criminologist within their stories, establishing the crime writing style for which Conan Doyle would later become famous.

By the mid- to late 19th century, naturalist writers—who believed that both genes and social factors determined personality—were examining the criminal condition. Notable works include the French author Émile Zola's novel about the eponymous domestic murderess *Thérèse Raquin* (1867) and Russian novelist Fyodor Dostoyevsky's *Crime and Punishment* (1866), which explored the mind of a psychopath.

Twenty years later, Conan Doyle invented Holmes, who arguably has had the greatest long-term impact and influence.

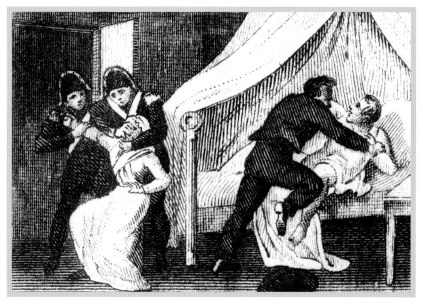

Holmes's predecessors

In some ways, the roots of crime fiction started with the real-life career of one notorious Frenchman, Eugène François Vidocq. A direct inspiration for many French writers, from Balzac to Gaboriau, Vidocq was a petty criminal and spy who later channeled his skills in a lawful way when he established the secret *Sûreté Nationale* in Paris. In fact, Balzac became Vidocq's close friend, using him as a model for the detectives in his novels, such as *Le Père Goriot* (1835), *Illusions perdues* (1837), and *La Cousine Bette* (1846). Balzac's most famous detective was Jacques Collin, often known by his alias Vautrin. Dumas also worked elements of Vidocq's activities into *Les Mohicans de Paris* (1854) in the form of the fictional Monsieur Jackal. And in *Les Misérables* (1862), Hugo based aspects of characters—like both the »

Eugène François Vidocq

Born in Arras, France, to a middle-class family, Eugène François Vidocq (1775–1857) turned to crime as a teenager. He fought as a French soldier in several battles, where he killed at least two opponents. After a spell in prison for crimes that included forgery and assault, he became involved in spying.

Vidocq then transformed himself. Towards the end of 1811, he decided to use his experience of the criminal world to help the French authorities, establishing *Sûreté Nationale*, within the Prefecture of Police in Paris.

Controversially, he recruited former lawbreakers, and even encouraged his agents to foster their contacts in the criminal underworld. He later resigned from the *Sûreté* and, in 1832, he founded the first private detective agency, *Le Bureau des Renseignements*. Vidocq was one of the first professional "criminologists," combining his intelligence-gathering skills with forensic methods. He even kept card indexes of known criminals and how they operated, thereby creating an early version of a crime database.

Charles Dickens (1812–1870) was the most popular writer in Victorian England, and a master of suspense. Like many authors of the period, he wrote novels for serialization in magazines.

the development of the genre that was to become one of the most important strands in popular publishing.

British crime mysteries

The first major British crime fiction writer was Wilkie Collins (1824–1889), who wrote *The Woman in White* (1860) and *The Moonstone* (1868), which were published around two decades before Conan Doyle introduced Holmes. Today, they remain superb examples of mysteries and conspiracies unravelled by inventive detection. Like many novels of the period, these were first published in serial form.

The giant of the English serial novel, Charles Dickens (1812–1870) also experimented with mystery stories, drawing elements of the developing genre into his novels such as *Oliver Twist* (1838) and *Our Mutual Friend* (1865). Two of his most notable detective stories were *Bleak House* (1853), with Inspector Bucket, and *The Mystery of Edwin Drood* (1870)—which remained unfinished at his death—featuring an early amateur private detective, Dick Datchery.

Writing around the same time was Irish author Joseph Sheridan Le Fanu (1814–1873), who created Gothic mystery novels featuring magic and the supernatural. But he also wrote novels that contained elements of a classic detective mystery, including *Wylder's Hand* (1864), *The Wyvern Mystery* (1869), and *In a Glass Darkly* (1872), which purported to be the memoirs of an "occult" detective, Dr. Hesselius.

reformed criminal Jean Valjean and the relentless police inspector Javert who was pursuing him—on Vidocq's astonishing career, which by then had been widely celebrated—however unreliably—in print and on stage. Émile Gaboriau even wrote about Vidocq's adventures in popular novels including his Monsieur Lecoq series, published from 1866.

Vidocq's fame also spread to the US, and Poe was apparently inspired by the French celebrity when he wrote what many believe to be the first pure detective story. Poe also used the terms "detection" and "ratiocination" (pp.306–09) to describe the methods of his fictional detective C. Auguste Dupin—lateral thinking being a key feature of his crime solving. Indeed, Conan Doyle acknowledged that Poe's stories were a model for later crime fiction, saying that three stories involving Dupin in particular provided "a root from which a whole literature has developed." The first of these tales, "The Murders in the Rue Morgue" (1841) is a model of the "locked room"

mystery, in which a crime—usually murder—is committed under seemingly impossible conditions. In the second tale, "The Mystery of Marie Roget" (1842), which is based on an actual murder case in New York, Dupin has to reconstruct the last days of a mysterious victim's life. The third story called "The Purloined Letter" (1844) combines a psychological duel between the detective and a blackmailer with the "hidden in plain sight" problem. Most of these foreign writers were read in Britain and influenced

Where was the detective story until Poe breathed the breath of life into it?
Arthur Conan Doyle
Poe Centennial Dinner (1909)

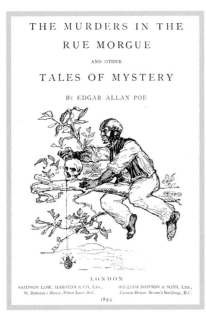

Edgar Allan Poe's 1841 story "The Murders in the Rue Morgue" was later published in this 1893 collection that included "The Mystery of Marie Roget".

The arrival of Holmes

In 1887, Conan Doyle published his first Holmes story, *A Study in Scarlet* (pp.36–45). In this novel, he included forensics (pp.310–15), detailed crime scene investigation, and careful character analysis. Once established as a key character in the *Strand* series, Holmes became a hit with an increasingly literate and enthusiastic reading public. It was therefore understandable that Conan Doyle's decision to kill off his greatest fictional creation in 1893 met with public uproar. It seems that Conan Doyle had not realized the intense appeal of his stories. But even without Holmes, popular crime fiction was here to stay, and would continue well into the 20th and 21st century in its many permutations.

Holmes's contemporaries

Apart from Holmes, there were other fictional detectives at this time who proved to be popular.

The English detective Sexton Blake, described as the "poor man's Sherlock Holmes," was one of these. The first Blake adventures were syndicated in newspapers and magazines from 1893, and penned by a variety of authors. The first was "The Missing Millionaire", by Harry Blyth. Like Holmes, Blake lived in Baker Street and had a tolerant landlady. Continuing until 1978 and adapted for stage, radio, and TV, there were over 4,000 Blake stories.

Another contemporary in crime fiction was G.K. Chesterton (1874–1936) who, in addition to writing the brilliant but murky police vs. anarchists thriller *The Man Who Was Thursday* (1908), created the unassuming Catholic ecclesiastical detective Father Brown. Brown solves problems using similar methods to Holmes, although, as a priest, he draws on his knowledge of the human

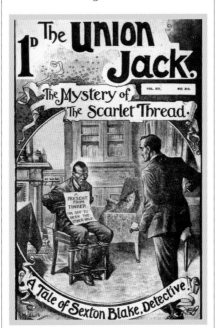

Nicknamed "Penny Dreadful," "The Union Jack" described itself as a "Library of high class fiction," and serialized many tales. This cover from 1900 features detective Sexton Blake.

All men thirst to confess their crimes more than tired beasts thirst for water.
G.K. Chesterton
The Illustrated London News (1908)

condition through hearing confessions. Across five volumes of short stories written from 1911 to 1935, Brown became a staple of the British crime fiction diet.

There were other fine writers who wrote under the long shadow of Holmes. Conan Doyle's brother-in-law, E.W. Hornung, introduced the gentleman thief/hero Raffles in *The Amateur Cracksman* (1899), and E.F. Bentley wrote the popular detective murder mystery *Trent's Last Case* (1913), in which his gentleman detective Philip Trent falls in love with one of the suspects and comes to a number of incorrect conclusions.

Crime-writing subgenres

Around the beginning of the 20th century, crime fiction could be divided into three main subgenres. There were stories about sleuths—as embodied by Holmes; pulp-crime fiction; and spy thrillers, often involving conspiracies (p.320). There was a huge dividing line between the type of detective mystery that Conan Doyle espoused, and what later became the more popular strands of sensationalist cliff-hangers typified by the latter two styles. »

The British "Golden Age"

The period between the two World Wars became known as the "Golden Age" of detective fiction. Modelled on the Holmes tales, stories from this era tend to take the form of classic murder mysteries, or "whodunits," featuring amateur detectives outsmarting the police, often in British upper-class settings. Agatha Christie (see right) was undoubtedly the most successful and well-known "Golden Age" author, but there were many others.

These included Dorothy L. Sayers with her Lord Peter Wimsey stories, the first being *Whose Body* (1923); Margery Allingham's Albert Campion tales, which began with *The Crime at Black Dudley* (1929); Ngaio Marsh's Inspector Alleyn mysteries, such as *A Man Lay Dead* (1934); and Leslie Charteris's Simon Templar stories, which were later made into a popular film and TV series, *The Saint*. Introduced in 1928, Templar was an amateur detective/knight living slightly outside the law, with an instinct for detection and righteousness.

Very few detective stories baffle me nowadays, but Mr. Carr's always do.
Agatha Christie
Crime writer (1890–1976)

John Dickson Carr (1906–1977) was another writer of detective fiction. Although American, he set most of his novels in England, where he lived for many years, so his works are often categorized as British crime fiction. His detectives include the decadent and charming but untidy Dr. Gideon Fell (possibly based on G. K. Chesterton), and the aristocratic Sir Henry Merrivale. *The Hollow Man* (1935), which was called *The Three Coffins* in the US, includes a chapter-long textbook lecture by Fell about his methodology for solving apparently impossible crimes. Carr also wrote an early biography of Conan Doyle.

Edgar Wallace (1875–1932), the highly prolific English writer—who also spent time in the US as a successful screenwriter—created a crime-writing phenomenon almost single-handedly. At his height, in the 1920s, he was selling more than a million books per year. His main works include *The Four Just Men* (1905), *The Green Archer* (1923), and the J.G. Reeder stories (collected in 1925).

The detective fiction queen

The queen of 20th-century detective fiction was Agatha Christie (1890–1976). She is rated as the world's best-selling novelist, with her sales ranking just behind the Bible and Shakespeare, and her books have been translated into 103 languages. Despite her high social status, her work was "middle brow," and therefore she could appeal to the general public across the world. During a long career, she published

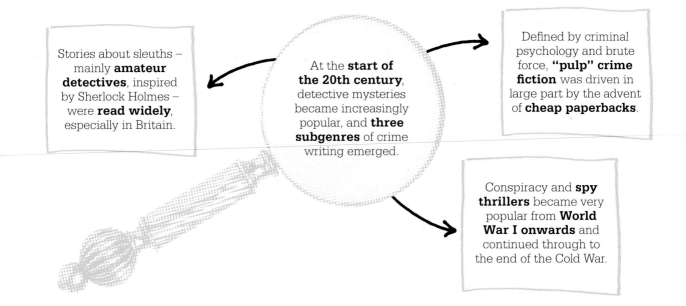

Stories about sleuths – mainly **amateur detectives**, inspired by Sherlock Holmes – were **read widely**, especially in Britain.

At the **start of the 20th century**, detective mysteries became increasingly popular, and **three subgenres** of crime writing emerged.

Defined by criminal psychology and brute force, **"pulp" crime fiction** was driven in large part by the advent of **cheap paperbacks**.

Conspiracy and **spy thrillers** became very popular from **World War I onwards** and continued through to the end of the Cold War.

The Strand Magazine ran from 1891 to 1950, serializing many writers' works. This cover from 1935 features Agatha Christie's Belgian detective Hercule Poirot in "The Crime in Cabin 66."

66 detective novels and 14 short stories, while also creating the world's longest-running play, *The Mousetrap* (1952). Other noteworthy books include *The Murder of Roger Ackroyd* (1926), which has been regularly nominated as the best crime novel ever written by The Crime Writers' Association, while *And Then There Were None* (1939) has sold over 100 million copies.

Christie had an inventive mind and created two main detectives: the Holmes-like Belgian former professional detective, Hercule Poirot, and the amateur yet brilliant observer of human nature, Miss Jane Marple. Both detectives used an acute psychological analysis of the protagonists in each story, linked with a close observation of the available and often overlooked details of apparently insignificant evidence—a lesson learned from Holmes. Poirot was first seen in *The Mysterious Affair at Styles* (1920), which also launched Christie's career, and he went on to feature in 33 novels. Marple debuted in a short story in 1926, "The Tuesday Night Club," and in novel form in *The Murder at the Vicarage* in 1930. She appeared in 11 further novels and more than 20 short stories. Like Chesterton's Father Brown, she is a retiring and contemplative character who modestly delves her way into each mystery. Both Poirot and Marple feature in numerous films played by a variety of actors.

The "Golden Age" in the US

S.S. Van Dine's (a pseudonym of Willard Huntingdon Wright, 1888–1939) aesthete and sleuth Philo Vance was among the first true champions in the US of the Holmesian approach to solving crimes. Van Dine introduced Vance after writing an exhaustive study of the genre, which led to *The Benson Murder Case* (1926) and 11 other masterful detective novels.

Cousins Frederic Dannay (1905–1982) and Manfred Bennington Lee (1905–1971)—both aliases—invented Ellery Queen. A gifted investigator, and often presented as the "author" of his books, Queen was very popular after the publication of the first novel, *The Roman Hat Mystery* (1929). Today, Queen has become a brand, appearing as a character in magazines, and theatrical, TV, and film adaptations.

However, the clearest inheritor of Holmes's cloak and deerstalker in the US is Rex Stout's clever but sedentary detective, Nero Wolfe (p.322). »

Nero Wolfe

One of the most improbable successors to the Holmes legacy in the US was Rex Stout's (1886–1975) oversized character Nero Wolfe. A consultant private detective, Wolfe lives in a "brownstone" house in upper Manhattan, where he is attended by his chef, Fritz, and assistant, Archie Goodwin who, like Watson, acts as the narrator.

Wolfe appears unchanged (aged 56) in 33 novels and over 40 novellas. He analyses crime by shutting his eyes and becoming immersed in a mystery while digesting a gourmet meal and reclining in his specially strengthened chair. He rarely leaves his home, but solves cases by gathering information, interrogating both the police and suspects, and using pure deduction.

Wolfe's background is a mystery. Some Sherlockians trace his roots to Eastern Europe; others believe that he is the illegitimate son of Irene Adler and Holmes. Like Holmes, Wolfe's deductions draw on his vast knowledge and experience, and demand a suspension of disbelief.

The "hard-boiled" school

In the 1930s and 1940s, another style of crime writing emerged in the US. The novels were unsentimental, realistic, and gritty, with cynical antiheroes for detectives who were quite different from Holmes. The style became known as the "hard-boiled" school of detective fiction. Dashiell Hammett (1894–1961) and the Anglo-American writer Raymond Chandler (1888–1959) are considered to be the founders of "hard-boiled" crime fiction.

Hammett's three leading protagonists—the unnamed "Continental Op" in *Red Harvest* (1929), Sam Spade in *The Maltese Falcon* (1930), and Nick Charles in *The Thin Man* (1934)—find themselves involved in mysteries that can be solved only by clever detective work. Raymond Chandler's sleuth, Philip Marlowe, though, is less inventive, often merely following a track of bodies and glamorous femmes fatales to frequently inscrutable but violent conclusions, in works such as *The Big Sleep* (1939) and *Farewell, My Lovely* (1940).

The Adventures of Ellery Queen was made into four television series. The first season in 1950 starred Richard Hart. Lee Bowman (pictured) took over after the death of Hart in January 1951.

Holmes's British legacy

Over a century after Holmes, the true legacy of Conan Doyle's invention can be seen in a number of British crime fiction writers.

P.D. James (1920–2014) wrote ingenious and intellectually driven stories, often set in remote locations. She introduced her female private eye Cordelia Gray in *An Unsuitable Job for a Woman* (1972) and later published a series of novels featuring Commander Adam Dalgliesh, beginning with *A Taste for Death* (1986). With her wonderful prose, James's crime fiction novels were soon considered to be works of serious literature.

Ruth Rendell (1930–2015), meanwhile, created a unique role for herself as an inventor of psychological crime narratives, also publishing under the name Barbara Vine. Her principal series of novels

Humphrey Bogart famously played Chandler's Philip Marlowe in the first film version of *The Big Sleep* in 1946. Lauren Bacall played Vivian Rutledge.

involve the carefully analytical Chief Inspector Wexford; this series began in 1964 with *From Doon with Death* and stretched over the course of 12 novels until 1983.

Colin Dexter (1930–) created the irascible Inspector Morse and his Watson-like companion, Lewis. Indeed, Dexter's format is similar to Conan Doyle's, as Lewis often carries out the legwork, while Morse solves

the mystery. Beginning with *Last Bus to Woodstock* (1975) the series extended to 13 novels until 1999.

Ian Rankin (1960–) never thought of his books as genre fiction, yet his Detective Inspector Rebus series, which began with *Knots and Crosses* (1987) and has continued through a further 18 titles to date, has established him as one of the leading modern crime writers. Rebus is a likeably unlikeable character, who follows his instinct using a combination of Holmesian logic and Philip Marlowe's strong-arm blundering.

Hinted at in Poe's crime fiction, and made explicit with Holmes—from his bouts of depression to his reliance on drugs—many of these latter-day sleuths are also damaged by romantic or family issues, alcohol dependency, and secrets or ghosts from their past, among other things.

Contemporary crime fiction

The legacy of Holmes continues with crime fiction writers throughout the world, but particularly in the US.

The US crime writer John D. Macdonald (1916–1986) invented Travis McGee—a Florida boat-owning freelancer who takes on cases by which he is intrigued or outraged. The reader is placed in the role of the observer and forced to interpret what McGee is up to as he unravels cases. McGee collects evidence and thinks the problems through carefully, gradually drawing together the clues and, like Holmes, using them to trap his villains.

The American-Canadian Ross Macdonald (the pseudonym of Kenneth Millar, 1915–1983) wrote a series of adventures about the Californian private detective Lew Archer. Although he may employ some violent tactics, Archer nevertheless manages to perform some excellent detective work.

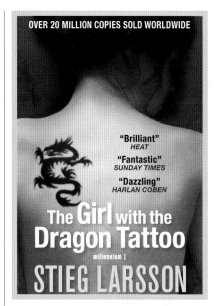

Swedish writer Stieg Larsson (1954–2004) planned this book as the first of ten, but only three were completed. The books were made into successful films.

Much like Holmes was a pioneer of using science as a detective, the US author Patricia Cornwell (1956–) has excelled in describing modern forensics in stomach-churning detail. Her heroine Kay Scarpetta uses her mouth-watering cookery skills to examine mortal remains and confront evil criminals in novels such as *The Body Farm* (1994). Another American, Karin Slaughter (1971–), who debuted with her novel *Blindsighted* in 2001, also describes forensic investigations in gory detail.

Crime fiction is now a well-established genre, particularly in France, Spain, Russia, Japan, and Scandinavia, and numerous non-English-speaking authors like Stieg Larsson and Pierre Lemaitre are proving to be enormously popular worldwide. Whatever the authors' origins or individual styles, there is no doubt that they have all gained from the legacy of Conan Doyle's indomitable Sherlock Holmes. ■

WHAT ONE MAN CAN INVENT, ANOTHER CAN DISCOVER
THE FANS OF SHERLOCK HOLMES

Sherlock Holmes mania began to emerge during 1891, with the publication of the first short stories in *The Strand Magazine*. The Great Detective soon became famous all over the world, and has remained an international phenomenon ever since.

A best-seller is born
The two novels in which Holmes first appeared, *A Study in Scarlet* (pp.36–45) and *The Sign of Four* (pp.46–55), had been moderately popular, but it was the short stories in the *Strand* that propelled the detective to new heights of fame. The stories carried illustrations by Sidney Paget on each page and, with their quick bursts of adventure and satisfying resolutions, proved perfect for the monthly format. Readers went Holmes—mad and the *Strand* quickly became Britain's best-selling magazine.

The dreadful event
The level of fans' enthusiasm, however, would not become clear—to Conan Doyle, at least—until, bored with his creation, he killed Holmes off in "The Final Problem" (pp.142–47) in 1893. The reaction to Holmes's death showed just how popular the ace detective had become. Readers were outraged; more than 20,000 of them canceled their subscriptions. Both the magazine and Conan Doyle received letters of anguished protests—just as Dickens did when he killed off Little Nell in *The Old Curiosity Shop*. People even wore black armbands in mourning and accosted Conan Doyle in the street. The author was completely taken aback. Holmes was merely a fiction, a figment of his imagination. The staff at *The Strand Magazine*, ever after, referred to Holmes's death as "the dreadful event."

Nearly a decade later, Conan Doyle brought Holmes back from the dead, going on to write another 32 Holmes stories. In the meantime, he accepted that Holmes was out

113 Sherlock Holmes fans gathered at University College, London in 2014, in an attempt to set a world record for the greatest number of people dressed as the famous sleuth.

Such is the worldwide appeal of Sherlock Holmes that five statues of the great detective have been erected across the globe from Scotland to Japan. Since 2014, the statue of Sherlock Holmes in London has become particularly lifelike: as part of the "Talking Statues" initiative, passers-by can swipe a nearby code with their smartphone to hear it deliver a monologue written by Anthony Horowitz and voiced by Ed Stoppard.

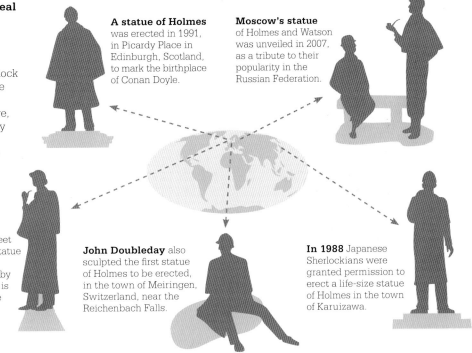

A statue of Holmes was erected in 1991, in Picardy Place in Edinburgh, Scotland, to mark the birthplace of Conan Doyle.

Moscow's statue of Holmes and Watson was unveiled in 2007, as a tribute to their popularity in the Russian Federation.

In 1999 Baker Street finally received a statue of its most famous resident. Sculpted by John Doubleday, it is located outside the tube station.

John Doubleday also sculpted the first statue of Holmes to be erected, in the town of Meiringen, Switzerland, near the Reichenbach Falls.

In 1988 Japanese Sherlockians were granted permission to erect a life-size statue of Holmes in the town of Karuizawa.

there in the world, and he never attempted to stop other people from trying their hand at writing about him, as they very quickly did.

Parodies of Holmes
The first authors to adapt Holmes parodied him, often with amusing variations of his name. In 1892, *The Idler* magazine published "The Adventures of Sherlaw Kombs," and in 1893 *Punch* magazine featured "The Adventures of Picklock Holes." Even famous authors created spoofs: in 1903 P. G. Wodehouse wrote "Dudley Jones, Bore-Hunter" for *Punch*, while Mark Twain produced a novelette called *A Double-Barrelled Detective Story*, in which Sherlock Holmes goes to California, only to make a complete fool of himself.

Holmes mania spread into mainland Europe too. A German magazine of 1908 described the Holmes craze as "a literary disease similar to Werther-mania and romantic Byronism." When two sensational murders occurred in Paris, newspapers ran imaginary interviews with Holmes to try to get to the bottom of the cases.

The Canon
In 1911, Ronald Knox, a young Oxford academic theologian, wrote an analysis of the Holmes stories,

You may marry him, murder him, or do anything you like to him.
Arthur Conan Doyle
To playwright William Gillette (1896)

Studies in the Literature of Sherlock Holmes. Intended as a spoof of detailed, scholarly textual analyses of the Bible, it used biblical terms—such as "the Canon" or the "Sacred Writings"—to refer to the stories of Holmes. Thereafter the complete collection of Conan Doyle's Holmes stories came to be called the canon, and the countless stories written by others are thus known as non-canonical works. Scholarly fans in North America came to call themselves Sherlockians, while in Britain they are more often known as Holmesians.

Non-canonical works
Holmes fans' appetite for the great detective was insatiable—they even began producing their own Holmes stories while Conan Doyle was still alive. For instance, in 1927, the year of the final Conan Doyle story, American teenager August Derleth began to write short »

August Derleth began to write the Solar Pons stories—the cover of the first British edition is shown here—when Conan Doyle politely declined his offer of continuing the Holmes tales.

stories about a detective called Solar Pons, "the Sherlock Holmes of Praed Street." Over the next decade, Derleth produced more than 70 stories, which were widely admired. Since then, countless other writers have tried to recreate Holmes, Conan Doyle's own son Adrian being among them.

Some of the stories are in the same vein as Conan Doyle's, but others import Holmes into other worlds, or even bring him into the present day. Some take aspects of Holmes's character and exaggerate them—his drug habit, for instance—while more radical stories transform him into a superhero who fights anything from vampires to Nazis (pp.340–43).

Holmes has also made numerous cameo appearances in other works. He was called in to solve *The Case of Emily V* (Keith Oatley, 1993), and teamed up with fictional detective Erast Fandorin in Boris Akunin's *Jade Rosary Beads* (2006). On film and television, the recreations of Holmes have been even more varied and imaginative (pp.328–35).

Sherlock Holmes societies

Today there are at least 400 groups devoted to Holmes worldwide. The most illustrious of these is probably the Baker Street Irregulars (BSI), founded in New York in 1934 by Christopher Morley, and named after Holmes's helpful band of little street urchins. Members have included such important figures as Isaac Asimov and Franklin D Roosevelt. The BSI is an invitation only group but oversees a host of Holmes "scion societies" across North America—ranging from the Red Circle of Washington to the Dancing Men of Providence. Each of these has its own obscure rituals, but in general, members meet to talk about the great detective, watch movies, dress up, and exchange views about details of the adventures. Another major

[The Game] must be played as solemnly as a county cricket match at Lord's; the slightest touch of extravagance... ruins the atmosphere.
Dorothy L Sayers
Unpopular Opinions (1951)

Holmes group is The Sherlock Holmes Society of London, which, since 1952, has published *The Sherlock Holmes Journal*, featuring Holmesian news, reviews, essays, and criticism.

Japan is home to more than 30 Holmes societies, among them the Japan Sherlock Holmes Club, which boasts 1,200 members. The country also has a statue of Holmes in Karuizawa by Japanese sculptor Satoh Yoshinori. Portugal has the Norah Creina Castaways of Lisbon, named after the ship

The Grand Game

More than 300 groups around the world are devoted to piecing together the "true" events of the lives of Holmes and Watson. Called the Grand Game after Holmes's famous exclamation, "the game is afoot", but also known as the Great Game or simply the Game, it relies on the tongue-in-cheek assumption that Holmes and Watson are real historical figures and the canon a record of true events. Arthur Conan Doyle's role is explained as that of literary agent.

Any discrepancies within the stories are taken as deliberate obfuscation or forgetfulness on Watson's part, rather than the inevitable mistakes of a fast-working author, and provide numerous inconsistencies for Grand Gamers to examine. Gamers might, for example, try to uncover the reason behind Watson's inconsistent mentions of his wife. They are particularly intrigued by the so-called "Great Hiatus"—the period between Holmes's death at Reichenbach and his reappearance in "The Empty House" (pp.162–67).

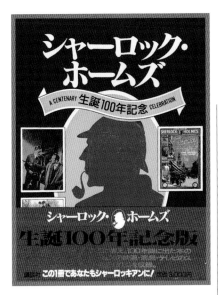

that went down off the Portuguese coast in "The Resident Patient" (pp.134–35), and there are also numerous Holmes societies in India, Russia, Germany, and around the world.

Holmesian London

Countless letters have been written by fans to Holmes at 221B Baker Street—from the 1930s, the actual occupants were the Abbey National Building Society, who had to take on a secretary to deal with the deluge of Holmes-related mail. When The Sherlock Holmes Museum opened, in 1990, at 239 Baker Street, it was eventually renumbered 221 by the Royal Mail, even though it sits between 237 and 241. In 1999, a bronze Holmes statue by John Doubleday (also creator of the Holmes statue in Meiringen, Switzerland) was unveiled outside Baker Street Underground station, in which there is also a mosaic

At the Sherlock Holmes Museum
on Baker Street, visitors can look inside a faithful recreation of the great detective's famous first floor study overlooking the street.

This 1987 Japanese edition of Allen Eyles's *Sherlock Holmes: A Centenary Celebration* was translated for the Japan Sherlock Holmes Club and is one of a number of publications by them.

wall-tile silhouette of Holmes. The detective has also left his mark in other parts of London. A plaque in the glamorous Criterion restaurant on Piccadilly Circus commemorates the spot where Watson is said to have first heard Holmes's name, and a faithful recreation of the detective's 221B study (originally created for the 1951 Festival of Britain) can be found in the appropriately named Sherlock Holmes pub, close to Trafalgar Square.

Popularity continues

Holmes mania looks set to continue well into the 21st century, over 100 years since the first story was penned. The popular BBC television series *Sherlock,* starring Benedict Cumberbatch and Martin Freeman, has spawned a host of new fans around the world. In 2014, devotees dressed in deerstalkers and capes gathered near University College, London in

an attempt to create a world record for the largest group of people dressed as Sherlock Holmes. Other incarnations of the great detective include being cast in a Bollywood musical; an appearance as an African American in modern-day Harlem, New York; starring in Japanese manga; teaming up with other fictional characters, such as Batman and Dracula in numerous comics; and even a role as the muppet Gonzo in *The Muppet Show* comic book.

More serious Sherlockians and Holmesians enjoy regular Sherlock Holmes debates that bring together the world's experts at London's University College, as well as numerous meetings of the various Sherlock Holmes societies.

From the original *Strand* magazines to Sherlock Holmes stamps, patches, posters, and beer coasters, Holmes memorabilia is big business. Fans still can't get enough of him, and it could be said that in his popularity lie the roots of fandom as we know it today. Sherlock Holmes's adaptability, and the public's enthusiasm, appear to be truly endless. ∎

THE BEST WAY OF SUCCESSFULLY ACTING A PART IS TO BE IT

SHERLOCK ON STAGE AND SCREEN

The combined magic of Conan Doyle's compelling fictional creation, and the evocative pictures by Sidney Paget that illustrated his adventures, have long made the detective-hero and his army-doctor companion a gift for dramatic portrayals. For well over 100 years, Sherlock Holmes has been a fixture of popular culture, starring in hundreds of plays, movies, and television shows, and even a Russian ballet.

These numerous appearances across a variety of different media have enhanced Sherlock Holmes's legendary status. Different aspects of his iconic character have been explored in each new adaptation and interpretation of his famous adventures. On stage and screen, the subsidiary characters that populate the stories, such as Mrs. Hudson, Professor Moriarty, Irene Adler, and Inspector Lestrade, have also become more prominent, adding even more detail and color to Holmes's unique world.

Curtain up

Conan Doyle had made several unsuccessful attempts to write for the stage when, in the 1890s, he created a five-act play featuring Sherlock Holmes. Charles Frohman, a US theater producer, expressed an interest in the work, but was unimpressed on reading it. He persuaded the author that the US actor and playwright William Gillette would be the ideal person to rewrite the script and take the lead role. Conan Doyle, happy to relinquish the project, agreed. Initially his only restriction was that Holmes should not fall in love; however, he was soon persuaded otherwise, writing to Gillette, "You may marry him, murder him, or do whatever you like to him."

> He has that rare quality which can be described as glamour... His impersonation of Holmes amazes me.
> **Arthur Conan Doyle**
> on Eille Norwood's performance

The play—the plot of which was drawn largely from "A Scandal in Bohemia" (pp.56–61) and "The Final Problem" (pp.142–47)—opened in New York in 1899. The critics sneered, but the public cheered, and William Gillette toured intermittently with the play for the rest of his life. He also appeared in a film adaptation in 1916, which was feared lost for many years, until, remarkably, a print of it was discovered in France in 2014. Conan Doyle did go on to write two plays that were performed on the London stage: a three-act version of "The Speckled Band" (pp.84–9) in 1910, and *The Crown Diamond*—a one-act drama later adapted as the short story "The Mazarin Stone" (pp.252–53).

Lights, Camera, Sherlock

To begin with, the film industry relied heavily on literary sources for material, and it was little surprise that the popular Sherlock Holmes stories became a recurring source of inspiration for silent movies. Indeed, between 1910 and 1920 more than 50 films were made featuring Holmes. These fell into one of two camps: either they attempted, with varying degrees

of success, to be true to the plots and characters of the stories, or they simply took the detective's basic characteristics and put him in new—and sometimes inappropriate—scenarios, and ignored most of his unique traits.

In the 1922 Goldwyn Pictures movie *Sherlock Holmes*, based on William Gillette's successful play, matinee idol John Barrymore played Holmes as a youthful, handsome, tousled-haired fellow. By contrast, Professor Moriarty was portrayed as a grotesque figure by German actor Gustav von Seyffertitz; so eerie and powerful was von Seyffertitz's performance that when the film was first released in Britain, its title was changed to *Moriarty*.

The British actor Eille Norwood is widely regarded as the greatest Holmes of the silent movie era—and the first actor to successfully embody the character beyond the pages of *The Strand Magazine*. He starred in 47 titles in two years for the Stoll film company, and while not possessing the gaunt, aquiline, Paget-like features, he was a

The Sign of Four (1923) was the final film in the Sherlock Holmes series made by Stoll Pictures. Conan Doyle enjoyed Eille Norwood's "masterly" portrayal of Holmes.

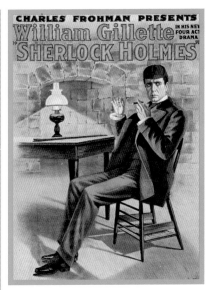

Premiering on Broadway in 1899, the Gillette-authored *Sherlock Holmes* was a big success, touring the US and the UK. It was also revived several times.

convincing Holmes. He even went as far as shaving his hairline to create the impression of Holmes's extra "frontal development."

Holmes talks!

Conan Doyle did not live to see the first Sherlock Holmes film to feature sound—*The Hound of the Baskervilles*, produced in the UK by Gainsborough Pictures in 1930—but this is perhaps just as well, since the film was not a success. During the rest of the 1930s, the performer who received the critics' thumbs-up for presenting "the perfect Holmes" was Londoner, Arthur Wontner. He starred in five features and faced Moriarty in two of them: *The Triumph of Sherlock Holmes* (1935) and *Silver Blaze* (1937).

Top billing

It is interesting to note that all the Holmes films up until the late 1930s were set in the period in which they were made, instead of in the »

Dressed to Kill (1946) was the fourteenth and final movie starring Rathbone and Bruce as Holmes and Watson. Its plot was based on "The Adventure of the Dancing Men."

Century Fox found a solution to this—they transformed him into a bumbling, comic character, raising his cinematic profile in the process. Meanwhile, with his charismatic screen presence and strong resemblance to the detective of Paget's illustrations, Basil Rathbone became the most authentic Holmes to that generation of moviegoers; his performance set the benchmark for the silver-screen portrayals that followed.

These two movies marked the beginning of a long run as Holmes and Watson for Rathbone and Bruce, and very shortly afterward they became involved in a highly successful, long-running radio show, *The New Adventures of Sherlock Holmes*. Fox no longer cared to finance further expensive, Victorian-themed films, and in 1942 Universal Pictures began a series of B movies starring Rathbone and Bruce as the Baker Street duo, transporting them to modern-day

Watson insists that I am the dramatist in real life... Some touch of the artist wells up within me, and calls insistently for a well staged performance.
Sherlock Holmes
The Valley of Fear (1915)

London. The first three Universal movies used the ongoing World War II as a backdrop, and Holmes found himself fighting the Germans and unmasking Nazi spies. This removal of the detective from his usual milieu had the effect of cutting him free from Conan Doyle's influence, thereby helping to promote him as an independent character. However, Rathbone grew tired of playing the role, and in 1946, after a total of 14 outings, he decided to bring his Holmes film

Victorian or early Edwardian era of the original stories. Also, the actor playing Watson was always set well down the cast list, far away from Holmes's star billing. All this was to change in 1939. In March, US film company Twentieth Century Fox released *The Hound of the Baskervilles*, featuring British actors Basil Rathbone and Nigel Bruce as Holmes and Watson, and set in the late Victorian period. Nigel Bruce received fourth billing and even Rathbone only second— below the romantic lead. The film was a surprise hit, and just months later Fox released a sequel, *The Adventures of Sherlock Holmes*, featuring the same actors. This time, the doctor was given equal, top billing with his Holmes.

Filmmakers had long grappled with the problem of Watson's role. In the stories, he is the narrator of the events, which is difficult to emulate on screen. Twentieth

Mrs. Hudson

Although she has no dialogue in the stories, landlady Mrs Martha Hudson is portrayed in numerous film and television adaptations, where she is used to show the human, sometimes humorous side of Holmes. She first made her mark in the Arthur Wontner movies as a cheeky Cockney (played by Minnie Rayner) who indulged in light-hearted banter with her lodger; in the Rathbone series she (Mary Gordon) was a motherly Scotswoman; and in *The Private Life of Sherlock*

Holmes, she (Irene Handl) was an East Londoner again, this time comically crotchety.

In the Jeremy Brett TV series, the character, played by Rosalie Williams, became more prominent. Mrs H's affection for her lodger was obvious, but she grew irritated with his ways as the series wore on. In Guy Ritchie's films, the landlady (Geraldine James) is stoical and rather stately, while in the BBC's *Sherlock*, she (Una Stubbs) is fond but despairing of Holmes, declaring "I'm your landlady, not your housekeeper!"

career to an end. In the 1950s he appeared briefly as Holmes on television and in an unsuccessful Broadway play.

The horror Holmes

After the international success of their technicolor treatments of *Frankenstein* and *Dracula* in the mid-1950s, the British company Hammer Films next turned their attention to Conan Doyle's chiller, *The Hound of the Baskervilles*. Horror-movie stalwart Peter Cushing took the lead—and was slightly alarmed to learn that producer James Carreras had presold his incarnation of the great detective as a "sexy Sherlock." Watson was played by another Hammer regular, André Morell, whose intention to portray him as "a real person and not just a butt for Holmes" resulted in a realistic and solid cinematic portrayal of the doctor.

Sir Nigel Films, a British company formed by the Sir Arthur Conan Doyle Estate to film the author's works, was the force behind another "horror Holmes": 1965's *A Study in Terror*. The movie's storyline pitted the world's greatest detective against its most vicious killer, Jack the Ripper. In a bid to capture the youth market, and cash in on the success of the Batman TV series that was very popular at the time, Holmes was billed as "Sherlock Holmes—the Original Caped Crusader."

Holmes faced Jack the Ripper again in 1979, in the superior British-Canadian *Murder by Decree*, with long-established Hollywood actors Christopher Plummer as Holmes and

In this gory Sherlock Holmes comic-book horror, released in 1965, the detective pits his wits against the real-life notorious Victorian serial killer, Jack the Ripper.

James Mason as Watson. The pair formed a warm relationship, displaying a more human side to the characters for the first time.

Holmes on the small screen

Sherlock Holmes's television career took off in the early 1950s, with productions in both the UK and

US. The first was a BBC six-part series (shown live, so no tapes exist). *Sherlock Holmes*, a 39-episode series made for the US market, was shot on a shoestring budget in France and broadcast in 1954. Wanting to appeal to younger viewers, its producer cast fresh-faced English »

Peter Cushing's Holmes with Bishop Frankland (Mr. Frankland in the novel) in a scene from Hammer Film's 1959 adaptation of *The Hound of the Baskervilles*.

actor Ronald Howard as Holmes; he gave a lively and appealing performance. His Watson, character actor Howard Marion Crawford, played the part in a buffoonish way.

In 1964, Douglas Wilmer donned the deerstalker in a second BBC series that kicked off with *The Speckled Band* and was followed by a further 12 stories the next year. His performance was closely modeled on that of Basil Rathbone, and was praised for its faithfulness

The stage lost a fine actor, even as science lost an acute reasoner, when [Holmes] became a specialist in crime.
Dr. Watson
"A Scandal in Bohemia" (1891)

to the original stories. However, Wilmer was unhappy with the scripts (sometimes even rewriting them himself) and the production values, and refused a second series.

In 1968, Peter Cushing stepped into Wilmer's shoes for a two-part adaptation of *The Hound of the Baskervilles*, which remains one of the most faithful versions of the story. However, once the rest of the 16-episode series—the first to be made in color—got under way, Cushing experienced similar problems to those encountered by Wilmer. But the actor's devotion to the character and attention to detail were unfailing: he requested that his costumes replicate those shown in the Paget illustrations, thus exploding the myth of the great detective's Inverness cape: "It's not an Inverness cape… it's a long overcoat with a hood."

Holmes on the radio
When Basil Rathbone gave up playing Holmes on screen, he also left the US radio series, but Nigel

Bruce continued to play Watson with other Sherlocks. In Britain, the great detective was a comparative latecomer to radio, and it was not until the 1950s that he was granted a series. The pairing of two distinguished actors, Carleton Hobbs as Holmes, with his high, reedy, alien tones, and Norman Shelley as Watson, with his dark plum pudding of a voice, proved successful, and they inhabited the parts intermittently from 1953 to 1969. Today, the duo sound decidedly middle-aged, but they were very popular at the time.

Perhaps the most illustrious of all radio Holmes and Watsons were Sir John Gielgud and Sir Ralph Richardson—two of Britain's greatest Shakespearean actors—who appeared on the BBC in 1954 in a short series.

In 1988, the BBC decided to adapt all of Conan Doyle's Sherlock Holmes tales for radio, including the novels, and within 10 years the whole canon had been recorded and broadcast.

Off-the-wall portrayals
Between the Peter Cushing television series of the late 1960s and the emergence of Jeremy Brett in the 1980s in one of the most notable of all depictions, there were a number of unusual Holmes portrayals. Perhaps the most refined of these was Robert Stephens in Billy Wilder's *The Private Life of Sherlock Holmes* (1970), an almost effeminate incarnation, with languid movements, a nasal drawl, and wavy hair. Mark Gatiss, the co-creator of the BBC's successful

The definitive Sherlock Holmes is really in everyone's head. No actor can fit into that category because every reader has his own ideal.
Jeremy Brett
TV Times interview (1991)

Sherlock television series, has said that the movie was "a template of sorts for Steven Moffat and me as we made our adaptation." James Bond star Roger Moore later presented a Simon Templar-like version in *Sherlock Holmes in New York* (1976); while acting heavyweight George C. Scott played a New York lawyer who thinks, and indeed acts, like the great detective in the bleak comedy *They Might Be Giants* (1971), featuring the first female Watson, Joanne Woodward. The mercurial Scottish-born stage actor Nicol Williamson was a neurotic and emotionally disturbed Holmes in 1976's *The Seven-Per-Cent Solution*, which saw Holmes being treated by Sigmund Freud for cocaine-induced psychosis.

In 1985, Spielberg's *Young Sherlock Holmes* billed itself as an "affectionate speculation" that addressed the question of what might have happened had Holmes and Watson first met at a boarding school. The ensuing mystery also introduces the young Moriarty and Inspector Lestrade. Holmes matures over the course of the action, acquiring a curly pipe and a deerstalker hat, and his doomed romance cleverly hints at why, in later life, he adopts a distant attitude toward women.

Holmes around the world

In the 1930s, the German film industry produced a number of Holmes movies, essentially adopting the character for use in a series of wild adventure films. The 1937 *De Hund Von Baskerville*, featuring a gun-toting Sherlock Holmes in a leather overcoat and flat cap, was a favorite of Adolf Hitler: in 1945, a copy of the movie was found in the Führer's private collection in the Berghof, his mountain residence. In 1967, Germany produced a television series based on the scripts for the BBC's Douglas Wilmer series, with stage actor Erich Schellow as a rather down-at-heel, drug-addicted version of the Baker Street sleuth.

Between 1979 and 1986, Soviet television screened a series of Sherlock Holmes films, split into 11 episodes. In 1986, a movie adaptation, *The Twentieth Century Approaches*, was made from the last four episodes. Produced by »

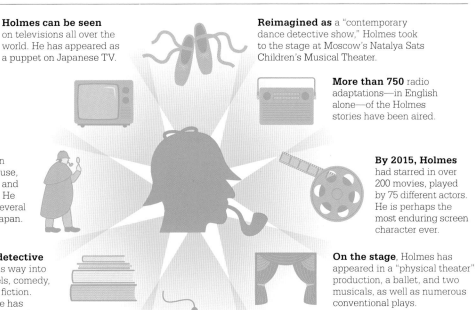

In Sherlock Holmes, Conan Doyle created a template that can be used in almost any art form or genre. Arguably, no other fictional character is so adaptable. The enduring flexibility of Holmes is itself a subject of study.

Holmes can be seen on televisions all over the world. He has appeared as a puppet on Japanese TV.

Reimagined as a "contemporary dance detective show," Holmes took to the stage at Moscow's Natalya Sats Children's Musical Theater.

More than 750 radio adaptations—in English alone—of the Holmes stories have been aired.

Holmes has been animated as a mouse, a duck, a bulldog, and even a cucumber. He has appeared in several manga series in Japan.

By 2015, Holmes had starred in over 200 movies, played by 75 different actors. He is perhaps the most enduring screen character ever.

The great detective has found his way into literary novels, comedy, and science fiction. In comics, he has teamed up with other fictional characters such as Batman.

On the stage, Holmes has appeared in a "physical theater" production, a ballet, and two musicals, as well as numerous conventional plays.

Holmes and his world were the subject of board games in the 1980s and computer games in the 2000s.

Animated appearances

Some of the most eccentric depictions of Holmes have been made for children—in the form of cartoons. As early as 1946, Daffy Duck met the detective in "The Great Piggy Bank Robbery." In 1986, Disney produced Basil, the Great Mouse Detective, who, along with his friend Dr. David Q. Dawson, lived beyond the baseboards at 221B Baker Street. Professor Rattigan, their Moriarty-like adversary, was voiced by Vincent Price.

In the 1980s, Holmes's ghost appeared in an episode of *Scooby Doo*, while in "Elementary, My Dear Turtle," the Teenage Mutant Ninja Turtles enlisted Holmes's help in thwarting Moriarty's bid for world domination. In the 1999 US television series *Sherlock Holmes in the 22nd Century*, the detective was revived by a biologist to combat a clone of Moriarty; in order to assist him, Inspector Lestrade's "compudroid" read Watson's journals and assumed the doctor's name, face, voice, and mannerisms. And in 2010, Holmes met Tom and Jerry in a full-length movie.

Lenfilm, the series featured Russian actors Vassily Livanov as Holmes and Vitaly Salomin as Watson; they were chosen for the "Englishness" of their appearance and for their likeness to the Paget drawings. The adaptations themselves remained very close to the original Conan Doyle plots, but tended to include a great deal of humor.

A definitive portrait?
During the 1980s and early 1990s, British actor Jeremy Brett gave what many consider to be the defining Holmes performance, in a series made by Granada Television. The intention was to create a truly authentic Holmes, and no actor before Brett had managed to embody so many of the attributes created by Conan Doyle. As Michael Cox, the series' producer, observed, Brett "had the voice, the actor's intelligence, the presence, the physique, the ability to jump over furniture, be convincing in a disguise, handle the horses, and whatever else that may be required."

For millions of fans all around the world, Brett *was* Holmes. In his mesmerizing performance, the controlled eccentricities, the mannered delivery, and the furious outbursts combined to create an

I think people fall in love, not with Sherlock Holmes or with Dr. Watson, but with their friendship.
Steven Moffat
Co-writer of BBC's *Sherlock*

Jeremy Brett portrayed Holmes in the 1984–1994 Granada Television series. The actor admitted that the role was "the hardest part I have ever played."

enduring portrayal of the great detective. Brett was partnered by two excellent but contrasting Watsons: David Burke, who gave a sensitive and at times jovial performance, and then Edward Hardwicke, who inhabited the role for eight years, combining a strong sense of loyalty and tolerance with quiet authority.

Holmes in the 21st century
In the 21st century, the world's fascination with the super sleuth of Baker Street is as strong as ever. In 2009 and 2011, two movies by British director Guy Ritchie presented an exaggerated, cartoonish, action-hero version of the great detective—played with anarchic relish by Robert Downey Jr.—with all his foibles and habits magnified or lampooned.

Meanwhile, on the small screen, two recent ventures have created a thoroughly modern reimagining of

Guy Ritchie's *Sherlock Holmes* (2009) is set in 1890s London. Robert Downey Jr. is a bohemian Holmes, while Jude Law is a tolerant, if often exasperated, Watson. A sequel was released in 2011.

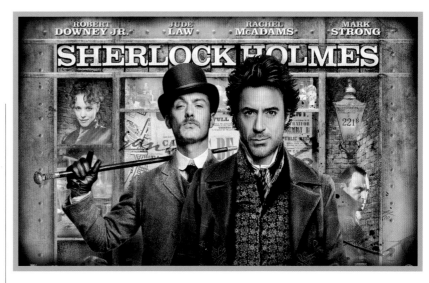

the detective and his world. In *Elementary*, which had its US premier in 2012, Sherlock Holmes (played by British actor Jonny Lee Miller) is a recovering drug addict who helps the New York City Police Department solve crimes. His female Watson (Lucy Liu) is a former surgeon who is initially appointed as his sober companion (to prevent him from relapsing), but becomes a pupil of sorts when they begin to investigate cases together. Canonical characters, such as Moriarty and Irene Adler (who becomes Holmes's lover), are gradually added to the mix and given unexpected twists.

Meanwhile, in the UK, a pair of self-confessed Sherlock Holmes fans, writers Steven Moffat and Mark Gatiss, conceived the notion of bringing Conan Doyle's protagonists into a contemporary, high-tech London. The first series of

Sherlock aired on the BBC in 2010, and its daring concept allowed the detective to manipulate modern technology in authentic Holmesian fashion to aid his investigations. He even has a website called "The Science of Deduction."

The show has been hugely successful all over the world, especially with a younger audience. Its fast-paced, humorous, and intriguing plots are packed with references to the original stories, and its lead actors are also of similar ages to the literary Holmes and Watson when they first met. Benedict Cumberbatch's Holmes is a geek, but despite his arrogance and, at times, lack of social skills, he is a fascinating individual. Martin Freeman's Watson is a fragile mixture of independence of thought and unabashed loyalty to his friend. Indeed, his violent reaction to Holmes's return after his "death" is more realistic than the rather tepid response of his literary counterpart. Andrew Scott's Moriarty is perhaps the most chilling portrayal of the villain and a wonderful foil to Holmes.

Since he first appeared in print more than 125 years ago, Sherlock Holmes has been an almost constant presence in the media. Conan Doyle's unstoppable creation has transcended literature to become a global phenomenon, continuing to fascinate and entertain fresh audiences. ∎

The BBC television series *Sherlock* brings Holmes and company firmly into the present day. Benedict Cumberbatch plays Holmes, while Martin Freeman's Watson records their exploits in a blog.

THE MANY FACES OF HOLMES

Ever since his first appearance on the page, Holmes has frequently been portrayed on stage and screen, with almost every decade offering new adaptations, adventures, and directions. It was Conan Doyle himself who initially penned the first Holmes-based drama, with his efforts later becoming the basis for William Gillette's play, *Sherlock Holmes* (1899). Unlike the books and stories in which much of Holmes is left to the reader's imagination, on screen in particular he is presented as a complete package—faults and all. While some portrayals are easily forgotten, many of the best, such as those of Rathbone, Cushing, Brett, and Cumberbatch have become the living embodiment of the great detective for successive generations.

SHERLOCK HOLMES
Stage (1899)

Originally written by Conan Doyle, the final version was reworked by William Gillette, who also directed and starred in the play. The story was based on material drawn from the canon, and despite Conan Doyle's original misgivings, he consented to allow Holmes to be married. For Holmesians, this play marks an influential adaptation, since it introduced the detective's now iconic bent briar pipe and his frequent use of a magnifying glass, and included the line, "Oh, this is elementary, my dear fellow."

THE FURTHER ADVENTURES OF SHERLOCK HOLMES
Film (1921–1923)

This was a series of short, silent films, each based on one of Conan Doyle's original stories; most are now lost. They starred English actor Eille Norwood, who, from the age of 60, made 47 films between 1921 and 1923, and was famous for his sharp features and piercing eyes. The films all stayed close to the originals, although there was no attempt at Victoriana—all were set in a London in which electricity, cars, and buses were the norm.

THE RETURN OF SHERLOCK HOLMES
Film (1929)

This was the first sound-era Holmes movie—a so-called "talkie." Paramount Pictures owned the rights to the characters of Holmes, Watson, and Moriarty but not to any specific story, so an original piece was concocted by borrowing various ideas from Conan Doyle. The movie presented the first of many dim-witted Watsons (here played by H. Reeves-Smith), and began with a murder via a trick cigarette case with a lethal needle—a device that Moriarty (Harry T. Morey) later tried to use on Holmes (Clive Brook). The closing lines of the movie also gave another first for Holmes: his trademark phrase, "Elementary, my dear Watson," which was never uttered in the canon itself.

THE HOUND OF THE BASKERVILLES
Film (1939)

This movie marked the first of Basil Rathbone's fourteen outings as Holmes, establishing him as one of the key actors in the role. Watson was portrayed as likable but buffoonish by Nigel Bruce, with Richard Greene as the romantic lead, Sir Henry Baskerville. This was the first movie to be set in the Victorian period, and in which the actor playing Watson received equal billing with Holmes. Although the action followed the original plot, the great spectral hound simply appeared as a large dog.

THE ADVENTURES OF SHERLOCK HOLMES
Film (1939)

"The strange case of the chinchilla fetish! The fiendish instrument that strangles, crushes, vanishes! The albatross of doom! The British crown jewels!" As the 20th Century Fox press release suggests, this movie, starring Rathbone as Holmes, had an adventurous plot. An original piece, it was claimed to be based on Gillette's 1899 play, *Sherlock Holmes*, in which Moriarty goads the detective, telling him of his plans for the crime of the century, for which Holmes would be discredited.

THE PEARL OF DEATH
Film (1944)

Starring Rathbone and Bruce as Holmes and Watson, this movie was one in a series of twelve made by Universal Studios. It was based on "The Adventure of the Six Napoleons," and sees Holmes making a rare mistake—the loss of a famous, and seemingly cursed, pearl that he must then recover. The movies in the series were all made cheaply and quickly, with no attempt at period settings. They are particularly notable for the humor between Holmes and Watson, as well as their array of macabre elements. Other movies in the series include *The Scarlet Claw* (1944) and *The Woman in Green* (1945).

SHERLOCK HOLMES
Television (1953–1954)

Lost in the mists of television history, this American series was made with the cooperation of Conan Doyle's son Adrian, who was eager to perpetuate his father's franchise. Holmes was played by a youthful Ronald Howard (age 39), with Howard Marion Crawford as Watson. It was filmed in France, meaning that some of the London locations appear curiously Gallic. New, non-canonical plots were utilized that took aspects from

Conan Doyle's stories, with the scripts written by blacklisted Hollywood writers working in Europe. This was the only Holmes television series produced in the US until *Elementary* in 2012.

THE HOUND OF THE BASKERVILLES
Film (1959)

This adaptation was produced by a company celebrated for its Gothic horror outings—Hammer Films. True to form, the dark, gruesome elements found in Conan Doyle's *The Hound of the Baskervilles* are graphically translated on screen. The cast included the classic pairing of Peter Cushing as Holmes and Christopher Lee as Sir Henry Baskerville. The movie was directed by Hammer's signature director, Terence Fisher, who had already reenergized the company's Frankenstein and Count Dracula franchises. It was the first of a projected series of movies that never materialized, although Cushing played Holmes again in later years.

A STUDY IN TERROR
Film (1965)

Directed by James Hill (better known for co-directing *Born Free* in 1966) this ingenious movie has Holmes hot on the trail of Jack the Ripper. The notorious murderer is terrorizing Victorian London's East End, and the only clues are the crest of an aristocratic family and a box containing surgical instruments with the scalpel missing. Bizarrely, in the UK the movie was marketed as a violent and sexually graphic exploitation movie, while in the US it was sold

as a camp, Batman-style comic-book caper. John Neville played a solid, energetic Holmes alongside Donald Houston as Watson.

SHERLOCK HOLMES
Television (1965–1968)

Produced by the BBC, this series initially cast Douglas Wilmer as a wry and amused Holmes. Like many of his fellow actors in the role, Wilmer bore a marked resemblance to the Sidney Paget illustrations in *The Strand Magazine*. He declined to do a second series, with the lead then going to Peter Cushing, himself a Holmesian, who had previously starred in Hammer's *The Hound of the Baskervilles* in 1959. The series adapted many of the original stories, starting with "The Adventure of the Speckled Band" and extended to 29 episodes, the later Cushing shows being filmed in full color.

THE PRIVATE LIFE OF SHERLOCK HOLMES
Film (1970)

This parody was directed by Billy Wilder, who also co-wrote it with I. A. L. Diamond. A non-canonical tale, it saw Holmes (played by Robert Stephens) and Watson (Colin Blakely) take on a particularly strange case that involved missing midgets, naval experiments, and the Loch Ness monster. Controversially for Holmes fans, it was also the first movie to feature jokes about a supposed gay relationship between Holmes and Watson. Accompanying the movie was a notably rich musical score by Miklos Rózsa, based on his own violin concerto.

THE SEVEN-PER-CENT SOLUTION
Film (1976)

An adaptation of a pastiche, this movie is based on Nicholas Meyer's imaginative 1974 novel of the same title (see p.341). It shows a cocaine-addicted Holmes becoming highly paranoid about being persecuted by mathematics expert Professor Moriarty, who is portrayed here as a feeble, elderly man. Holmes is persuaded to follow Moriarty to Vienna, unaware that Watson and Mycroft Holmes have a hidden agenda—they want him to be treated for his addiction by the world-famous psychoanalyst Sigmund Freud. The cast included Nicol Williamson as the blighted Holmes, Laurence Olivier as Moriarty, and Alan Arkin as Freud.

THE CRUCIFER OF BLOOD
Stage (1978)

Written and directed by Paul Giovanni, this play was based on *The Sign of Four*. It first opened on Broadway, and employed state-of-the-art lighting to recreate the river chase scene on stage. It later opened in London and Los Angeles, where Jeremy Brett played Watson. In 1991, it was turned into a movie starring Charlton Heston.

MURDER BY DECREE
Film (1979)

Of the various, often outlandish, treatments of theories about the British royal family's involvement in the Jack the Ripper killings, this was one of the most accomplished. The movie dealt with largely discredited theories about Jack's identity, and this British/Canadian co-production boasted Christopher Plummer as an emotionally-charged incarnation of Holmes. The great detective is enlisted after the grisly dispatch of the third prostitute to die at the Ripper's hands, "Long Liz" Stride, and discovers the involvement of the British Prime Minister, the Home Secretary, and the Freemasons.

THE ADVENTURES OF SHERLOCK HOLMES
Television (1984–1994)

Produced by Granada Television, this adaptation ran over six series, and featured 41 episodes based on the original stories. The great detective was played by Jeremy Brett, who for many devotees is the archetypal Holmes, portraying him as deeply intense and edgy. Watson was initially played by David Burke, then later by the long-serving Edward Hardwicke. The series was immensely popular, being broadcast in the UK and the US, and is widely considered to be the most faithful representation of Conan Doyle's stories to date. The later series produced were entitled *The Return*, *The Casebook*, and *The Memoirs*.

THE MASKS OF DEATH
Film (1984)

This movie marks the last appearance as Holmes by Peter Cushing, who, then 71 years old, needed persuasion to take the part. Watson was played by fellow big-screen veteran John Mills, age 76. Set in 1913, the now-retired detective is brought in by the police after bodies are found in the Thames River, their faces frozen in a rictus of terror, but with no visible causes of death. In a separate, or possibly linked, case, he is asked to find a missing prince in order to prevent war between Britain and Germany.

SHERLOCK'S LAST CASE
Stage (1987)

Written by Charles Marowitz and directed by A. J. Antoon, this play is sometimes confused with one of the same name produced by Matthew Lang in 1974. This play was a dark comedy with Holmes, played by Frank Langella, receiving death threats from the evil son of the late Moriarty, and then being imprisoned by a frustrated Watson. Marowitz added some interesting changes to the Holmes formula, and the play was well reviewed.

THE SECRET OF SHERLOCK HOLMES
Stage (1988)

This play was written by Jeremy Paul, who had previously created several episodes of the Granada Television series featuring Jeremy Brett as Holmes. By the time of the play, the troubled actor had an ambiguous attitude to the character, and the results on stage were considered controversial. The drama featured just two characters, with Edward Hardwicke as Watson. Although the play received poor reviews, the actors' performances were praised. The "secret" alluded to in the title, as in Nicholas Meyer's *The Seven-Per-Cent Solution*, was that the Machiavellian Moriarty was a concoction of Holmes's drug-addled brain.

SHERLOCK HOLMES... THE DEATH AND LIFE
Stage (2008)

This is the second Holmes play written by David Stuart Davies, and as in the first, Roger Llewellyn was cast as the great detective. Rather than following a canonical tale or creating a simple pastiche, Davies explored the relationship between a fictional character and his creator. In the play, Conan Doyle is now tired of Holmes, and desperate to rid himself of his famous character, he creates the evil Moriarty to do his bidding. Holmes, of course, proves more resilient than Conan Doyle anticipated, and the adventure begins. This was an interesting play, where characters flitted between fantasy and reality.

SHERLOCK HOLMES
Film (2009)

Directed by Guy Ritchie, who is best known for his "Cockney crime" movies, this is a tongue-in-cheek rebooting of the Holmes genre that sees the detective transformed into a Hollywood-style action hero. Set in Victorian London, it is a non-canonical tale with Holmes and Watson played by Robert Downey Jr. and Jude Law. The plot, which has elements of science fiction and the supernatural, sees the detective pair form an unlikely alliance with former enemy Irene Adler. Together they must first save Britain, the US, and then the whole world from the late Lord Blackwood—recently raised from the dead. At the end, Adler reveals her connections to Moriarty, opening the prospect of a sequel, which followed in 2011.

SHERLOCK
Television (2010–)

Produced by the BBC, and starring Benedict Cumberbatch as Holmes, and Martin Freeman as Watson, this innovative series remolded the great detective for the twenty-first century audience. Hence Holmes gains a mobile phone and GPS, but loses his famous "three-pipe problem" to multiple nicotine patches. The series co-creators, Stephen Moffat and Mark Gatiss, based some episodes on Conan Doyle's originals. Existing characters, were repurposed, such as Irene Adler, here seen as a dominatrix, and new ones introduced. These included Holmes's parents, played by Wanda Ventham and Timothy Carlton, the real-life parents of Benedict Cumberbatch.

SHERLOCK HOLMES: A GAME OF SHADOWS
Film (2011)

This was the sequel to the 2009 movie staring Robert Downey Jr., again directed by Guy Ritchie. It has the same light-hearted, fast-paced, all-action approach as the original movie, and sees Watson having ended the detecting partnership in order to marry his sweetheart, Mary Morstan. Now working alone, Holmes uncovers a plot by Moriarty to embroil all of Europe in war, which will benefit his recently acquired munitions and arms supplies manufacturers. Naturally, the newly married Watson is soon at Holmes's side in the case. This sequel introduced Stephen Fry as Mycroft, Holmes's brother, and Jared Harris as a chillingly quiet Moriarty.

ELEMENTARY
Television (2012–)

Set in modern-day New York, this series was produced by CBS Television Studios. Holmes, played by Jonny Lee Miller, has been sent to New York from London by his father to help him recover from his drug addiction. To watch over and support him, his father has employed a former surgeon, Dr. Joan Watson, played by Lucy Liu. Holmes's previous detective work for Scotland Yard is known to the NYPD, which naturally makes use of his services, and Watson becomes Holmes's new apprentice. Interestingly, this was the first Holmes television series produced in the US since Ronald Howard's outings in 1953. Having proved popular with viewers, several series have been produced.

MR. HOLMES
Film (2015)

Starring Sir Ian McKellen as the great detective, this movie is set just after World War II. Holmes, now in his nineties and long-since retired, shies away from the fame of his younger days, wishing only to tend to his bees in solitude. Where once he battled criminals, now he fights senility, as he struggles with short-term memory loss. The movie centers on Holmes's last case, and his annoyance at the way Watson (now deceased) embellished the facts and changed the outcome when publishing the story. Eager to set the record straight, Holmes must try to remember the events as they happened so many years before. This movie is a moving portrayal of Holmes at his most human.

HOLMES BY OTHER HANDS

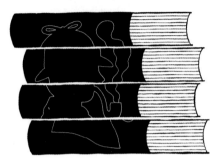

Many authors have attempted to create new adventures for the great detective, and while some have offered clever variations on the originals, others fatally lack their fire and invention. Even during Conan Doyle's lifetime, writers were eager to take on the Holmesian mantle, including Vincent Starrett, who wrote *The Adventure of the Unique Hamlet* in 1920. Other pastiches soon followed, but the first significant work came in 1944 with the Ellery Queen anthology, *The Misadventures of Sherlock Holmes*. As the 20th century progressed, Holmes's opponents became increasingly bizarre. Pitted against Dracula, and battling H. G. Wells's Martians with Professor Challenger, it is no wonder that he later seeks help from psychoanalyst Sigmund Freud.

THE EXPLOITS OF SHERLOCK HOLMES
Adrian Conan Doyle & John Dickson Carr (1954)

Consisting of twelve short stories, this was a collaboration between Conan Doyle's son and Dickson Carr, a celebrated writer of golden-age crime fiction. Their plan was to extrapolate plot ideas from hints given by Watson in the original canon, and for them to write each new story together. The tales include "The Adventure of the Highgate Miracle" and "The Adventure of the Abbas Ruby." They are regarded as hit-or-miss by Holmes fans, but enjoyed some success. Several of the stories appeared in *Collier's Weekly* magazine, like the originals.

SHERLOCK HOLMES VS. JACK THE RIPPER
Ellery Queen/Paul Fairman (1966)

Also known as *Ellery Queen vs. Jack the Ripper*, this is a skillful novelization of James Hill's 1965 film. Here, Fairman writes as Ellery Queen, mystery writer and amateur detective, who takes the place of Holmes in a plot where a decadent aristocracy is not to be trusted. It is considered the first real modern Holmes pastiche, and also marks the first of numerous encounters between the detective and fellow Victorian Jack the Ripper.

THE PRIVATE LIFE OF SHERLOCK HOLMES
Michael & Mollie Hardwick (1970)

This novelization was based on *The Private Life of Sherlock Holmes*, the largely parodic 1970 screenplay by Billy Wilder and I. A. L. Diamond (p.337). Adhering closely to the original storyline, this adventure features many mysterious elements, including a distraught woman, an absent husband, a Scottish castle, and even the Loch Ness monster. It also makes a comic play on the nature of Holmes's and Watson's friendship. The idea that they were a gay couple was fully explored later in 1971, in Larry Townsend's camp, bawdy tale, *The Sexual Adventures of Sherlock Holmes*.

THE FURTHER ADVENTURES OF SHERLOCK HOLMES: THE PEERLESS PEER
Philip José Farmer (1974)

In this quirky and inventive tale, set during World War I, respected American science-fiction writer Farmer sends an aged Holmes and Watson in pursuit of a devilish new weapon in Africa. It marks another occasion where the pair encounter a well-known fictional character—this time, Lord Greystoke, better known as Tarzan. It is an exciting tale with elements of the science-fiction genre.

THE RETURN OF MORIARTY
John Gardner (1974)

Gardner had already proved himself a successful pasticheur with his Boysie Oaks espionage novels—comic riffs on Ian Fleming's James Bond—before turning his attention to Holmes. Set in evocatively described Victorian London, Moriarty is center stage, having been brought back from the dead, like Holmes before him. The plot is ripe with criminality, and is richly conveyed, with Moriarty and Sal Hodges, his prostitute-mistress, at its heart. Together they manipulate everything from blackmail to murder. In 1975 Gardner wrote a sequel, *The Revenge of Moriarty*.

THE SEVEN-PER-CENT SOLUTION
Nicholas Meyer (1974)

A bestseller in New York when first published, this novel offers an abundance of new ideas to the Holmes genre, and often emulates Conan Doyle's own elegant writing style. The case involves a sinister kidnapping and the threat of war, though as the title suggests, the detective's drug addiction is central. To cure his dependence, Holmes needs help, turning to none other than psychoanalyst Sigmund Freud. Meyer later wrote the Holmes pastiches *The West End Horror* (1976) and *The Canary Trainer* (1993).

THE GIANT RAT OF SUMATRA
Richard L. Boyer (1976)

To most Holmes devotees, the references to cases that were not included in the canon provoke keen speculation, and none more so than the mention of the "Giant Rat of Sumatra" in "The Adventure of the Sussex Vampire." According to Holmes, it is "a story for which the world is not yet prepared." This tale is allegedly based on a manuscript found in a London bank vault after Watson's demise. Featuring death and a murderous animal, it has similarities to *The Hound*

of the Baskervilles, although the perpetrator is a surprise—an old face from the canon. Other Holmes short stories by Boyer include "The Adventure of Bell Rock Light" and "The Adventure of the Eyrie Cliff."

EXIT SHERLOCK HOLMES
Robert Lee Hall (1977)

Crossing over into science fiction, this is a highly inventive novel that has both Holmes and his brother, Mycroft, lined up once again against a revivified Moriarty. Holmes, now retired, features only sparingly, and it is Watson who plays the central role, which may frustrate Holmes fans. However, the book reveals many hitherto undisclosed "facts." Where did Holmes acquire his astonishing skills? What are the secrets of his shadowy brother? And what is the relationship between Holmes and Moriarty? There is a particularly unexpected twist at the end.

THE LAST SHERLOCK HOLMES STORY
Michael Dibdin (1978)

This is a darkly Gothic novel, almost phantasmagorical, in which Holmes and Watson are on the trail of Jack the Ripper in the East End of Victorian London. Unusually, Conan Doyle himself appears as a character, a medical friend of Watson given permission by him to write up the case, and Moriarty also features in the tale. While the plot follows the familiar Ripper murders, as other authors have done, Dibdin's approach is highly audacious. The novel is considered by Holmesians as controversial, and divides opinion.

THE HOLMES– DRACULA FILE
Fred Saberhagen (1978)

This is a highly original Holmes novel, narrated equally by Watson, and the greatest of all supernatural villains, Count Dracula. Set in London in 1878, it is a suspense-filled tale featuring a mad scientist, plague-infested rats, and bloodless corpses that combines the worlds of both Conan Doyle and Bram Stoker. Unlike other Holmes/ Dracula encounters by different authors, here they work together, although a more surprising and controversial relationship is later revealed. Holmes also encounters Count Dracula in *Sherlock Holmes vs Dracula: The Adventure of the Sanguinary Count* by Loren D. Estelman (1979).

TEN YEARS BEYOND BAKER STREET
Cay Van Ash (1984)

In another pairing of literary worlds and fictional characters, this novel pits Conan Doyle's Holmes against Sax Rohmer's infamous villain of the Far East, Dr. Fu Manchu. Set in 1914, in a richly-described Wales, the plot is as much an action adventure as it is a crime story, which at one point sees Holmes and his client, Dr. Petrie, facing certain death in an abandoned mine. This book is well regarded by Holmes fans for the authenticity of Watson's narration. It is also notable that, like Holmes in many of Conan Doyle's original stories, Fu Manchu makes few appearances, with the plot focusing mainly on his pursuit. In 1971, Van Ash wrote *Master of Villainy,* a biography of Sax Rohmer.

THE BEEKEEPER'S APPRENTICE
Laurie R. King (1994)

This is the first in a series of Holmes novels by King, in which she details the adventures of the aging detective, seen from the viewpoint of Mary Russell, a 15-year-old American girl living in Sussex following the death of her parents. In this first outing, Holmes is training his new apprentice in the art of deduction, and the two are soon investigating a sinister kidnapping. With its strong female lead character and villain, this book is noted for its feminist current. King outraged many Holmesians by marrying off the asexual detective to the feisty Russell in the second book in the series, *A Monstrous Regiment of Women* (1995). He was, of course, first married with Conan Doyle's consent in Gillette's 1899 play, *Sherlock Holmes* (p.336).

THE MANDALA OF SHERLOCK HOLMES
Jamyang Norbu (1999)

This novel follows Conan Doyle's ascetic hero during his "Great Hiatus," as he travels through India and Tibet in the guise of Norwegian explorer Sigerson. The premise is that the author, Norbu, discovered a long-lost account of Holmes's time there, written by his then companion, a Bengali spy named Huree Chunder Mookerjee—a character from Rudyard Kipling's *Kim* (1901). The plot centers on Holmes's battle to protect the young thirteenth Dalai Lama from assassination by an evil master criminal, and the story becomes increasingly mystical.

THE PATIENT'S EYES: THE DARK BEGINNINGS OF SHERLOCK HOLMES
David Pirie (2001)

In the first in his series, Pirie features Conan Doyle himself as Watson to the Holmes of the remarkable doctor Joseph Bell (on whom Holmes was modeled). This account presents Bell and Conan Doyle as partners in a criminal investigation, tackling the hidden menace and sexual hypocrisy of Victorian life. The fictional Conan Doyle is intrigued by the symptoms displayed by a young woman with an unusual eye complaint; she is also haunted by visions of a phantom cyclist. The murder of a wealthy Spanish businessman monopolizes the two detectives' attention, until the matter of the patient's eyes and the solitary cyclist looms large.

THE FINAL SOLUTION
Michael Chabon (2004)

In this concise tale, the great detective is painfully aged, long-forgotten, and in seclusion at the time of World War II. Living in quiet retirement in the countryside, the elderly man in his late 80s (who is never named) is known only to the locals as a once-celebrated detective—his world is now one of sedate beekeeping rather than crime. He is visited by Linus Steinman, nine years old and mute, who has fled Nazi Germany with just one companion, an African gray parrot, who holds a puzzle. What is behind the baffling lists of German numbers the bird repeatedly utters? There is a deep melancholy infusing this story of the greatest of Victorian detectives, alienated and ignored by the world of the 1940s.

THE VEILED DETECTIVE
David Stuart Davies (2004)

Everything that was previously believed about Holmes and Watson is turned completely on its head in this inventive novel. Opening at the start of their friendship, Watson isn't Watson, Mrs. Hudson is an actress, and both are employed by Moriarty to spy and report back on the young detective to prevent him from ever getting too close to the criminal mastermind. Even Mycroft isn't what he seems. The plot cleverly weaves together Conan Doyle's *A Study in Scarlet* and "The Final Problem," reworking the earliest days of Holmes's and Watson's lives together, and culminating with an alternative take on that fateful day at the Reichenbach Falls.

DUST AND SHADOW: AN ACCOUNT OF THE RIPPER KILLINGS BY DR. JOHN H. WATSON
Lyndsay Faye (2009)

This novel is yet another bloody encounter with Jack the Ripper for Holmes, but very different from Michael Dibdin's *The Last Sherlock Holmes Story* and the others. With assiduous historical detail, the world of early tabloid journalism (with Holmes himself a victim of character assassination), and fledgling clinical psychology are evoked in this relentless pursuit by Holmes of one of the world's first serial killers. This novel is a highly regarded Holmes pastiche.

THE HOUSE OF SILK
Anthony Horowitz (2011)

Unlike in many other pastiches where Holmes has been reinvented, here Horowitz has stuck closely to the original canon, and forged a loyal facsimile in Conan Doyle's style. Set in Victorian London, the plot is twisting and, at times, dramatic. It contains many familiar Conan Doyle motifs: a rich client whose family is not all it seems; a gruesome knife murder; a detailed, violent backstory set in America involving brutal Irish expatriates; and some elaborate Holmesian deductions. Written for modern readers, it touches on many themes forbidden to Conan Doyle.

PROFESSOR MORIARTY: THE HOUND OF THE D'URBERVILLES
Kim Newman (2011)

This is an audacious take on the Holmes saga where seven of the original cases are retold, focusing on Moriarty's and Moran's previously unknown involvement. The tales are even retitled to reflect their new perspective: *The Study in Scarlet* becomes "A Volume in Vermilion," while "The Greek Interpreter" becomes "The Greek Invertebrate." Here, Moriarty and Moran are portrayed at their most cruel and villainous, and are seen at the heart of an international crime web, of which Holmes is not fully aware. Mirroring Moriarty's role in Conan Doyle's original canon, Holmes himself is barely referred to in the first stories, and only makes a full appearance in the final tale, "The Problem of the Final Adventure."

THE BREATH OF GOD
Guy Adams (2011)

Set at the end of the 19th century, this novel has a strong sense of the paranormal. Someone is found crushed to death in London, yet despite being surrounded by snow, there are no footprints. It is up to Holmes and Watson to illuminate the mystery, and they travel to Scotland to meet the only person who may be able to help—the real-life sinister occultist and novelist Aleister Crowley. Narrated by the recently widowed Watson, Holmes is largely absent for much of the story, which instead features an interesting mix of real-life and fictional characters, such as the runic expert and demonologist Julian Carswell—borrowed from M. R. James's ghoulish short story, "Casting the Runes" (1911).

DEAD MAN'S LAND
Robert Ryan (2012)

Following an acrimonious disagreement with Holmes, this novel sees Watson working with the Royal Army Medical Corps in war-torn France during 1914. A series of deaths takes place, quite unlike the wholesale slaughter of the trenches, involving grotesque and mutilated bodies—the victims seemingly scared to death. Working by himself, Watson is obliged to investigate the mystery, and the flare-lit horrors of World War I become the stage for grisly nocturnal graveyard raids. Holmes features only in the shadows, often obliquely referred to as "the old man," yet there is constant hope for a reconciliation between the two great former friends.

SHERLOCK HOLMES: GODS OF WAR
James Lovegrove (2014)

This is a tense and action-packed novel in which an aged Watson, visiting the now-retired Holmes at his cottage on the Sussex Downs, comes across the body of a man who has fallen from a great height. Is it murder or suicide? The dead man's lover reveals that he had some Egyptian hieroglyphics tattooed on his body, and questions are raised over other recent deaths—is this the work of a clandestine society?

SHERLOCK HOLMES: THE SPIRIT BOX
George Mann (2014)

In this intriguing novel, Mann utilizes themes from his previous books featuring his supernatural protagonists, Newbury and Hobbes. It is set in 1915, amid scenes of destruction as World War I Zeppelins rain bombs onto London below. The aging Holmes and Watson are leading separate lives until reunited by Holmes's brother, Mycroft. Rich and powerful members of society have been behaving erratically before taking their own lives in bizarre fashions. Mycroft knows something is afoot when a British member of Parliament gives a pro-German speech before jumping naked into the Thames River; a senior military adviser advocates surrendering to Germany before feeding himself to a tiger at London Zoo; and an eminent suffragette jumps to her death under a train having renounced the movement. Someone or something must be behind these events, and Holmes and Watson duly investigate.

CONAN DOYLE'S OTHER WORKS

Sir Arthur Conan Doyle is undoubtedly best known for the Holmes canon, which is widely regarded as his defining work. Before creating the great detective, however, he had previously published a number of short, dark mysteries, including "The Captain of the Polestar" (1883) and "J. Habakuk Jephson's Statement" (1884), a fictional account of the *Mary Celeste*, which were both inspired by his time as a ship's doctor. Holmes brought Conan Doyle huge public acclaim, but he soon tired of his creation, wishing instead to concentrate on "better things." He wrote many other works during the "Great Hiatus" and after *The Case Book of Sherlock Holmes*, including historical epics, fantasy adventures, and deep psychological pieces. Sadly for the author, none are as well remembered.

THE MYSTERY OF CLOOMBER
(1889)

Published a year after *A Study in Scarlet*, this is a Gothic mystery set in Scotland involving a family secret and long-awaited revenge. The appearance of the three mysterious Buddhist monks in a remote area has distinct echoes of Wilkie Collins's *The Moonstone* (1868), one of Conan Doyle's favorite novels as a youth.

MICAH CLARKE
(1889)

Conan Doyle's first critical success as a novelist, this novel records the events of the Monmouth Rebellion of 1685 that sought to replace the Catholic King James with a Protestant rival. Events are seen through the eyes of Micah Clarke, a young boy who falls under the influence of a world-weary soldier of fortune. Becoming disillusioned with the religious extremism around him, Micah concludes that tolerance is vital for the good of us all. Micah may have expressed Conan Doyle's own views as a disillusioned former Catholic.

THE WHITE COMPANY
(1891)

This historic novel was Conan Doyle's first attempt to emulate Sir Walter Scott, who he admired. Set in England, France, and Spain, it follows the campaign of Edward, the Black Prince, to restore Peter of Castile to the throne in 1366–67. The hero, a knight, is Sir Nigel Loring, who Conan Doyle returns to in his later novel, *Sir Nigel*, in 1906.

THE REFUGEES
(1893)

Set during the reign of King Louis XIV of France (1638–1715), the central theme of this historic novel is the persecution of Protestant Huguenots through the revocation of their civil rights. Well-researched and richly detailed, it follows the tale of a Huguenot guardsman, Amory de Catinat, and his eventual emigration to America, where many Protestants settled.

THE PARASITE
(1894)

Written when his first wife was terminally ill, this is considered to be one of Conan Doyle's most personally revealing tales, exploring the power of the mind and sexual obsession. Here, the repellent parasitic mesmerist, Miss Penclosa, controls the minds of the young Professor Gilroy and his fiancée, and is determined to destroy their relationship. Unsuccessful, it was later withdrawn by Conan Doyle.

THE STARK MUNRO LETTERS
(1895)

A departure in style for Conan Doyle, this is a thinly disguised biographical piece in which he drew on various incidents from his own life. It takes the form of twelve long letters written by J. Stark

Munro, a recent medical graduate, to his friend Herbert Swanborough in the US. The letters detail his failed attempt to build a medical practice with the brilliant but unorthodox James Cullingworth, reflecting Conan Doyle's early life.

THE EXPLOITS OF BRIGADIER GERARD
(1895)

Based on the real-life Baron de Marbot, Conan Doyle's comic character, Brigadier Gerard, is a swaggering, vain officer in Napoleon's army, yet is also brave, imaginative, and resourceful. He initially appeared in the pages of *The Strand Magazine*, with the first short stories published in book form in 1896. *The Adventures of Gerard* followed in 1903.

RODNEY STONE
(1896)

Set against a backdrop of bare-knuckle boxing at the time of the Prince Regent, this novel weaves together the coming-of-age of the narrator, Rodney Stone, and a murder mystery. Conan Doyle drew on the life of famous dandy Beau Brummell and many contemporary chronicles to capture the flavor of the period. He came to regard this novel as one of his successes.

THE TRAGEDY OF THE KOROSKO
(1898)

This novel tells the story of a group of European tourists who, while sailing up the Nile in a boat called the *Korosko*, are attacked and abducted by a marauding band of Dervish warriors. It is a clear defense of British Imperialism, and in particular, its reach into North Africa. It also reveals the very great suspicion of Islam felt by many Europeans at the time.

THE LOST WORLD
(1912)

This fantasy novel introduces another of Conan Doyle's fascinating characters: Professor George Edward Challenger, an irascible, red-haired explorer, much given to losing his temper with anyone who disagrees with him. Like Holmes, Professor Challenger was based on a real person, here William Rutherford, a professor of physiology who had lectured at the University of Edinburgh while Conan Doyle studied medicine. The imaginative plot concerns Challenger's expedition to a plateau in the Amazon basin, where dinosaurs still survive. Highly influential, it inspired many later works in which prehistoric monsters are loose in the modern world, including the 1993 movie *Jurassic Park*. Challenger returned in the novels *The Poison Belt* (1913) and *The Land of Mist* (1926).

THE COMING OF THE FAIRIES
(1922)

Conan Doyle wrote this piece having been fooled by the "Cottingley Fairies." In 1917, two young cousins, Elsie Wright and Frances Griffiths, claimed that there were fairies in their garden, and produced their own photographs as proof. Duped, Conan Doyle enthusiastically endorsed the girls' story, hoping to encourage the belief in spiritualism. It had the opposite effect; he was mocked in the press, and his credulity was called into question. The truth only came out in 1983 when the perpetrators said they'd always felt guilty for fooling Conan Doyle, and for holding him up to the ridicule he suffered.

THE MARACOT DEEP
(1929)

Subtitled *The Lost World Under the Sea*, this was Conan Doyle's last work. It is a short novel about the discovery of the sunken city of Atlantis by a team of explorers led by Professor Maracot. He is accompanied on the adventure by Cyrus Headley, a young research zoologist, and Bill Scanlan, an expert mechanic who built the submersible that carries them to the bottom of the Atlantic. This tale is regarded as being part science fiction and part spiritualist sermon, with the Atlanteans demonstrating the movement's high ideals.

TALES OF UNEASE
(2000)

This is a compilation of short stories written by Conan Doyle between 1890 and 1921. It includes "The Ring of Thoth" (1890) about an ancient Egyptian mummy coming back to life, which, along with his "Lot No. 249" (1892), inspired the 1932 movie *The Mummy*, featuring Boris Karloff. Also, his atmospheric ghost story, "The Captain of the Polestar" (1883), echoes images from the climax of Mary Shelley's 1818 Gothic classic, *Frankenstein*.

INDEX

ACKNOWLEDGMENTS

Dorling Kindersley would like to thank Andrew Heritage for his assistance in planning and commissioning the book; Antara Moitra, Vineetha Mokkil, Tejaswita Payal, and Ira Pundeer for proofreading; Helen Peters for the index; Sam Atkinson, Hannah Bowen, Lizzie Davey, Helen Fewster, Ashwin Khurana, Stuart Neilson, Andy Szudek, and Cressida Tuson for editorial assistance; and Stephen Bere for design assistance.

PICTURE CREDITS

The publisher would like to thank the following for their kind permission to reproduce their photographs:

(Key: a-above; b-below/bottom; c-center; f-far; l-left; r-right; t-top)

15 Alamy Images: INTERFOTO (tr). **Museum of London:** (bl). **18 Rex Features:** Associated Newspapers (br). **19 Corbis:** (tr). **20 Getty Images:** SSPL / Glenn Hill (bl). **21 Alamy Images:** Dean Hoskins (br). **22 Alamy Images:** David Angel (crb). **23 Alamy Images:** Pictorial Press Ltd (br). **24 Getty Images:** Culture Club (bl). **25 Getty Images:** Time Life Pictures / Mansell / The LIFE Picture Collection (bl). **26 Alamy Images:** Hemis (bl). **27 Alamy Images:** AF Fotografie (bl). **28 Alamy Images:** Mary Evans Picture Library (bl). **29 Getty Images:** UniversalImagesGroup (tr). **The Library of Congress, Washington DC:** LC-USZ62-136386 (bl). **30 Getty Images:** Time Life Pictures / Mansell / The LIFE Picture Collection (tr). **31 Rex Features:** ITV (tr). **40 Alamy Images:** Mary Evans Picture Library (tr). **43 Alamy Images:** @ csp archive (bl); Mary Evans Picture Library (tr). **44 Corbis:** (bl). **TopFoto.co.uk:** ullsteinbild (tr). **45 AF Fotografie:** Private Collection (br). **50 Getty Images:** Roger Viollet Collection (tc). **Toronto Public Library:** (bl). **51 Alamy Images:** ILN (tr). **Museum of London:** (tl). **52 Rex Features:** Everett Collection (tl). **53 Alamy Images:** Chronicle (br). **Bridgeman Images:** Private Collection / Bourne Gallery, Reigate, Surrey (tr). **57 Rex Features:** ITV (tr). **58 Alamy Images:** Photos 12 / Archives du 7e Art / Hartswood Films (bl). **60 Getty Images:** Culture Club (t). **61 Getty Images:** Hulton Archive (bl). **63 Rex Features:** ITV (br). **64 Corbis:** (clb, tr). **65 Mary Evans Picture Library:** (tl). **67 Alamy Images:** Baker Street Scans (tr). **69 Getty Images:** Hulton Archive (tl). **71 Dreamstime.com:** Alexei Novikov (br). **72 Getty Images:** Time Life Pictures / Mansell / The LIFE Picture Collection (bl). **75 Alamy Images:** Baker Street Scans (br). **77 Rex Features:** Everett Collection (br). **79 TopFoto.co.uk:** City of London / HIP (tl). **Getty Images:** Hulton Archive / Culture Club (br). **Museum of London:** (br). **83 Alamy Images:** Heritage Image Partnership Ltd (tr). **85 Alamy Images:** Mary Evans Picture Library (tl). **86 Bridgeman Images:** Private Collection / Archives Charmet (t). **88 Rex Features:** ITV (tl). **89 Bridgeman Images:** © Look and Learn / Illustrated Papers Collection (br). **91 Alamy Images:** Baker Street Scans (tr). **93 Alamy Images:** coin Alan King (bl). **94 Alamy Images:** The National Trust Photolibrary (br). **95 Alamy Images:** Everett Collection Historical (tr). **97 Dorling Kindersley:** The Natural History Museum, London (bc). **Rex Features:** Everett Collection (tr). **99 Rex Features:** ITV (tr). **101 Alamy Images:** Baker Street Scans (tr). **107 Getty Images:** The Print Collector / Print Collector (tr). **108 Getty Images:** Popperfoto (tr). **110 Rex Features:** ITV (tr). **111 AF Fotografie:** Private Collection (cra). **113 Corbis:** Bettmann (tl). **115 Alamy Images:** Mary Evans Picture Library (tr). **117 Corbis:** Fine Art Photographic Library (b). **118 Getty Images:** Time Life Pictures / Mansell / The LIFE Picture Collection (tr). **119 Getty Images:** Hulton Archive / Ann Ronan Pictures / Print Collector (tr). **121 Rex Features:** Everett Collection (tr). **122 Alamy Images:** Baker Street Scans (bl). **124 Getty Images:** Universal History Archive (tl). **125 Getty Images:** Hulton Archive (bl). **127 Getty Images:** Hulton Archive / Oxford Science Archive / Print Collector (tl); Universal History Archive (tl). **129 Alamy Images:** Baker Street Scans (br). **130 The Library of Congress, Washington DC:** LC-USZ62-79139 (cb). **131 Corbis:** Christie's Images (b). **132 Getty Images:** Hulton Archive (c). **133 Getty Images:** De Agostini (bl). **135 Alamy Images:** Mary Evans Picture Library (tr). **137 Corbis:** Peter Aprahamian (bl). **Rex Features:** ITV (tl). **139 Getty Images:** Hulton Archive / English Heritage / Heritage Images (tl). **141 Alamy Images:** Baker Street Scans (br). **143 Mary Evans Picture Library:** © The Boswell Collection, Bexley Heritage Trust (tl). **144 Getty Images:** Time Life Pictures / Mansell / The LIFE Picture Collection (tl). **Rex Features:** ITV (br). **146 Evgeny Murtola:** (bl). **147 The Sherlock Holmes Museum (www.sherlock-holmes.co.uk):** (tl). **156 Alamy Images:** Pictorial Press Ltd (bl). **157 Alamy Images:** AF Fotografie (bl). **Photoshot:** UPPA (tr). **159 Alamy Images:** AF Fotografie (bl). **Mary Evans Picture Library:** Peter Higginbotham Collection (tr). **160 Alamy Images:** Derek Stone (b). **161 Alamy Images:** John Warburton-Lee Photography (tc). **163 Alamy Images:** Mary Evans Picture Library (tl). **165 Rex Features:** ITV (bc). **166 Courtesy of Pobjoy Mint Ltd:** (br). **Getty Images:** Transcendental Graphics (tl). **169 Rex Features:** ITV (tl). **172 Alamy Images:** Mary Evans Picture Library (tr). **174 Rex Features:** Everett Collection (bc). **175 Mary Evans Picture Library:** (tl).

176 Alamy Images: Chronicle (br). **177 Alamy Images:** thislife pictures (tl). **179 TopFoto.co.uk:** (tl). **180 Corbis:** Lebrecht Authors / Lebrecht Music & Arts (tc). **181 Rex Features:** ITV (tr). **183 Getty Images:** Hulton Archive / Guildhall Library & Art Gallery / Heritage Images (bl). **185 Corbis:** (tr). **186 Bridgeman Images:** Ashmolean Museum, University of Oxford, UK (br). **187 Alamy Images:** Pictorial Press Ltd (tr). **189 Rex Features:** Universal History Archive / UIG via Getty images (tr). **191 Corbis:** Alan Copson / 145 / Ocean (bl). **Images courtesy of The Strand Magazine (www.strandmag.com):** (tr). **195 akg-images:** (tl). **197 Alamy Images:** Lordprice Collection (tl). **Getty Images:** Universal History Archive (bl). **198 Getty Images:** Hulton Archive / Print Collector (c). **199 Images courtesy of The Strand Magazine (www.strandmag.com):** (br). **201 Alamy Images:** Chronicle (bl). **203 Alamy Images:** Lordprice Collection (bl). **204 Rex Features:** ITV (tl). **205 Alamy Images:** Chronicle (tl). **206 Rex Features:** ITV (tl). **216 Alamy Images:** INTERFOTO (tr). **218 Alamy Images:** Gary Lucken (cla); Tony Watson (tl). **219 The Library of Congress, Washington DC:** LC-DIG-ds-01522 (tr). **TopFoto.co.uk:** (bl). **220 Alamy Images:** Lebrecht Music and Arts Photo Library (bl). **221 Alamy Images:** North Wind Picture Archives (tr). **222 Alamy Images:** Photos 12 (br). **223 Rex Features:** ITV (t). **225 Alamy Images:** Mary Evans Picture Library (c). **226 By permission of The British Library:** (br). **228 The Library of Congress, Washington DC:** LC-DIG-ggbain-03246 (bl). **229 Rex Features:** ITV (t). **230 Alamy Images:** adam parker (br). **231 Getty Images:** Hulton Archive / Print Collector (t). **233 Alamy Images:** Historical image collection by Bildagentur-online (tr). **235 Alamy Images:** REDA &CO srl / Paroli Galperti (tr). **237 Lebrecht Music and Arts:** Lebrecht Authors (tr). **238 Science & Society Picture Library:** Science Museum (tr). **239 Getty Images:** Hulton Archive / General Photographic Agency (tr). **241 Alamy Images:** Chronicle (bl). **242 Corbis:** Underwood & Underwood (tl). **243 Alamy Images:** Pictorial Press Ltd (tl). **Rex Features:** ITV (tl). **244 Alamy Images:** Patrick Guenette (cb). **246 Alamy Images:** Mary Evans Picture Library (cb). **247 Alamy Images:** Classic Image (bl). **253 Getty Images:** Hulton Archive / Museum of London / Heritage Images (b). **Images courtesy of The Strand Magazine (www.strandmag.com):** (tr). **255 Alamy Images:** INTERFOTO (tr). **257 Alamy Images:** Chronicle (br). **258 Rex Features:** ITV (t). **259 Alamy Images:** Mary Evans Picture Library (bl). **261 Getty Images:** Buyenlarge (tl). **263 Getty Images:** The Natural History Museum (bl). **Rex Features:** ITV (tr). **265 Alamy Images:** LatitudeStock / David Williams (t). **268 Alamy Images:** UIG / Leemage (bl). **269 Alamy Images:** Mary Evans Picture Library (t). **271 Alamy Images:** Chronicle (tr). **273 Rex Features:** ITV (tr). **274 Alamy Images:** Pictorial Press Ltd (br). **275 Getty Images:** Universal History Archive (t). **280 Images courtesy of The Strand Magazine (www.strandmag.com):** (tl). **281 Image courtesy of Biodiversity Heritage Library. http://www.biodiversitylibrary.org:** Princeton Theological Seminary Library (archive.org) (tr). **282 Corbis:** Minden Pictures / Hiroya Minakuchi (tr). **283 Alamy Images:** eye35. pix (bl). **285 Alamy Images:** North Wind Picture Archives (bl). **287 Getty Images:** Hulton Archive / Art Media / Print Collector (tl). **288 akg-images:** Paul Almasy (crb). **289 Getty Images:** DEA PICTURE LIBRARY (t). **296 Getty Images:** F J Mortimer (bl). **297 Getty Images:** DEA PICTURE LIBRARY (tr). **298 Corbis:** Arcaid / English Heritage / York & Son (tr). **301 Bridgeman Images:** Wakefield Museums and Galleries, West Yorkshire, UK (tr). **The Art Archive:** Museum of London (bl). **302 Alamy Images:** Chronicle (tl). **303 Alamy Images:** Mary Evans Picture Library (bl). **305 Getty Images:** Hulton Archive / Museum of London / Heritage Images (tr). **306 Alamy Images:** The Art Archive / Gianni Dagli Orti (cb). **308 Alamy Images:** Mary Evans Picture Library (tl). **309 Science Photo Library:** Sheila Terry (bl). **310 Science Photo Library:** Sheila Terry (crb). **311 Getty Images:** Hulton Archive / Museum of London / Heritage Images (tr). **312 Alamy Images:** Pictorial Press Ltd (br). **313 Getty Images:** Hulton Archive / Oxford Science Archive / Print Collector (br). **314 Getty Images:** SSPL (tl). **315 Getty Images:** Edward Gooch (tl); Hulton Archive / Topical Press Agency (tr). **317 Alamy Images:** Mary Evans Picture Library (bl). **TopFoto.co.uk:** RV1893-13 (tr). **318 Science Photo Library:** NEW YORK PUBLIC LIBRARY (tl). **319 Bridgeman Images:** Private Collection (tl). **Getty Images:** Hulton Archive (cb). **321 Alamy Images:** Mary Evans Picture Library (tr). **322 Getty Images:** DuMont (tr). **Kevin Gordon / / kevingordonportraits.com :** (tl). **323 Hodder & Stoughton:** Cover Of The Girl With The Dragon Tattoo By Stieg Larsson (tl). **Rex Features:** Everett Collection (tl). **324 TopFoto.co.uk:** PA Photos (bl). **326 Roland Smithies / luped.com:** (tl). **327 Alamy Images:** Gregory Wrona (br). **Roland Smithies / luped.com:** (tl). **329 AF Fotografie:** (cb). **The Library of Congress, Washington DC:** LC-USZC2-1459 (tr). **330 The Ronald Grant Archive:** (tl). **331 Alamy Images:** Universal History Archive (br). **332 Alamy Images:** AF archive (tl). **334 Alamy Images:** AF archive (tl, tr). **335 Alamy Images:** Photos 12 / Archives du 7e Art / Hartswood Films (bl); World History Archive (tr)

All other images © Dorling Kindersley
For more information see: **www.dkimages.com**